Allez, viens!

Holt French

Level 1

HOLT, RINEHART AND **WINSTON**

Harcourt Brace & Company

Austin • New York • Orlando • Atlanta • San Francisco • Boston • Dallas • Toronto • London

Director Lawrence Haley

Executive Editor Robert Didsbury

Editorial Staff Julie Barnett, Marion Bermondy, Priscilla Blanton, Lisa Bruce, Séverine Champeny, Dana Chicchelly, Craig Gilchrist, Jamie Jones, Heidi Miller, Cherie Mitschke, Pamela Pate, Stan Rappaport, Dana Riggs, Dianne Schrader, Kim Smith; Beth Goerner, *Department Secretary.*

Editorial Permissions Carrie Jones

Design, Production, and Photo Research Pun Nio, *Senior Art Director;* Candace Moore, *Designer;* Jennifer Dix, Leslie Kell, Bob Prestwood, Alicia Sullivan, Jane Thurmond, *Design Staff;* Bob Bretz, Donna McKennon, *Media Designers;* Betty Wong, *Design Secretary;* Gene Rumann, *Production Supervisor;* Amber P. Martin, *Production Assistant;* George Previlige, *Manufacturing Manager;* Jenine Street, *Manufacturing Coordinator;* Simira Davis, *Photo Researcher;* Angi Cartwright, Victoria Smith, *Photo Research Staff.*

Video Production Video Materials produced by Edge Productions, Inc., Aiken, S. C.

ACKNOWLEDGMENTS

For permission to reprint copyrighted material, grateful acknowledgment is made to the following sources:

Air Afrique: Adaptation of "Menu" from Air Afrique.

Air France: Front of boarding pass, "Carte d'accès à bord."

A. Leconte, Éditeur: Cover of *Paris Monumental.*

Bayard Presse International: Title and illustrations from pages 51–53 from "Sondage : les lycéens ont-ils le moral?" from *Phosphore,* September 1989. Copyright © 1989 by Bayard Presse International.

Cacharel: Four photographs from *RENTREE TRES CLASSE A PRIX PETITS:* Nouvelles Galeries Lafayette.

Canal B: Logo for Canal B, 94 MHz (Bruz).

Casino France: Advertisement, "Nouvelle Collection Claude Saint Genest," from *Femme Actuelle,* no. 496, page 29, March 28-April 3, 1994.

Cathédrale d'images: Advertisement, "Cathédrale d'images" from *Évasion Plus.*

Château Musée de l'Empéri: Advertisement, "Château Musée de l'Empéri," from *Évasion Plus.*

Clip FM: Logo, "Clip FM, 88.7 MHz" (Chalon/Saone.) Created by Christian Bernard.

Comité Français d'Éducation pour la Santé, 2 rue Auguste Comte 92170 Vanves: "Les Groupes d'Aliments" from *Comment équilibrer votre alimentation.*

C'Rock Radio: Logo from C'Rock Radio, 89.5 MHz (Vienne).

Editions Estel Blois France: Front and back of postcard, "Arènes d'Arles," no. 10033 Z.

ACKNOWLEDGMENTS continued on page 374, which is an extension of the copyright page.

AUTHORS

Emmanuel Rongiéras d'Usseau
Le Kremlin-Bicêtre, France

Mr. Rongiéras d'Usseau contributed to the development of the scope and sequence for the chapters, created the basic material and listening scripts, selected realia, and wrote activities.

John DeMado
Washington, CT

Mr. DeMado helped form the general philosophy of the French program and wrote activities to practice basic material, functions, grammar, and vocabulary.

CONTRIBUTING WRITERS

Jayne Abrate
The University of Missouri
Rolla Campus
Rolla, MO

Sally Adamson Taylor
Publishers Weekly
San Francisco, CA

Linda Bistodeau
Saint Mary's University
Halifax, Nova Scotia

Betty Peltier
Consultant
Batz-sur-Mer, France

REVIEWERS

Dominique Bach
Rio Linda Senior High School
Rio Linda, CA

Jeannette Caviness
Mount Tabor High School
Winston-Salem, NC

Jennie Bowser Chao
Consultant
East Lansing, MI

Pierre F. Cintas
Penn State University
Ogontz Campus
Abington, PA

Donna Clementi
Appleton West High School
Appleton, WI

Cathy Cramer
Homewood High School
Birmingham, AL

Jennifer Jones
U.S. Peace Corps volunteer
Côte d'Ivoire 1991–1993
Austin, TX

Joan H. Manley
The University of Texas at El Paso
El Paso, TX

Jill Markert
Pflugerville High School
Pflugerville, TX

Inge McCoy
Southwest Texas State University
San Marcos, TX

Gail Montgomery
Foreign Language Program
Administrator
Greenwich, CT Public Schools

Agathe Norman
Consultant
Austin, TX

Audrey O'Keefe
Jordan High School
Los Angeles, CA

Sherry Parker
Selvidge Middle School
Ballwin, MO

Sherron N. Porter
Robert E. Lee High School
Baton Rouge, LA

Marc Prévost
Austin Community College
Austin, TX

Norbert Rouquet
Consultant
La Roche-sur-Yon, France

Michèle Shockey
Gunn High School
Palo Alto, CA

Ashley Shumaker
Central High School West
Tuscaloosa, AL

Antonia Stergiades
Washington High School
Massillon, OH

Frederic L. Toner
Texas Christian University
Fort Worth, TX

Jeannine Waters
Harrisonburg High School
Harrisonburg, VA

Jo Anne S. Wilson
Consultant
Glen Arbor, MI

FIELD TEST PARTICIPANTS

Marie Allison
New Hanover High School
Wilmington, NC

Gabrielle Applequist
Capital High School
Boise, ID

Jana Brinton
Bingham High School
Riverton, UT

Nancy J. Cook
Sam Houston High School
Lake Charles, LA

Rachael Gray
Williams High School
Plano, TX

Priscilla Koch
Troxell Junior High School
Allentown, PA

Katherine Kohler
Nathan Hale Middle School
Norwalk, CT

Nancy Mirsky
Museum Junior High School
Yonkers, NY

Myrna S. Nie
Whetstone High School
Columbus, OH

Jacqueline Reid
Union High School
Tulsa, OK

Judith Ryser
San Marcos High School
San Marcos, TX

Erin Hahn Sass
Lincoln Southeast High School
Lincoln, NE

Linda Sherwin
Sandy Creek High School
Tyrone, GA

Norma Joplin Sivers
Arlington Heights High School
Fort Worth, TX

Lorabeth Stroup
Lovejoy High School
Lovejoy, GA

Robert Vizena
W.W. Lewis Middle School
Sulphur, LA

Gladys Wade
New Hanover High School
Wilmington, NC

Kathy White
Grimsley High School
Greensboro, NC

iii

To the Student

*Some people have the opportunity to learn a new language by living in another country.
Most of us, however, begin learning another language and getting acquainted with a foreign
culture in a classroom with the help of a teacher, classmates, and a book.
To use your book effectively, you need to know how it works.*

Allez, viens! *(Come along!)* takes you to six different French-speaking locations. Each location is introduced with photos and information on four special pages called Location Openers.

There are twelve chapters in the book, and each one follows the same pattern.

The two Chapter Opener pages announce the chapter theme and list the objectives. These objectives set goals that you can achieve by the end of the chapter.

Mise en train *(Getting started)* The next part of the chapter is an illustrated story that shows you French-speaking people in real-life situations, using the language you'll be learning in the chapter. You'll also have fun watching this story on video.

Première, Deuxième, Troisième Etape *(First, Second, Third Part)* Following the opening story, the chapter is divided into three parts, called **étapes**. At the beginning of each **étape** there's a reminder of the objective(s) you'll be aiming for in this part. In order to communicate, you'll need the French expressions listed in boxes called **Comment dit-on... ?** *(How do you say . . . ?)*. You'll also need vocabulary; look for new words under the heading **Vocabulaire**. You won't have trouble finding grammar, for you're sure to recognize the headings **Grammaire** and **Note de Grammaire**. Now all you need is plenty of practice. In each **étape** there are listening, speaking, reading, and writing activities for you to do individually, with a partner, or in groups. By the end of the **étape**, you'll have achieved your objective(s).

This book will also help you get to know the cultures of the people who speak French.

Panorama Culturel *(Cultural Panorama)* On this page of the chapter you'll read interviews with French-speaking people around the world. They'll talk about themselves and their lives, and you can compare their culture to yours. You'll watch these interviews on video or listen to them on audiocassette or CD.

Note Culturelle *(Culture Note)* These notes provide a lot of interesting cultural information.

Rencontre Culturelle *(Cultural Encounter)* This page in six of the chapters offers a firsthand encounter with French-speaking cultures.

Lisons! *(Let's read!)* After the three **étapes**, one or more reading selections related to the chapter theme will help you develop your reading skills.

Mise en pratique *(Putting into practice)* A variety of activities gives you opportunities to put into practice what you've learned in the chapter in new situations. You'll improve your listening skills and practice communicating with others orally and in writing.

Que sais-je? *(What do I know?)* On this page at the end of the chapter, a series of questions and short activities will help you decide how well you've done.

Vocabulaire *(Vocabulary)* On the last page of the chapter, you'll find a French-English vocabulary list. The words are grouped by **étape** and listed under the objectives they support. You'll need to know these words and expressions for the Chapter Test.

Throughout the book, you'll get a lot of help.

De bons conseils *(Good advice)* Check out the helpful study hints in these boxes.

Tu te rappelles? *(Do you remember?)* Along the way, these notes will remind you of things you might have forgotten.

A la française *(The French way)* Be on the lookout for these boxes, too. They'll give you additional language tips to help you sound more like a native speaker.

Vocabulaire à la carte *(Your choice of vocabulary)* From these lists, you'll be able to choose extra words and expressions you might want to use when you talk about yourself and your interests.

At the end of your book, you'll find more helpful material, including a list of the communicative expressions you'll need, a summary of the grammar you've studied, supplementary vocabulary, and French-English, English-French vocabulary lists with the words you'll need to know in bold type.

Allez, viens! Come along on an exciting trip to a new culture and a new language.

Bon voyage!

Allez, viens! Contents

Come along—to a world of new experiences!

Allez, viens! offers you the opportunity to learn the language spoken by millions of people in countries in Europe, Africa, Asia, and around the world. Let's find out what those countries are.

CHAPITRE PRELIMINAIRE
Allez, viens!

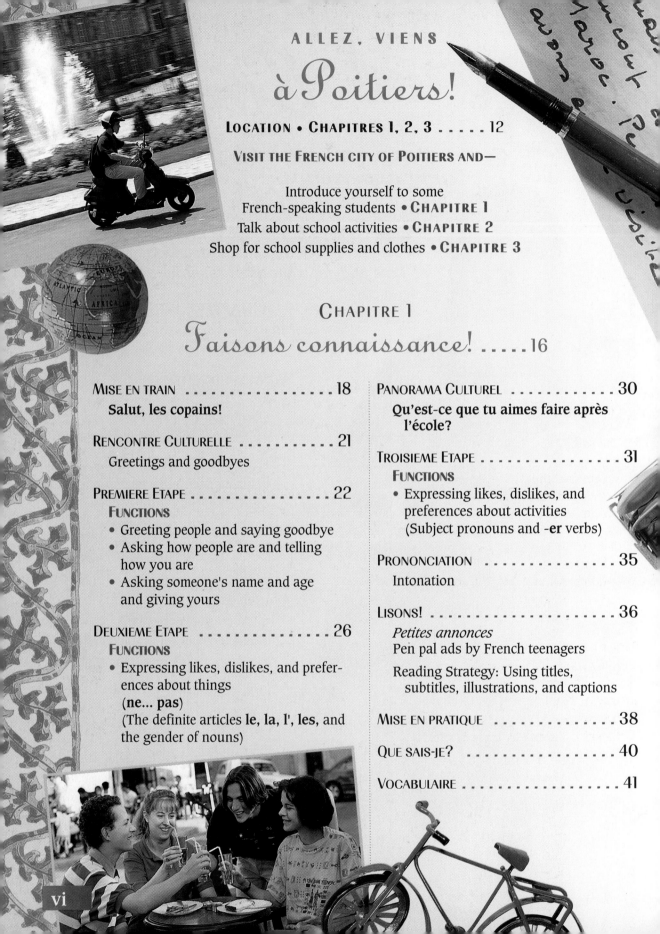

ALLEZ, VIENS

à Poitiers!

CHAPITRE 1

Faisons connaissance! 16

CHAPITRE 2
Vive l'école! 42

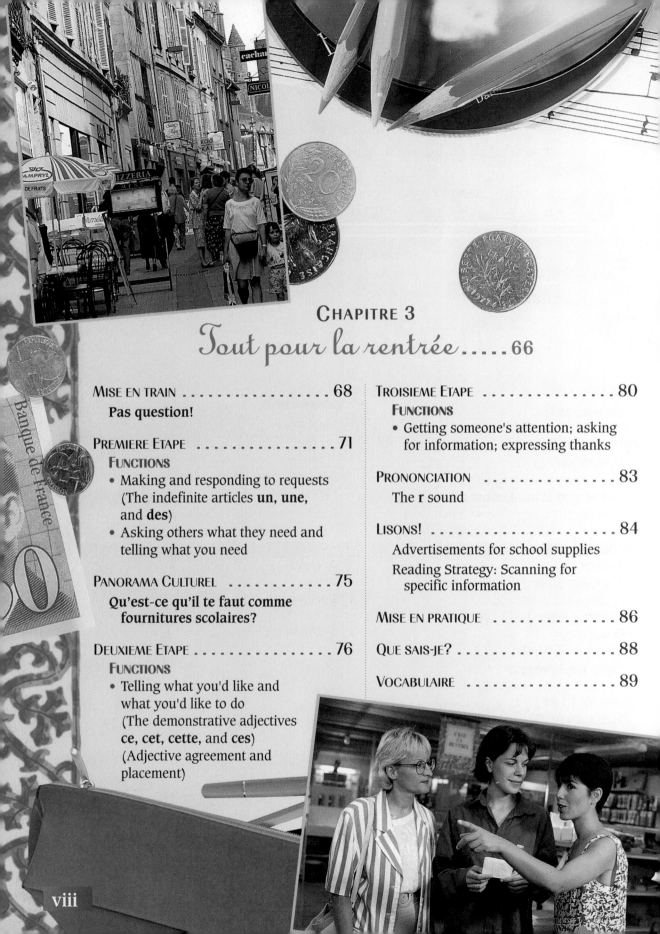

CHAPITRE 3
Tout pour la rentrée 66

ALLEZ, VIENS

à Québec!

CHAPITRE 4

Sports et passe-temps 94

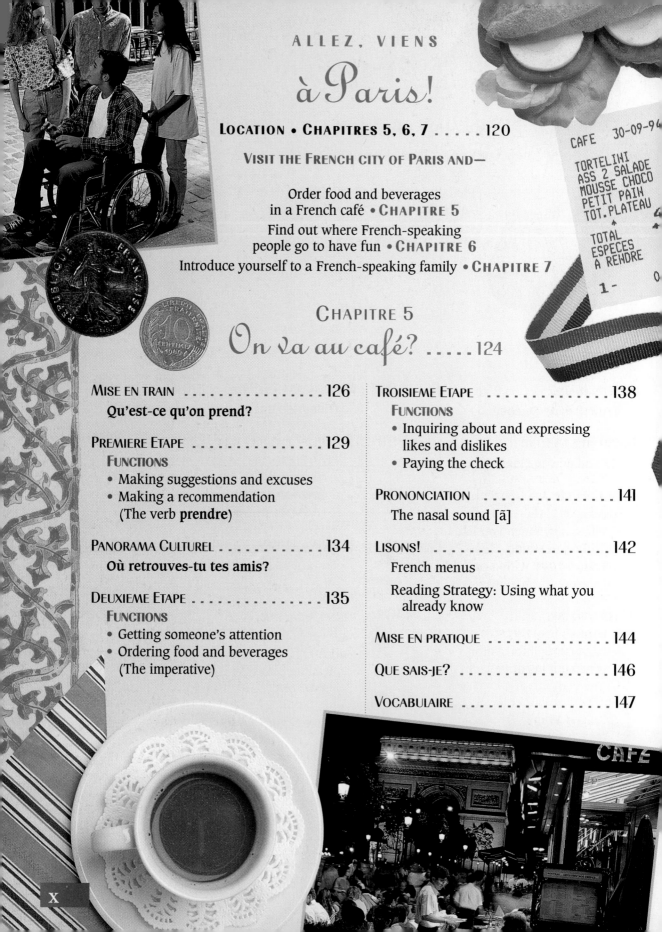

ALLEZ, VIENS

à Paris!

VISIT THE FRENCH CITY OF PARIS AND—

Order food and beverages
in a French café • CHAPITRE 5

Find out where French-speaking
people go to have fun • CHAPITRE 6

Introduce yourself to a French-speaking family • CHAPITRE 7

CHAPITRE 5

On va au café? 124

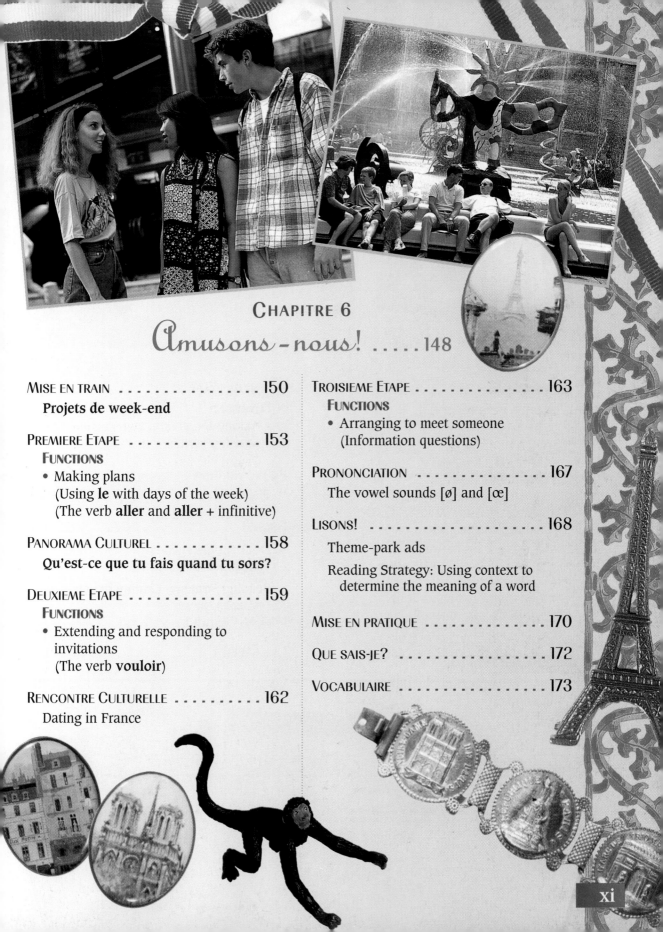

CHAPITRE 6
Amusons-nous! 148

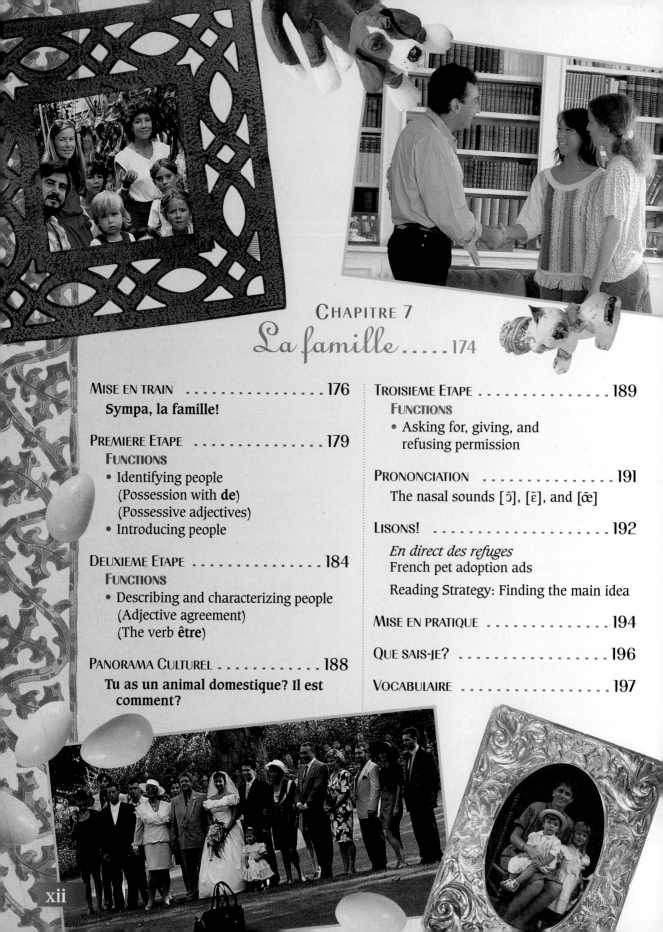

CHAPITRE 7
La famille 174

ALLEZ, VIENS

à Abidjan!

CHAPITRE 8
Au marché 202

ALLEZ, VIENS

en Arles!

VISIT THE FRENCH CITY OF ARLES AND—

Talk about weekend activities • CHAPITRE 9

Find out how French-speaking teenagers feel about fashion • CHAPITRE 10

Make vacation plans • CHAPITRE 11

CHAPITRE 9

Au téléphone 232

CHAPITRE 10
Dans un magasin de vêtements 256

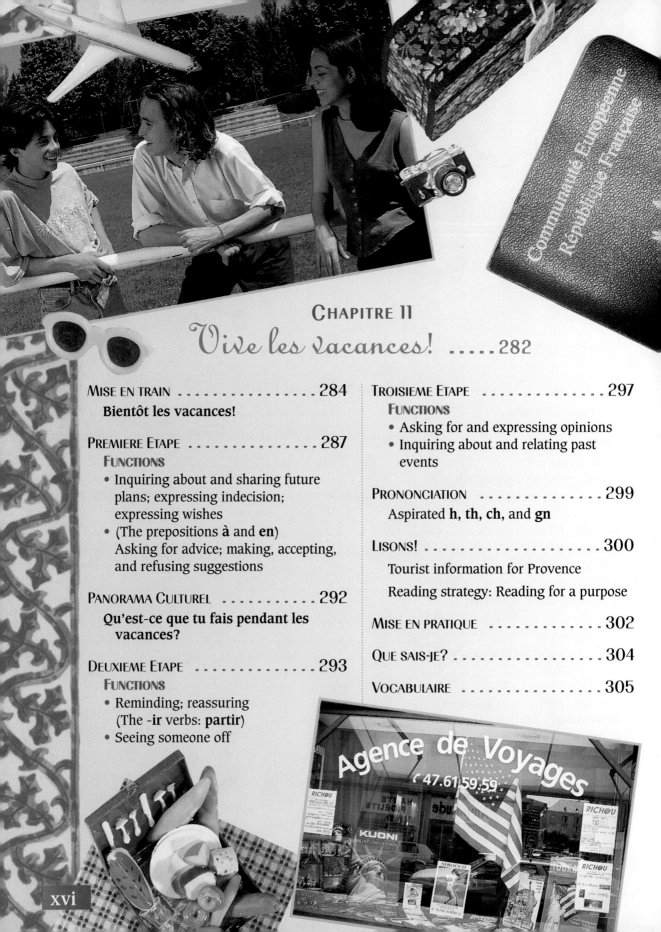

CHAPITRE 11
Vive les vacances! 282

ALLEZ, VIENS

à Fort-de-France!

LOCATION • CHAPITRE 12 306

VISIT THE CAPITAL OF MARTINIQUE AND—

Ask directions
around town • **CHAPITRE 12**

CHAPITRE 12

En ville 310

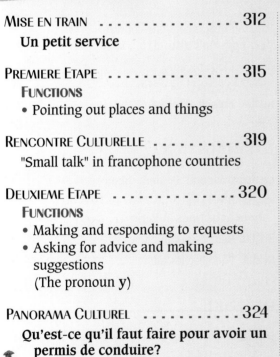

Cultural References

La France

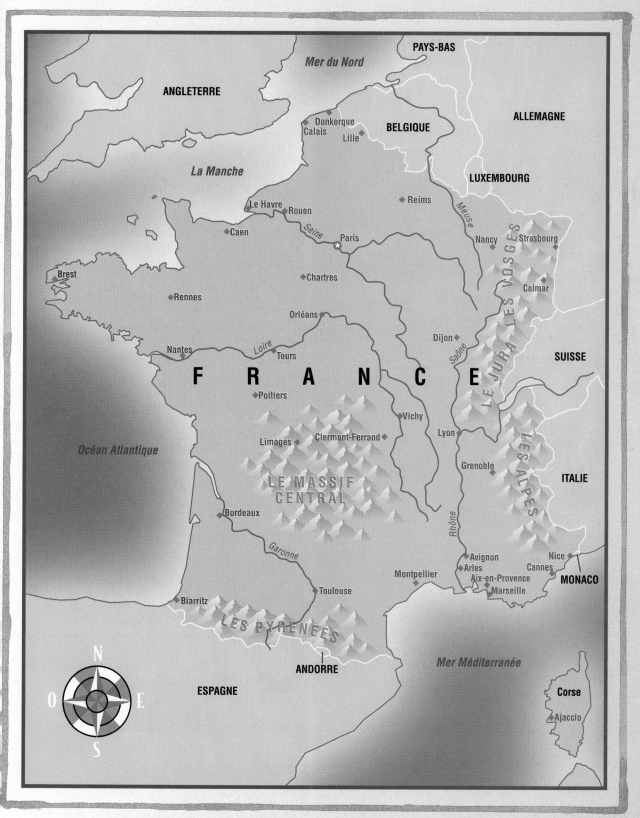

ANGLETERRE

Mer du Nord

PAYS-BAS

ALLEMAGNE

BELGIQUE

La Manche

Dunkerque
Calais
Lille

LUXEMBOURG

Reims

Meuse

Le Havre
Rouen

Seine

Caen

Nancy

Strasbourg

Paris

Brest

Chartres

Colmar

Rennes

Orléans

Dijon

Saône

SUISSE

Nantes

Loire

Tours

F R A N C E

Poitiers

Vichy

Lyon

Océan Atlantique

Limoges

Clermont-Ferrand

Grenoble

ITALIE

LE MASSIF
CENTRAL

Bordeaux

Rhône

Garonne

Avignon
Arles
Aix-en-Provence
Marseille

Nice
Cannes

MONACO

Montpellier

Biarritz

Toulouse

LES PYRÉNÉES

ANDORRE

Mer Méditerranée

Corse

ESPAGNE

N
O   E
S

Ajaccio

L'Afrique francophone

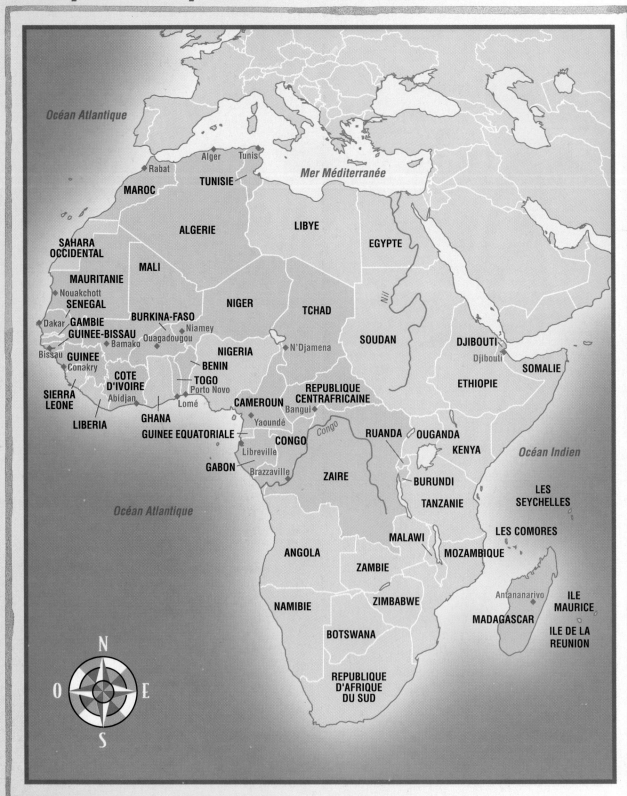

Océan Atlantique

Mer Méditerranée

Alger Tunis

Rabat

MAROC TUNISIE

ALGERIE LIBYE

EGYPTE

SAHARA
OCCIDENTAL

MALI

MAURITANIE

Nouakchott

SENEGAL NIGER TCHAD

Dakar GAMBIE BURKINA-FASO

GUINEE-BISSAU Niamey

Ouagadougou N'Djamena

Bamako

Bissau GUINEE NIGERIA SOUDAN DJIBOUTI

Conakry BENIN Djibouti

COTE TOGO SOMALIE

D'IVOIRE Porto Novo

SIERRA Abidjan Lomé CAMEROUN REPUBLIQUE ETHIOPIE

LEONE Yaoundé CENTRAFRICAINE

LIBERIA GHANA Bangui

GUINEE EQUATORIALE RUANDA OUGANDA

CONGO KENYA Océan Indien

Libreville

GABON Brazzaville ZAIRE BURUNDI

Nil

Congo

TANZANIE LES
SEYCHELLES

LES COMORES

MALAWI

ANGOLA MOZAMBIQUE

ZAMBIE

Antananarivo ILE
MAURICE

NAMIBIE ZIMBABWE MADAGASCAR ILE DE LA
REUNION

BOTSWANA

REPUBLIQUE
D'AFRIQUE
DU SUD

Océan Atlantique

N
O   E
S

L'Amérique francophone

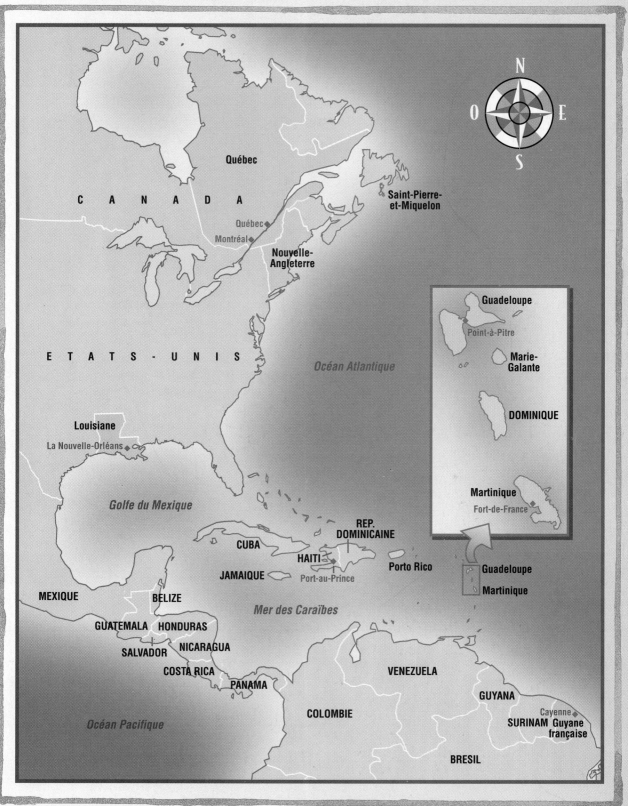

CHAPITRE PRÉLIMINAIRE
Allez, viens!

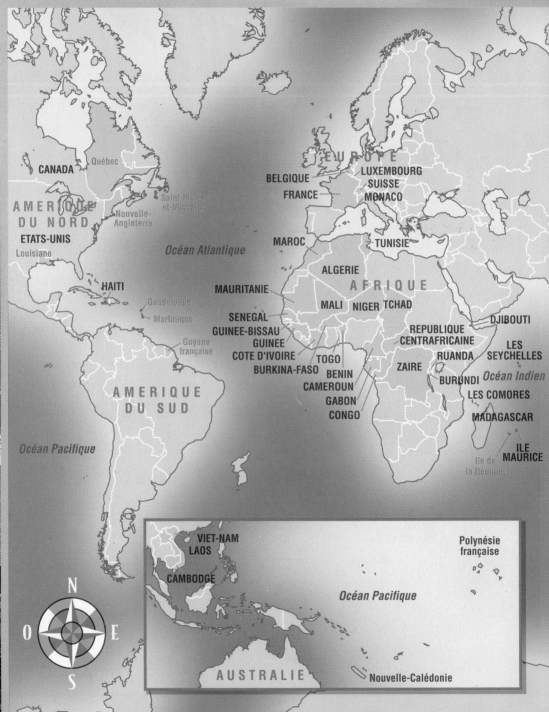

CANADA
Québec

AMÉRIQUE
DU NORD

Saint-Pierre-
et-Miquelon
Nouvelle-
Angleterre

ÉTATS-UNIS
Louisiane

Océan Atlantique

HAITI
Guadeloupe
Martinique

Guyane
française

AMÉRIQUE
DU SUD

Océan Pacifique

EUROPE

BELGIQUE
FRANCE

LUXEMBOURG
SUISSE
MONACO

MAROC
TUNISIE

ALGERIE

MAURITANIE
AFRIQUE

MALI   NIGER TCHAD

SENEGAL
GUINEE-BISSAU
GUINEE
COTE D'IVOIRE
BURKINA-FASO

TOGO
BENIN
CAMEROUN
GABON
CONGO

REPUBLIQUE
CENTRAFRICAINE

ZAIRE

RUANDA

BURUNDI

DJIBOUTI

LES
SEYCHELLES

Océan Indien

LES COMORES

MADAGASCAR

Ile de
la Réunion

ILE
MAURICE

N
O   E
S

VIET-NAM
LAOS

CAMBODGE

Polynésie
française

Océan Pacifique

AUSTRALIE

Nouvelle-Calédonie

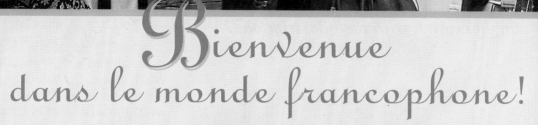

Bienvenue
dans le monde francophone!

Welcome to the French-speaking world!

You know, of course, that French is spoken in France, but did you know that French is spoken by many people in North America? About one-third of Canadians speak French, mostly in Quebec province **(le Québec).** In the United States, about 400,000 people in New England **(la Nouvelle Angleterre),** whose ancestors immigrated from Canada, speak or understand French. French is also an official language in the state of Louisiana **(la Louisiane).**

French is the official language of France's overseas possessions. These include the islands of Martinique **(la Martinique)** and Guadeloupe **(la Guadeloupe)** in the Caribbean Sea, French Guiana **(la Guyane française)** in South America, the island of Réunion **(la Réunion)** in the Indian Ocean, and several islands in the Pacific Ocean. French is also spoken in Haïti **(Haïti).**

Did you know that French is also widely used in Africa? Over twenty African countries have retained French as an official language. Many people in West and Central African countries, such as Senegal **(le Sénégal),** the Republic of Côte d'Ivoire **(la République de Côte d'Ivoire),** Mali **(le Mali),** Niger **(le Niger),** and Chad **(le Tchad),** speak French. In North Africa, French has played an important role in Algeria **(l'Algérie),** Tunisia **(la Tunisie),** and Morocco **(le Maroc).** Although Arabic is the official language of these North African countries, French is used in many schools across North Africa and in parts of the Middle East.

Take a minute to find France on the map. Several of the countries bordering France use French as an official language. It's the first or second language of many people in Belgium **(la Belgique),** Switzerland **(la Suisse),** Luxembourg **(le Luxembourg),** and Andorra **(l'Andorre),** as well as in the principality of Monaco **(Monaco).**

As you look at the map, what other places can you find where French is spoken? Can you imagine how French came to be spoken in these places?

TU LES CONNAIS? *Do you know them?*

In science, politics, technology, and the arts, French-speaking people have made important contributions. How many of these pictures can you match with their descriptions?

a.

b.

c.

1. **Léopold Senghor** (b. 1906)

   A key advocate of **Négritude**, which asserts the values and the spirit of black African civilization, Senghor is a man of many talents. He was the first black African high school teacher in France. He was President of Senegal from 1960 to 1980. He won the **Grand Prix International de Poésie** for *Nocturnes,* a book of poetry.

2. **Isabelle Adjani** (b. 1955)

   A talented actress and producer, Isabelle Yasmine Adjani is well known for her award-winning roles in French films. In the 1980s, Adjani publicly acknowledged her Algerian heritage and began a personal campaign to raise consciousness about racism in France.

3. **Victor Hugo** (1802-1885)

   Novelist, poet, and political activist, Hugo led the Romantic Movement in French literature. In his most famous works, *Notre-Dame de Paris (The Hunchback of Notre Dame)* and *Les Misérables,* he sympathizes with the victims of poverty and condemns a corrupt political system.

4. **Surya Bonaly** (b. 1974)

   Surya Bonaly is a four-time gold-medal winner in the European Figure-Skating Championships and a silver medalist in the 1993 and 1994 World Championships.

d.

e.

g.

h.

5. *Jacques Cousteau* (b. 1910)

Jacques-Yves Cousteau first gained worldwide attention for his undersea expeditions as the commander of the *Calypso* and for inventing the aqualung. In order to record his explorations, he invented a process for filming underwater.

6. *Céline Dion* (b. 1968)

A native of Quebec, Dion is a bilingual singer. After recording nine albums in French, she began to learn English and has since produced several albums in English. She performed the award-winning title song for the movie *Beauty and the Beast*.

7. *Gérard Depardieu* (b. 1948)

Gérard Depardieu is a popular actor, director, and producer, who has appeared in over 70 films. His performance in the 1990 movie *Green Card*, which won him a Golden Globe award, marked his American film debut.

8. *Marie Curie* (1867–1934)

Along with her husband Pierre, Marie Curie won a Nobel prize in physics for her study of radioactivity. Several years later, she also won an individual Nobel prize for chemistry. Marie Curie was the first woman to teach at the Sorbonne in Paris.

POURQUOI APPRENDRE LE FRANÇAIS?

Why learn French?

When you study a language, you learn much more than vocabulary and grammar. You learn about the people who speak the language and the influence they've had on our lives. Francophone (French-speaking) cultures continue to make notable contributions to many fields, including art, literature, movies, fashion, cuisine, science, and technology.

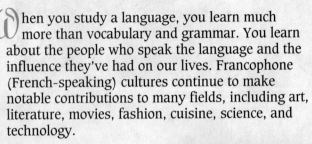

Someday you may live, travel, or be an exchange student in one of the more than 30 countries all over the world where French is spoken. You can imagine how much more meaningful your experience will be if you can talk to people in their own language.

Being able to communicate in another language can be an advantage when you're looking for employment in almost any field. As a journalist, sportscaster, hotel receptionist, tour guide, travel agent, buyer for a large company, lawyer, engineer, economist, financial expert, flight attendant, diplomat, translator, teacher, writer, interpreter, publisher, or librarian, you may have the opportunity to use French in your work. Did you know that over 600 American companies have offices in France?

Perhaps the best reason for studying French is for the fun of it. Studying another language is a challenge to your mind, and you'll get a great feeling of accomplishment the first time you have a conversation in French.

QUI SUIS-JE? *Who am I?*

Here's how you introduce yourself to young people who speak French.

To ask someone's name:
Tu t'appelles comment?

To give your name:
Je m'appelle...

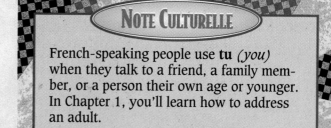

NOTE CULTURELLE

French-speaking people use **tu** *(you)* when they talk to a friend, a family member, or a person their own age or younger. In Chapter 1, you'll learn how to address an adult.

 Here's a list of some popular French names for girls and boys. Can you find your name, or a name similar to yours?

NOMS de FILLES

Delphine
Christelle
Nathalie
Aurélie
Laurence
Karine
Céline
Laetitia
Elodie
Valérie
Sophie
Virginie
Sandrine
Séverine
Claudine
Sabrina
Dominique
Emilie
Corinne
Audrey
Stéphanie
Julie

NOMS de GARÇONS

Bernard   Vincent   Pierre
Stéphane   Etienne
Eric   Gilles
Jean   Marc
Daniel   Laurent
Philippe   David
Frédéric   Christian
Cédric   Mathieu
Nicolas   Christophe
           Jérôme
Michel   Olivier

1 Présente-toi! *Introduce yourself!*

 If you like, choose a French name for yourself. Introduce yourself to two or three students in the class, using your own name or your new French name. Ask them their names, too.

L'ALPHABET

The French alphabet looks the same as the English alphabet. The difference is in pronunciation. Look at the letters and words below as your teacher pronounces them or as you listen to the audio recording. Which letters sound similar in English and French? Which ones have a different sound?

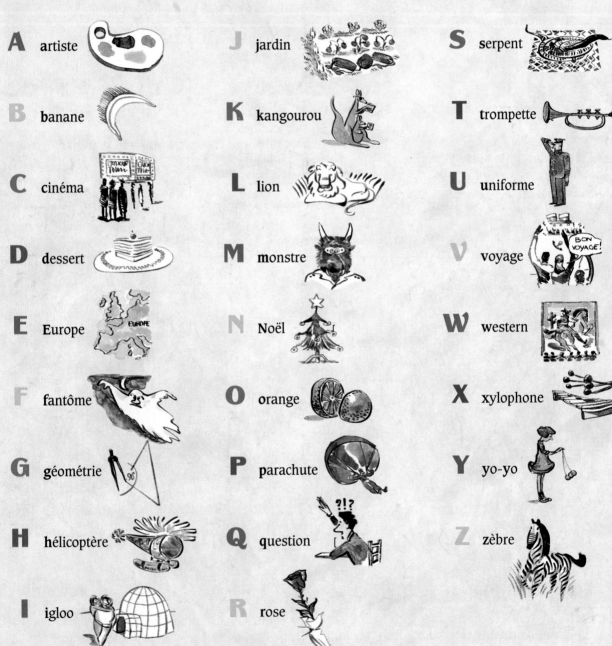

A artiste

B banane

C cinéma

D dessert

E Europe

F fantôme

G géométrie

H hélicoptère

I igloo

J jardin

K kangourou

L lion

M monstre

N Noël

O orange

P parachute

Q question

R rose

S serpent

T trompette

U uniforme

V voyage

W western

X xylophone

Y yo-yo

Z zèbre

Have you noticed that many French words look like English words? Words in different languages that look alike are called *cognates*. Although they're pronounced differently, cognates often have the same meaning in French and English. You may not realize it, but you already know hundreds of French words.

Can you figure out what these words mean?

carotte   chocolat   adresse   musique   examen

2 Le dictionnaire

Scan the French-English vocabulary list in the back of your book to see if you can find ten cognates.

3 Ecoute! *Listen!*

Write down the words as you hear them spelled. Then, match the words you've written with the pictures. Be careful! One of the words isn't a cognate.

a.

b.

c.

d.

e.

f.

4 Tu t'appelles comment?

Can you spell your name, pronouncing the letters in French?

LES ACCENTS *Accent marks*

*H*ave you noticed the marks over some of the letters in French words? These marks are called accents. They're very important to the spelling, the pronunciation, and even the meaning of French words.

- The **accent aigu** (´) tells you to pronounce an *e* similar to the *a* in the English word *date:*

    éléphant   Sénégal

- The **accent grave** (`) tells you to pronounce an *e* like the *e* in the English word *jet:*

    zèbre   chèque

    However, an **accent grave** over an *a* or *u* doesn't change the sound of these letters:

    à   où

- The **accent circonflexe** (ˆ) can appear over any vowel, and it doesn't change the sound of the letter:

    pâté   forêt   île   hôtel   flûte

- The **cédille** (¸) under a *c* tells you to pronounce the *c* like an *s*:

    français   ça

- When two vowels appear next to each other, a **tréma** (¨) over the second one tells you to pronounce each vowel separately:

    Noël   Haïti

- You usually will not see accents on capital letters.

    île   Ile   état   Etats-Unis

- When you spell a word aloud, be sure to say the accents, as well as the letters.

5 Ecoute!
Write down the words as you hear them spelled.

LES CHIFFRES DE 0 A 20 *Numbers from 0 to 20*

How many times a day do you use numbers? Giving someone a phone number, checking grades, and getting change at the store all involve numbers. Here are the French numbers from 0 to 20.

0 zéro	1 un	2 deux	3 trois
4 quatre	5 cinq	6 six	7 sept
8 huit	9 neuf	10 dix	11 onze
12 douze	13 treize	14 quatorze	15 quinze
16 seize	17 dix-sept	18 dix-huit	19 dix-neuf

20 vingt

Note Culturelle

When you count on your fingers, which finger do you start with? The French way is to start counting with your thumb as number *one,* your index finger as *two,* and so on. How would you show *four* the French way? And *eight?*

6 Ecoute!

Listen as Nicole, Paul, Vincent, and Corinne tell you their phone numbers. Then, match the numbers with their names.

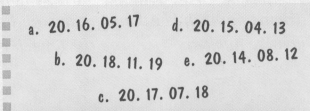

a. 20. 16. 05. 17   d. 20. 15. 04. 13

b. 20. 18. 11. 19   e. 20. 14. 08. 12

c. 20. 17. 07. 18

1. Nicole
2. Paul
3. Vincent
4. Corinne

7 Devine! *Guess!*

Think of a number between one and twenty. Your partner will try to guess your number. Help out by saying **plus** *(higher)* or **moins** *(lower)* as your partner guesses. Take turns.

8 Plaques d'immatriculation *License plates*

Look at the license plates pictured below. Take turns with a partner reading aloud the numbers and letters you see.

90 ZD 972

Québec
WFW 547
11 QC Je me souviens

1.

4.

275 PS 13

2463 RP 13

2.

5.

6904 RD 13

1869 AR 01 CI

3.

6.

A L'ECOLE *At school*

*Y*ou should familiarize yourself with these common French instructions. You'll hear your teacher using them in class.

Ecoutez! *Listen!*
Répétez! *Repeat!*
Levez-vous! *Stand up!*
Levez la main! *Raise your hand!*
Asseyez-vous! *Sit down!*
Ouvrez vos livres à la page... !
  Open your books to page . . . !

Fermez la porte! *Close the door!*
Sortez une feuille de papier!
  Take out a sheet of paper!
Allez au tableau!
  Go to the blackboard!
Regardez la carte! *Look at the map!*

9 Ecoute!

Listen to the teacher in this French class tell his students what to do. Then, decide which student is following each instruction.

Allez, viens
à Poitiers !

Poitiers — ville d'art et d'histoire

Poitiers

Capital of Poitou-Charentes

Population: more than 100,000

Points of interest: the Futuroscope theme park, the Saint-Pierre Cathedral, the Palais de Justice

Museums: Sainte-Croix, Hypogée des Dunes

Industries: agriculture, fishing, electrical and mechanical manufacturing, forestry, furniture production

Famous people: Saint Hilaire, Diane de Poitiers, Aliénor d'Aquitaine

Regional specialties: goat cheese, nougat, snails, cream-cheese pastries, chocolates

ANGLETERRE
Lille
BELGIQUE
ALLEMAGNE
LUXEMBOURG
Paris
Chartres
Strasbourg
SUISSE
Tours
Poitiers
FRANCE
Océan Atlantique
Lyon
ITALIE
Bordeaux
Nice
Arles
Aix-en-Provence
CORSE
ESPAGNE
Mer Méditerranée

N

Poitiers

Poitiers is famous for its art and history. It was here in 732 A.D. that Charles Martel defeated the Saracens in the Battle of Poitiers. Home to an important university and attractions such as a futuristic park devoted to cinematic technology, Poitiers is also a very modern city.

① People of all ages enjoy **le Futuroscope**, a popular futuristic theme park filled with cinematic exhibits. Of particular interest are the 360-degree theater, and the **Kinémax** with its 600-square-meter screen.

② The heart of French cities and towns is called **le centre-ville**. In Poitiers, it is the bustling center of town where people gather in cafés and frequent the many shops.

③ At least once a week, French towns usually have an outdoor market such as this **marché aux fleurs**.

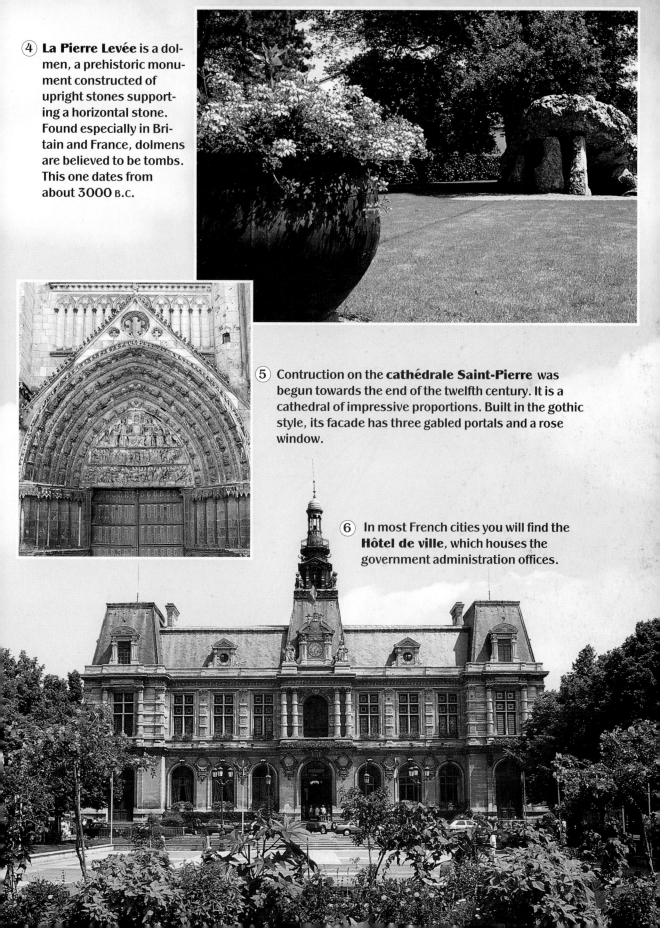

④ **La Pierre Levée** is a dolmen, a prehistoric monument constructed of upright stones supporting a horizontal stone. Found especially in Britain and France, dolmens are believed to be tombs. This one dates from about 3000 B.C.

⑤ Contruction on the **cathédrale Saint-Pierre** was begun towards the end of the twelfth century. It is a cathedral of impressive proportions. Built in the gothic style, its facade has three gabled portals and a rose window.

⑥ In most French cities you will find the **Hôtel de ville**, which houses the government administration offices.

1 Faisons connaissance!

① Bonjour!

When you meet new people, it's fun to find out what you have in common with them—and even what you don't!

In this chapter you will learn

- to greet people and say goodbye; to ask how people are and tell how you are; to ask someone's name and age and give yours
- to express likes, dislikes, and preferences about things
- to express likes, dislikes, and preferences about activities

And you will

- listen to French-speaking students tell what they like to do
- read about French-speaking teenagers who are looking for pen pals
- write a letter of introduction to a pen pal
- find out how French-speaking people greet one another

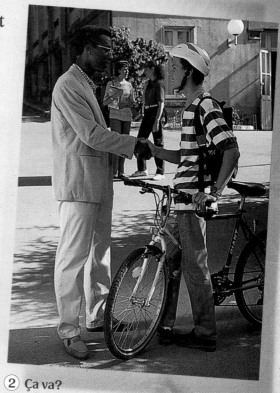

② Ça va?

③ J'aime les pâtisseries!

Mise en train

Salut, les copains!

What can you tell about these teenagers just by looking at their photos?

Claire

Bonjour! Ça va? Je m'appelle Claire. J'ai 15 ans. Je suis française, de Poitiers. J'adore le cinéma. Mais j'aime aussi danser, lire, voyager et écouter de la musique.

Djeneba

Salut! Je m'appelle Djeneba. J'ai 16 ans. Je suis ivoirienne. J'aime étudier, mais j'aime mieux faire du sport. C'est super cool!

Ahmed

Salut! Je m'appelle Ahmed. Je suis marocain. J'aime tous les sports, surtout le football. J'aime aussi faire du vélo.

Thuy

Salut! Ça va? Je m'appelle Thuy. J'ai 14 ans. Je suis vietnamienne. J'aime faire les magasins. En général, je n'aime pas la télévision. J'aime mieux aller au cinéma.

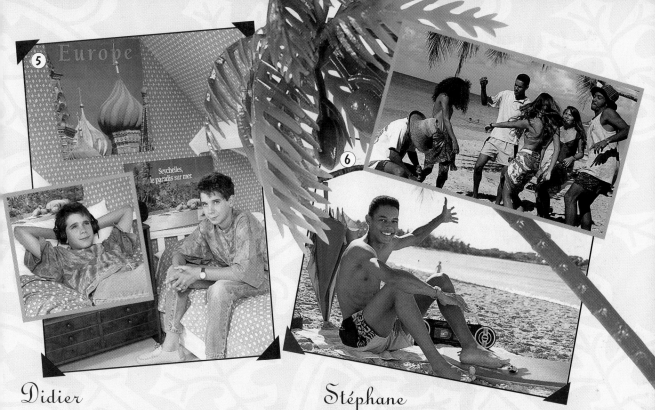

Didier

Salut! Je m'appelle Didier. J'ai 13 ans. Je suis belge. J'aime écouter de la musique. J'aime aussi les vacances. J'aime surtout voyager!

Stéphane

Bonjour! Je m'appelle Stéphane. J'ai 15 ans et je suis martiniquais. J'aime la plage, la mer, le soleil, la musique et j'aime aussi nager. J'aime surtout danser.

André

Tiens, bonjour! Comment ça va? Je m'appelle André. J'ai 17 ans et je suis suisse. Je parle français et allemand. J'aime beaucoup la télévision. J'aime aussi parler au téléphone avec mes copains.

Emilie

Bonjour! Je m'appelle Emilie. J'ai 16 ans. Je suis québécoise. J'adore faire du sport, surtout du ski et du patin. J'aime bien aussi faire de l'équitation.

1 Tu as compris? *Did you understand?*

Answer the following questions about the teenagers you've just met. Look back at **Salut, les copains!** if you have to. Don't be afraid to guess.

1. What are these teenagers talking about?
2. What information do they give you in the first few lines of their introductions?
3. What are some of the things they like?
4. Which of them have interests in common?

2 Vrai ou faux? *True or false?*

According to **Salut, les copains!**, are the following statements true **(vrai)** or false **(faux)**?

1. André aime parler au téléphone.
2. Ahmed n'aime pas le sport.
3. Stéphane aime écouter de la musique.
4. Claire aime voyager et danser.
5. Didier n'aime pas voyager.
6. Emilie aime faire de l'équitation.
7. Thuy aime la télévision.
8. Djeneba n'aime pas faire du sport.

3 Cherche les expressions *Look for the expressions*

Look back at **Salut, les copains!** How do the teenagers . . .

1. say hello?
2. give their name?
3. give their age?
4. say they like something?

4 Qui est-ce? *Who is it?*

Can you identify the teenagers in **Salut, les copains!** from these descriptions?

1. Elle est québécoise.
2. Il parle allemand.
3. Il a quinze ans.
4. Il aime voyager.
5. Elle adore le ski.
6. Elle n'aime pas la télévision.
7. Il adore le football.
8. Elle aime étudier.

5 Et maintenant, à toi *And now, it's your turn*

Which of the students in **Salut, les copains!** would you most like to meet? Why? Jot down your thoughts and share them with a classmate.

Rencontre Culturelle

Look at what the people in these photos are doing.

—Salut, Mireille!
—Salut, Lucien!

—Bonjour, maman!
—Bonjour, mon chou!

—Salut, Lucien!
—Salut, Jean-Philippe!

—Salut, Agnès!
—Tchao, Mireille!

—Bonjour, Monsieur
  Balland.
—Bonjour, Marc.

—Au revoir, Monsieur
  Legrand.
—Au revoir, Isabelle.

Qu'en penses-tu?   *What do you think?*

1. How do the teenagers greet adults? Other teenagers? What gestures do they use?
2. How do they say goodbye? What gestures do they use?
3. Is this similar to the way you greet people and say goodbye in the United States?

Savais-tu que...?   *Did you know . . . ?*

In France, girls kiss both girls and boys on the cheek when they meet. The number of kisses varies from two to four depending on the region. Boys shake hands with one another. Teenagers may kiss adults who are family members or friends of the family, but they shake hands when they greet other adults.

To address adults who aren't family members, teenagers generally use the titles **madame, mademoiselle,** or **monsieur. Mme, Mlle,** and **M.** are the written abbreviations of these titles.

PREMIERE ETAPE

Greeting people and saying goodbye; asking how people are and telling how you are; asking someone's name and age and giving yours

COMMENT DIT-ON... ?

Greeting people and saying goodbye

To anyone:	**Bonjour.** *Hello.*	**Au revoir.** *Goodbye.*
		A tout à l'heure. *See you later.*
		A bientôt. *See you soon.*
		A demain. *See you tomorrow.*
To someone your own age or younger:	**Salut.** *Hi.*	**Salut.** *Bye.*
		Tchao. *Bye.*

6 Ecoute!

Imagine you overhear the following short conversations on the street in Poitiers. Listen carefully and decide whether the speakers are saying hello or goodbye.

7 Comment le dire? *How should you say it?*

How would you say hello to these people in French?

Mme Leblanc   M. Diab   Nadia   Eric   Mme Desrochers

8 Comment répondre? *How should you answer?*

How would you respond to the greeting from each of the following people?

1.   2.   3.   4.

COMMENT DIT-ON... ?

Asking how people are and telling how you are

To ask how your friend is: **Comment ça va?** *or* **Ça va?**

To tell how you are:

Super! *Great!*
Très bien. *Very well.*

Ça va. *Fine.*
Comme ci, comme ça. *So-so.*
Pas mal. *Not bad.*
Bof! *(expression of indifference)*

Pas terrible. *Not so great.*

To keep a conversation going: **Et toi?** *And you?*

9 Ecoute!

You're going to hear a student ask Valérie, Jean-Michel, Anne, Marie, and Karim how they're feeling. Are they feeling good, fair, or bad?

10 Méli-mélo! *Mishmash!*

Work with a classmate to rewrite this conversation in the correct order, using your own names. Then, act it out with your partner. Remember to use the appropriate gestures.

Très bien. Super! Et toi? Tchao. Salut,... ! Ça va? Bon. Alors, à tout à l'heure! Bonjour,... !

11 Et ton voisin (ta voisine)? *And your neighbor?*

Create a conversation with a partner. Be sure to greet your partner, ask how he or she is feeling, respond to any questions your partner asks you, and say goodbye. Don't forget to include the gestures you learned in the **Note Culturelle** on page 23.

COMMENT DIT-ON... ?
Asking someone's name and giving yours

—Tu t'appelles comment?
—Je m'appelle Magali.

To ask someone his or her name:
Tu t'appelles comment?

To ask someone else's name:
Il/Elle s'appelle comment? *What is his/her name?*

To give your name:
Je m'appelle...

To give someone else's name:
Il/Elle s'appelle... *His/Her name is . . .*

12 Écoute!

Listen as some French teenagers tell you about their friends. Are they talking about a boy (**un garçon**) or a girl (**une fille**)?

13 Ecoute!

You're going to hear a song called **S'appeler rap.** Which of the following names are mentioned in the song?

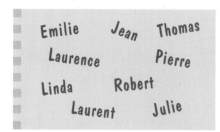

Emilie   Jean   Thomas

Laurence   Pierre

Linda   Robert

Laurent   Julie

14 Je te présente... *Let me introduce ...*

Select a French name for yourself from the list of names on page 5, or ask your teacher to suggest others. Then, say hello to a classmate, introduce yourself, and ask his or her name. Now, introduce your partner to the rest of the class, using **il s'appelle** or **elle s'appelle.**

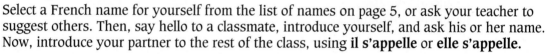

COMMENT DIT-ON... ?

Asking someone's age and giving yours

To find out someone's age:
Tu as quel âge?

To give your age:
J'ai douze **ans.**
treize
quatorze
quinze
seize
dix-sept
dix-huit

15 Ecoute!

Listen as Bruno, Véronique, Laurent, and Céline introduce themselves to you. Write down each student's age.

16 Faisons connaissance! *Let's get to know one another!*

Create a conversation with two other classmates. Introduce yourself, ask your partners' names and ages, and ask how they are.

17 Mon journal *My journal*

A good way to learn French is to use it to express your own thoughts and feelings. From time to time, you'll be asked to write about yourself in French in a journal. As your first journal entry, identify yourself—give your name, your age, and anything else important to you that you've learned how to say in French.

DEUXIEME ETAPE

Expressing likes, dislikes, and preferences about things

COMMENT DIT-ON... ?

Expressing likes, dislikes, and preferences about things

To ask if someone likes something:
Tu aimes les hamburgers?

To say that you like something:
J'adore le chocolat.
J'aime bien le sport.
J'aime les hamburgers.

To say that you dislike something:
Je n'aime pas les hamburgers.

To say that you prefer something:
J'aime mieux le chocolat.
Je préfère le français.

J'aime la pizza.

Je n'aime pas la pizza.

Note de *Grammaire*

Look at the sentences in the illustrations to the left. Can you figure out when to use **ne (n')... pas**?

You put **ne (n')... pas** around the verb **aime** to make the sentence negative. Notice the contraction **n'** before the vowel.

J'aime le sport.
Je **n'**aime **pas** le sport.

18 Ecoute!

a. Listen to Paul and Sophie Dubois discuss names for their baby girl. Which of the names does Paul prefer? And Sophie?

Claude   Sandrine   Claudette
Laetitia   Claudine

b. Do you agree with Paul and Sophie's choices? With a partner, discuss whether you like or dislike the names Paul and Sophie mention. What's your favorite French girl's name? And your favorite French boy's name? You might refer to the list of names on page 5.

— Tu aimes... ?
— Non. J'aime mieux...

19 Quel film?   *Which movie?*

With two of your classmates, decide on a movie you all like.

— J'aime *Aliens*®! Et toi?
— Moi, je n'aime pas *Aliens*®. Tu aimes *Star Trek*®?
— Oui, j'aime *Star Trek*®, mais j'aime mieux *Casablanca*!

CASABLANCA RE
1942. 1h40. Film d'aventures américain en noir et blanc de Michael Curtiz avec Humphrey Bogart, Ingrid Bergman, Paul Henreid, Conrad Veidt, Claude Rains.
Casablanca à l'heure de Vichy. Un réfugié américain retrouve une femme follement aimée et fuit la persécution nazie. Une distribution étincelante et une mise en scène efficace.
• V.O. Saint Lambert 96

les amis (m.)

le cinéma

le ski

le football

le magasin

la plage

le vélo

la glace

l'école (f.)

le français

les frites (f.)

le chocolat

l'anglais (m.)

les examens (m.)

les vacances (f.)

les escargots (m.)

You can probably guess what these words mean:

les concerts (m.)   les hamburgers (m.)   les maths (f.)   la pizza   le sport

20 Ecoute!

Listen as several French teenagers call in to a radio talk-show poll of their likes and dislikes. Match their names with the pictures that illustrate the activities they like or dislike.

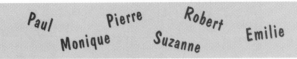

Paul   Pierre   Robert   Emilie
Monique   Suzanne

a.

b.

Salut, Jean!   Salut, Elodie!

c.

d.

e.

f.

𝒢rammaire   The definite articles **le**, **la**, **l'**, and **les**

There are four ways to say *the* in French: **le**, **la**, **l'**, and **les**. These words are called *definite articles*. Look at the articles and nouns below. Can you tell when to use **les**? When to use **l'**?

le français	la glace	l'école	les escargots
le football	la pizza	l'anglais	les magasins

- As you may have guessed, you always use **les** before plural nouns.
- Before a singular noun, you use **l'** if the noun begins with a vowel sound, **le** if the noun is masculine, or **la** if the noun is feminine. How do you know which nouns are masculine and which are feminine? One general rule to follow is that normally, nouns that refer to males are masculine (**le garçon** *the boy*) and those that refer to females are feminine (**la fille** *the girl*). There are no hard-and-fast rules for nouns that refer to neither males nor females; you'll just have to learn the definite article **le**, **la**, **l'**, or **les** that goes with each one.

---

21 Et toi, qu'est-ce que tu aimes?

Lucie and Gilbert are talking about the things they like. With a partner, complete their conversation according to the pictures.

LUCIE   Moi, j'aime bien . Et toi?

GILBERT   Moi, j'aime mieux . J'aime bien aussi sortir avec  .

J'adore le sport aussi. Et toi, tu aimes le sport?

LUCIE   Oui, j'adore et j'aime bien aussi.

How can you remember if a noun is masculine or feminine? Here are a few hints. Choose the one that works best for you.

De bons Conseils

- Practice saying each noun aloud with **le** or **la** in front of it. (NOTE: This won't help with nouns that begin with vowels!)
- Write the feminine nouns in one column and the masculine nouns in another. You might even write the feminine nouns in one color and the masculine nouns in a second color.
- Make flash cards of the nouns, writing the feminine and masculine nouns in different colors.

---

22 Tu aimes...?   *Do you like . . . ?*

Choose six things from the vocabulary on page 27. Next, write down which of those things you like and which you dislike. Then, with a partner, try to guess each other's likes and dislikes by asking **Tu aimes... ?**

A la française

Two common words you can use to connect your ideas are **et** *(and)* and **mais** *(but)*. Here's how you can use them to combine sentences.

J'aime les hamburgers. J'aime le chocolat.
J'aime les hamburgers **et** le chocolat.

J'aime le français. Je n'aime pas les maths.
J'aime le français, **mais** je n'aime pas les maths.

---

23 Mon journal

In your journal, write down some of your likes and dislikes. Use **et** and **mais** to connect your sentences. You might want to illustrate your journal entry.

PANORAMA CULTUREL

Gabrielle • Québec

Fabienne • Martinique

Caroline • France

What do you like to do when you have free time? Do you think teenagers in French-speaking countries like to do the same things? Here's what some students had to say about their favorite leisure-time activities.

Qu'est-ce que tu aimes faire après l'école?

«J'aime lire. J'aime écouter de la musique. J'aime parler... discuter avec mes amis.»

—Gabrielle

«Alors, quand j'ai du temps libre, j'aime aller au cinéma, aller à la plage, lire et puis voilà, c'est tout.»

—Fabienne

«Après l'école, j'aime regarder la télévision, aller à la piscine ou lire des livres.»

—Caroline

Qu'en penses-tu?

1. What do all three of these people have in common?
2. What interests do you and your friends share with these people?
3. What do these people do that isn't commonly done where you live?
4. Which of these people would you most like to meet? Why?

Savais-tu que...?

In general, teenagers everywhere enjoy the same kinds of activities you do. However, some activities do tend to be especially popular in certain areas, such as badminton and hockey in Canada, dancing and soccer in West Africa, and soccer and cycling in France. In many francophone countries, students have a great deal of homework, so they do not have very much leisure time after school. Of course, people are individuals, so their tastes vary. In French, you might say **Chacun ses goûts!** *(To each his own!)*.

TROISIEME ETAPE

Expressing likes, dislikes, and preferences about activities

Vocabulaire

Stéphanie adore **regarder la télé.**

Etienne aime **sortir avec les copains.**

Nicolas aime **parler au téléphone.**

Olivier aime **dormir.**

Danielle aime **étudier.**

Sylvie aime bien **faire du sport.**

Michèle aime **faire les magasins.**

Hervé aime **faire le ménage.**

Raymond aime **faire de l'équitation.**

Serge aime **voyager.**

Eric aime **écouter de la musique.**

Laurence aime bien **nager.**

Solange adore **danser.**

Annie aime **lire.**

TROISIEME ETAPE

trente et un **31**

24 Ecoute!

You're going to hear six students tell you what they like or don't like to do. For each statement you hear, decide which of the students pictured on page 31 is speaking.

COMMENT DIT-ON... ?

Expressing likes, dislikes, and preferences about activities

To ask if someone likes an activity:
Tu aimes voyager?

To tell what you like to do:
J'aime voyager.
J'adore danser.
J'aime bien dormir.

To tell what you don't like to do:
Je n'aime pas aller aux concerts.

To tell what you prefer to do:
J'aime mieux regarder la télévision.

25 Sondage *Poll*

a. Complete the following poll.

1. J'aime...
a. faire de l'équitation.
b. sortir avec les copains.
c. parler français.
d. dormir.
e. écouter le professeur.
f. faire du sport.

2. Chez moi, j'aime...
a. regarder la télévision.
b. écouter de la musique.
c. dormir.
d. parler au téléphone.

3. Avec mes copains, j'aime mieux...
a. faire du sport.
b. manger au restaurant.
c. faire les magasins.
d. danser.
e. nager.
f. aller au cinéma.

4. J'aime surtout...
a. le chocolat.
b. les hamburgers.
c. la salade.
d. les frites.
e. la pizza.

5. J'aime aussi...
a. le ski.
b. le vélo.
c. le volley.
d. le basket-ball.

6. Je n'aime pas...
a. les escargots.
b. la pollution.
c. l'école.
d. la violence.
e. les dentistes.
f. les examens.

b. Compare your responses to the poll with those of a classmate. Which interests do you have in common?

Grammaire Subject pronouns and -er verbs

The verb **aimer** has different forms. In French, the verb forms change according to the subjects just as they do in English: *I like, you like,* but *he* or *she likes.*

Look at the chart below. Most **-er** verbs, that is, verbs whose infinitive ends in **-er**, follow this pattern.

aimer *(to like)*

J'aime	Nous aim**ons**
Tu aim**es** ⎱ les vacances.	Vous aim**ez** ⎱ les vacances.
Il/Elle aime	Ils/Elles aim**ent**

- The forms **aime, aimes,** and **aiment** sound the same.
- The subject pronouns in French are **je** *(I)*, **tu** *(you)*, **il** *(he or it)*, **elle** *(she or it)*, **nous** *(we)*, **vous** *(you)*, **ils** *(they)*, and **elles** *(they)*.
- Notice that there are two pronouns for *they*. Use **elles** to refer to a group of females. Use **ils** to refer to a group of males or a group of males and females.
- **Tu** and **vous** both mean *you*. Use **vous** when you talk to more than one person or to an adult who is not a family member. Use **tu** when you talk to a friend, family member, or someone your own age.
- Noun subjects take the same verb forms as their pronouns.

Philippe aime la salade.	**Sophie et Julie aiment** faire du sport.
Il aime la salade.	**Elles aiment** faire du sport.

26 «Tu» ou «vous»?

During your trip to France, you meet the following people. Would you use **tu** or **vous** to greet them? How would you ask them if they like a certain thing or activity?

M. et Mme Roland   Mlle Normand   Flore et Loïc   Lucie

27 Qu'est-ce qu'ils aiment faire?

Your French pen pal wants to know what your friends like to do. Use the following photographs as cues.

Julio

Robert

Mark, David et Thomas

Pam

Marie

Eric

Karen

Blair

Emily et Raymond

28 Les vedettes! *Celebrities!*

a. Make a list of three public figures you admire (movie stars, musicians, athletes, . . .). Write down one or two things you think each person might like to do.

Shaquille O'Neal aime faire du sport, surtout du basket-ball!

b. Now, get together with a classmate. Tell your partner what one of the celebrities you've chosen likes to do. Use **il** or **elle** instead of the person's name. Your partner will try to identify the celebrity. Take turns.

29 Enquête *Survey*

Get together with three classmates. Ask questions to find out who shares your likes and dislikes. After you've discovered what you have in common, report your findings to the rest of the class.

> Paul et moi, nous aimons le français et l'anglais, mais nous n'aimons pas le sport.

30 Mon journal

Expand upon your previous journal entry. Write about the activities you like and dislike. Tell which activities you and your friends like to do together. Find or draw pictures to illustrate the activities.

PRONONCIATION

Intonation

As you speak, your voice rises and falls. This is called *intonation*.

A. A prononcer

In French, your voice rises at the end of each group of words within a statement and falls at the end of a statement. Repeat each of the following phrases:

J'aime les frites, les hamburgers et la pizza.

Il aime le football, mais il n'aime pas le vélo.

If you want to change a statement into a question, raise your voice at the end of the sentence. Repeat these questions.

Tu aimes l'anglais?

Tu t'appelles Julie?

B. A écouter

Decide whether each of the following is a statement or a question.

C. A écrire

You're going to hear two short dialogues. Write down what the people say.

LISONS!

When you look through French magazines, you'll often find a section called **Petites annonces** where people place personal or business ads.

DE BONS CONSEILS

You can often figure out what a reading selection is about simply by looking at the titles, subtitles, illustrations, and captions.

A. Look at the pictures and titles of this article from a French magazine. What do you think the article is about?

B. Do you remember what you've learned about cognates? Can you find at least five cognates in this article?

C. What do you think **Petites annonces** means?

D. Which of the pen pals would you choose if you were searching for the following?

Quelqu'un qui *(someone who)*...

aime faire les boutiques

aime les animaux

parle français et espagnol

aime la musique et le cinéma

aime le rap et la techno

PETITES

Christiane Saulnier
Marseille

Si vous aimez la télévision, les animaux et les vacances, qu'est-ce que vous attendez pour m'écrire et m'envoyer votre photo! Je voudrais correspondre avec des filles ou des garçons de 13 à 16 ans. J'attends votre réponse avec impatience!

Karim Marzouk
Tunis, Tunisie

J'adorerais recevoir des lettres de personnes habitant le monde entier; j'adore voyager, écouter de la musique, aller au concert et lire sur la plage. J'aime bien les langues et je parle aussi l'arabe et l'espagnol. A bientôt.

Mireille Lacombe
Nantes

J'ai 15 ans et je voudrais bien correspondre avec des filles et des garçons de 13 à 17 ans. J'aime le rap et surtout la techno. Je fais aussi de l'équitation. Ecrivez-moi vite et je promets de vous répondre (photos S.V.P.)!

Didier Kouassi
Abidjan, Côte d'Ivoire

La techno me fait délirer et je suis aussi très sportif. Je cherche des correspondants filles ou garçons entre 15 et 17 ans. N'hésitez pas à m'écrire!

ANNONCES

Laurence Simon
La Marin, Martinique

J'ai 16 ans, je suis dingue de sport, j'aime les soirs de fête entre copains. Le week-end, j'aime faire les magasins. Alors, si vous me ressemblez, dépêchez-vous de m'écrire. Réponse assurée à 100%!

Etienne Hubert
Poitiers

Je suis blond aux yeux bleus, assez grand, timide mais très sympa. J'aime sortir et j'aime lire la science-fiction. Je cherche des amis entre 14 et 16 ans. Répondez vite!

Hugues Vallet
la Rochelle

Je voudrais correspondre avec des filles et des garçons de 16 à 18 ans. J'aime sortir, délirer et faire les boutiques. Je suis fan de Vanessa Paradis et de Julia Roberts. Alors, j'attends vos lettres!

Amélie Perrin
Périgord

Je voudrais correspondre avec des jeunes de 14 à 17 ans qui aiment faire la fête, écouter de la musique et aller au cinéma. Moi, j'étudie la danse et la photographie. Ecrivez-moi et je me ferai une joie de vous répondre.

Vous voulez correspondre avec des gens sympa? Écrivez votre petite annonce en précisant vos nom, prénom, âge et adresse, et en y joignant une photo d'identité.

E. Several of your friends are looking for pen pals. Based on their wishes, find a good match for each of them in **Petites annonces.**

> My pen pal should like sports.

> I'd like to hear from someone who likes going out.

> I'm looking for a pen pal who likes to go to the movies.

> It would be great to have a pen pal who enjoys shopping.

> I'd like to hear from someone from Africa.

> I'd like a pen pal who likes to travel.

F. If you want to place an ad for a pen pal, what should you do?

G. Jot down a few things you might like to include in your own letter requesting a pen pal. Using your notes, write your own request for a pen pal like the ones you read in **Petites Annonces.**

MISE EN PRATIQUE

CHAPITRE 1 CHAPITRE 1 CHAPITRE 1 CHAPITRE 1 CHAPITRE 1 CHAPITRE 1 CHAPITRE 1 CHAPITRE 1 CHAPITRE 1 CHAPITRE 1 CHAPITRE 1 CHAPITRE 1

1 Do the following photos represent French culture, American culture, or both?

1.

2.

3.

4.

5.

2 **L'Organisation internationale de correspondants (l'O.I.C.)**, a pen pal organization you wrote to, has left a phone message on your answering machine. Listen carefully to the message and write down your pen pal's name, age, phone number, likes, and dislikes.

3 Tell a classmate in French about your new pen pal.

Name:

Age:

Likes:

Dislikes:

Robert Perrault
25, Boulevard Saint
92700 TANNAY
FRANCE

Bonjour.
Je suis bien content d'être ton
correspondant. J'ai quinze ans.
J'aime bien sortir avec les copains
et écouter de la musique aussi,
mais j'aime pas danser. J'adore
la pizza et la glace au chocolat.
Et toi? Le week-end, j'adore faire du
sport. J'aime bien le vélo, mais pendant les vacances, j'aime mieux
nager; c'est super! Tu aimes nager
aussi? J'espère que oui. Écris-moi.
A bientôt,
Robert

4 You've received your first letter from Robert Perrault. Read it twice— the first time for general understanding, the second time for details. Then, answer the questions below in English.

1. How old is Robert?

2. What sports does he like?

3. What foods does he like?

4. What doesn't he like to do?

5 Now, answer Robert's letter. Begin your reply with **Cher Robert.** Be sure to . . .

• introduce yourself.

• ask how he's doing.

• tell about your likes and dislikes.

• ask him about other likes and dislikes he might have.

• answer his questions to you.

• say goodbye.

6

J E U   D E   R O L E

A French exchange student has just arrived at your school. How would you find out his or her name? Age? Likes and dislikes? Act out the scene with a partner. Take turns playing the role of the French student.

Can you greet people and say goodbye? p. 22

Can you ask how people are and tell how you are? p. 23

Can you ask someone's name and age and give yours? pp. 24–25

Can you express likes, dislikes, and preferences? pp. 26, 32

Can you use what you've learned in this chapter?

1 How would you say hello and goodbye to the following people? What gestures would you use?

    1. a classmate   2. your French teacher

2 Can you ask how someone is?

3 If someone asks you how you are, what do you say if . . .

    1. you feel great?   2. you feel OK?   3. you don't feel well?

4 How would you . . .

    1. ask someone's name?   2. tell someone your name?

5 How would you . . .

    1. find out someone's age?   2. tell someone how old you are?

6 Can you tell what you like and dislike, using the verb **aimer**?

    1. horseback riding   4. shopping
    2. soccer   5. the movies
    3. going out with friends

7 Can you ask a friend in French if he or she likes . . .

a.

b.

c.

d.

e.

8 Can you tell in French what these people like, dislike, or prefer?

    1. Robert never studies.
    2. Emilie thinks reading is the greatest.
    3. Hervé prefers pizza.
    4. Nathalie never goes to the beach.
    5. Nicole is always cycling or playing soccer.

PREMIERE ETAPE

Greeting people and saying goodbye

Bonjour! *Hello!*
Salut! *Hi! or Goodbye!*
Au revoir! *Goodbye!*
A tout à l'heure! *See you later!*
A bientôt. *See you soon.*
A demain. *See you tomorrow.*
Tchao! *Bye!*
madame (Mme) *ma'am; Mrs.*
mademoiselle (Mlle) *miss; Miss*
monsieur (M.) *sir; Mr.*

Asking how people are and telling how you are

(Comment) ça va? *How's it going?*
Ça va. *Fine.*
Super! *Great!*
Très bien. *Very well.*
Comme ci, comme ça. *So-so.*
Bof! *(expression of indifference)*
Pas mal. *Not bad.*
Pas terrible. *Not so great.*
Et toi? *And you?*

Asking someone's name and giving yours

Tu t'appelles comment? *What's your name?*
Je m'appelle... *My name is . . .*
Il/Elle s'appelle comment? *What's his/her name?*
Il/Elle s'appelle... *His/Her name is . . .*

Asking someone's age and giving yours

Tu as quel âge? *How old are you?*
J'ai... ans. *I am . . . years old.*
douze *twelve*
treize *thirteen*
quatorze *fourteen*
quinze *fifteen*
seize *sixteen*
dix-sept *seventeen*
dix-huit *eighteen*

DEUXIEME ETAPE

Expressing likes, dislikes, and preferences about things

Moi, j'aime (bien)... *I (really) like . . .*
Je n'aime pas... *I don't like . . .*
J'aime mieux... *I prefer . . .*
Je préfère... *I prefer . . .*
J'adore... *I adore . . .*
Tu aimes... ? *Do you like . . . ?*
les amis (m.) *friends*
l'anglais (m.) *English*
le chocolat *chocolate*
le cinéma *the movies*
les concerts (m.) *concerts*
l'école (f.) *school*
les escargots (m.) *snails*
les examens (m.) *tests*
le football *soccer*
le français *French*
les frites (f.) *French fries*
la glace *ice cream*
les hamburgers (m.) *hamburgers*
les magasins (m.) *stores*
les maths (f.) *math*
la pizza *pizza*
la plage *beach*
le ski *skiing*
le sport *sports*
les vacances (f.) *vacation*
le vélo *biking*

Other useful expressions

et *and*
mais *but*
non *no*
oui *yes*

TROISIEME ETAPE

Expressing likes, dislikes, and preferences about activities

aimer *to like*
danser *to dance*
dormir *to sleep*
écouter de la musique *to listen to music*
étudier *to study*
faire de l'équitation *to go horseback riding*
faire les magasins *to go shopping*
faire le ménage *to do housework*
faire du sport *to play sports*
lire *to read*
nager *to swim*
parler au téléphone *to talk on the phone*
regarder la télé *to watch TV*
sortir avec les copains *to go out with friends*
voyager *to travel*

Other useful expressions

aussi *also*
surtout *especially*

For subject pronouns, see page 33.

2
Vive l'école!

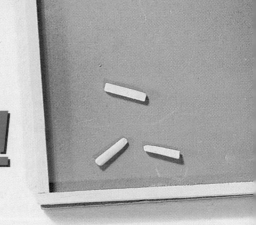

① — J'adore le sport!
— Moi aussi!

When school starts, new schedules are the main topic of conversation, at least for a while. What classes do you have? How do you feel about them?

In this chapter you will learn

- to agree and disagree
- to ask for and give information
- to ask for and express opinions

And you will

- listen to French-speaking students talk about their classes
- read a French student's class schedule
- write about your own classes
- compare schools in francophone countries with schools in the United States

② J'ai latin à dix heures quinze.

③ Les arts plastiques, c'est génial!

Mise en train

La rentrée

Where do you think these teenagers are?
What do you think they're talking about?
How do you know?

Les jeunes de Poitiers :

Claire   Delphine   Marc

et du Texas :

Jérôme   Ann

C'est la première semaine de cours...

Tu as quel cours maintenant?

Allemand. J'adore. Et toi, tu as quoi?

Sciences nat.

Ecoutez. Je ne veux pas être en retard. Bon courage!

Pourquoi?

C'est difficile, les sciences nat.

Mais non, c'est passionnant. Et le prof est sympa.

2

Qu'est-ce qu'il y a?

Oh rien. J'ai maths.

Alors, les garçons, ça boume?

3

Super.

Bof. Pas terrible.

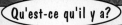

Tu n'aimes pas les maths?

4

Non, c'est nul.

CHAPITRE 2   Vive l'école!

1 Tu as compris?

Answer the following questions about **La rentrée**.

1. What are the students discussing?
2. What do you think **La rentrée** means?
3. What class do they all have together?
4. Why are they in a hurry at the end of the conversation?
5. What is Jérôme worried about?

2 Vrai ou faux?

1. Ann est américaine.
2. Jérôme n'aime pas l'espagnol.
3. Ann et Marc n'aiment pas les maths.
4. Jérôme a allemand.
5. Marc n'a pas sport cet aprèm.

3 Cherche les expressions

In **La rentrée**, what do the students say to . . .

1. ask what class someone has?
2. tell why they like a class?
3. tell why they don't like a class?
4. tell which class they prefer?
5. ask what time it is?

4 Ils aiment ou pas?

Do these students like or dislike the subjects or teachers they're talking about?

1. «Les sciences nat, c'est passionnant.»
2. «Les maths, c'est nul.»
3. «C'est super intéressant, les maths.»
4. «Le prof est sympa.»

5 Qu'est-ce qui manque?   *What's missing?*

Choose the correct words from the box to complete these sentences based on **La rentrée**.

1. Après maths, Marc a _____.
2. Jérôme a _____.
3. Jérôme aime mieux _____ que l'allemand.
4. On a tous sport à _____ heures.
5. On est en retard! Il est _____ heures.

> géographie   allemand   quatorze
>
> huit   l'espagnol

6 Et maintenant, à toi

Which students in **La rentrée** share your own likes or dislikes about school subjects?

VOCABULAIRE

l'algèbre (f.)	*algebra*	la chorale	*choir*	la musique	*music*
la biologie	*biology*	le cours de développement		le cours	*course, school subject*
la chimie	*chemistry*	personnel et social (DPS)	*health*	les devoirs (m.)	*homework*
la géométrie	*geometry*	la danse	*dance*	l'élève (m./f.)	*student*
la physique	*physics*	le latin	*Latin*	le professeur	*teacher*

*You can abbreviate **Education Physique et Sportive** as **EPS.** In conversation, students often say **le sport** instead of **EPS.**

7 Ecoute!

On the first day of school, Céline and Aurélie are looking for their French class. As you listen to their conversation, look at the drawing of the school on page 47 and write the numbers of the classrooms they're looking into.

8 Ils aiment quels cours? *What subjects do they like?*

Name three subjects Nicole and Gérard probably like, according to their interests.

Nicole

Gérard

9 C'est qui? *Who is it?*

Tell your partner what subject one of these students likes, without naming the person. Your partner will try to guess the person's name. Take turns until you've identified all of the students.

Michel

— Il aime le français.
— C'est Michel.

Julien

Nathalie

Virginie

Guillaume

Franck

Karine

Study at regular intervals. It's best to learn language in small chunks and to review frequently. Cramming will not usually work for French. Study at least a little bit every day, whether you have an assignment or not. The more often you review words and structures, the easier it will be for you to understand and participate in class.

NOTE CULTURELLE

In France and other countries that follow the French educational system, the grade levels are numbered in descending order. When students begin junior high (**le collège**) at about 10 or 11 years of age, the grade they are in is called **sixième**. Then they go into **cinquième, quatrième,** and **troisième.** The grade levels at the high school (**le lycée**) are called **seconde, première,** and **terminale.**

Le baccalauréat, or le bac, is a national exam taken at the end of study at a **lycée.** Not all students take the **bac,** but those who plan to go on to a university must pass it. It's an extremely difficult oral and written test that covers all major subjects. Students spend the final year of the **lycée, la terminale,** preparing for this exam. There are several kinds of **baccalauréat** exams, each appropriate to a major field of study. For example, students who specialize in literature and languages take **le bac A2,** students of math and physical science take **le bac C.**

Bac 1991 : 75 % de reçus

Taux de réussite au baccalauréat d'enseignement général par série (en %) :

Séries	Total	dont filles
A1 - Lettres, sciences	73,4	74,8
A2 - Lettres, langues	76,3	76,9
A3 - Lettres, arts plastiques	70,1	71,1
B - Economique et social	68,7	70,7
C - Maths et sc. physiques	84,3	88,2
D - Maths et sc. de la nature	74,2	78,0
D' - Sciences agro. et tech.	69,0	63,2
E - Sciences et techniques	75,2	73,8
Total France métropolitaine	**74,9**	**76,3**

Un élève entrant en sixième a 57 % de chances de devenir bachelier, contre 30 % en 1980.

10 Mon journal

Make a list of your favorite school subjects in your journal. If you were taking these subjects in France, which **bac** do you think you would take?

Je ferais le bac... (*I would take* **bac** . . .)

COMMENT DIT-ON... ?

Agreeing and disagreeing

To agree:

Oui, beaucoup. *Yes, very much.*
Moi aussi. *Me too.*
Moi non plus. *Neither do I.*

To disagree:

Moi, non. *I don't.*
Non, pas trop. *No, not too much.*
Moi, si. *I do.*
Pas moi. *Not me.*

11 Ecoute!

Listen as Hélène and Gérard talk about the subjects they like and dislike. Which one do they agree on? Which one do they disagree on?

12 Parlons! *Let's talk!*

Ask your partner's opinion about several subjects and then agree or disagree. Take turns.

— Tu aimes les arts plastiques?
— Non, pas trop.
— Moi, si.

Note de *G*rammaire

Use **si** instead of **oui** to contradict a negative statement or question.

— Tu **n'**aimes **pas** la biologie?
— Mais **si!** J'adore la bio!

13 Ça te plaît? *Do you like it?*

Get together with two classmates. Find at least two things or activities that you all like. Then, tell the rest of the class what you agree on.

ELEVE 1 — J'aime les hamburgers. Et toi?
ELEVE 2 — Oui, beaucoup.
ELEVE 3 — Moi aussi.
ELEVE 1 — Nous aimons tous *(all)* les hamburgers.

le cinéma   le foot   les concerts
la pizza   faire du sport
écouter de la musique
la glace   faire les magasins   le ski

COMMENT DIT-ON...?
Asking for and giving information

To ask about someone's classes:	To tell what classes you have:
Tu as quels cours aujourd'hui? *What classes do you have . . . ?*	**J'ai** arts plastiques et physique.
Tu as quoi le matin? *What do you have . . . ?*	**J'ai** algèbre, DPS et sport.
Vous avez espagnol l'après-midi? *Do you have . . . ?*	Oui, **nous avons** aussi espagnol et géo.

14   On a quoi?   *What do we have?*

a. Find out what subjects your partner has in the morning and in the afternoon.

— Tu as quoi le matin
  (l'après-midi)?
— Bio, algèbre et chorale.
  Et toi?
— Moi, j'ai algèbre, chimie,
  chorale et DPS.

b. Now, tell the rest of the class
which subjects you and your
partner have in common.

  Marc et moi, nous avons
  algèbre et chorale.

VOCABULAIRE

le matin	*in the morning*
l'après-midi	*in the afternoon*
aujourd'hui	*today*
demain	*tomorrow*
maintenant	*now*

Grammaire   The verb avoir

Avoir is an irregular verb. That means it doesn't follow the pattern of the -**er** verbs you learned in Chapter 1.

avoir *(to have)*

J' **ai**		Nous **avons**	
Tu **as**	chimie maintenant.	Vous **avez**	chimie maintenant.
Il/Elle/On **a**		Ils/Elles **ont**	

As you saw in Chapter 1, you often use an article (**le, la, l'**, or **les**) before a noun. When you're telling which school subjects you have, however, you don't use an article.

15 Ils ont quels cours?

Some students are day-dreaming about the future. What classes are they taking to prepare for these careers?

Ils ont géométrie, physique et géographie.

1.

2.

3.

4.

VOCABULAIRE

Voilà l'emploi du temps de Stéphanie Lambert.

EMPLOI DU TEMPS				NOM: Stéphanie Lambert			CLASSE: 3ᵉ	
		LUNDI	**MARDI**	**MERCREDI**	**JEUDI**	**VENDREDI**	**SAMEDI**	**DIMANCHE**
MATIN	**8h00**	Allemand	Arts plastiques	Mathématiques	Mathématiques	Français		L
	9h00	Français	Arts plastiques	Anglais	Sciences nat	Français	Anglais	
	10h00	**Récréation**	**Récréation**	**Récréation**	**Récréation**	**Récréation**	TP physique	I
	10h15	EPS	Allemand	Français	EPS	Sciences nat	TP physique	
	11h15	Sciences nat	**Etude**	Histoire/Géo	**Etude**	Arts plastiques	**[Sortie]**	B
	12h15	**Déjeuner**	**Déjeuner**	**[Sortie]**	**Déjeuner**	**Déjeuner**	**APRES-MIDI**	
APRES-MIDI	**14h00**	Histoire/Géo	Mathématiques	**APRES-MIDI**	Histoire/Géo	Allemand	**LIBRE**	R
	15h00	Anglais	Physique/Chimie	**LIBRE**	Physique/Chimie	Mathématiques		
	16h00	**Récréation**	**[Sortie]**		**Récréation**	**[Sortie]**		E
	16h15	Mathématiques			Arts plastiques			
	17h15	**[Sortie]**			**[Sortie]**			

16 Tu comprends?

Answer the following questions about Stéphanie Lambert's schedule on page 52.

1. Can you find and copy the words in the schedule that refer to days of the week?
2. **Déjeuner** and **Récréation** don't refer to school subjects. What do you think they mean?
3. What do you think **14h00** means?
4. If **étudier** means *to study,* what do you think **Etude** means?*
5. You know that **sortir** means *to go out.* What do you think **Sortie** means?
6. Can you list two differences between Stéphanie's schedule and yours?

17 Vrai ou faux?

Decide whether the following statements are true (**vrai**) or false (**faux**) according to Stéphanie's schedule. Correct the false statements.

1. Le lundi et le jeudi, elle a histoire.
2. Stéphanie a arts plastiques le lundi.
3. Le vendredi, elle a allemand.
4. Stéphanie a sport le lundi et le jeudi.
5. Elle a étude le mercredi.
6. Elle n'a pas cours le samedi.

18 Ecoute!

Look at Stéphanie's schedule as you listen to three of her friends call her on the phone. They're going to tell her what subjects they have on a certain day of the week. Do they have the same subjects as Stéphanie on that day?

VOCABULAIRE

You've already learned the numbers 0–20. Here are the numbers 21–59 in French.

21 vingt et un	22 vingt-deux	23 vingt-trois	24 vingt-quatre	25 vingt-cinq
26 vingt-six	27 vingt-sept	28 vingt-huit	29 vingt-neuf	30 trente
31 trente et un	32 trente-deux	40 quarante	41 quarante et un	42 quarante-deux
50 cinquante	51 cinquante et un	52 cinquante-deux	59 cinquante-neuf	

---

* In casual conversation, students use **perm** to say *study hall.*

19 Quels sont les nombres?

1. Say these numbers in French.
   a. 25 b. 37 c. 46 d. 53

2. Write the numerals for these numbers.
   a. vingt-huit b. trente-quatre c. quarante et un d. cinquante-cinq

COMMENT DIT-ON... ?

Telling when you have class

To find out at what time someone has a certain class:
Tu as maths **à quelle heure**?

To tell at what time you have a certain class:
J'ai maths **à neuf heures**.

huit heures **dix heures quinze** **sept heures vingt** **quinze heures trente** **seize heures quarante-cinq**

20 Ecoute!

Listen as Jérôme answers Ann's questions about his schedule. At what time does he have these classes: **anglais, espagnol, histoire,** and **maths?**

À la française

In casual conversation, you might try using the abbreviated forms of words just as French teenagers do. For example, **la récréation** can be abbreviated to **la récré.** Do you recall the abbreviated forms of the words listed below? If not, look for them in **La rentrée** or in Stéphanie's schedule.

les sciences naturelles
la géographie
l'éducation physique et sportive
l'après-midi
les mathématiques
le professeur

 **NOTE CULTURELLE**

Although in familiar conversation people may use the 12-hour system to give the time, they use the 24-hour system (**l'heure officielle**) to give schedules for transportation, schools, stores, and movies. For example, the school day generally begins at 8h00 (**huit heures**) and continues until 17h00 (**dix-sept heures**) or 18h00 (**dix-huit heures**) with a break from 12h00 (**douze heures**) to 14h00 (**quatorze heures**). You will learn about the 12-hour system in Chapter 6.

21 Une journée chargée

A busy day

Claudine is busy today. What does she have at each of the times listed?

A huit heures, elle a géographie.

1. 8h00

2. 9h35

3. 11h50

4. 14h05

5. 16h20

22 Nos emplois du temps   *Our schedules*

a. You and your partner prepare schedules showing only the times classes meet at your school. Take turns asking at what time you each have the classes listed here. Fill in each other's schedule, writing the subjects next to the appropriate times.

— Tu as histoire à quelle heure?
— A onze heures trente.

b. Now complete the schedules by asking what subjects you each have at the remaining times.

— Tu as quoi à treize heures?

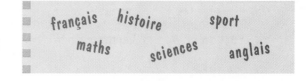

français   histoire   sport
maths   sciences   anglais

23 Mon journal

In your journal, make a list of your classes. Include the days and times you have them, and the names of your teachers.

PANORAMA CULTUREL

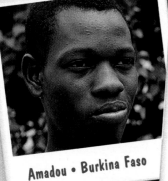

Amadou • Burkina Faso

Yannick • Martinique

Patrice • Québec

What is your school day like? At what time does it start and end? What classes do you have? Here's what some francophone students had to say about their school day.

Tu as quels cours?

«A l'école, j'ai comme cours français, anglais, sciences physiques, sciences naturelles, éducation civique et morale, géographie physique.»

—Amadou

«Comme je suis en première S, j'ai de l'économie. Je fais de l'anglais, du portugais, du français, de l'éducation physique, de l'histoire, de la géographie et des maths.»

Tu peux décrire ton emploi du temps?

«Je commence à huit heures. Je termine à midi. J'ai l'interclasse de midi à deux heures et [j'ai cours] de deux heures à dix-sept heures.»

—Yannick

«Comme cours, j'ai le français, l'anglais, les maths. J'ai aussi éducation physique. J'ai l'art plastique, l'informatique... beaucoup de matières comme ça.»

—Patrice

Qu'en penses-tu?

1. What classes do you have in common with these students?
2. What subjects were mentioned that aren't taught at your school?
3. Would you like to trade schedules with any of these students? Why or why not?

Savais-tu que...?

Students in francophone countries commonly have Wednesday afternoons free and attend classes on Saturday mornings. In general, they follow the same core curriculum, which includes French, math, science, history, geography, physical education, and at least one foreign language. Courses like industrial arts and band are not often taught.

COMMENT DIT-ON... ?
Asking for and expressing opinions

To ask someone's opinion:
Comment tu trouves ça?
Comment tu trouves le cours de biologie?

To express a favorable
    opinion:
C'est... *It's . . .*
    facile. *easy.*
    génial. *great.*
    super. *super.*
    cool. *cool.*
    intéressant.
      interesting.
    passionnant.
      fascinating.

To express indifference:

C'est pas mal.
  It's not bad.
Ça va.

To express an unfavorable
    opinion:
C'est... *It's . . .*
    difficile. *hard.*
    pas terrible. *not*
      so great.
    pas super. *not*
      so hot.
    zéro. *a waste of*
      time.
    nul. *useless.*
    barbant. *boring.*

^A la **française**

In informal conversation, French speakers will often leave out the **ne** in a negative sentence.

    J'aime pas les hamburgers, moi.
    C'est pas super, la géo.

In writing, you should include the **ne** in negative sentences.

24 Ecoute!

Listen as Aurélie and Eric talk about their subjects. Which ones does Eric like? Which doesn't he like? And Aurélie?

les sciences nat   la géo
l'anglais   l'allemand
l'espagnol
l'histoire   les maths

NOTE CULTURELLE

The French system of grading is based on a scale of 0–20. A score of less than 10 isn't a passing grade. Students are usually pleased with a score of 10 or higher. They must work very hard to receive a 17 or an 18, and it's very rare to earn a 19 or a 20.

25 Qu'est-ce qu'on se dit? *What are they saying to themselves?*

What do you think these students are saying to themselves?

1. L'histoire, c'est…

2. La géométrie, c'est…

3. L'algèbre, c'est…

4. La biologie, c'est…

5. L'espagnol, c'est…

6. Les arts plastiques, c'est…

26 Comment tu trouves?

With your partner, discuss how you feel about your classes.

— Tu as maths?
— Oui, à neuf heures.
— Comment tu trouves ça?
— C'est super!

27 La vie scolaire *School life*

Read this letter that your new pen pal Laurent wrote to you after his first day of class. Then, write your reply.

- Cher/Chère … ,

Ça va au lycée? Tu aimes tes cours? Moi, mes cours sont super! J'adore les maths, c'est facile. Mais la physique, c'est turbant. Et la bio, c'est difficile. Et toi? Tu aimes les sciences? Pas moi. J'aime mieux les langues. C'est génial, et c'est plus intéressant. J'ai sport l'après-midi. J'aime bien; c'est cool. Et toi? Tu as sport aussi? Ça te plaît?

A bientôt,
Laurent

28 Un sondage

What is your favorite in each of the following categories? Ask three of your classmates how they like your favorites.

— Comment tu trouves *Jurassic Park*®?
— C'est pas terrible.

les groupes
(musical groups)   les films

les cours   les bandes dessinées
(comic strips)

P R O N O N C I A T I O N

Liaison

In French you don't usually pronounce consonants at the end of a word, such as the **s** in **les** and the **t** in **c'est**. But you do pronounce some final consonants if the following word begins with a vowel sound. This linking of the final consonant of one word with the beginning vowel of the next word is called **liaison**.

les examens	C'est intéressant.	vous avez	deux élèves
z	t	z	z

A. A prononcer

Repeat the following phrases and sentences.

les maths / les escargots
nous n'aimons pas / nous aimons
C'est super./ C'est intéressant.
les profs / les élèves

B. A lire

Take turns with a partner reading the following sentences aloud. Make all necessary liaisons.

1. Ils ont maths.
2. Elles ont histoire.
3. Elles aiment l'espagnol.
4. Elle a deux examens lundi.
5. Vous avez cours le samedi?
6. Nous aimons les arts plastiques.

C. A écrire

You're going to hear two short dialogues. Write down what you hear.

LISONS!

*H*ow do most American students feel about their classes and their teachers? Do you think French students feel the same way?

A. First, look at the illustrations. Based on what you see, do you think you're going to read . . .

1. price lists?
2. math exercises?
3. results from a survey?
4. ads from a sales catalogue?

B. Now, scan the titles and texts. Based on the titles and the drawings, do you think these articles are about . . .

1. teenagers' favorite pastimes?
2. grades given to students on exams?
3. students' attitudes toward school?
4. prices at several stores?

C. Here are some cognates from the graph entitled **Profs.** What do you think these words mean in English?

distants   respectueux
compétents   absents

SONDAGE

PROFS
Dans l'ensemble, jugez-vous que la majorité de vos professeurs sont...

assidus	trop souvent absents
86 %	8
compétents	incompétents
80 %	13 %
intéressants	pas intéressants
68 %	25 %
respectueux	méprisants
64 %	21 %
amicaux	distants
48 %	43%

les lycéens ont-ils le moral?

ENTHOUSIASME
Le matin, quand vous allez au lycée, êtes-vous habituellement...

...très content
6 %

58 %

...assez content

52 %

Et pourquoi êtes-vous content ?

• Parce que vous retrouvez vos copains _____ **69 %**
• Parce que vos études vous intéressent _____ **45 %**
• Parce que l'ambiance du lycée vous plaît _____ **28 %**
• Parce que c'est toujours mieux qu'à la maison ___ **12 %**
• Parce que vous y retrouvez votre petit(e) copain(ine) **9 %**
• Parce que vos professeurs sont sympas _____ **9 %**

Ne se prononcent pas ___ **1 %**

Sur 100 lycéens contents d'aller au lycée, soit 58 % de l'échantillon. Total supérieur à 100, les interviewés ayant pu donner 2 réponses.

...peu content

29 %

40 %

...pas content du tout

11 %

Et pourquoi êtes-vous mécontent ?

• Parce que vos professeurs vous énervent _____ **36 %**
• Parce que l'ambiance est déplorable _____ **34 %**
• Parce que votre travail scolaire vous prend trop de temps et vous empêche un peu de vivre _____ **33 %**
• Parce qu'après tout on est mieux à la maison ___ **22 %**
• Parce que vos études vous ennuient _____ **22 %**
• Parce que vous ne supportez pas d'être traité comme un gosse ___ **13 %**

Ne se prononcent pas ___ **2 %**

Sur 100 lycéens mécontents d'aller au lycée, soit 40 % de l'échantillon. Total supérieur à 100, les interviewés ayant pu donner 2 réponses.

D. Knowing that the words at each end of the bar on the graph are opposites, what do you think the following words mean?
1. **assidus**
2. **incompétents**
3. **pas intéressants**
4. **méprisants**
5. **amicaux**

E. According to the graph . . .
1. do French students generally have a positive or negative image of their teachers?
2. how do most of the students feel about their teachers?
3. what do they criticize the most?

F. Look at the drawings for **Enthousiasme.** What do you think the following categories mean in English? Which category is the best? Which is the worst?

peu content   très content

pas content du tout

assez content

G. According to the percentages, do most of the students have a positive or a negative attitude when they go to the **lycée?**

H. Conduct the same surveys in your class and compile the results. How do the attitudes of your classmates compare with those of the French **lycéens?**

1 Listen as André, a French exchange student, tells you how he feels about his American schedule. What is his reaction to his schedule in general? At what times does he have the following subjects: **chimie, sport, latin, informatique**?

2 Answer these questions according to Eliane's schedule.

1. Eliane a quoi le lundi matin?
2. Elle a quels cours le jeudi après-midi?
3. Quels jours et à quelle heure est-ce qu'elle a histoire? Anglais? Maths?

EMPLOI DU TEMPS   NOM: Eliane Soulard   CLASSE: 3^e

		LUNDI	MARDI	MERCREDI	JEUDI	VENDREDI	SAMEDI	DIMANCHE
MATIN	8h00	Anglais	Arts plastiques	Histoire/Géo	Mathématiques	Musique		L
	9h00	Français	Musique	Anglais	Sciences nat	Arts plastiques	Anglais	I
	10h00	Récréation	Récréation	Récréation	Récréation	Récréation	TP physique	B
	10h15	EPS	Mathématiques	Sciences nat	EPS	Sciences nat	TP physique	R
	11h15	Sciences nat	Etude	Arts plastiques	Etude	Français	[Sortie]	E
	12h15	Déjeuner	Déjeuner	[Sortie]	Déjeuner	Déjeuner	APRES-MIDI	
APRES-MIDI	14h00	Arts plastiques	Mathématiques	APRES-MIDI	Histoire/Géo	Physique	LIBRE	
	15h00	Musique	Physique	LIBRE	Physique	Anglais		
	16h00	Récréation	[Sortie]		Récréation	[Sortie]		
	16h15	Mathématiques			Français			
	17h15	[Sortie]			[Sortie]			

3 Tell three classmates whether or not you like Eliane's schedule and why. Then, ask them if they like it.

> J'aime l'emploi du temps d'Eliane. Elle a étude et arts plastiques. C'est cool! Et vous?

4 How does an American class schedule compare with Eliane's? With a partner, make a list of similarities and differences.

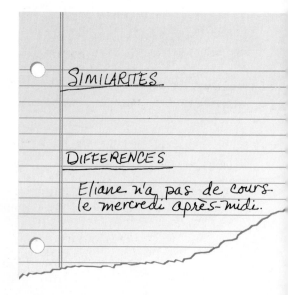

SIMILARITES

DIFFERENCES

Eliane n'a pas de cours le mercredi après-midi.

5 Answer these questions according to Eliane's report card.

1. What are Eliane's best subjects?
2. What would she probably say about French class? Music class? Science class?

BULLETIN TRIMESTRIEL

Année scolaire : 19 **95** - 19 **96**

NOM et Prénom: _Soulard Eliane_   Classe de: **3ᵉ**

MATIERES D'ENSEIGNEMENT	Moyenne de l'élève	OBSERVATIONS
Français	5	Montre peu d'enthousiasme
Anglais	8	Assez mauvais travail!
Mathématiques	18	Très bonne élève!
Histoire-Géographie	11	Travail moyen
Sciences naturelles	17	Élève sérieuse
Education physique	12	Un peu paresseuse
Physique-Chimie	18	Très douée pour la physique
Arts plastiques	14	Bon travail.
Musique	15	Fait des efforts.

Ce bulletin doit être conservé précieusement par les parents.
Il n'en sera pas délivré de duplicata.

---

6 Create your ideal schedule showing subjects, days, and times. Write it down in the form of a French **emploi du temps.** Then, compare your ideal schedule with a partner's.

7

JEU DE ROLE

Create a conversation with two classmates. Talk about . . .

a. the subjects you like best and your opinion of them.
b. the subjects you don't like and your opinion of them.
c. whether or not you agree with your classmates' likes and dislikes.

Can you use what you've learned in this chapter?

Can you agree and disagree? p. 50

1 How would you agree if your friend said the following? How would you disagree with your friend?

1. J'adore l'histoire!
2. J'aime les sciences nat. Et toi?
3. Je n'aime pas le français.

Can you ask for and give information? pp. 51, 54

2 How would you ask . . .

1. what subjects your friend has in the morning?
2. what subjects your friend has in the afternoon?
3. what subjects your friend has on Tuesdays?
4. if your friend has music class?
5. if your friend has English today?

3 How would you say in French that the following students have these classes, using the verb **avoir**?

1. you / French and choir
2. Paul / physics
3. we / gym
4. Francine and Séverine / Spanish

4 How would you ask your friend at what time he or she has these classes?

 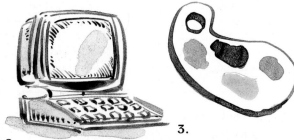 

1.   2.   3.

Can you tell when you have class? p. 54

5 How would you tell your friend that you have the following classes at the times given?

1. 9h15   2. 11h45   3. 15h50

Can you ask for and express opinions? p. 57

6 How would you tell your friend that your geography class is . . .

1. fascinating?   2. not so great?   3. boring?

VOCABULAIRE

PREMIERE ETAPE

School subjects

l'algèbre (f.) *algebra*
l'allemand (m.) *German*
les arts (m.) plastiques *art class*
la biologie *biology*
la chimie *chemistry*
la chorale *choir*
le cours de développement
    personnel et social (DPS)
    health
la danse *dance*
l'éducation (f.) physique et
    sportive (EPS) *physical
    education*

l'espagnol (m.) *Spanish*
la géographie *geography*
la géométrie *geometry*
l'histoire (f.) *history*
l'informatique (f.) *computer
    science*
le latin *Latin*
la musique *music*
la physique *physics*
les sciences (f.) naturelles
    natural science
le sport *gym*
les travaux (m.) pratiques *lab*

School-related words

le cours *course*
les devoirs (m.) *homework*
l'élève (m./f.) *student*
le professeur (le prof) *teacher*

Agreeing and disagreeing

Oui, beaucoup. *Yes, very much.*
Moi aussi. *Me too.*
Moi, non. *I don't.*
Non, pas trop. *No, not too much.*
Moi non plus. *Neither do I.*
Moi, si. *I do.*
Pas moi. *Not me.*

DEUXIEME ETAPE

Asking for and giving information

Tu as quels cours... ? *What
    classes do you have . . . ?*
Tu as quoi... ? *What do you
    have . . . ?*
J'ai... *I have . . .*
Vous avez... ? *Do you have . . . ?*
Nous avons... *We have . . .*
avoir *to have*

Telling when you have class

Tu as... à quelle heure? *At what
    time do you have . . . ?*
à... heures *at . . . o'clock*
à... heures quinze *at . . . fifteen*

à... heures trente *at . . . thirty*
à... heures quarante-cinq *at . . .
    forty-five*
aujourd'hui *today*
demain *tomorrow*
maintenant *now*
le matin *in the morning*
l'après-midi *in the afternoon*
le lundi *on Mondays*
le mardi *on Tuesdays*
le mercredi *on Wednesdays*
le jeudi *on Thursdays*
le vendredi *on Fridays*
le samedi *on Saturdays*
le dimanche *on Sundays*

Parts of the school day

la récréation *break*
l'étude *study hall*
le déjeuner *lunch*
la sortie *dismissal*
l'après-midi libre *afternoon off*

Numbers

See p. 53 for the numbers 21
    through 59.

TROISIEME ETAPE

Asking for and expressing opinions

Comment tu trouves... ? *What do
    you think of . . . ?*
Comment tu trouves ça? *What
    do you think of that/it?*
Ça va. *It's OK.*

C'est... *It's . . .*
    super *super*
    cool *cool*
    facile *easy*
    génial *great*
    intéressant *interesting*
    passionnant *fascinating*

pas mal *not bad*
barbant *boring*
difficile *difficult*
nul *useless*
pas super *not so hot*
pas terrible *not so great*
zéro *a waste of time*

3

Tout pour la rentrée

① C'est combien, cette calculatrice?

At the start of a new school year, French students have to buy supplies, including their textbooks, at the store. They may also buy things that are less essential for school, like compact discs and clothes.

In this chapter you will learn

- to make and respond to requests; to ask others what they need and tell what you need
- to tell what you'd like and what you'd like to do
- to get someone's attention; to ask for information; to express thanks

And you will

- listen to teenagers talk about what they need for school
- read a page from a French catalogue
- write a list of supplies you need for your classes
- find out about the school supplies French teenagers buy

② Il me faut un sac.

③ Je voudrais ce tee-shirt.

Mise en train

Claire   Mme Millet   La vendeuse

 ## Pas question!

Where are Claire and Mme Millet?
What do you think they are shopping for?

Alors, qu'est-ce qu'il te faut?

Eh bien, des crayons, des stylos, une gomme, une calculatrice, un pot de colle...

Pardon, mademoiselle, vous avez des trousses, s'il vous plaît?

Bien sûr. Là, à côté des cahiers.

Merci.

C'est combien, ces cahiers-ci?

12 F.

Ah, regarde, maman, une calculatrice-traductrice.

C'est pour les maths ou pour l'anglais?

Euh, il me faut une calculatrice pour les maths... Mais une calculatrice-traductrice, c'est pratique pour l'anglais.

1 Tu as compris?

Answer the following questions based on **Pas question!**

1. What is the relationship between Claire and Mme Millet? How do you know?
2. Where are they?
3. What are they doing there?
4. Why does Claire need a calculator?
5. What is Mme Millet's main concern?
6. What do you think of Claire's decision at the end of **Pas question!**?

2 Claire ou sa mère?

Does **elle** in each of the following sentences refer to Claire or Mme Millet?

1. Elle aime la calculatrice à 590 F.
2. Elle voudrait une calculatrice-traductrice.
3. Elle aime mieux le sac à 70 F.
4. Elle aime mieux le sac vert.
5. Elle va aller à l'école sans sac.
6. Elle n'achète pas un sac à 215 F.

3 Cherche les expressions

Can you find an expression in **Pas question!** to . . .

1. ask what someone needs?
2. tell what you need?
3. get a salesperson's attention?
4. ask the price of something?
5. say you like something?
6. say you don't like something?

4 Mets en ordre

Put these sentences about **Pas question!** in chronological order.

1. Mme Millet asks the price of a calculator.
2. Mme Millet asks a salesperson if she has any pencil cases.
3. Claire says she will go to school without a bag.
4. Mme Millet asks Claire what she needs for school.
5. Mme Millet asks the price of the notebooks.
6. Claire points out a bag she likes.

5 Et maintenant, à toi

What do you think will happen next in the story? Discuss your ideas with a partner.

Making and responding to requests; asking others what they need and telling what you need

VOCABULAIRE

un stylo

un crayon

une gomme

une règle

un sac (à dos)

un taille-crayon

un livre

une trousse

un classeur

une calculatrice

des feuilles (f.) de papier

un cahier

De bons conseils

Make flashcards to learn new words. On one side of a card, write the French word you want to learn. (If the word is a noun, include an article to help you remember the gender.) On the other side, paste or draw a picture to illustrate the meaning of the word. Then, ask a classmate to show you the picture while you try to name the object, or use the cards to test yourself.

---

6 Ecoute!

Listen as Hafaïdh and Karine check the contents of their bookbags. Then, look at the pictures and decide which bag belongs to each of them.

a.

b.

c.

7 Objets trouvés
Lost and found

When Paulette gets home from the store, she realizes that she forgot to put some of her school supplies into her bag. Look at the receipt showing what she bought and make a list, in French, of the missing items.

Elle n'a pas le...

```
VEN 13-05-94              3004
  047CA BELLIOT Stephanie

GOMME CAOUTCH.           3.30
CRAYONS GRAH.            5.15
REGLE GRADUEE            5.20
CAH. BROUILLON          1.90
COPIES DBLES PF GC       4.25
CLASSEUR 17X22          16.15
TROUSSE                 28.10
SOUS/TOTAL             64.05

TOTAL                   64.05

                       100.00
REÇU                    35.95
RENDU

00617     7 ARTC     16:36TM
```

NOTE CULTURELLE

In large stores in France, customers are expected to place their items on the conveyer belt and then remove and bag them as well. Most stores provide small plastic sacks, but many shoppers bring their own basket (**un panier**) or net bag (**un filet**). Although bar-code scanners were a French invention, they first caught on in the United States. Now they're becoming more common in France, especially in larger stores.

8 Devine!

Write down the name of one of the objects from the **Vocabulaire** on page 71. Don't let the other members of your group know what you've chosen. They will then take turns guessing which object you chose.

—C'est un taille-crayon?
—Oui, c'est ça. *or* Non, ce n'est pas ça.

—Tu as une calculatrice, Paul?
—J'ai un stylo, un crayon, une règle et des feuilles de papier, mais je n'ai pas de calculatrice!

COMMENT DIT-ON... ?
Making and responding to requests

To ask someone for something:
Tu as un stylo?
Vous avez un crayon?

To respond:
Oui. **Voilà.** *Here.*
Non. **Je regrette. Je n'ai pas de** crayons. *Sorry. I don't have . . .*

*G*rammaire The indefinite articles **un, une,** and **des**

The articles **un** and **une** both mean *a* or *an.* Use **un** with masculine nouns and **une** with feminine nouns. Use **des** *(some)* with plural nouns. Notice that **un, une,** and **des** change to **de** after **ne... pas.**

J'ai **un** crayon, mais je n'ai pas **de** papier.

9 **Ecoute!**

Listen as Nadine asks her friends for some school supplies. Match her friends' responses to the appropriate pictures.

  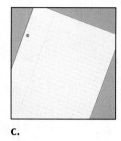 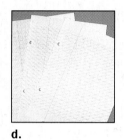 

a.   b.   c.   d.   e.

10 **Tu as ça, toi?**

With a partner, take turns pointing out the differences you notice between Christophe's desk and Annick's.

Regarde! Christophe a une gomme, mais Annick n'a pas de gomme.

COMMENT DIT-ON... ?

Asking others what they need and telling what you need

To ask what someone needs:

Qu'est-ce qu'il te faut pour la bio?
What do you need for . . . ?
(informal)

Qu'est-ce qu'il vous faut pour la géo?
What do you need for . . . ? (formal)

To tell what you need:

Il me faut un stylo et un classeur.

---

11 Qu'est-ce qu'il te faut?

Make a list of your school subjects. Exchange lists with a partner. Then take turns asking each other what you need for various classes.

> — Qu'est-ce qu'il te faut pour les maths?
> — Il me faut une calculatrice et un crayon.

12 Aide-mémoire

Write a note to remind yourself of the school supplies you need to buy for two or three of your classes.

13 Un petit service

You're late for class, and you've forgotten your supplies. Ask a friend if he or she has what you need. Your friend should respond appropriately. Then, change roles.

> — Oh là là! J'ai histoire! Il me faut un stylo et un cahier. Tu as un stylo?
> — Non, je regrette.
> — Zut! *(Darn!)*

Vocabulaire à la carte

Here are some additional words you can use to talk about your school supplies.

un compas	*a compass*
des crayons (m.) **de couleur**	*some colored pencils*
un feutre	*a marker*
du liquide correcteur	*some correction fluid*
du ruban adhésif (m.)	*some transparent tape*
une tenue de gymnastique	*a gym suit*

PANORAMA CULTUREL

Séverine • Martinique

Onélia • France

Marius • Côte d'Ivoire

We asked some francophone students what supplies they bought for the opening of school, **la rentrée**. Here's what they had to say.

Qu'est-ce qu'il te faut comme fournitures scolaires?

«Alors, donc pour l'école j'ai acheté un nouveau sac à dos, des livres pour étudier, des vêtements, entre autres des jeans, des chaussures, bien sûr et puis bon, des tee-shirts, des jupes, des robes.»

—Séverine

«Il faut des classeurs, des cahiers, des crayons, des règles, des instruments de géométrie, [une] calculatrice pour les mathématiques, des feuilles... C'est tout.»

—Onélia

«Pour l'école, il faut des règles, des bics, des stylos, des cahiers, des livres et la tenue.»

—Marius

Qu'en penses-tu?

1. What school supplies did you have to purchase for the school year?
2. What did these students buy that is usually provided by schools in the United States?
3. What are the advantages and disadvantages of each system?
4. What other items do you usually buy at the beginning of a school year?

Savais-tu que...?

In French-speaking countries, students usually buy their own textbooks and even maintain their own grade book, **un livret scolaire.** Some schools require students to purchase school uniforms. A store that specializes in school supplies, textbooks, and paper products is called **une librairie-papeterie.**

DEUXIEME ETAPE

Telling what you'd like and what you'd like to do

VOCABULAIRE

Qu'est-ce qu'on va acheter?

Hervé regarde **un short.**

Odile regarde **des baskets.**

Denis regarde **un roman.**

Stéphane regarde **un disque compact/un CD.**

Dorothée regarde **un jean.**

Mme Roussel regarde **un ordinateur.**

M. Beauvois regarde **une montre.**

M. Prévost regarde **un portefeuille.**

You can probably figure out what these words mean:

un bracelet	un magazine	une radio	une télévision
une cassette	un poster	un sweat-shirt	une vidéocassette
un dictionnaire	un pull-over	un tee-shirt	

---

14 Ecoute!

Several shoppers in the **Vocabulaire** are going to tell you what they would like to buy. As you listen to each speaker, look at the illustrations above and identify the person. Write down his or her name.

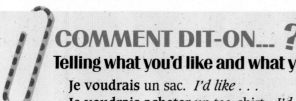

COMMENT DIT-ON... ?

Telling what you'd like and what you'd like to do

Je **voudrais** un sac. *I'd like . . .*
Je **voudrais acheter** un tee-shirt. *I'd like to buy . . .*

15 Ecoute!

Since Georges doesn't have time to go shopping for school supplies, you've offered to get them. Listen as Georges tells you what he needs and write down what you have to buy at the store.

16 Vive le week-end!

What would you like to do this weekend? Find three classmates who want to do the same thing.

—Je voudrais sortir avec des copains. Et toi?
—Moi aussi. *or* Moi, je voudrais faire du sport.

faire les magasins
dormir
danser
écouter de la musique
parler au téléphone
étudier
regarder la télévision
nager
sortir avec des copains
faire le ménage
faire du sport

17 Un cadeau   *A gift*

Make a list of what you would like to buy for . . .

1. a friend who likes horror movies and books.
2. a friend who loves sports.
3. someone who's always late for class.
4. a friend who loves music.
5. someone who loves French.
6. your best friend.

18 Mon journal

You earned 100 dollars this summer. Write down three or four items you'd like to buy for yourself.

Grammaire   The demonstrative adjectives ce, cet, cette, and ces

Ce, cet, and **cette** mean *this* or *that.* **Ces** means *these* or *those.*

	Singular	Plural
Masculine before a consonant sound	**ce** stylo	**ces** stylos
Masculine before a vowel sound	**cet** examen	**ces** examens
Feminine	**cette** école	**ces** écoles

When you want to specify *that* as opposed to *this*, add **-là** *(there)* to the end of the noun.

—J'aime **ce** sac.
—Moi, j'aime mieux **ce** sac-**là**.

19 Le cadeau parfait *The perfect gift*

Claire is shopping for a gift for her mother. The salesperson is making suggestions. Choose the correct articles to complete their conversation.

LE VENDEUR   Vous aimez **(ce/cette)** montre, mademoiselle?

CLAIRE   Oui, mais ma mère a déjà **(un/une)** montre.

LE VENDEUR   Euh, **(ces/ce)** roman, il vous plaît?

CLAIRE   Non, elle n'aime pas lire.

LE VENDEUR   Elle aime **(la /l')** musique?

CLAIRE   Oui. Elle adore le jazz.

LE VENDEUR   **(Cet/Cette)** cassette de Wynton Marsalis, peut-être?

CLAIRE   C'est une bonne idée.

20 Qu'est-ce que tu aimes mieux?

Take turns with a partner asking and answering questions about the items below.

— Tu aimes ce sac?
— Non. J'aime mieux ce sac-là!

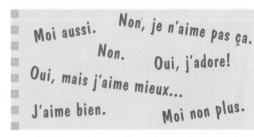

Moi aussi.   Non, je n'aime pas ça.

Non.

Oui, j'adore!

Oui, mais j'aime mieux...

J'aime bien.   Moi non plus.

1.

2.

3.

4.

Vocabulaire

J'aime le sac...	Moi, j'adore la trousse...		J'aime le sac...	Moi, j'adore la trousse...
ROUGE	ROUGE		ROSE	ROSE
ORANGE	ORANGE		BLANC	BLANCHE
JAUNE	JAUNE		GRIS	GRISE
VERT	VERTE		NOIR	NOIRE
BLEU	BLEUE		MARRON	MARRON
VIOLET	VIOLETTE			

21 Vrai ou Faux?

Read the statements below and tell whether they're true (vrai) or false (faux) according to the picture. Correct the false statements.

1. Claire a un sac jaune.
2. Claire et Thierry ont des tee-shirts bleus.
3. Claire a un short marron.
4. Thierry a des baskets bleues.
5. Thierry a un classeur rouge.
6. Claire et Thierry ont des shorts noirs.

*G*rammaire Adjective agreement and placement

Did you notice in the **Vocabulaire** on page 78 that the spelling of the colors changes according to the nouns they describe?

	Singular	*Plural*
Masculine	le classeur vert	les classeurs vert**s**
Feminine	la gomme vert**e**	les gommes vert**es**

- Usually, you add an **e** to make an adjective feminine; however, when an adjective ends in an unaccented **e**, you don't have to add another **e**: **le classeur rouge, la gomme rouge.**

- Some adjectives have irregular feminine forms: **blanc, blanche; violet, violette.**

- Usually, you add an **s** to make an adjective plural; however, when an adjective ends in an **s**, you don't have to add another **s**: **les crayons gris.**

- Some adjectives don't change form. Two examples are **orange** and **marron.**

- What do you notice about where the adjectives are placed in relation to the nouns they describe?*

22 Chasse au trésor *Scavenger hunt*

Copy the list of items below. Ask your classmates if they have the items on your list. When you find someone who does, write his or her name next to the item.

un tee-shirt violet   une montre blanche   un poster de France

des baskets bleues   un roman de science-fiction   un short rose

une trousse violette   un stylo rouge

une cassette de musique classique   un portefeuille gris

* Colors and many other adjectives are placed **after** the nouns they describe.

VOCABULAIRE

60	70	71	72
soixante	soixante-dix	soixante et onze	soixante-douze

80	81	90
quatre-vingts	quatre-vingt-un	quatre-vingt-dix

91	100	101
quatre-vingt-onze	cent	cent un

200	201
deux cents	deux cent un

23 Ecoute!

Listen to four French disc jockeys announce the dial frequencies of their radio stations. Then, match the frequency to the station logo.

NOTE CULTURELLE

If you ask about prices in French stores, they will be given in **francs,** the French monetary unit. In addition to French francs, there are Swiss francs, Belgian francs, Luxembourg francs, and C.F.A. **(Communauté financière africaine)** francs in many African countries. There are 100 **centimes** in one French franc. Coins are available in denominations of 5, 10, and 20 centimes, 1/2 franc, 1 franc, and 2, 5, 10, and 20 francs. Bills come in denominations of 20, 50, 100, 200, and 500 francs. The size of the bill varies according to the amount—the larger the bill, the more it's worth—and each bill carries the picture of a French author, artist, or philosopher.

Prices can be said and written in two ways, either **quarante-cinq francs cinquante** (45F50) or **quarante-cinq cinquante** (45,50). Notice that a comma is used instead of a decimal point.

24 Ça fait combien? *How much is it?*

How much money is shown in each illustration? Give the totals in French.

1.

2.

25 C'est combien?

Look at the drawing of the store display below. How much money does each of these customers spend in **Papier Plume**?

1. Alain achète deux stylos et une trousse.
2. Geneviève achète un classeur, un dictionnaire et un cahier.
3. Paul achète six crayons et un taille-crayon.
4. Marcel achète une règle, une gomme et un stylo.
5. Sarah achète deux cahiers et un dictionnaire.
6. Cécile achète une règle et une calculatrice.

26 Mon journal

Do you budget your money? Make a list of the items you've bought in the last month and the approximate price of each in francs. To convert American prices to francs, look up the current exchange rate in the newspaper.

COMMENT DIT-ON... ?
Getting someone's attention; asking for information; expressing thanks

To get someone's attention:
Pardon, monsieur/madame/
mademoiselle.
Excusez-moi, monsieur/madame/
mademoiselle.

To ask how much something costs:
C'est combien?

To express thanks:
Merci.

27 Ecoute!

In a department store in France, you overhear shoppers asking salespeople for the prices of various items. As you listen to the conversations, write down the items mentioned and their prices.

28 Jeu de rôle

You're in a French **librairie-papeterie** buying school supplies. For each item you want, get the salesperson's attention and ask how much the item costs. The salesperson will give you the price. Act out this scene with a partner. Then, change roles.

29 Les magazines

You've decided to subscribe to a French magazine. Take turns with a partner playing the roles of a customer and a salesperson. Use the advertisement to discuss the prices of several magazines.

Abonnez-vous à :

FEMME A LA MODE	(12 numéros) France 210 FF
DECOUVERTE SCIENTIFIQUE	(22 numéros) France 499 FF
L'AFRIQUE DE NOS JOURS	(12 numéros) France 250 FF, Europe 250 FF, Dom-Tom 250 FF, Afrique 265 FF
TÉLÉ-TUBE	(52 numéros) France et Dom-Tom 580 FF, USA $140, Canada $180, Autres pays 855 FF
LA VOIX DU MONDE	(52 numéros) France 728 FF
LES GRANDS MOUVEMENTS DE L'ECONOMIE	(12 numéros) France 170 FF
LA VIE SPORTIVE	(12 numéros) France 215 FF

PRONONCIATION

The r sound

The French **r** is quite different from the American *r.* To pronounce the French **r**, keep the tip of your tongue pressed against your lower front teeth. Arch the back of your tongue upward, almost totally blocking the passage of air in the back of your throat.

A. A prononcer

Repeat the following words.

1. Raoul	rouge	roman	règle
2. crayon	trente	calculatrice	barbe
3. terrible	intéressant	Europe	quarante
4. poster	rare	vert	montre

B. A lire

Take turns with a partner reading the following sentences aloud.

1. Fermez la porte.
2. Regardez le livre de français.
3. Prenez un crayon.
4. Ouvrez la fenêtre.
5. Je voudrais une montre.
6. Je regrette. Je n'ai pas de règle.

C. A écrire

You're going to hear a short dialogue. Write down what you hear.

LISONS!

$\mathcal{L}$ook at the information presented on this page. Where would you expect to find a text like this? Would you normally use information like this for a specific purpose? What would it be?

A. At what time of year would you expect to see an advertisement like this?

B. When you buy school supplies, what is most important to you? Color? Price? Brand name?

C. Working with a partner, scan the ad for information about price, size, and quantity. Make a list of the words you find in the text that fit each of these categories.

D. What do you think **les 3** means?

E. The word **écolier** is used to describe the notebook. Do you recognize a word you've learned before in this word? What do you think **écolier** means?

F. What is the most expensive item? The least expensive?

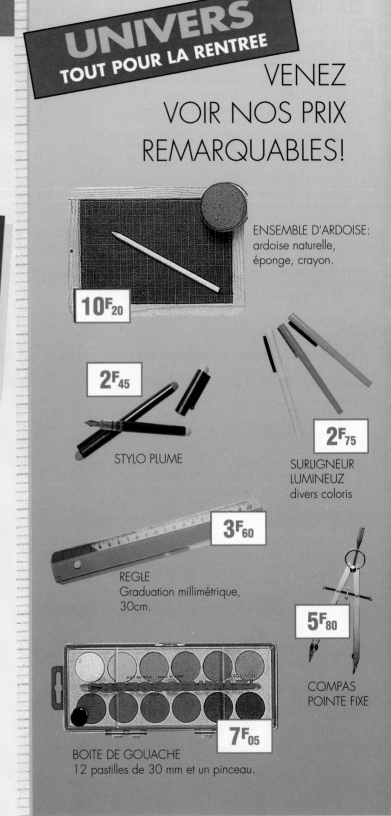

UNIVERS
TOUT POUR LA RENTREE

VENEZ
VOIR NOS PRIX
REMARQUABLES!

10F20

ENSEMBLE D'ARDOISE:
ardoise naturelle,
éponge, crayon.

2F45

STYLO PLUME

2F75

SURLIGNEUR
LUMINEUZ
divers coloris

3F60

REGLE
Graduation millimétrique,
30cm.

5F80

COMPAS
POINTE FIXE

7F05

BOITE DE GOUACHE
12 pastilles de 30 mm et un pinceau.

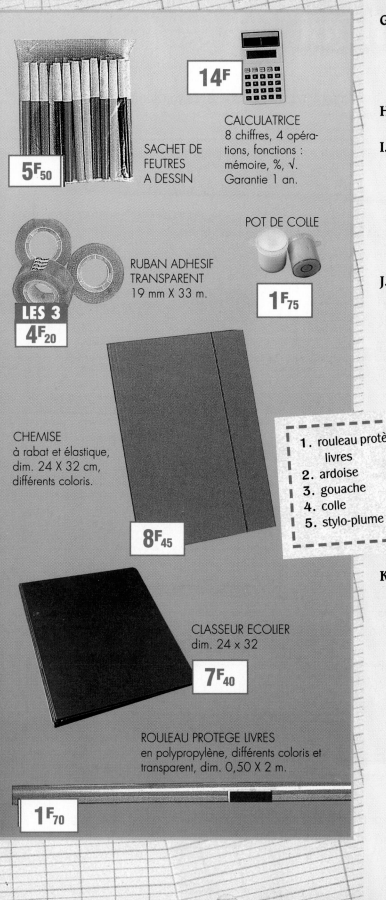

SACHET DE FEUTRES A DESSIN

5F50

14F

CALCULATRICE
8 chiffres, 4 opérations, fonctions : mémoire, %, √. Garantie 1 an.

POT DE COLLE

RUBAN ADHESIF TRANSPARENT
19 mm X 33 m.

1F75

LES 3
4F20

CHEMISE
à rabat et élastique, dim. 24 X 32 cm, différents coloris.

8F45

CLASSEUR ECOLIER
dim. 24 x 32

7F40

ROULEAU PROTEGE LIVRES
en polypropylène, différents coloris et transparent, dim. 0,50 X 2 m.

1F70

G. What item(s) in this ad might each of these people ask for?
1. a secretary
2. an architect
3. an artist

H. Do you think these are good prices? How can you tell?

I. What do you think these cognates mean?

adhésif   coloris

éponge   transparent

J. There are probably some items in this advertisement that you don't normally buy for school. Match the French words for these items with the English definitions. Look at the text and the pictures if you need help.

1. rouleau protège-livres
2. ardoise
3. gouache
4. colle
5. stylo-plume

a. a writing slate
b. glue
c. fountain pen
d. a roll of plastic material used to protect books
e. paint

K. If you had 50F to spend on school supplies, which items in the ad would you buy? Remember, you need supplies for all of your classes.

1 You want to buy your friend a birthday gift. Listen as she gives you some ideas and then make a list of the things she would like.

2 You and a friend are browsing through a magazine. Point out several items you like and several you dislike.

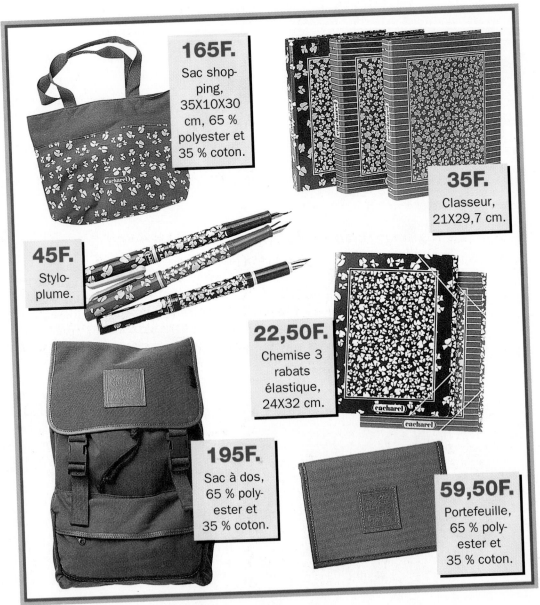

165F.
Sac shopping, 35X10X30 cm, 65 % polyester et 35 % coton.

35F.
Classeur, 21X29,7 cm.

45F.
Stylo-plume.

22,50F.
Chemise 3 rabats élastique, 24X32 cm.

195F.
Sac à dos, 65 % polyester et 35 % coton.

59,50F.
Portefeuille, 65 % polyester et 35 % coton.

3 Make a list in French of two or three of the items pictured above that you'd like to buy. Include the colors and prices of the items you choose.

4 Tell your partner about the items you've chosen in Activity 3. Give as much detail as you can, including the color and price.

5 Your friend has been passing notes to you during study hall. Write a response to each one.

Tu as une feuille de papier?

Il me faut un stylo!

Qu'est-ce qu'il faut pour l'algèbre?

Qu'est-ce qu'il faut pour la chimie?

6 If you were in France, what differences would you notice in these areas?

1. money   **2.** school supplies   **3.** stores

7 Create your own store and write a list of the merchandise you have for sale. You might have a bookstore **(une librairie-papeterie),** a music store **(une boutique de disques),** or even a gift shop **(une boutique de cadeaux).** On your list of merchandise, describe each item and give its price. You might even illustrate your list with drawings or clippings from a newspaper or magazine.

8

JEU DE ROLE

Visit the "store" your partner created and decide on something you'd like to buy. Your partner will play the role of the salesperson. Get the salesperson's attention, tell what you want, ask the price(s), pay for your purchases, thank the salesperson, and say goodbye. Your partner should respond appropriately. Then change roles. Remember to use **madame, monsieur,** or **mademoiselle,** and **vous.**

Can you use what you've learned in this chapter?

Can you make and respond to requests? p. 72

1 How would you ask for the following items using the verb **avoir**? How would you respond to someone's request for one of these items?

1.

2.

3.

Can you ask others what they need? p. 74

2 How would you ask your friend what he or she needs for each of these school subjects?

1.

2.

3.

Can you tell what you need? p. 74

3 How would you tell a friend that you need . . .

1. a calculator and an eraser for math?
2. a binder and some sheets of paper for Spanish class?
3. some pens and a notebook for English?
4. a pencil and a ruler for geometry?
5. a backpack and a book for history?

Can you tell what you'd like and what you'd like to do? p. 77

4 How would you tell your friend that you'd like . . .

1. those white sneakers?
2. this blue bag?
3. that purple and black pencil case?
4. to listen to music and talk on the phone?
5. to go shopping?

Can you get someone's attention, ask for information, and express thanks? p. 82

5 What would you say in a store to . . .

1. get a salesperson's attention?
2. politely ask the price of something?
3. thank a clerk for helping you?

VOCABULAIRE

PREMIERE ETAPE

Making and responding to requests

Tu as... ?   *Do you have . . . ?*
Vous avez... ?   *Do you have . . . ?*
Voilà.   *Here.*
Je regrette.   *Sorry.*
Je n'ai pas de...   *I don't have . . .*

Asking others what they need and telling what you need

Qu'est-ce qu'il vous faut pour... ?
  What do you need for . . . ?
  (formal)

Qu'est-ce qu'il te faut pour... ?
  What do you need for . . . ?
  (informal)
Il me faut...   *I need . . .*
un   *a; an*
une   *a; an*
des   *some*

School supplies

un cahier   *notebook*
une calculatrice   *calculator*
un classeur   *loose-leaf binder*
un crayon   *pencil*

des feuilles (f.) de papier   *sheets of paper*
une gomme   *eraser*
un livre   *book*
une règle   *ruler*
un sac (à dos)   *bag; backpack*
un stylo   *pen*
un taille-crayon   *pencil sharpener*
une trousse   *pencil case*

Other useful expressions

Zut!   *Darn!*

DEUXIEME ETAPE

Telling what you'd like and what you'd like to do

Je voudrais...   *I'd like . . .*
Je voudrais acheter...   *I'd like to buy . . .*

For school and fun

des baskets (f.)   *sneakers*
un bracelet   *a bracelet*
une cassette   *cassette tape*
un dictionnaire   *dictionary*
un disque compact/un CD
  compact disc/CD
un jean   *(a pair of) jeans*
un magazine   *magazine*

une montre   *watch*
un ordinateur   *computer*
un portefeuille   *wallet*
un poster   *poster*
un pull-over   *a pullover*
une radio   *a radio*
un roman   *novel*
un short   *(a pair of) shorts*
un sweat-shirt   *a sweatshirt*
un tee-shirt   *T-shirt*
une télévision   *a television*
une vidéocassette   *a videotape*
ce, cet, cette   *this; that*
ces   *these; those*
-là   *there (noun suffix)*

Colors

blanc(he)   *white*
bleu(e)   *blue*
gris(e)   *grey*
jaune   *yellow*
marron   *brown*
noir(e)   *black*
orange   *orange*
rose   *pink*
rouge   *red*
vert(e)   *green*
violet(te)   *purple*

TROISIEME ETAPE

Getting someone's attention; asking for information; expressing thanks

Pardon.   *Pardon me.*
Excusez-moi.   *Excuse me.*
C'est combien?   *How much is it?*
Merci.   *Thank you.*

A votre service.   *At your service; You're welcome.*
s'il vous/te plaît   *please*
franc   *(the French monetary unit)*
soixante   *sixty*
soixante-dix   *seventy*
quatre-vingts   *eighty*

quatre-vingt-dix   *ninety*
cent   *one hundred*
deux cents   *two hundred*

Other useful expressions

Bien sûr.   *Of course.*

Allez, viens à Québec!

Le château Frontenac

Québec

Capitale de la province du Québec

Population : plus de 574.400

Points d'intérêt : le château Frontenac, l'université de Laval, la terrasse Dufferin, le musée du Québec, les fortifications de Québec, les chutes Montmorency, le mont Sainte-Anne, Québec Expérience

Québécois célèbres : Samuel de Champlain, François de Montmorency-Laval, le marquis de Montcalm

Ressources et industries : dérivés du bois, du cuir et de l'érable; tourisme

Spécialités : ragoût de boulettes, tourtière, cretons, soupe aux pois, tarte au sucre, tarte à la ferlouche

Baie d'Hudson

TERRE-NEUVE

QUÉBEC

Sept-Îles

Golfe du St-Laurent

Chicoutimi

I.P.E.

NOUVEAU-BRUNSWICK

ONTARIO

Québec

Montréal

NOUVELLE-ECOSSE

Lac Huron

ETATS-UNIS

Océan Atlantique

N

Québec

Quebec City, one of the oldest cities in North America, is the capital of **La Nouvelle-France**, as the French-speaking part of Canada used to be called. The **Québécois** people are fiercely proud of their heritage and traditions, and they work hard to maintain their language and culture. The narrow streets and quaint cafés of **Vieux-Québec** have an old-world feeling, but Quebec is also a dynamic, modern city — as exciting as any you'll find in North America!

1 Typical houses in **Vieux-Québec.**

2 The spectacular **chutes Montmorency** are just outside of the city.

3 Musicians, jugglers, and other entertainers perform frequently in the streets of **Vieux-Québec.**

4 **Le quartier Petit-Champlain** is a picturesque shopping district filled with boutiques and cafés.

⑤ **La rue du Trésor** is where local artists sell their work. This street in the heart of the old section of town is very popular among tourists.

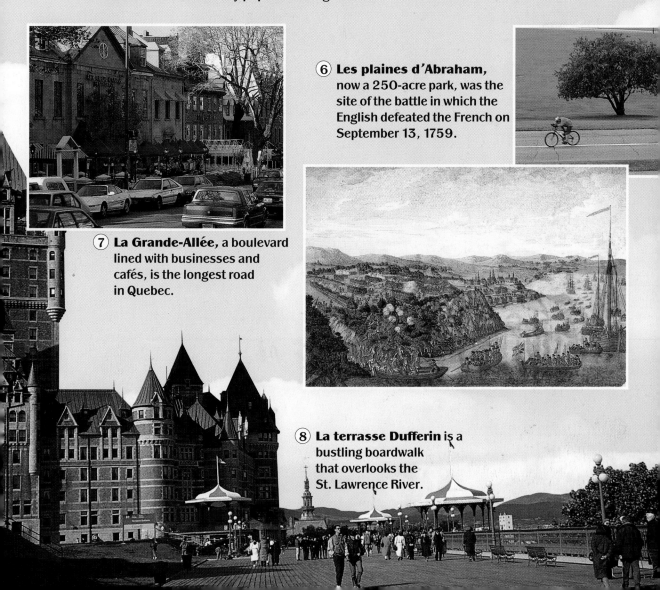

⑥ **Les plaines d'Abraham,** now a 250-acre park, was the site of the battle in which the English defeated the French on September 13, 1759.

⑦ **La Grande-Allée,** a boulevard lined with businesses and cafés, is the longest road in Quebec.

⑧ **La terrasse Dufferin** is a bustling boardwalk that overlooks the St. Lawrence River.

4

Sports et passe-temps

1st essay

① On aime faire du théâtre!

Teenagers in French-speaking countries find plenty of time for hobbies. They play sports, watch television, listen to music, take photos, and go out with friends. Many of their spare-time activities are similar to yours.

In this chapter you will learn

- to tell how much you like or dislike something
- to exchange information
- to make, accept, and turn down suggestions

And you will

- listen to French-speaking students talk about what they do for fun
- read about a sports camp in Canada
- write about your hobbies and what you do to have fun
- find out about sports and hobbies in francophone countries

② On fait du patin à glace de temps en temps.

③ En automne, on fait du vélo.

Mise en train

Nouvelles de Québec

Emilie is eager to get to know her American pen pal Leticia. What kind of information do you think Emilie might include in a letter to her new pen pal?

Salut, Leticia!

Comment ça va? Juste une petite lettre pour accompagner ces photos, une brochure sur le mont Sainte-Anne, une montagne près de Québec et aussi une cassette vidéo sur Québec... et sur moi! Comme ça, tu as une idée des activités ici... C'est l'automne à Québec et il fait déjà froid! Heureusement, il y a du soleil, mais il y a du vent. Quel temps est-ce qu'il fait à San Diego? Est-ce qu'il fait froid aussi? J'aime beaucoup Québec. C'est très sympa. Il y a beaucoup de choses à faire. En automne, je fais du patin et de la natation. J'adore le sport. En été, je fais du deltaplane et de la voile. Au printemps, je fais de l'équitation et je joue au tennis. Et en hiver, bien sûr, je fais du ski. C'est super ici pour le ski. Il neige de novembre à avril! Tu imagines? Est-ce qu'il neige à San Diego? Qu'est-ce qu'on fait comme sport? Du ski? Du base-ball? Quand il fait trop froid, je regarde la télévision et j'écoute de la musique. J'adore le rock et la musique québécoise. Et toi? Qu'est-ce que tu écoutes comme musique? Qu'est-ce qu'on fait à San Diego les fins de semaine? J'ai aussi une autre passion : de temps en temps, je fais des films avec un caméscope. C'est le fun! Tu sais, c'est super, Québec. Et la Californie, c'est comment? C'est le fun ou pas?

A très bientôt

Emilie

① Ça, c'est notre café préféré.

② La musique, c'est super!
Tu fais de la musique, toi?

③ Au printemps, on joue
au tennis. J'adore!

④ C'est mon copain Michel.
En été, on fait du vélo.

⑤ En automne, on fait
de l'équitation.

⑥ C'est moi! En hiver,
on fait du patin.

1 Tu as compris?

Answer the following questions about Emilie's letter to Leticia. Don't be afraid to guess.

1. What is Emilie sending to Leticia along with her letter?
2. What are some of Emilie's hobbies and pastimes?
3. What would she like to know about Leticia and San Diego?
4. What does Emilie tell Leticia about the city of Quebec?
5. What else have you learned about Emilie from her letter?

2 C'est Emilie?

Tell whether Emilie would be likely or unlikely to say each of the statements below.

1. «J'adore faire du sport.»
2. «Le ski? Ici on n'aime pas beaucoup ça.»
3. «Pour moi, Québec, c'est barbant en hiver.»
4. «Faire des films avec un caméscope, pour moi, c'est passionnant.»
5. «Je regarde la télé en hiver quand il fait trop froid.»
6. «La musique? Bof! Je n'aime pas beaucoup ça.»

3 Cherche les expressions

In **Nouvelles de Québec**, what does Emilie say to . . .

1. greet Leticia?
2. ask how Leticia is?
3. ask about the weather?
4. tell what she likes?
5. express her opinion about something?
6. inquire about California?
7. say goodbye?

4 Les saisons et les sports

D'après la lettre d'Emilie, quels sports est-ce qu'elle fait? En quelle saison? Choisis des sports pour compléter ces phrases.

1. Au printemps, Emilie fait...
2. En hiver, elle fait...
3. En automne, elle fait...
4. En été, elle fait...

de l'équitation   du ski
du deltaplane
de la voile
du patin   de la natation

5 Et maintenant, à toi

Emilie fait beaucoup de choses! Tu fais les mêmes choses? Pour chaque activité, réponds **Moi aussi** ou **Moi non**.

1. Emilie fait du ski.
2. Elle écoute de la musique.
3. Emilie fait des films avec un caméscope.
4. Elle fait de l'équitation.
5. Quand il fait trop froid pour sortir, Emilie regarde la télé.
6. Emilie joue au tennis.

What do you know about Quebec? What impressions do you get of Quebec when you look at these photos?

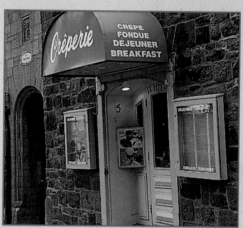

Qu'en penses-tu?

1. What things do you see that are typically American?
2. What do you see in these photos that you wouldn't see in the United States?

Savais-tu que... ?

One of the first things you'll notice about Quebec City is its fascinating blend of styles—old and new, European and North American. Old Quebec (**Vieux-Québec**) is filled with quaint neighborhood cafés and shops that maintain the old-world flavor of Europe. And yet, it is surrounded by a vibrant, modern city with high-rise hotels, office buildings, and a complex network of freeways. All of these elements together give the city its unique character.

Telling how much you like or dislike something

VOCABULAIRE

Qu'est-ce que tu aimes faire après l'école?

jouer au foot(ball)

jouer au football américain

faire de la vidéo

faire du roller en ligne

faire du patin à glace

faire du théâtre

faire de l'athlétisme

faire du vélo

faire de la natation *

You can probably guess what these activities are:

faire de l'aérobic	faire du ski	jouer au basket(-ball)	jouer à des jeux vidéo
faire du jogging	faire du ski nautique	jouer au golf	jouer au tennis
faire des photos	jouer au base-ball	jouer au hockey	jouer au volley(-ball)

6 Ecoute!

Listen to this conversation between Philippe and Pascal. List at least two activities Pascal likes and two he doesn't like.

* Remember that **nager** also means *to swim.*

7 Qu'est-ce que tu aimes faire?

Ariane and Serge are telling each other about the activities they like to do after school. Complete their conversation by substituting the activities suggested by the pictures.

ARIANE   Qu'est-ce que tu aimes faire après l'école?

SERGE   Moi, j'aime avec mes copains. Et toi?

ARIANE   Moi, j'aime et j'adore .

SERGE   Tu aimes ? On va jouer à la plage demain. Tu viens?

ARIANE   Non, merci. J'aime mieux avec des copains.

8 Télé 7 jours

While you're staying with a friend, you both decide to watch sports on TV. Take turns checking the days and times of the sports you'd like to watch.

— Le tennis de table, c'est quel jour?
— Samedi.
— A quelle heure?
— A vingt heures trente.

La semaine en direct	
GOLF Open de Belgique	Samedi à 14.00 — *TV Sport*
BASKET-BALL Levallois/Villeurbanne	Samedi à 20.25 — *TV Sport*
TENNIS DE TABLE G.P. de Paris	Sam. à 20.30 — *Paris Première*
FOOTBALL Botafogo/Corinthians	Samedi à 0.00 — *TV Sport*
ATHLÉTISME Finale Coupe du monde	Sam. à 22.00 — *Eurosport*
TENNIS Tournoi indoor féminin à Tokyo	Mer. à 18.00 — *TV Sport*
FOOT AMÉRICAIN Kansas City/Los Angeles	Mar. à 19.30 — *TV Sport*

COMMENT DIT-ON... ?

Telling how much you like or dislike something

To tell how much you like something:

J'aime **beaucoup** le sport. *I like . . . a lot!*

J'aime **surtout** faire du ski. *I especially like . . .*

To tell how much you dislike something:

Je n'aime **pas tellement** le football. *I don't like . . . too much.*

Je n'aime **pas beaucoup** le volley-ball. *I don't like . . . very much.*

Je n'aime **pas du tout** la natation. *I don't like . . . at all.*

You can use the expressions in bold type alone as short answers:

— Tu aimes faire du sport?

— Oui, **beaucoup!** *or*

Non, **pas tellement.**

9 Ecoute!

On a school trip to Quebec, you listen to your classmate talk to a Canadian student. Write down at least one sport or game each speaker likes and one each speaker dislikes.

10 Pas d'accord!

You and a Canadian exchange student want to watch sports on TV, but you can't agree on what to watch. Each time one of you finds something you like, the other doesn't like it and changes the channel. Act this out with a partner.

— Oh, voilà le football. J'aime bien le football. Et toi, tu aimes?

— Pas beaucoup. Regarde, un match de tennis. Tu aimes le tennis?

11 Qu'est-ce que je lui achète?

What should I buy him/her?

Your visit to Canada is about over. You'd like to buy gifts for several of the students you've met, so you ask a Canadian classmate about their interests. Create a conversation with a partner.

—Qu'est-ce que Marc aime faire?
—Il aime beaucoup le football.
—Il aime le tennis?
—Non, pas tellement.

> faire des photos
> faire de la vidéo
> jouer au golf
> jouer au hockey
> faire du ski   lire
> jouer à des jeux vidéo

Marc

Isabelle

Jean-Paul

Antoine

Anne-Marie

*G*rammaire   Question formation

You've already learned to make a yes-or-no question by raising the pitch of your voice at the end of a sentence. Another way to ask a yes-or-no question is to say **est-ce que** before a statement and raise your voice at the very end.

Est-ce que tu aimes faire du vélo?

12 Et toi?

With a partner, discuss the sports and hobbies you both like to do. Take turns asking and answering questions. Be sure to vary the kinds of questions you ask.

— Est-ce que tu aimes jouer au football américain?
— Non! J'aime mieux faire de l'aérobic, du théâtre et du roller en ligne.

*V*ocabulaire *à la carte*

faire un pique-nique	*to have a picnic*
faire de la randonnée	*to go hiking*
faire des haltères	*to lift weights*
faire de la gymnastique	*to do gymnastics*
faire du surf	*to surf*
faire de la voile	*to go sailing*

13 Enquête

Poll five of your classmates about the sports and hobbies they like to do. Which activity is the most popular? Which is the least popular?

Exchanging information

COMMENT DIT-ON...?
Exchanging information

To find out a friend's interests:
Qu'est-ce que tu fais comme sport? *What sports do you play?*
Qu'est-ce que tu fais pour t'amuser? *What do you do to have fun?*

To tell about your interests:
Je fais de l'athlétisme. *I do . . .*
Je joue au volley-ball. *I play . . .*
Je ne fais pas de ski. *I don't . . .*
Je ne joue pas au foot. *I don't play . . .*

Note de *G*rammaire

Du, de la, and **de l'** usually become **de** (or **d'**) in a negative sentence.

Je ne fais pas **de** jogging.
Je ne fais pas **d'**athlétisme.

14 Qu'est-ce que tu fais pour t'amuser?

With a partner, take turns asking each other about your sports and hobbies.

— Qu'est-ce que tu fais pour t'amuser?
— Je fais du jogging et du ski. Et toi?
— Moi, je...

*G*rammaire   The verb **faire**

The irregular verb **faire** is used in many different expressions.

faire*(to do, to play, or to make)*

Je **fais**		Nous **faisons**	
Tu **fais**	du sport.	Vous **faites**	du sport.
Il/Elle/On **fait**		Ils/Elles **font**	

- The subject pronoun **on** is used with the **il/elle** form of the verb. In conversational French, **on** usually means *we.*
  Le samedi, **on** fait du sport. *On Saturdays, we play sports.*

- In some situations, **on** can mean *people in general, they,* or *you.*
  En France, **on** parle français.

- You will have to use context, the surrounding words and phrases, to tell how a speaker is using **on.**

15 Quels sports?

Complete the following conversation with the correct forms of the verb **faire**.

— Tu __1__ quels sports?
— Moi, je __2__ surtout du ski et du patin.
— Et tes copains, qu'est-ce qu'ils __3__ comme sport?
— Michel __4__ de la natation et Hélène __5__ du roller en ligne.
— Hélène et toi, est-ce que vous __6__ du sport ensemble?
— Oui, nous __7__ souvent du vélo.

16 Au cercle français *At the French Club*

Based on the activities shown in the photos, talk about some of the activities you do or don't do with your friends.

Mes copains et moi, on fait...

1. 2. 3. 4. 5.

17 Jean et Luc

Jean and Luc are identical twins. They even enjoy the same activities. Tell what activities they do, based on what you see in their room.

Qu'est-ce que tu fais quand...

il fait beau?

il fait chaud?

il fait froid?

il fait frais?

il pleut?

il neige?

18 C'est agréable ou désagréable?

Tell a partner if these activities are pleasant (**agréable**) or unpleasant (**désagréable**).

1. faire du vélo quand il fait froid
2. faire de la natation quand il fait chaud
3. regarder la télé quand il neige
4. faire du jogging quand il fait frais
5. jouer au football américain quand il pleut

19 Et toi?

Qu'est-ce que tu aimes faire quand...

1. il fait froid?
2. il pleut?
3. il fait beau?
4. il neige?

NOTE CULTURELLE

Francophone countries, like most other countries of the world, use the metric system, so temperature is measured in degrees centigrade or Celsius rather than Fahrenheit. This means that the freezing point of water is 0°C, and its boiling point is 100°C. A comfortable temperature would be 25°C (77°F). If the température were more than 35°C, it would be very hot. If the temperature were 18°C (64.4°F), you would probably need a jacket.

Printemps :	mi-mars à mi-mai	
Eté :	mi-mai à mi-septembre	
Automne :	mi-septembre à mi-novembre	
Hiver :	mi-novembre à mi-mars	

QUEBEC

	Température moyenne		moyenne ensoleille-ment (h)
	Minimale °C	Maximale °C	
Janvier	-14	-6	97
Février	-13	-5	113
Mars	-8	0	140
Avril	0	8	172
Mai	6	16	220
Juin	12	21	224
Juillet	14	24	248
Août	13	23	219
Septembre	9	18	153
Octobre	3	11	116
Novembre	-2	3	74
Décembre	-12	-5	76

20 Il fait quel temps?

In these months, what is the weather usually like where you live?

1. en mai
2. en février
3. en juillet
4. en octobre
5. en avril
6. en décembre

Il fait froid.   Il pleut.
Il neige.   Il fait frais.
Il fait beau.   Il fait chaud.

Tu te rappelles?

Do you remember the endings that you learned to use with the verb **aimer** in Chapter 1? Those endings are exactly the same for all regular **-er** verbs, which include many French verbs. Here's how the verb **jouer** fits the pattern.

jouer *(to play)*

Je **joue**
Tu **joues**   } au tennis.
Il/Elle/On **joue**

Nous **jouons**
Vous **jouez**   } au tennis.
Ils/Elles **jouent**

21 Ecoute!

Listen as a newspaper reporter asks three Canadian teenagers, Paul, Anne, and Julie, about their hobbies and pastimes. Then, answer the questions below.

1. Which teenagers don't watch TV?
2. Which ones like to listen to music?
3. Which ones play hockey?
4. Which ones like to dance?
5. Which teenagers like to go to the movies?

22 Prisonnier des neiges

Imagine that you've been snowed in during a winter storm. Write a note to a friend telling him or her about the weather, what you're doing to pass the time, and how you feel about the situation.

VOCABULAIRE

Qu'est-ce que tu fais...

en vacances?

le soir?

le week-end?

en automne?

en hiver?

au printemps?

en été?

23 Un questionnaire

To help pair up campers for activities, a camp counselor has sent out the survey you see on the right. Give one answer in each category.

24 Et toi?

Tell other students in your class what activities you do in each season and ask what they do. Try to find someone who does at least two of the same things that you do.

— En hiver, je fais du patin à glace. Et toi?
— Moi non! Quand il fait froid, j'écoute de la musique.

25 Une lettre

In preparation for a visit to Canada, you've decided to write to your French-Canadian pen pal. Write a brief paragraph, asking about your pen pal's sports and hobbies and telling which ones you do and don't do.

1. En automne, je...
a. fais du patin à glace.
b. joue au hockey.
c. écoute de la musique.
d. fais du ski.
e. fais autre chose.

2. En hiver, je...
a. joue au football américain.
b. joue au foot.
c. fais du théâtre.
d. joue au volley.
e. fais autre chose.

3. Au printemps, je...
a. joue au base-ball.
b. fais de l'athlétisme.
c. fais du vélo.
d. fais de la vidéo.
e. fais autre chose.

4. En été, je...
a. fais de la natation.
b. fais du roller en ligne.
c. regarde la télé.
d. fais du ski nautique.
e. fais autre chose.

PANORAMA CULTUREL

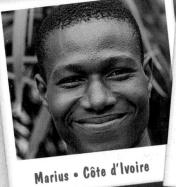

Marius • Côte d'Ivoire

Aljosa • France

Mélanie • Québec

What sports do you play? Where do you go to practice them? We asked some young people about their favorite sports. Here's what they had to say.

Qu'est-ce que tu fais comme sport?

«Je fais beaucoup de sport, mais surtout le football. Je fais le football et le skate, le patin à roulettes et puis j'aime aussi le tennis.»

—Marius

«Comme sport, j'aime bien faire le tennis. J'aime bien aller à la piscine, voilà. J'aime bien [le] bowling.»

—Aljosa

«Avec mes amies, moi je fais beaucoup de sport. Je fais partie de l'équipe intersco-laire de volley-ball et de badminton de l'école. Je fais de la natation. Je fais du patinage. Je fais de la course. Je fais du tennis aussi souvent l'été. L'hiver, je patine.»

—Mélanie

Qu'en penses-tu?

1. Which of these students enjoy the same sports that you do?
2. Which sports that they mention are not played in your area?
3. Can you guess which sports are associated with the following events and places?*

   a. La Coupe du monde

   b. Le Grand Prix de Monaco

   c. Le Tour de France

   d. Roland-Garros

Savais-tu que... ?

While schools in francophone countries do offer extracurricular sports, serious athletes often participate through clubs outside of school. Activities such as swimming, tennis, or volleyball are often organized by parent volunteers or communities. In France, recreation centers (**Maisons des jeunes et de la culture** or **MJC**) sponsor all kinds of social, cultural, and educational activities for young people.

* a. soccer b. auto racing c. cycling d. tennis (the French Open)

COMMENT DIT-ON... ?

Making, accepting, and turning down suggestions

To make a suggestion:

On fait du patin?
How about . . . ?

On joue au foot?
How about . . . ?

To accept a suggestion:

D'accord. *OK.*
Bonne idée. *Good idea.*
Oui, c'est génial!
Allons-y! *Let's go!*

To turn down a suggestion:

Désolé(e), mais je ne peux pas.
Sorry, but I can't.
Ça ne me dit rien.
That doesn't interest me.
Non, c'est barbant!

26 Ecoute!

Listen as Germain calls his friends Lise, Renaud, Philippe, and Monique to suggest activities for the weekend. Do his friends accept or turn down his suggestions?

27 Qu'est-ce qu'on fait?

Write down one or two things that you'd like to do this weekend. Then, find three classmates who'd like to join you.

— On fait du jogging ce week-end?
— Le jogging, c'est barbant! *or* D'accord. C'est génial, le jogging.

Grammaire Adverbs of frequency

- To tell how often you do something, use **quelquefois** (*sometimes*), **de temps en temps** (*from time to time*), **une fois par semaine** (*once a week*), **souvent** (*often*), **d'habitude** (*usually*), and **ne... jamais** (*never*).

- Short adverbs usually come after the verb. Longer adverbs can be placed at the beginning or the end of a sentence. Put **d'habitude** at the beginning of a sentence and **une fois par semaine** at the end. Put **ne... jamais** around the verb, as you do with **ne... pas**.

    Je fais **souvent** du ski.
    D'habitude, je fais du ski au printemps.
    Je fais du ski **une fois par semaine.**
    Je **ne** fais **jamais** de ski.

28 Ecoute!

Listen as Emile, a reporter for the school newspaper in Quebec City, interviews his classmates about sports. How often does each person practice sports?

29 L'agenda de Pauline *Pauline's planner*

Pauline is an active, French-Canadian teenager. Based on her calendar, take turns with a partner asking about her activities and how often she does them.

— Est-ce qu'elle fait de l'aérobic?
— Oui, de temps en temps.

NOVEMBRE

DIMANCHE	LUNDI	MARDI	MERCREDI	JEUDI	VENDREDI	SAMEDI
		1 jogging	2 photo	3 jogging	4 théâtre	5 patin à glace
6 aérobic	7 jogging	8 photo	9	10 jogging	11	12 jogging
13 photo	14 jogging	15	16 aérobic	17 jogging	18 théâtre	19
20 patin à glace	21 jogging	22 jogging	23 photo	24 ski	25	26 aérobic
27 jogging	28	29 jogging	30 photo			

30 Moi, je fais souvent...

With a partner, discuss your favorite pastimes and how often you do them. Ask questions to keep the conversation going.

— Qu'est-ce que tu fais pour t'amuser?
— En été, je fais souvent du ski nautique. Et toi?
— Je fais du vélo. Et toi? Tu fais du vélo... ?

> le week-end?   en vacances?
> quand il fait froid?   en été?
> quand il fait beau?

31 Sondage

a. Make a chart like the one shown here. In the left-hand column, list the activities you enjoy. In the middle column, tell when you do them, and in the right-hand column, tell how often.

ACTIVITE	SAISON	FREQUENCE
Je fais du ski. Je fais...	en hiver	de temps en temps

b. Now, share this information with three other classmates. Ask questions to find out what you have in common and what you don't.

— Je fais du ski de temps en temps.
— Pas moi! Je ne fais jamais de ski.

32 Le sportif

Your French pen pal Lucien is coming to visit soon. Read his letter and tell whether he would answer **D'accord** or **Ça ne me dit rien** if you were to suggest the following activities.

1. On fait de la vidéo ce week-end?
2. On fait du ski nautique?

3. On joue au foot?
4. On fait de la natation ce soir?
5. On joue au football américain ce week-end?

> Salut!
> J'espère que ça va. Moi, ça va bien. Je fais beaucoup de sport maintenant. Et toi, tu aimes faire du sport? Moi, j'aime jouer au foot, mais je n'aime pas trop le football américain; c'est barbant. D'habitude, le week-end, je joue au tennis ou je fais de la natation. La natation, c'est génial. Mais je n'aime pas faire du ski nautique; c'est nul. Quand il fait froid, je fais de l'aérobic. A part le sport, quelquefois, je fais de la vidéo. Et toi? Qu'est-ce que tu fais le week-end? Ecris-moi vite!
> A bientôt,
> Lucien

33 Cher Lucien, ...

Now, answer Lucien's letter. Be sure to . . .

- tell him what activities you like and why you like them;
- tell him when and how often you do each activity;

- tell him what you don't like to do and why not;
- suggest one or two things you might do together and when.

34 Une interview

a. You are a guest at a French-Canadian school and you'll soon be interviewed on local television. You've received a list of questions you'll be asked. Write down your answers.

1. Tu fais souvent du sport?
2. Qu'est-ce que tu fais comme sport en hiver?
3. Tu regardes souvent la télé?
4. Qu'est-ce que tu fais le week-end?
5. Qu'est-ce que tu fais en vacances?
6. Tu fais quoi le soir?
7. Tu écoutes souvent de la musique? (Du rock? Du jazz? De la musique classique?)
8. Qu'est-ce que tu fais quand il fait froid?

b. With a partner, take turns asking and answering the questions.

35 Mon journal

Using the information in the chart you made for Activity 31, tell about your favorite weekend and after-school activities, and how often you do them. Give your opinions of the activities, too.

PRONONCIATION

The sounds [u] and [y]

The sound [u] occurs in such English words as *Sue, shoe,* and *too.* The French [u] is shorter, tenser, and more rounded than the vowel sound in English. Listen to these French words: **tout, nous, vous.** The sound [u] is usually represented by the letter combination **ou.**

The sound [y] is represented in the words **salut, super,** and **musique.** This sound does not exist in English. To pronounce [y], start by saying [i], as in the English word *me.* Then, round your lips as if you were going to say the English word *moon,* keeping your tongue pressed behind your lower front teeth.

A. A prononcer

Now, practice first the sound [u] and then [y]. Repeat these words.

1. vous
2. nous
3. douze
4. rouge
5. cours
6. joue
7. tu
8. musique
9. nul
10. étude
11. une
12. du

B. A lire

Take turns with a partner reading the following sentences aloud.

1. Salut! Tu t'appelles Louis?
2. J'ai cours aujourd'hui.
3. Tu aimes la trousse rouge?
4. Elle n'aime pas du tout faire du ski.
5. Nous aimons écouter de la musique.
6. Vous jouez souvent au foot?

C. A écrire

You're going to hear a short dialogue. Write down what you hear.

LISONS!

What are your favorite free-time activities? In this reading you will get some additional information about the hobbies enjoyed by francophone students.

A. How many of the *W* questions are answered in the introduction of this reading?
   1. *What* subjects do these surveys cover?
   2. *Who* organized the surveys? *Who* responded to the surveys?
   3. *Where* were the surveys conducted? In which areas of the country?
B. Now, look at the illustrations to see if you can figure out the topics that will be covered in each poll.
C. Which poll is the most general? What three topics are covered in detail? Why do you think these topics were chosen?

LES JEUNES

Sondage exclusif

Pour fêter son 20ᵉ anniversaire, *Vidéo-Presse* te présente une étude exclusive portant sur les habitudes et les goûts des jeunes. Plus de 500 jeunes de diverses régions du Québec ainsi que du reste du Canada ont répondu aux questions.

LOISIRS
Quels sont tes loisirs préférés? 1

83% Sports
Ça bouge!

51% Lecture
Et dire qu'on pense que les jeunes ne lisent pas!

27% Musique
Surtout chez les jeunes de 14 ans.

24% Télévision
Surprise! nous ne sommes pas toujours devant la télé.

18% Bricolage
Surtout chez les 12 ans et moins.

15% Ordinateur
À surveiller! Qu'en sera-t-il dans deux ans?

6% Jeux de société

3% Collections

Julie marque un toucher.

SPORTS
Es-tu un vrai sportif? 2

«Moi, j'aime la gymnastique artistique, la natation et le ski» (*école Saint-Clément, Ville Mont-Royal*).
Le ski et la natation sont les activités préférées autant chez les garçons que chez les filles et à tous les groupes d'âge. Les garçons regardent plus d'émissions sportives et lisent plus d'articles sur le sport que les filles.

Savais-tu que... ?
• 6 répondants sur 10 font plus de trois heures d'activités sportives par semaine.
• Sur un total de 10 joueurs de hockey, 2 sont des filles.
• Les filles jouent plus au tennis et au basketball que les garçons.
• 9 garçons sur 10 jouent au baseball.
• 7 garçons sur 10 pratiquent le judo, le karaté, le tae kwon do.

AU MICRO

LIVRES
Qu'est-ce que tu aimes lire? 3

BD
Astérix
Archie

Boule et Bill
Garfield
Gaston La Gaffe
Lucky Luke

ROMANS
Alerte au lac des loups
Anne la maison
aux pignons verts
Agathe Christie
Annie-Croche
Le dernier des raisins
Les filles de Caleb

LECTURES PRÉFÉRÉES

FILLES
1 — Romans
2 — Bandes dessinées
3 — Revues
4 — Poésie

GARÇONS
1 — Bandes dessinées
2 — Revues
3 — Romans
4 — Documentaires
5 — Poésie

LECTEURS ET LECTRICES AYANT PARTICIPÉ À L'ENQUÊTE

Garçons **530**

Filles **640**

MUSIQUE
Les lauréats du Gala Vidéo-Presse 4

Les lecteurs de Vidéo-Presse sont branchés. Des mordus de la musique!

VIP

1. New kids on the block
2. Roch Voisine
3. Metalica
4. Michael Jackson
5. Rock et belles oreilles
6. Samantha Fox
7. Bon Jovi
8. Michel Rivard
9. Paula Abdoul
10. Def Leppard
11. Prince
12. Beatles, Elvis...

Les abonnés de *Vidéo-Presse* ne font pas qu'écouter de la musique, ils en jouent (54%). La flûte, le piano et la guitare sont les trois instruments les plus joués.

ORIGINE DES RÉPONSES

Ontario **4 %**

Québec **37 %**

Manitoba **59 %**

Quels sont tes loisirs préférés?

D. What are the two most popular pastimes? Which pastimes have the fewest supporters?

E. Which activity do the fourteen-year-olds prefer? The twelve-year-olds?

F. Are you surprised by these results? Why or why not?

Es-tu un vrai sportif?

G. Which sports do both boys and girls like?

H. Which sports do girls play more often than boys? Which do boys play more often than girls?

I. Do more boys than girls watch sports on TV? Who reads more about sports?

Qu'est-ce que tu aimes lire?

J. Look at the entries under the heading **BD.** Do you remember what **roman** means? Can you figure out what **BD (bande dessinée)** means?

K. Do boys and girls have the same taste in their choice of reading? What are the similarities and differences?

Les lauréats du Gala

L. Do you recognize some of these names? Which ones?

M. What information is contained in the paragraph below the survey results?

N. Now, conduct a poll of your classmates on one of the topics covered in this survey. Are your results similar to the ones you read here?

MISE EN PRATIQUE

1 Listen to this radio commercial for the **Village des Sports,** a resort in Quebec. List at least one activity offered in each season.

2 You've decided to spend part of your vacation at the **Village des Sports.** Read the information you've received about the resort. Then, complete the application form on the next page.

Village des Sports

c'est l'fun fun fun!

en hiver comme en été

Le plus grand centre du sport au Canada offre du plaisir pour toute la famille.
Services d'accueil, de restauration et de location sur place.

EN ETE
- le tennis
- le volley
- l'athlétisme
- le base-ball
- le roller en ligne
- le ski nautique
- la natation
- l'équitation
- la voile

EN AUTOMNE
- le football
- l'équitation
- la randonnée
- le volley

EN HIVER
- le hockey
- le ski
- le patin à glace
- la luge

AU PRINTEMPS
- le base-ball
- la randonnée
- le roller en ligne
- le tennis

Village des Sports
1860, boul. Vlaicartier
(418) 844-3725
à 24 km du centre-ville de Québec via
la route 371 Nord

Vos activités préférées

Nom _____

Prénom _____

Né(e) le _____

Domicile _____

_____

J'aime surtout _____

_____

De temps en temps, j'aime _____,

_____

Je n'aime pas tellement _____

_____.

Village des Sports

3 **a.** You've arrived at the **Village des Sports.** You meet your three roommates, get to know them, and ask them about the activities they enjoy.

b. You and your roommates decide to participate in an activity together. Each of you suggests an activity until you all agree on one.

4 Write to your French class back home to tell all about your activities at the **Village des Sports.** Mention the activities you're doing, what you like, what you don't like, and what the weather is like there. You might also tell something about your roommates.

5 What differences are there between the way students in your area and students in Quebec spend their free time?

6

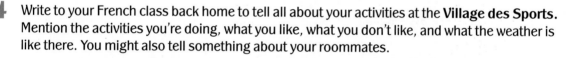

JEU DE ROLE

You're a famous Canadian athlete. Your partner, a reporter for the local television station, will interview you about your busy training routine. Tell the interviewer what you do at different times of the year, in various weather conditions, and how often. Then, take the role of the reporter and interview your partner, who will assume the identity of a different Canadian athlete.

Can you use what you've learned in this chapter?

Can you tell how much you like or dislike something? p.102

1 Can you tell someone how much you like or dislike these activities?

1.   2.   3.   4.   5.

2 Can you tell someone which sports and activities you enjoy a lot? Which ones you don't enjoy at all?

Can you exchange information? p.104

3 How would you tell someone about a few of your sports and hobbies, using the verbs **jouer** and **faire**?

4 How would you find out if someone plays these games?

1.   2.   3.

Can you make, accept, and turn down suggestions? p.110

5 How would you suggest that . . .

1. you and a friend go waterskiing?
2. you and your friends play baseball?

6 If a friend asked you to go jogging, how would you accept the suggestion? How would you turn it down?

7 How would you tell someone in French . . .

1. what you do in a certain season?
2. what you like to do in a certain month?
3. what you do in certain weather?
4. what you like to do at a certain time of day?

PREMIERE ETAPE

Telling how much you like or dislike something

Beaucoup. *A lot.*
surtout *especially*
Pas tellement. *Not too much.*
Pas beaucoup. *Not very much.*
Pas du tout. *Not at all.*

Sports and hobbies

faire de l'aérobic *to do aerobics*
de l'athlétisme *to do track and field*
du jogging *to jog*
de la natation *to swim*
du patin à glace *to ice-skate*
des photos *to take pictures*
du roller en ligne *to in-line skate*
du ski *to ski*
du ski nautique *to water-ski*
du théâtre *to do drama*
du vélo *to bike*
de la vidéo *to make videos*
jouer au base-ball *to play baseball*
au basket(-ball) *to play basketball*
au foot(ball) *to play soccer*
au football américain *to play football*
au golf *to play golf*
au hockey *to play hockey*
à des jeux vidéo *to play video games*
au tennis *to play tennis*
au volley(-ball) *to play volleyball*

Other useful expressions

Est-ce que *(Introduces a yes-or-no question)*

DEUXIEME ETAPE

Exchanging information

Qu'est-ce que tu fais comme sport? *What sports do you play?*
Qu'est-ce que tu fais pour t'amuser? *What do you do to have fun?*
Je fais... *I play/do . . .*
Je joue... *I play . . .*
Je ne fais pas de... *I don't play/do . . .*
Je ne joue pas... *I don't play . . .*
faire *to do, to play, to make*
jouer *to play*

Weather

Qu'est-ce que tu fais quand... *What do you do when . . .*
il fait beau? *it's nice weather?*
il fait chaud? *it's hot?*
il fait frais? *it's cool?*
il fait froid? *it's cold?*
il pleut? *it's raining?*
il neige? *it's snowing?*

Seasons, months and times

Qu'est-ce que tu fais... *What do you do . . .*
le week-end? *on weekends?*
le soir? *in the evening?*
en vacances? *on vacation?*
au printemps? *in the spring?*
en été? *in the summer?*
en automne? *in the fall?*
en hiver? *in the winter?*
en janvier?
en février?
en mars?
en avril?
en mai?
en juin?
en juillet?
en août?
en septembre?
en octobre?
en novembre?
en décembre?

Other useful expressions

on *we, people in general, they, you*

TROISIEME ETAPE

Making, accepting, and turning down suggestions

On... ? *How about . . . ?*
D'accord. *OK.*
Bonne idée. *Good idea.*
Allons-y! *Let's go!*
Oui, c'est... *Yes, it's . . .*
Désolé(e), mais je ne peux pas. *Sorry, but I can't.*
Ça ne me dit rien. *That doesn't interest me.*
Non, c'est... *No, it's . . .*

Other useful expressions

quelquefois *sometimes*
une fois par semaine *once a week*
de temps en temps *from time to time*
souvent *often*
ne... jamais *never*
d'habitude *usually*

Allez, viens à Paris!

L'avenue des Champs-Elysées et l'Arc de Triomphe

Paris

Capitale de la France

Population : plus de 2.150.000; région parisienne : plus de 10.000.000

Points d'intérêt : la tour Eiffel, l'Arc de Triomphe, la cathédrale de Notre-Dame, le centre Georges Pompidou, la basilique du Sacré-Cœur

Musées : l'Orangerie, le musée du Louvre, le musée d'Orsay, le musée de l'Homme, le musée Rodin

Parcs et jardins : le jardin du Luxembourg, le Champ-de-Mars, le jardin des Tuileries

Parisiens célèbres : Charles Baudelaire, Colette, Victor Hugo, Edith Piaf, Auguste Rodin, Jean-Paul Sartre

Industries : haute couture, finance, technologie, transport, tourisme

Paris

Paris is a city that has no equal. It is the intellectual and cultural capital of the French-speaking world and also the largest city in Europe, if you include the greater Parisian area. Whether you like to visit museums, go to the theater, sit in cafés, or stroll along tree-lined boulevards, there's something for everyone here. Paris is one of the world's most beautiful and exciting cities!

① **Le centre Georges Pompidou** houses a major library and the National Museum of Modern Art. Outside, you can see jugglers, magicians, and all kinds of entertainers. It is one of Paris' most popular tourist attractions.

② Many of the streets in the **Montmartre** district are lined with artists who sell their works and will even paint your portrait.

③ In the shadow of **la cathédrale de Notre-Dame,** booksellers, called **bouquinistes,** sell rare books and posters along the banks of the river Seine.

④ In Paris, the terrace of a café is a wonderful place to sit and watch the world go by.

⑤ **La tour Eiffel** was erected as a temporary exhibit for the Centennial Exposition in 1889 and has been the object of controversy ever since. It is 320.75 meters tall, including the television antenna added in 1956. To reach the top platform, ride one of the hydraulic elevators or climb the 1,792 stairs!

⑥ The Paris subway, **le métro,** is one of the world's most efficient mass-transit systems.

⑦ **Le stade Roland-Garros** is the site of the French Open, one of the grand-slam tennis tournaments.

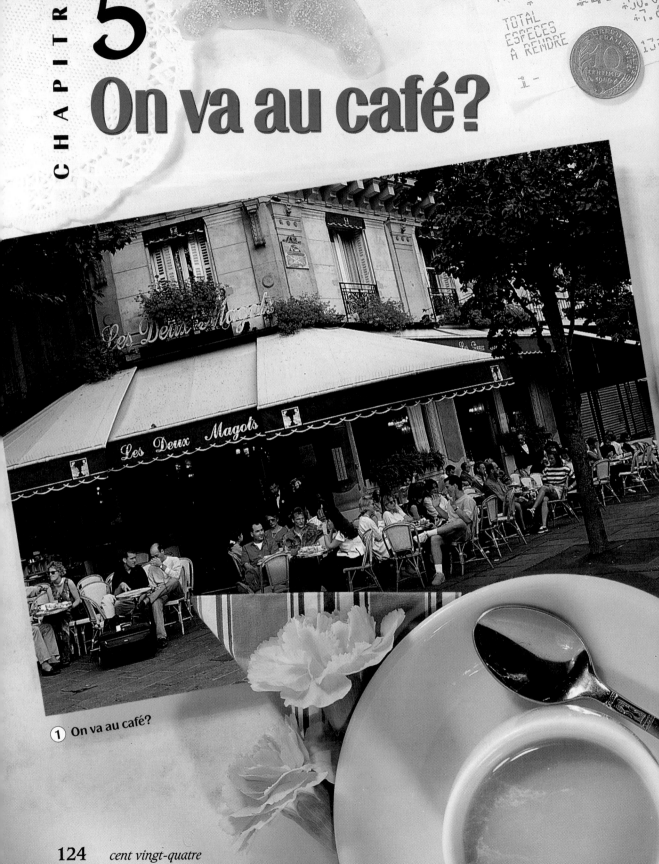

On va au café?

① On va au café?

Where are your favorite places to meet and relax with your friends? In France, people of all ages meet at cafés to talk, have a snack, or just watch the people go by!

In this chapter you will learn

- to make suggestions; to make excuses; to make a recommendation
- to get someone's attention; to order food and beverages
- to inquire about and express likes and dislikes; to pay the check

And you will

- listen to people ordering in a café
- read a café menu
- write about your food and drink preferences
- find out about French cafés

② Miam, miam! Je vais prendre un croque-monsieur.

③ L'addition, s'il vous plaît.

Mise en train

Qu'est-ce qu'on prend?

Where does this story take place?
What are the people doing? Why do
you think they look upset at the end?

1. **On va au café?**
   Oui, d'accord.
   Si tu veux. Tu viens, Mathieu?
   Désolé. J'ai des devoirs à faire. A demain!

2. Qu'est-ce que vous prenez?
   Je vais prendre une menthe à l'eau.
   Euh... je ne sais pas.

3. C'est combien, un croque-monsieur?
   22 F.

LA CARTE

CAFE	8 F
CHOCOLAT	10 F
JUS DE FRUIT	13 F
COCA	14
LIMONADE	11
SANDWICH	16
HOT-DOG	17
GLACE	12 F

SERVICE ◆ COMPRIS

1 Tu as compris?

1. What is the relationship between the teenagers in **Qu'est-ce qu'on prend?**
2. Where are they at the beginning of the story?
3. Where do they decide to go?
4. What does each person order?
5. Who has trouble deciding what to order?
6. What is the problem at the end of the story?

2 Mets en ordre

Mets les phrases suivantes en ordre d'après **Qu'est-ce qu'on prend?**

1. Thuy commande une menthe à l'eau.
2. Simon demande l'addition.
3. Simon propose à Isabelle, Thuy et Mathieu d'aller au café.
4. Isabelle ne retrouve pas son argent.
5. Le serveur apporte l'addition.
6. Isabelle commande un jus d'orange.

3 Les deux font la paire

Choisis la bonne réponse, d'après **Qu'est-ce qu'on prend?**

1. On va au café?
2. Qu'est-ce que vous prenez?
3. C'est combien, un croque-monsieur?
4. Vous avez des pizzas?
5. Qu'est-ce que vous avez comme jus de fruit?

a. Nous avons du jus d'orange, du jus de pomme...
b. Je vais prendre une menthe à l'eau.
c. Désolé. J'ai des devoirs à faire.
d. Vingt-deux francs.
e. Non, je regrette.

4 Cherche les expressions

Look back at **Qu'est-ce qu'on prend?** What do the students say to . . .

1. suggest that everyone go to the café?
2. give an excuse?
3. ask what someone's going to order?
4. order food?
5. ask what kind of fruit juice the restaurant serves?
6. ask how much something costs?
7. ask for the check?

5 Et maintenant, à toi

Isabelle is in an embarrassing situation. What is she going to do? Have you or has someone you know ever been in a similar situation? Take turns with a partner sharing these experiences.

Making suggestions; making excuses; making a recommendation

COMMENT DIT-ON... ?
Making suggestions; making excuses

To make suggestions:

On va au café? *How about going to the café?*
On fait du ski?
On joue au base-ball?

To make excuses:

Désolé(e). J'ai des devoirs à faire. *Sorry. I have homework to do.*
J'ai des courses à faire. *I have errands to do.*
J'ai des trucs à faire. *I have some things to do.*
J'ai des tas de choses à faire. *I have lots of things to do.*

6 Ecoute!

Listen to the following dialogues. Do the speakers accept or turn down the suggestions?

Tu te rappelles ?

Do you remember the following ways to accept a suggestion?

D'accord.
Bonne idée.

Do you remember the following ways to turn down a suggestion?

Ça ne me dit rien. J'aime mieux…
Désolé(e), mais je ne peux pas.

7 Qu'est-ce qu'on fait?

Suggest that your friends do these activities with you after class. They will either accept or turn down your suggestions and make excuses. Then, accept or decline their suggestions.

—On… ?
—D'accord,… *or* Désolé(e),…

1.

2.

3.

4.

5.

8 Un petit mot

You and your friend have agreed to go to the café on Saturday. You can't make it. Write your friend a note saying that you can't go, make an excuse, and suggest another activity at another time.

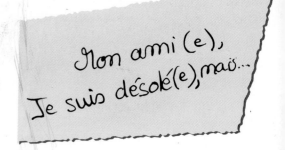

Mon ami (e),
Je suis désolé(e), mai…

9 Ecoute!

Look at the picture. As the boys tell the waiter what they would like, decide which boy is ordering.

Didier   Minh   Paul   Mamadou   Nabil

10 Vous désirez?

Now, take the role of the server in Activity 9. Write down each boy's order.

11 La fête internationale

Your French class is going to participate in an international food fair at school. Make a list of some of the foods and drinks you'd like to serve.

COMMENT DIT-ON... ?

Making a recommendation

To recommend something to eat or drink:

Prends une limonade. (informal) *Have . . .*
Prenez un sandwich. (formal) *Have . . .*

Grammaire The verb prendre

Prendre is an irregular verb.

prendre *(to take; to have food or drink)*

Je **prends**
Tu **prends** ⎱ des frites.
Il/Elle/On **prend** ⎰

Nous **prenons**
Vous **prenez** ⎱ un croque-monsieur.
Ils/Elles **prennent** ⎰

12 Qu'est-ce qu'ils prennent?

13 Qu'est-ce que je vais prendre?

You and your friends are deciding what to order in a café. Tell one another whether you are hungry or thirsty. Then, recommend something to eat or drink.

—Moi, j'ai très faim.
—Prends un sandwich.
—D'accord! Bonne idée.

or

—Non, je voudrais un croque-monsieur.

De bons conseils

Resist the temptation to match English with French word-for-word. In many cases, it doesn't work. For example, in English you say *I am hungry,* while in French you say **J'ai faim** (literally, *I have hunger*).

PANORAMA CULTUREL

Déjan • France

Clémentine • France

Armande • Côte d'Ivoire

Where do you go to meet with your friends? Here's what some francophone students had to say about where they go and what they do.

Où retrouves-tu tes amis?

«J'aime bien aller au café après l'école. On va jouer un peu au baby, au flipper et après, je rentre chez moi faire les devoirs. On a un parc à côté de chez nous et on rencontre tous nos amis.»

—Déjan

«Nous allons dans des cafés ou chez d'autres amis. Quand il fait beau, [on va] à la piscine. Ça dépend du temps qu'il fait.»

—Clémentine

«Je vais à la maison, soit chez moi, ou bien chez eux [mes amis]. Puis on va à l'Alocodrome, enfin pour prendre un peu d'aloco, puis on revient à la maison.»

—Armande

Qu'en penses-tu?

1. Where do these students go to meet their friends?
2. Do you and your friends like to go to the same places and do the same things as these teenagers?

Savais-tu que... ?

Many cultures have a particular kind of place where people gather. In many francophone countries, a café is more than just a place to eat; it's a social institution! Cafés primarily serve beverages. They may also serve bread (**pain**) or flaky crescent rolls (**croissants**) in the morning, and some cafés serve lunch. If you order something, you may stay in a café as long as you like. In some African countries, people like to go to open-air restaurants called **maquis**. They usually open only in the evening and serve traditional snack foods such as fried plantains (**aloco**), as well as full meals.

Getting someone's attention; ordering food and beverages

COMMENT DIT-ON... ?

Getting someone's attention; ordering food and beverages

To get the server's attention:

Excusez-moi.
Monsieur!   Madame!   Mademoiselle!
La carte, s'il vous plaît. *The menu, please.*

The server may ask:

Vous avez choisi? *Have you decided/chosen?*
Vous prenez? *What are you having?*

You might want to ask:

Vous avez des jus de fruit?
Qu'est-ce que vous avez comme sandwiches? *What kind of . . . do you have?*
Qu'est-ce que vous avez comme boissons? *What do you have to drink?*

To order:

Je voudrais un hamburger.
Je vais prendre un coca, **s'il vous plaît.** *I'll have . . . , please.*
Un sandwich, **s'il vous plaît.** *. . . , please.*
Donnez-moi un hot-dog, **s'il vous plaît.** *Please give me . . .*
Apportez-moi une limonade, **s'il vous plaît.** *Please bring me . . .*

14 Ecoute!

Listen to these remarks and decide whether the server (**le serveur/la serveuse**) or the customer (**le client/la cliente**) is speaking.

15 Méli-mélo!

Unscramble the following conversation between a server and a customer. Then, act it out with a partner.

> —Qu'est-ce que vous avez comme sandwiches?
> —Bien sûr.
> —Eh bien, donnez-moi un sandwich au fromage, s'il vous plaît.
> —Vous avez choisi?
> —Nous avons des sandwiches au jambon, au saucisson, au fromage...

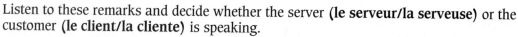

A la française

If you need time to think during a conversation, you can say **Eh bien**... and pause for a moment before you continue speaking.

> —Vous prenez, mademoiselle?
> —Eh bien... un steak-frites, s'il vous plaît.

At first you'll have to make a conscious effort to do this. The more you practice, the more natural it will become.

16 On prend un sandwich?

You've stopped at a café for lunch. Get the server's attention, look at the menu, and order. Take turns playing the role of the server.

Les sandwiches

La carte pomme de pain :

LE LYONNAIS — ROSETTE DE LYON — 450 CALORIES
LE COMTE — COMTÉ DU JURA — 430 CALORIES
LE PARISIEN — JAMBON AU TORCHON — 333 CALORIES
LE SAVOYARD — JAMBON CRU — 347 CALORIES
LE SPECIAL — JAMBON/CRUDITÉS — 400 CALORIES
LE PROVENCAL — OEUFS/CRUDITÉS — 400 CALORIES
LE CORDON BLEU — JAMBON AU TORCHON / COMTÉ — 530 CALORIES
LE VILLAGEOIS — VOLAILLE/CRUDITÉS — 360 CALORIES
LE NICOIS — THON/CRUDITÉS — 420 CALORIES

pomme de pain
LA MAISON DU SANDWICH...

Vos suggestions ou remarques nous intéressent
Écrivez-nous à :
POMME DE PAIN
173, rue Saint-Martin - 75003 Paris

*G*rammaire The imperative

Did you notice the subject **vous** isn't used in **Donnez-moi...** and **Apportez-moi...** ? When you give a command in French, you leave off the subject pronoun **tu** or **vous**, just as we leave off the subject pronoun *you* in English.

- When you write the **tu** form of an -**er** verb as a command, drop the final **s** of the usual verb ending.

  Tu écoutes... ⟶ **Ecoute!**

  Tu regardes... ⟶ **Regarde!**

- If the verb isn't a regular -**er** verb, the spelling of the command form doesn't change.

  Tu fais... ⟶ **Fais** les devoirs!

  Tu prends... ⟶ **Prends** un hot-dog, Paul!

- Remember to use the **tu** form when you talk with family members and people your own age or younger. Use the **vous** form when you talk with people older than you or with more than one person.

  Prenez un coca, Marc et Eve.

17 Apporte-moi quelque chose!

You and your friends are entertaining a French exchange student at your home. You decide to go out and get something to eat or drink. Ask in French what everyone wants and write down the orders. Read the orders back to verify them.

—Qu'est-ce que tu vas prendre?
—Euh... apporte-moi un hamburger et un coca.   *(later)*
—Tu vas prendre un hamburger, des frites et un coca, c'est ça?
—Oui.

18 Que prendre?

You don't know what to order at the café. The server makes some suggestions for you, but you don't like the suggestions. Take turns playing the server.

—Prenez un sandwich au fromage.
—Non, je n'aime pas le fromage.
—Alors, prenez un sandwich au jambon.
—Non, apportez-moi un hot-dog, s'il vous plaît.

19 A la crêperie

You and some friends get together at a **crêperie** to have some ice cream. Look at the menu and order. Take turns playing the server.

NOTE CULTURELLE

In France, waiters and waitresses are considered professionals. In better restaurants, waiters and waitresses must not only be good servers but they must also be knowledgeable about food and wine. Even in simple restaurants or cafés, servers take great pride in their work. Contrary to what you may have seen in American movies, it is impolite to address a waiter as **Garçon.** It is more polite to say **Monsieur** to a waiter, and **Madame** or **Mademoiselle** to a waitress. It is expected that diners will take time to enjoy their food, so service in French restaurants may seem slow to Americans. It is not uncommon for a meal to last several hours.

La Crêperie Normande

NOS GLACES

Parfait	35
Café ou Chocolat Liégeois	38
Mystère	45
Meringue Royale Meringue - Glace - Chantilly	55
Coupe Melba	55
Banana Split Banane - Glace fraise - Noisette - Chantilly	55

20 Mon journal

Make a list of the foods and drinks you like to have when you go out with your friends. Then, mention several items you'd try if you were at a café in France.

TROISIEME ETAPE

*Inquiring about and expressing likes and dislikes;
paying the check*

COMMENT DIT-ON... ?

Inquiring about and expressing likes and dislikes

To ask how someone likes the food or drink:
Comment tu trouves ça? *How do you like it?*

To say you like your food/drink:
C'est... *It's . . .*
  bon! *good!*
  excellent! *excellent!*
  délicieux! *delicious!*

To say you don't like your food/drink:
C'est... *It's . . .*
  pas bon. *not very good.*
  pas terrible. *not so great.*
  dégoûtant. *gross.*

21 Ecoute!

Listen to the following remarks. Do the speakers like or dislike the food they've been served?

NOTE CULTURELLE

French speakers have a tendency to use understatement (**la litote**). For instance, if the food were bad, they might say **C'est pas terrible**. Similarly, rather than saying something is really good, they would say **C'est pas mauvais**.

22 A mon avis...

The school cafeteria is thinking of adding some items to the menu. A poll is being taken among the students. Discuss each of the items below with a partner.

1.

2.

3.

4.

23 Ça, c'est bon

You and your partner are in a café. Ask if your partner has decided what to order and tell what you think of his or her choice.

> — Tu as choisi? Qu'est-ce que tu vas prendre?
> — Euh... je vais prendre des escargots.
> — Les escargots? C'est dégoûtant! *or* Bonne idée. C'est délicieux.

24 Chère correspondante

Your French pen pal Cécile asked you what teenagers in America eat or drink when they get together. Write a brief note in French telling her what you and your friends have when you go out and what you think of it.

COMMENT DIT-ON...?
Paying the check

To ask for the check:

L'addition, s'il vous plaît. *The check, please.*

To ask how much it is:

C'est combien, un sandwich?
Ça fait combien, s'il vous plaît?
How much is it, . . . ? (total)

The server might answer:

Oui, tout de suite. *Yes, right away.*
Un moment, s'il vous plaît.

C'est huit **francs.**
Ça fait cinquante **francs.** *It's . . . francs.* (total)

25 Ecoute!

Listen to the following remarks. Are the speakers ordering or getting ready to pay the check?

Tu te rappelles ?

Here are the numbers from 20–100.

20 vingt	50 cinquante	80 quatre-vingts
30 trente	60 soixante	90 quatre-vingt-dix
40 quarante	70 soixante-dix	100 cent

```
        LA GIRAFE
      Port de Cavalaire
      Tél : 94 64 40 31

 28-09-96

 CROQUE-MONSIEUR 23,00
 STEAK-FRITES     29,00
 EAU MINERALE      9,00
 COCA             14,00

 TOTAL           75,00 F

 La Direction souhaite
  que cet instant de
 détente vous ait été
      AGREABLE
```

26 Ça fait combien, chacun?

You and your friend have just finished eating at a café. Look at the check, tell what you had (**Moi, j'ai pris...**), and figure out how much each of you owes.

> —Moi, j'ai pris...
> —Ça fait... francs.

27 Qu'est-ce qu'on dit?

Write what you think the people in this scene are saying. Then, with a partner, compare what you both have written.

CAFE SPORT

Sandwiches		BOISSONS	
Fromage	15 F	Jus de fruit	13 F
Jambon	19 F	orange, pomme,	
Saucisson	18 F	pamplemousse	
Hamburger	22 F	Limonade	11 F
Hot-dog	17 F	Café	8 F
Steak-frites	33 F	Cola	14 F
Croque-monsieur	22 F	Eau minérale	10 F
Pizza	20 F	Chocolat	10 F
Frites	10 F		
Glace	12 F		

28 Jeu de rôle

Act out a scene in a café. One student is the server and the others are customers. The customers should get the server's attention, order, comment on the food, and then pay the check.

The nasal sound [ã]

Listen carefully to the vowel sounds in the following words: **ans, en.** These words contain the nasal sound [ã]. It's called a nasal sound because part of the air goes through the back of your mouth and nose when you make the sound. Listen to the English word *sandwich,* and the French **sandwich.** Is the first syllable pronounced the same in the two words? The sound in French is a pure nasal sound, with no trace of the *n* sound in it. In English you say *envy,* but in French you say **envie.** The nasal sound [ã] has four possible spellings: **an, am, en,** and **em.**

These letter combinations don't always represent a nasal sound. If another vowel follows the **n** or the **m,** or if the **n** or **m** is doubled, there may not be a nasal sound. You'll have to learn the pronunciation when you learn the word.

Listen to the following pairs of words and compare the sounds.

Fr*an*ce/*ani*mal   pr*en*d/pr*ene*z   j*am*bon/*ami*   *en*vie/*enn*emi

A. A prononcer

Repeat the following words.

en France	attendez	comment	soixante
anglais	dimanche	jambon	temps
orange	tellement	vent	souvent

B. A lire

Take turns with a partner reading the following sentences aloud.

1. Il a cent francs.
2. J'ai un excellent roman allemand.
3. Elle a danse et sciences nat vendredi.
4. Moi, je vais prendre un sandwich au jambon.

C. A écrire

You're going to hear a short dialogue. Write down what you hear.

LISONS!

$\mathcal{D}$o you like to go out to eat with your friends? Where do you like to go?

DE BONS CONSEILS

When you're faced with something new to read, look for anything that is familiar, anything that will help you identify the type of reading selection that you're dealing with. For example, a quick glance at these reading selections tells you that they're menus. Since you're familiar with menus, you should have a general idea of the kind of information these will contain, even if you don't know what all the words mean.

A. When you look at menus, what information are you usually looking for? Can you find this type of information on these menus?

B. French cuisine is enjoyed the world over. However, you can often find dishes from other cultures at French cafés and restaurants.

   1. Which items on the menus are American?

   2. What French words might you find on American menus?

   3. What other French words do you know that are related to food and restaurants?

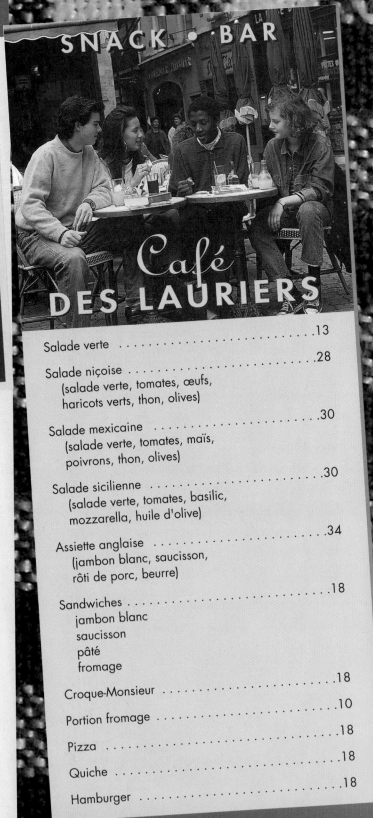

SNACK • BAR

Café DES LAURIERS

Salade verte	13
Salade niçoise	28
(salade verte, tomates, œufs, haricots verts, thon, olives)	
Salade mexicaine	30
(salade verte, tomates, maïs, poivrons, thon, olives)	
Salade sicilienne	30
(salade verte, tomates, basilic, mozzarella, huile d'olive)	
Assiette anglaise	34
(jambon blanc, saucisson, rôti de porc, beurre)	
Sandwiches	18
jambon blanc	
saucisson	
pâté	
fromage	
Croque-Monsieur	18
Portion fromage	10
Pizza	18
Quiche	18
Hamburger	18

Fontaine Elysée

SANDWICHES

Jambon Cru	30
Jambon de Paris	24
Pâté	24
Mixte	36
Roquefort aux Noix	28
Croque-Monsieur	30
Omelette Jambon	35
Omelette Fromage	35
Omelette Mixte	41
Hot-Dog 1 Saucisse	32
Hot-Dog 2 Saucisses	57
Escargots (les 6)	52

BOISSONS FRAICHES

Eau minérale, limonade	26
Cola	28
Jus de fruit	28
raisin, poire, abricot,	
pamplemousse, ananas	

SPECIALITES

COUPE CHAMPS-ELYSEES :
Chocolat - Pistache -
Caramel - Sauce Chocolat -
Mandarine Impériale -
Chantilly 53

BANANA SPLIT : Glace
Vanille - Chocolat - Banane
Fruit - Sauce Chocolat -
Chantilly 44

COUPE MELBA : Vanille -
Pêche Fruit - Chantilly -
Sauce Fraise 44

BOISSONS CHAUDES

Café express	15
Décaféiné	15
Double express	30
Double décaféiné	30
Grand crème ou chocolat	27
Café ou chocolat viennois	32
Cappuccino	33

C. Which café lists the beverages served? Do you recognize any of them? What is the difference between **BOISSONS FRAICHES** and **BOISSONS CHAUDES**?

D. How many different cognates can you find on the menus? (You should be able to find at least ten!)

E. Read the following statements about your friends' likes and dislikes. Which café would you recommend to each one?

1. Chantal a soif, mais elle n'a pas faim. Elle aime les jus de fruit.
2. Michel adore la glace.
3. Jean-Paul est végétarien.
4. Mai voudrait des escargots.
5. Alain aime les quiches.

F. Judging from the menus, what are the differences between the two cafés? What is the specialty of each one?

G. If your parents invited you to go out, which café would you choose? Why? Which would you choose if you had to pay?

H. If you had 100 F to spend, what would you order?

I. Now, make your own menu. Plan what you want to serve and how you want the menu to look. Will you have any illustrations? Don't forget to include prices.

MISE EN PRATIQUE

1 In which café would you most likely hear these conversations?

Café de Paris

15, Place du Palais - 75004 Paris
Téléphone 43-54-20-21

Nos glaces

Coupe Melba	50
Coupe Nougat	46
Banana Split	42

Nos boissons

Eau minérale	14
Jus de fruit	16
Café	10
Thé	8

SERVICE COMPRIS 15%

87, Avenue Victor Hugo -
75017 Paris
Tél. 45-62-52-53

Sandwiches

Croque-monsieur	30
Sandwich au jambon	25
Sandwich au fromage	20
Sandwich au rosbif	25

Boissons

Orangina, Coca	10
Eau minérale	12
Café	8
Jus de fruit	14

Café Américain

135, Boulevard d'Argençon • 75008 Paris • Téléphone 44-15-30-33

★ Pizzas ★

Trois fromages	50
Suprême	65

★ Boissons ★

Coca	12
Limonade	15
Eau minérale	13

★ Plats ★

Couscous	50
Steak-frites	45

SERVICE COMPRIS 15%

2 You and your partner are hungry. Suggest that you go to a café, decide what you both want to eat, and choose one of the cafés above.

3 Read the following dialogue. Then, answer the questions below.

SERVEUR	Vous avez choisi?
CHANTAL	Je vais prendre un sandwich au fromage.
SERVEUR	Et comme boisson?
CHANTAL	Un jus d'orange, s'il vous plaît.
SERVEUR	Et pour vous, monsieur?
GILLES	Est-ce que vous avez des sandwiches au saucisson?
SERVEUR	Non. Je regrette.
GILLES	Tant pis. Alors, apportez-moi un croque-monsieur et un café, s'il vous plaît.
SERVEUR	Merci.

87, Avenue Victor Hugo
75017 Paris
Tél. 45-62-52-53

2 sandwiches au fromage   30
1 jus d'orange   14
2 cafés   16
1 croque-monsieur   22

TOTAL   89F

1. Qu'est-ce que Chantal va prendre?
2. Qu'est-ce que Gilles voudrait *(would like)*?
3. Qu'est-ce que Gilles va prendre?
4. Est-ce que l'addition est correcte?

4 From what you know about French cafés, are these statements true or false?

1. If you don't see **service compris** on the menu, you should leave a tip.
2. To call the waiter, you should say **Garçon!**
3. It is acceptable to stay in a French café for a long time, as long as you've ordered something to eat or drink.
4. If a French person says **C'est pas mauvais,** he or she doesn't like the food.

5 The French Club at your school is going to have a picnic to raise money. Plan the picnic with two classmates. Decide on the time and place, the food, and the activities. Don't forget to talk about how much each item will cost. Jot down all your decisions.

6 Now that you've made your plans for the French Club picnic, create a poster to announce it. Include the food and the activities that you've planned, the price, the date, and the location. Make your poster attractive with drawings or pictures from magazines to illustrate the food and activities.

7

JEU DE ROLE

The day of the French Club picnic has arrived. One person in your group will act as host, the others will be the guests. The host will ask people what they want. Guests will tell what they want and talk about how they like the food and drink. After eating, suggest activities and decide which one you'll participate in.

Can you use what you've learned in this chapter?

Can you make suggestions, excuses, and recommendations?
p. 129, 132

1 How would you suggest to a friend that you . . .
1. go to the café?
2. play tennis?

2 How would you turn down a suggestion and make an excuse?

3 How would you recommend to a friend something . . .
1. to eat?
2. to drink?

Can you get someone's attention and order food and beverages?
p. 135

4 In a café, how would you . . .
1. get the server's attention?
2. ask what kind of sandwiches they serve?
3. ask what kind of drinks they serve?

5 How would you say that you're . . .
1. hungry?
2. thirsty?

6 How would you order . . .
1. something to eat?
2. something to drink?

7 How would you tell what people are having, using the verb **prendre**?

1. il 2. tu 3. nous 4. ils

Can you inquire about and express likes and dislikes?
p. 138

8 How would you ask a friend how he or she likes a certain food?

9 How would you tell someone what you think of these items?

 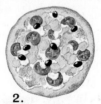 

1. 2. 3. 4.

Can you pay the check? p. 139

10 How would you ask how much each item in number 9 costs?

11 How would you ask for the check?

12 How would you ask what the total is?

PREMIERE ETAPE

**Making suggestions;
making excuses**

On va au café? *How about going
to the café?*
On... ? *How about . . . ?*
Désolé(e). J'ai des devoirs à
faire. *Sorry. I have homework
to do.*
J'ai des courses à faire. *I have
errands to do.*
J'ai des trucs à faire. *I have some
things to do.*
J'ai des tas de choses à faire. *I
have lots of things to do.*

Foods and beverages

un sandwich au jambon *ham
sandwich*
  au saucisson *salami sandwich*
  au fromage *cheese sandwich*
un hot-dog *hot dog*
un croque-monsieur *toasted
cheese and ham sandwich*
un steak-frites *steak and French
fries*
une eau minérale *mineral water*
une limonade *lemon soda*
un coca *cola*
un jus d'orange *orange juice*

un jus de pomme *apple juice*
un café *coffee*
un chocolat *hot chocolate*

Making a recommendation

Prends/Prenez... *Have . . .*
prendre *to take or to have (food
or drink)*

Other useful expressions

avoir soif *to be thirsty*
avoir faim *to be hungry*

DEUXIEME ETAPE

**Getting someone's
attention**

Excusez-moi. *Excuse me.*
Monsieur! *Waiter!*
Madame! *Waitress!*
Mademoiselle! *Waitress!*
La carte, s'il vous plaît. *The
menu, please.*

**Ordering food and
beverages**

Vous avez choisi? *Have you
decided/chosen?*

Vous prenez? *What are you
having?*
Vous avez... ? *Do you have . . . ?*
Qu'est-ce que vous avez
comme... ? *What kind of . . .
do you have?*
Qu'est-ce que vous avez comme
boissons? *What do you have
to drink?*
Je voudrais... *I'd like . . .*

Je vais prendre... , s'il vous plaît.
I'll have . . . , please.
... , s'il vous plaît. *. . . , please.*
Donnez-moi..., s'il vous plaît.
Please give me . . .
Apportez-moi... , s'il vous plaît.
Please bring me . . .

TROISIEME ETAPE

**Inquiring about and
expressing likes and
dislikes**

Comment tu trouves ça? *How do
you like it?*
C'est... *It's . . .*
  bon! *good!*
  excellent! *excellent!*
  délicieux! *delicious!*

pas bon. *not very good.*
pas terrible. *not so great.*
dégoûtant. *gross.*

Paying the check

L'addition, s'il vous plaît. *The
check, please.*
Oui, tout de suite. *Yes, right
away.*

Un moment, s'il vous plaît. *One
moment, please.*
C'est combien,... ? *How much
is . . . ?*
Ça fait combien, s'il vous plaît?
How much is it, please?
C'est... francs. *It's . . . francs.*
Ça fait... francs. *It's . . . francs.*

Amusons-nous!

① On va au centre Pompidou?

Teenagers everywhere love to go out with their friends. In Paris there are so many events and activities that it is almost impossible to choose. If you were in Paris, what would you want to do?

In this chapter you will learn

- to make plans
- to extend and respond to invitations
- to arrange to meet someone

And you will

- listen to French teenagers talk about where they go to have fun
- read brochures and advertisements
- write about your plans for the weekend
- find out what French-speaking young people do and where they go to have fun

② On se retrouve au métro Palais-Royal?

③ Je voudrais bien aller au cinéma.

Mise en train

Projets de week-end

What do you think Mathieu and Isabelle are talking about? Why do you think so?

CHAPITRE 6   Amusons-nous!

1 Tu as compris?

Answer the following questions according to **Projets de week-end**. Don't be afraid to guess.

1. What are Isabelle's plans for tomorrow?
2. What day and time of day is it?
3. Can you name three places where Mathieu suggests they go?
4. Can you name three things that Isabelle prefers to do?
5. What do they finally agree to do? What problem remains?

2 Vrai ou faux?

1. Isabelle aime aller au zoo.
2. Isabelle a un cours de danse.
3. Mathieu aime la musique de Patrick Bruel.
4. Isabelle aime bien les musées.
5. Isabelle veut voir un film d'horreur dimanche après-midi.

3 Mets en ordre

Mets les phrases en ordre d'après **Projets de week-end.**

1. Isabelle propose d'aller au palais de Chaillot.
2. Mathieu propose d'aller au zoo.
3. Isabelle propose d'aller au Sacré-Cœur.
4. Mathieu ne veut pas faire de promenade.
5. Isabelle refuse d'aller au concert.
6. Isabelle accepte d'aller au cinéma.

4 Où est-ce qu'on veut aller?

Choisis les activités qu'Isabelle veut faire et les activités que Mathieu préfère.

> aller voir un film comique
>
> aller à un concert   aller voir un film d'horreur   faire une promenade au palais de Chaillot
>
> aller au musée
>
> aller au zoo   faire un tour en bateau   aller au Sacré-Cœur

5 Invitations et refus

Match Mathieu's suggestions for weekend activities with Isabelle's refusals.

Tu veux...

1. aller au concert de Patrick Bruel?
2. aller au Louvre?
3. aller au zoo?
4. aller voir *Dracula*?

Désolée, mais...

a. je déteste les zoos.
b. je préfère aller voir un film comique.
c. je n'aime pas trop les musées.
d. je n'ai pas envie.

6 Et maintenant, à toi

How would you react to Mathieu and Isabelle's suggestions for the weekend? Which would you choose to do? Why? Compare your answers with a partner's.

COMMENT DIT-ON... ?

Making plans

To ask what a friend's planning to do:
> **Qu'est-ce que tu vas faire** demain? *What are you going to do . . . ?*
> **Tu vas faire quoi** ce week-end? *What are you going to do . . . ?*

To tell what you're going to do:
> Vendredi, **je vais** faire du vélo. *I'm going to . . .*
> Samedi après-midi, **je vais** aller au café.
> Dimanche, **je vais** regarder la télé.
> **Pas grand-chose.** *Not much.*
> **Rien de spécial.** *Nothing special.*

7 Ecoute!

Listen as Sophie asks Thérèse about her plans for the weekend. Write down at least three things Thérèse plans to do.

8 Qu'est-ce que tu vas faire?

a. Write down three activities you have planned for the weekend.

b. Now, tell your partner what you plan to do and ask about his or her plans.

> Je vais voir un film. Et toi, qu'est-ce que tu vas faire?

Note de *G*rammaire

If you want to say that you do an activity regularly on a certain day of the week, use the article **le** before the day of the week.

> Je fais du patin à glace **le mercredi** *(on Wednesdays)*.

To say that you are doing something only on one particular day, use the day of the week without an article before it.

> Je vais faire du patin à glace **mercredi** *(on Wednesday)*.

VOCABULAIRE

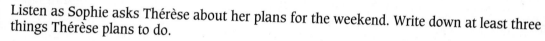

regarder un match	*to watch a game (on TV)*
manger quelque chose	*to eat something*
voir un film	*to see a movie*
voir un match	*to see a game (in person)*
voir une pièce	*to see a play*
faire une promenade	*to go for a walk*
faire les vitrines	*to window-shop*
faire un pique-nique	*to have a picnic*
aller à une boum	*to go to a party*

Grammaire   The verb aller

Aller is an irregular verb.

aller *(to go)*

Je **vais** ⎫
Tu **vas** ⎬ au café.
Il/Elle/On **va** ⎭

Nous **allons** ⎫
Vous **allez** ⎬ au café.
Ils/Elles **vont** ⎭

- You can use a form of the verb **aller** plus the infinitive of another verb to say that you're *going to do something* in the future.

  Je vais jouer au base-ball demain.

- To say that you're not going to do something in the near future, put **ne... pas** around the conjugated form of the verb **aller**.

  Je *ne* vais *pas* jouer au base-ball demain.

9 Ecoute!

Listen to the following sentences and decide whether the people are talking about what they're doing or what they're going to do.

10 Qu'est-ce qu'ils vont faire?

What are the people in the pictures going to do?

1.

2.

3.

4.

5.

6.

CHAPITRE 6   Amusons-nous!

A la française

The French often use the present tense of a verb to say that something will happen in the near future, just as we do in English.

Samedi matin, je vais jouer au tennis. *Saturday morning, I'm going to play tennis.*

Samedi matin, je joue au tennis. *Saturday morning, I'm playing tennis.*

11 Qu'est-ce qu'il va faire?

Qu'est-ce que Pierre va faire aux Etats-Unis?

1.

2.

3.

4.

5.

6.

12 Enquête

Ask the members of your group what they're going to do this weekend and tell them what you're planning. Then, tell the class what you're all planning to do.

—Qu'est-ce que tu vas faire ce week-end, Nicole?
—Samedi après-midi, je vais faire du ski nautique. Et toi?
—Moi, je vais voir un match de volley. *(to the class)*
—Je vais voir un match et Nicole va faire du ski nautique samedi après-midi.

> One of the best ways to practice your French is to talk to yourself! You can do this at any time in any place, either quietly under your breath or aloud. For example, if you're learning to say where you're going and what you're going to do, tell yourself in French what you're planning to do. Any time you're in a conversation, think about what you would say in French. In this way you'll learn to apply your French to your life, and you'll become more fluent.

VOCABULAIRE

Where do you and your friends like to go in your spare time?

au restaurant

au cinéma

au parc

au stade

au zoo

au centre commercial

à la plage

à la piscine

au musée

à la Maison des jeunes

au théâtre

à la bibliothèque

13 Où vas-tu?

Où est-ce que tu vas pour faire ces activités?

1. Je vais faire de la natation...
2. Je vais faire les vitrines...
3. Je vais voir un film...
4. Je vais manger quelque chose...
5. Je vais voir un match...
6. Je vais voir une pièce...

a. au cinéma.
b. au théâtre.
c. au centre commercial.
d. à la piscine.
e. au café.
f. au stade.

14 Projets de week-end

Christine and Alain are talking about where they like to go on weekends. Complete their conversation according to the pictures.

CHRISTINE   Moi, j'adore aller   avec mes copains. Après, on va

souvent . Et toi?

ALAIN   Moi, j'aime mieux aller . J'adore le sport. J'aime bien

aller aussi. On y joue souvent au foot.

CHRISTINE   Qu'est-ce que tu vas faire ce week-end? On va ?

ALAIN   Ah, non, je n'aime pas trop nager. Tu veux aller  ?

15 Qu'est-ce que tu aimes faire?

a. Ask your partner if he or she likes to go to the places pictured below. Take turns.

1.

2.

3.

4.

b. Now, take turns suggesting that you go to one of these places. Then, accept or reject each other's suggestions.

—On va... ?
—D'accord. *or*
   Non,...

Tu te rappelles ?

The preposition **à** generally means *to* or *at*. It combines with **le** to form **au** and with **les** to form **aux**, but it doesn't combine with **la** or **l'**.

On prend un coca **au** café?
Ils aiment faire du théâtre **à la** Maison des jeunes.

16 Mon journal

Tu as des projets pour le week-end? Qu'est-ce que tu vas faire? Où vas-tu? Quand?

Vendredi après-midi, je vais faire mes devoirs.

PANORAMA CULTUREL

Julie • Côte d'Ivoire

Arnaud • France

Céline • Viêt-nam

When you go out with your friends, where do you go? What do you do? We asked some French-speaking students what they like to do on weekends with their friends. Here's what they said.

Qu'est-ce que tu fais quand tu sors?

«Quand je sors, je me balade. Je vais manger un peu. Souvent, on va jouer de la musique. On joue au tennis... souvent, au basket aussi.»

—Julie

«Je vais au cinéma. Je vais dans une discothèque. J'achète des disques.»

—Arnaud

«Je vais à la patinoire, ou [je vais] faire les boutiques, ou [je vais] aux restaurants, enfin dans les fast-foods, ou alors je vais faire du sport, du tennis. Je vais nager.»

—Céline

Qu'en penses-tu?

1. Do you and your friends like to do any of the things these teenagers mentioned?
2. Do they mention anything that you wouldn't or couldn't do? Why wouldn't you or couldn't you do these things?
3. What do you and your friends like to do that isn't mentioned?

Savais-tu que...?

Teenagers around the world generally like to do the same things. They usually have favorite places where they go to meet with their friends, just as you do. In most towns, students can find films, plays, concerts, and **discothèques** to go to in their free time. Dance parties **(boums)** are very popular. Most cities in France also have a **Maison des jeunes et de la culture (la MJC)** where a variety of activities, such as photography, music, dance, drama, arts and crafts, and computer science are available to young people.

COMMENT DIT-ON... ?
Extending and responding to invitations

To extend an invitation:

Allons au parc! *Let's go . . . !*
Tu veux aller au café **avec moi?** *Do you want to . . . with me?*
Je voudrais aller faire du vélo. **Tu viens?** *Will you come?*
On peut faire du ski. *We can . . .*

To accept an invitation:

D'accord.
Bonne idée.
Je veux bien. *I'd really like to.*
Pourquoi pas? *Why not?*

To refuse an invitation:

Ça ne me dit rien.
J'ai des trucs à faire.
Désolé(e), je ne peux pas.
Désolé(e), je suis occupé(e).
  Sorry, I'm busy.

17 Ecoute!

Ecoute ces dialogues.
Est-ce qu'on accepte
ou refuse l'invitation?

LES MONUMENTS LES PLUS VISITÉS :

l'abbaye du Mont-Saint-Michel	826 000 entrées
l'arc de triomphe de l'Etoile	775 000
le château de Chambord	730 000
la Sainte-Chapelle	696 000
le château de Haut-Kœnigsbourg	591 000
les tours de Notre-Dame de Paris	452 000
le château d'Azay-le-Rideau	425 000

LES MUSÉES LES PLUS VISITÉS :

le Louvre	3,4 millions d'entrées payantes
Versailles	2,5
Orsay	2,0
Picasso	340 000
Fontainebleau	291 000
l'Orangerie	254 000

18 Et toi? Tu veux?

Choisis la bonne réponse.

1. J'ai faim.
2. Je voudrais faire un pique-nique.
3. Tu ne viens pas?
4. Je voudrais voir un match de foot.
5. Tu veux voir une pièce?

a. Allons au parc!
b. J'ai des trucs à faire.
c. Pourquoi pas? Allons au théâtre!
d. Tu veux aller au café?
e. Allons au stade!

19 Tu acceptes?

Your partner will invite you to participate in some of the following activities. Accept or refuse, telling where you're going or what you're going to do instead. Exchange roles.

1.

2.

3.

4.

5.

6.

---

*G*rammaire The verb **vouloir**

Vouloir is an irregular verb.

vouloir *(to want)*

Je **veux**	Nous **voulons**
Tu **veux** ⎬ aller au café.	Vous **voulez** ⎬ aller au café.
Il/Elle/On **veut**	Ils/Elles **veulent**

Je voudrais *(I would like)* is a more polite form of **je veux**.

20 Qu'est-ce qu'ils veulent faire ce soir?

1. Pierre et Marc

2. Alain

3. Robert et Lise

4. Elodie et Guy

5. Mes copains

6. David et Monique

21 Invitations pour le week-end

You're making plans for the upcoming weekend. Take turns with a partner suggesting activities and accepting or politely refusing the suggestions.

23 A la boum!

The French club is having a party. Invite three students. Before they accept or refuse your invitation, they want to know what you're planning to do. Tell them about the activities you're planning. Your friends will either accept or refuse.

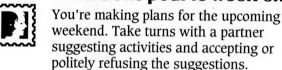

danser — écouter de la musique québécoise — voir un film français — parler français avec des copains — manger des escargots

22 Vous voulez faire quoi?

You and your friends can't decide what to do this weekend. Each of you makes a suggestion, and the others react to it. See if you can find three things you'd all like to do.

—Vous voulez faire du vélo?
—Oui, je veux bien.
—Moi, je ne veux pas. Je n'aime pas faire du vélo.

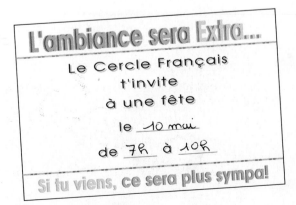

L'ambiance sera Extra...

Le Cercle Français
t'invite
à une fête

le _10 mai_

de _7h_ à _10h_

Si tu viens, ce sera plus sympa!

RENCONTRE CULTURELLE

Qu'en penses-tu?

1. Judging from these photos, how would you describe a typical date in France?
2. Do American teenagers usually go out on dates in groups or in couples? Which do you think is preferable? Why?
3. What do you think is the best age to begin dating? Why?

Savais-tu que... ?

French teenagers tend to go out in groups. They usually do not "date" in the same way American teenagers do. They do not generally pair off into couples until they are older. Those who do have a boyfriend or girlfriend still go out with a group — but they almost always pay their own way.

ENTRÉE
POUR UNE
PERSONNE

COMMENT DIT-ON... ?
Arranging to meet someone

To ask when:	To tell when:
Quand?	**Lundi./Demain matin./Ce week-end.**
Quand ça?	**Tout de suite.** *Right away.*

To ask where:	To tell where:
Où?	**Au café.**
	Devant le cinéma. *In front of . . .*
Où ça?	**Dans** le café. *In . . .*
	Au métro Saint-Michel. *At the . . . subway stop.*
	Chez moi. *At . . . house.*

To ask with whom:	To tell with whom:
Avec qui?	**Avec** Ahmed et Nathalie.

To ask at what time:	To tell at what time:
A quelle heure?	**A dix heures du matin.** *At ten in the morning.*
	A cinq heures de l'après-midi. *At five in the afternoon.*
	A cinq heures et quart. *At quarter past five.*
	A cinq heures et demie. *At half past five.*
	Vers six heures. *About six o'clock.*

To tell time:

Quelle heure est-il?   **Il est six heures.** *It's six o'clock.*
What time is it?   **Il est six heures moins le quart.** *It's quarter to six.*
   Il est six heures moins dix. *It's ten to six.*
   Il est midi. *It's noon.*/**Il est minuit.** *It's midnight.*

To confirm:

Bon, on se retrouve à trois heures. *OK, we'll meet . . .*
Rendez-vous mardi au café. *We'll meet . . .*
Entendu. *OK.*

24 Ecoute!

While you're waiting to use a public phone in Paris, you overhear a young woman inviting a friend to go out. Listen to the conversation and then choose the correct answers to these questions.

1. Sylvie parle **avec qui?**
   a. Marc   **b.** Anna   **c.** Paul

2. Elle va **où?**
   a. Au musée   **b.** Au parc   **c.** Au stade

3. **À quelle heure?**
   a. 1h30   **b.** 10h15   **c.** 12h00

4. **Où** est-ce qu'ils se retrouvent?
   a. au métro Solférino   **b.** dans un café   **c.** devant le musée

---

NOTE CULTURELLE

You've already learned that train, airline, school, and other official schedules use a 24-hour system called **l'heure officielle.** When you look in an entertainment guide such as *Pariscope,* you may see that a movie starts at 20h00, which is 8:00 P.M. In everyday conversation, however, people use a 12-hour system. For example, for 1:30 P.M., you may hear, **une heure et demie de l'après-midi,** rather than **treize heures trente.** Expressions such as **et demie, et quart,** and **moins le quart** are used only in conversational time, never in official time.

---

25 A quelle heure?

skip une

Où est-ce que Christian et Noëlle vont aujourd'hui? Qu'est-ce qu'ils vont faire? A quelle heure?

1. 9h00   2. 12h00   3. 5h45   4. 8h30

26 Ecoute!

Listen to these three messages on your answering machine and write down who they're from and where you're being invited to go. Listen a second time and write down the meeting time and place.

27 Qu'est-ce que tu vas faire ce soir?

a. Make a list of at least three things that you're going to do tonight. Be sure to include the time and place.

b. Now, ask what your partner is going to do tonight. Then, continue to ask questions about his or her plans.

*G*rammaire   Information questions

There are several ways to ask information questions in French.

* People often ask information questions using only a question word or phrase. They will sometimes add **ça** after it to make it sound less abrupt.

> **Où ça?**
> **Quand ça?**

* Another way to ask an information question is to attach the question word or phrase at the end of a statement.

> Tu vas **où?**
> Tu veux faire **quoi?**
> Tu vas au cinéma **à quelle heure?**
> Tu vas au parc **avec qui?**

* Still another way is to begin an information question with the question word or phrase, followed by **est-ce que (qu').**

> **Où est-ce que** tu vas?
> **Qu'est-ce que** tu veux faire ce soir?
> **Avec qui est-ce que** tu vas au cinéma?
> **A quelle heure est-ce qu'**on se retrouve?

28 On va où?

Some friends are inviting you to join them. Ask questions to get more information about their plans. Complete the conversation with the appropriate words or phrases.

— Tu veux aller au cinéma?
—
— Demain soir.
—
— Vers six heures.
—
— Au cinéma Gaumont.
—
— Avec Catherine et Michel.
— D'accord!
— Bon, on se retrouve...

29 Qu'est-ce qu'on fait chez toi?

You'd like to find out more about what teenagers in France normally do. Write down at least six questions to ask about your pen pal's classes, activities, and hobbies.

30 Allons au cinéma!

Look at the movie schedule below. Choose a movie you want to see and invite your partner to go with you. When you've agreed on a movie to see, decide at which time you want to go and arrange a time and place to meet.

Le Beaumont   **15, Bd des Italiens • 75002 PARIS**

○ **Blanche-Neige et les 7 nains,** *v.f.* Séances : 12h, 14h15, 16h30, 18h45, 20h15

○ **Dinosaures,** *v.f.* Séances : 11h55, 13h55, 15h55

○ **Hamlet,** *v.o.* Séances : 13h40, 16h15, 18h55, 21h30

○ **Tous les matins du monde,** Séances : 11h30, 14h, 16h30, 19h, 21h30

○ **Fievel au Far West,** *v.o.* Séances : 13h30, 15h, 16h30

○ **Madame Doubtfire,** *v.o.* Séances : 11h05, 13h45, 16h20, 19h, 21h35

○ **Frankenstein junior,** *v.o.* Séances : 21h

○ **Les voyages de Gulliver,** *v.f.* Séances : 13h30, 16h30

○ **Les tortues Ninja II,** *v.f.* Séances : 12h30, 14h, 16h

○ **Casablanca,** *v.o.* Séances : 16h30, 19h

---

31 Ça te dit?

A friend has written you this note suggesting some things to do this weekend. Write an answer, reacting to each invitation and making suggestions of your own.

> Salut! Ça va? Tu veux faire quoi ce week-end? Moi, je voudrais faire les magasins vendredi soir et jouer au tennis samedi après-midi. On va au ciné samedi soir vers huit heures et demie. Tu viens? Et dimanche matin, tu veux aller au café? Qu'est-ce que tu en penses? Fabienne

32 Mon journal

What are you and your friends going to do during the next school vacation? Write about your plans. Tell what you're going to do, with whom, when, where, and so on.

PRONONCIATION

The vowel sounds [ø] and [œ]

The vowel sound [ø] in **veux** is represented by the letter combination **eu.** It is pronounced with the lips rounded and the tongue pressed against the back of the lower front teeth. To produce this sound, first make the sound **è**, as in **algèbre**, and hold it. Then round the lips slightly to the position for closed **o**, as in **photo**. Repeat these words.

jeudi	veux	peu	deux

The vowel sound [œ] in the word **heure** is similar to the sound in **veux** and is also represented by the letters **eu.** This sound is more open, however, and occurs when these letters are followed by a consonant sound in the same syllable. To produce this sound, first make the sound **è**, as in **algèbre,** and hold it. Then round the lips slightly to the position for open **o**, as in **short**. Repeat these words.

classeur	feuille	heure

A. A prononcer

Repeat the following words.

1. jeudi   déjeuner   peux
2. deux   veut   mieux
3. ordinateur   jeunes   heure
4. feuille   classeur   veulent

B. A lire

Take turns with a partner reading each of the following sentences aloud.

1. Tu as deux ordinateurs? On peut étudier chez toi jeudi?
2. Tu veux manger des escargots? C'est délicieux!
3. On va à la Maison des jeunes? A quelle heure?
4. Tu as une feuille de papier? Je n'ai pas mon classeur.

C. A écrire

You're going to hear a short dialogue. Write down what you hear.

LISONS!

Where do you like to go on the weekend? Look at these brochures to see where Parisians go for fun.

DE BONS CONSEILS

When you run across a word you don't know, use context to guess the meaning of the word. You automatically use this strategy in your own language. For example, you may not know the English word *dingo*, but when you see it in a sentence, you can make an intelligent guess about what it means. Read this sentence: *He thought that the kangaroos and the koala bears were cute, but that the dingos were mean-looking.* You can guess that a *dingo* is a possibly vicious animal found in Australia. It is, in fact, a wild dog.

A. What kinds of places do these brochures describe?

B. Look at the brochure for **Parc Astérix.** Here are some questions you should consider if you were planning a day trip there with your friends.

1. During which months would you not be able to go on this trip?
2. On which days of the week can you take this trip to **Parc Astérix?**
3. If you took the trip in the advertisement, what time would you leave from Paris?
4. What time would you leave the park for the trip back?
5. What do you think **bienv-**

Bienvenue
Welcome
Welkom

PARC ASTERIX

Bienvenue en Gaule pour une journée mémorable !

Pour passer une journée partagée entre l'émotion et l'aventure. Pour retrouver cette bonne humeur légendaire et communicative. Pour faire un voyage mémorable en Gaule, au pays du bien-vivre et de l'histoire...

Venez au Parc Astérix! Astérix et tous ses amis vous y attendent...

Départ de Paris les mercredi et samedi à 9h, du 10 avril au 2 octobre. Retour du site à 18h et arrivée à Paris vers 19h30.

Prix par personne: **340 F**
Enfants de 3 à 11 ans inclus: **260 F**

Le prix inclut l'hébergement.

CALENDRIER SAISON 1994 :
Ouverture : 15 mars au 15 novembre.
Tous les jours de 10h à 19h. (juillet et août)
Le samedi, nocturne jusqu'à 23h.

TARIFS :
Individuels : Adultes : 68 F.
Enfants : 48 F (de 3 à 13 ans).

RESTAURATION
Deux restaurants de 300 places chacun et 2 kiosques proposent des menus de différentes régions de France (un restaurant ouvert le samedi soir). Aire de pique-nique aménagée.

MUSEUM NATIONAL D'HISTOIRE NATURELLE
PARC ZOOLOGIQUE DE PARIS
BOIS DE VINCENNES

OUVERT TOUS LES JOURS
de 9 h à 17 h ou 17 h 30 l'hiver - de 9 h à 18 h ou 18 h 30 l'été*

TARIF*
Entrée 40 F - Tarif Réduit 20 F - Groupes Scolaires 10 F

ACCES
Métro : Porte Dorée, Saint-Mandé-Tourelle - Bus : 46-86-325-PC

*Sauf modification

53 Av. de Saint-Maurice - 75012 PARIS - Tel. : 44.75.20.10 - Fax : 43.43.54.73

Le Pays FRANCE MINIATURE, c'est la France comme vous ne l'avez jamais vue! Sur une immense carte en relief, sont regroupées les plus belles richesses de notre patrimoine : 166 monuments historiques, 15 villages typiques de nos régions, les paysages et les scènes de la vie quotidienne à l'échelle 1/30ème... au cœur d'un environnement naturel extraordinaire.

6. If you go with three friends and one of you brings your ten-year-old sister, how much will it cost? How much is it in American money?

C. One of your friends just came back from **France Miniature** and told you about it. Check the brochure to see if what he said was accurate or not.

1. "I saw more than 150 monuments!"
2. "There were twenty villages represented."
3. "The size of everything was on a scale of 1/25."
4. "It was more expensive than **Parc Astérix.**"
5. "We stayed until midnight."
6. "We went on my birthday, June 15th."

D. Imagine you and a friend want to go to the **Parc zoologique de Paris.**

1. How can you get there? Can you take a bus? The metro? At which metro stop would you get off?
2. How much is it going to cost? Will it make a difference if you're students?
3. How late can you stay in the summer? In the winter?
4. What are some of the animals you'll get to see?
5. At what time do the pelicans eat? The pandas?
6. What are the restrooms near? How many picnic areas are there? What is near the first-aid station? Where can you buy a gift?

E. Which of these places would you like to go to most? Why?

La tour Eiffel est le monument parisien le plus connu au monde. Elle a été édifiée pour l'exposition universelle de 1889 sous l'impulsion de son concepteur de génie Gustave Eiffel. Avec ses 300 m, c'est l'édifice le plus haut du monde. Il s'agit d'un véritable chef-d'œuvre de légèreté et de résistance. Montée par l'ascenseur de 10h à 23h : 16 à 47 F, par les escaliers 8F. Tél.: 45 55 91 11

Une vue exceptionnelle du Musée d'Orsay

Musée d'Orsay

LE PLUS ELEGANT MUSEE DE PARIS L'architecte italienne Gae Aulenti a implanté dans l'ancienne gare d'Orsay une somptueuse scénographie, développée en un jeu de niveaux, magnifique écrin pour l'art français du 19e siècle : impressionniste, art décoratif, dessins, sculptures et photographies.
1, rue de Bellechasse, 7e. Tél. : 40 49 48 84. Tous les jours sauf le lundi de 10h à 17h30. Nocturne le jeudi jusqu'à 21h45.

PARISTORIC : LE FILM

2 000 ans d'émotions sur écran géant
2000 years of emotion on a giant screen

Adulte 70 F
Jeune 40 F

20 F off

réduction à la caisse sur présentation du guide **Paris Midnight**

■ SEANCE A CHAQUE DEBUT D'HEURE DE 9H A 21H
■ EVERY DAY, EVERY HOUR ON THE HOUR 9 A.M. TO 9 P.M.

Espace Hebertot, métro : Villiers/Rome
78 bis, bd des batignolles, 75017 Paris
Tél. : 42 93 93 46 — Fax : 42 93 93 48

1 Look over the advertisements and answer the questions below.

1. Which places offer a view of Paris?
2. Where can you see a free concert?
3. Where can you hear a movie about the history of Paris?
4. Where can you see nineteenth-century French art?
5. Where can you see ancient art?
6. Which places offer you a discount?
7. Which places list their prices?
8. Which attractions are closed on Mondays?
9. Which attractions are closed on Tuesdays?
10. Which advertisements tell you the name of the nearest subway stop?

2 Your French friends are discussing which Paris attraction to visit. Listen to their conversation and write down the attraction they decide on. Listen again and tell when and where they agree to meet.

3 Invite your partner to one of the places advertised above. Your partner will either accept or decline your invitation. Take turns.

Notre-Dame de Paris, c'est l'un des monuments les plus visités au monde. Ascension en haut de la tour (386 marches) de 10h à 17h : 27F, visite de la crypte de 10h à 16h30 : 23F, visite du trésor de 10h à 18h, dimanche de 14h à 18h : 15F. Concerts gratuits tous les dimanches à 17h45. Visites et ascension fermées les jours fériés.

Architecte : I. M. Pei

L O U V R E

Palais du Louvre
75001 Paris
Tél. (1) 40 20 51 51
Métro : Palais-Royal, Louvre

Antiquités égyptiennes, orientales, grecques, étrusques et romaines. Peintures. Sculptures. Mobilier et objets d'art. Arts graphiques.
Ouvert de 9h à 18h. Nocturne les lundi et mercredi jusqu'à 21h45. Fermé le mardi.

LA VUE PARISIENNE

à 209m!

To the top in 38 seconds!

TOUR MONTPARNASSE
Tous les jours, tous les soirs
56ᵉ Étage et Terrasse

VISITE PANORAMIQUE
Métro Montparnasse-Bienvenüe
Téléphone 45 38 52 56

20% de réduction sur le prix d'entrée à la visite panoramique, 59ème étage de la Tour Montparnasse. Présentez ce bon au guichet de la Tour. Valable pour 5 personnes maximum.

20% reduction off the admission price to the 59th floor of the Montparnasse Tower. To receive your discount, present this coupon to the Tower ticket booth, (coupon permits 5 persons discount maximum).

S. A. MONTPARNASSE 56 - Tour Montparnasse
33, avenue du Maine - 75015 PARIS - Tél. 45.38.52.56 - Fax. 45.38.69.96

---

(4) Using what you've learned about French culture, answer the following questions.

1. Where do French young people like to go to have fun?

2. Would a French teenager be surprised at American dating customs? Why?

(5) a. You have one day in Paris to do whatever you like. Make a list of where you're going and at what time you plan to go there.

b. Write a note to your French class back home telling everyone what you plan to do during your day in Paris.

6

J E U   D E   R O L E

Get together with some classmates. Choose one place in Paris you'd all like to visit and decide on a meeting time and place. Make sure that the Paris attraction you choose to visit will be open when you plan to go. Act this out with your group.

Can you use what you've learned in this chapter?

Can you make plans?
p. 153

1 How would you say that these people are going to these places?

1. je   2. nous   3. Anne et Etienne

2 How would you tell what you're planning to do this weekend?

3 How would you invite a friend to . . .

1. go window shopping?   3. go see a basketball game?
2. go for a walk?   4. go to the café?

**Can you extend
and respond to
invitations?**
p. 159

4 How would you accept the following invitations? How would you refuse them?

1. Je voudrais aller faire du ski. Tu viens?   3. On va au restaurant. Tu viens?
2. Allons à la Maison des jeunes!   4. Tu veux aller au cinéma?

5 How would you say that the following people want to go to these places?

1. Ahmed   2. Isabelle et Ferdinand   3. Mon amie et moi

**Can you arrange to
meet someone?**
p. 163

6 If someone invited you to go to the movies, what are three questions you might ask to find out more information?

7 What are some possible answers to the following questions?

1. Où ça?   3. A quelle heure?
2. Avec qui?   4. Quand ça?

PREMIERE ETAPE

Making plans

Qu'est-ce que tu vas faire... ? *What are you going to do . . . ?*
Tu vas faire quoi...? *What are you going to do . . . ?*
Je vais... *I'm going . . .*
Pas grand-chose. *Not much.*
Rien de spécial. *Nothing special.*

Things to do

aller à une boum *to go to a party*
faire une promenade *to go for a walk*
faire un pique-nique *to have a picnic*

faire les vitrines *to window-shop*
manger quelque chose *to eat something*
regarder un match *to watch a game (on TV)*
voir un film *to see a movie*
voir un match *to see a game (in person)*
voir une pièce *to see a play*
aller *to go*
au/à la *to, at*

Places to go

la bibliothèque *the library*
le centre commercial *the mall*

le cinéma *the movie theater*
la Maison des jeunes et de la culture (MJC) *the recreation center*
le musée *the museum*
le parc *the park*
la piscine *the swimming pool*
la plage *the beach*
le restaurant *the restaurant*
le stade *the stadium*
le théâtre *the theater*
le zoo *the zoo*

DEUXIEME ETAPE

Extending invitations

Allons... ! *Let's go . . . !*
Tu veux... avec moi? *Do you want . . . with me?*
Tu viens? *Will you come?*
On peut... *We can . . .*

Accepting an invitation

D'accord. *OK.*
Bonne idée. *Good idea.*

Je veux bien. *I'd really like to.*
Pourquoi pas? *Why not?*

Refusing invitations

Ça ne me dit rien. *That doesn't interest me.*
J'ai des trucs à faire. *I've got things to do.*
Désolé(e), je ne peux pas. *Sorry, I can't.*

Désolé(e), je suis occupé(e). *Sorry, I'm busy.*
vouloir *to want*

Other useful expressions

je voudrais... *I'd like . . .*

TROISIEME ETAPE

Arranging to meet someone

Quand (ça)? *When?*
tout de suite *right away*
Où (ça)? *Where?*
dans *in*
devant *in front of*
au métro... *at the . . . metro stop*
chez... *at . . . ('s) house*
Avec qui? *With whom?*
avec... *with . . .*
A quelle heure? *At what time?*

A cinq heures. *At five o'clock.*
  et demie *half past*
  et quart *quarter past*
  moins le quart *quarter to*
  moins cinq *five to*
Quelle heure est-il? *What time is it?*
Il est midi. *It's noon.*
Il est minuit. *It's midnight.*
Il est midi (minuit) et demi. *It's half past noon (midnight).*
vers *about*

Bon, on se retrouve... *OK, we'll meet . . .*
Rendez-vous... *We'll meet . . .*
Entendu. *OK.*

Other useful expressions

ce week-end *this weekend*
demain *tomorrow*
est-ce que *(introduces a yes-no question)*

CHAPITRE

7 La famille

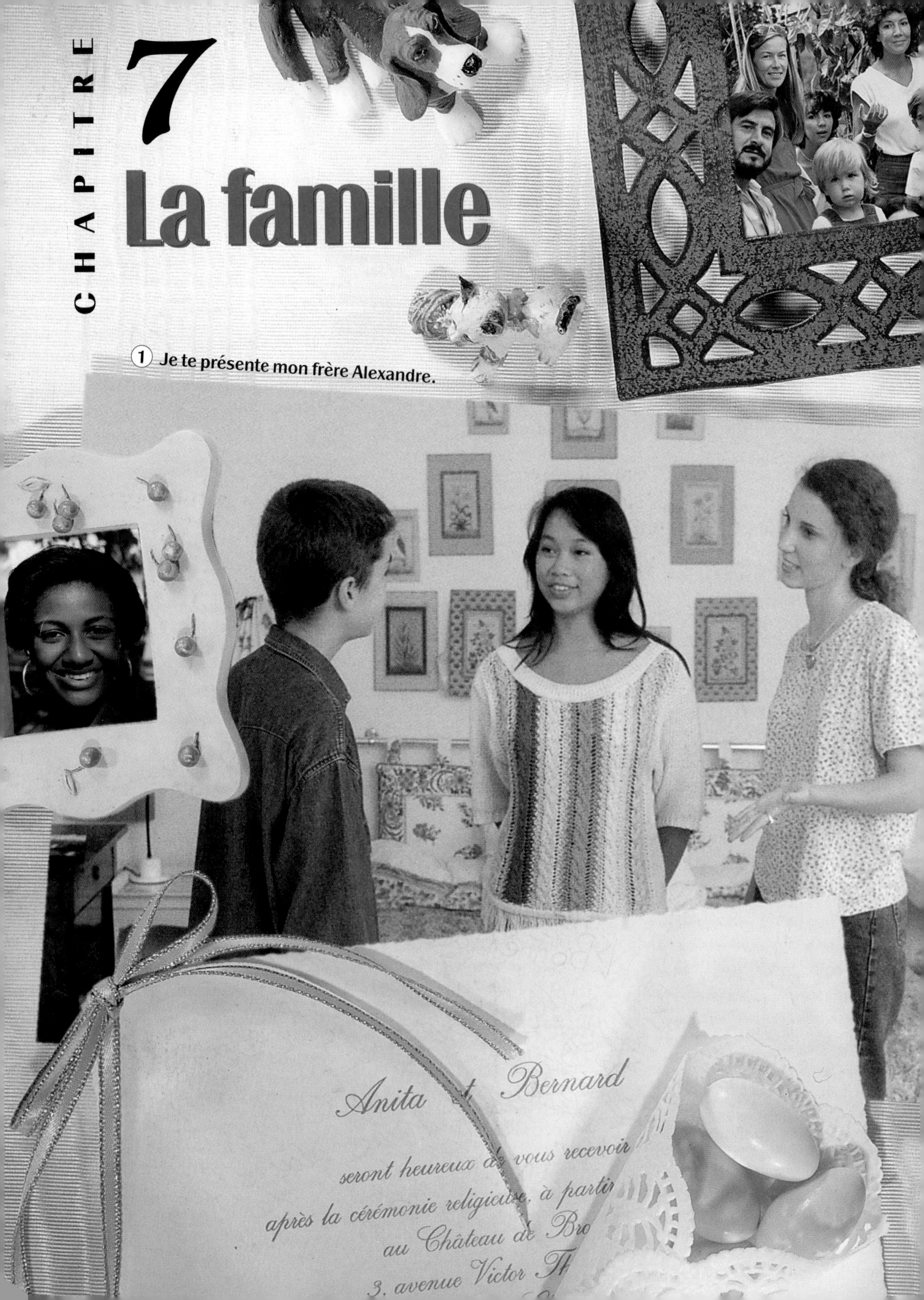
Anita et Bernard
seront heureux de vous recevoir
après la cérémonie religieuse, à partir
au Château de Bro
3, avenue Victor Th

1 Je te présente mon frère Alexandre.

Families provide support and nurturing for their members. Being part of a family also involves duties and responsibilities. Do you think families in francophone cultures are different from families here in the United States?

In this chapter you will learn

- to identify and introduce people
- to describe and characterize people
- to ask for, give, and refuse permission

And you will

- listen to French-speaking teenagers talk about their families
- read magazine articles about pets
- write a description of someone you know
- find out about pets in France

② Ma cousine? Comment est-elle? Elle est très gentille!

③ Je peux aller au cinéma ce soir, s'il te plaît?

Mise en train

Sympa, la famille!

Look at the people pictured in the photo album.
Can you guess how they're related to Isabelle?

Tiens, j'adore regarder les photos. Je peux les voir?

Bien sûr!

Ce sont mes grands-parents. Ils sont heureux sur cette photo. Ils fêtent leur quarantième anniversaire de mariage.

C'est une photo de papa et maman.

Là, c'est mon oncle et ma tante, le frère de ma mère et sa femme. Et au milieu, ce sont leurs enfants, mes cousins. Ils habitent tous en Bretagne. Ça, c'est Loïc. Il a 18 ans.

Et elle, c'est ma cousine Patricia. Elle est très intelligente. En maths, elle a toujours 18 sur 20!

C'est Julie. Elle a 8 ans. Elle est adorable.

Loïc

Ma tante

Julie

Patricia

Mon oncle

Là, c'est moi. Quel amour de bébé, n'est-ce pas? Je suis toute petite... peut-être un an et demi.

⑤

⑥

C'est mon frère Alexandre. Il a 11 ans. Il est parfois pénible.

⑦

C'est ma tante du côté de mon père. Elle s'appelle Véronique. Ça, c'est son chat Musica. Elle adore les animaux. Elle a aussi deux chiens!

Et toi, tu n'as pas de frères ou de sœurs?

Non. Je suis fille unique.

Tu as de la chance.

1 Tu as compris?

Answer these questions about **Sympa, la famille!**

1. What are Isabelle and Thuy talking about?
2. Does Isabelle have brothers or sisters? If so, what are their names?
3. Where do her cousins live?
4. Who are some of the other family members she mentions?
5. How does Isabelle feel about her family? How can you tell?

2 Vrai ou faux?

1. Julie a huit ans.
2. Julie est blonde.
3. Les cousins d'Isabelle habitent à Paris.

4. Tante Véronique n'a pas d'animaux.
5. Thuy a un frère.

3 Quelle photo?

De quelle photo est-ce qu'Isabelle parle?

1. Il a onze ans.
2. Elle s'appelle Véronique. Ça, c'est son chat, Musica.
3. C'est une photo de papa et maman.

4. En maths, elle a toujours 18 sur 20.
5. J'ai un an et demi, je crois...
6. Elle a huit ans.

a.

b.

c.

d.

e.

f.

4 Cherche les expressions

In **Sympa, la famille!**, what does Isabelle or Thuy say to . . .

1. ask permission?
2. identify family members?
3. describe someone?
4. pay a compliment?
5. tell someone's age?
6. complain about someone?

5 Et maintenant, à toi

How does Isabelle's family resemble or differ from families you know?

PREMIERE ETAPE

Identifying and introducing people

COMMENT DIT-ON... ?
Identifying people

To identify people:

C'est ma tante Véronique.
Ce sont mes cousins Loïc et Julie. *These/those are . . .*
Voici mon frère Alexandre. *Here's . . .*
Voilà Patricia. *There's . . .*

6 C'est qui?

With a partner, take turns creating identities for the people in this picture.

VOCABULAIRE

Les membres de la famille Ménard

**Ma grand-mère et mon grand-père
Eugénie et Jean-Marie Ménard**

**Ma tante
Véronique, la
sœur de mon
père**

**Mon père et ma mère Raymond
et Josette Ménard**

**Mon oncle et ma tante, Guillaume
et Micheline Ménard**

**Mon frère
Alexandre**

C'est moi!

Mes cousines Patricia et Julie, et mon cousin Loïc

Mon chien **Mon chat**

Mon canari **Mon poisson**

7 Qui est-ce?

Which member of Isabelle Ménard's family
does each of these statements refer to?

Le frère de Véronique, c'est Raymond.

1. C'est le père de Véronique.
2. C'est la mère de Véronique.
3. C'est le grand-père de Julie.
4. C'est la mère de Patricia.
5. Ce sont les sœurs de Loïc.
6. C'est le cousin de Patricia.

Note de *Grammaire*

Use **de (d')** to indicate relationship
or ownership.

C'est la mère **de** Paul.
That's Paul's mother.
Voici le chien **d'**Agnès.
Here's Agnès' dog.
C'est le copain **du** prof.
That's the teacher's friend.

8 Ecoute!

Alain montre des photos de sa famille à Jay. De quelle photo est-ce qu'il parle?

a.   b.   c.   d.   e.

---

*G*rammaire Possessive adjectives

	Before a masculine singular noun	Before a feminine singular noun	Before a plural noun
my	mon	ma	mes
your	ton	ta	tes
his/her	son	sa	ses
our	notre	notre	nos
your	votre	votre	vos
their	leur	leur	leurs

(masculine singular: frère; feminine singular: sœur; plural: frères)

- **Son, sa,** and **ses** may mean either *her* or *his.*

  C'est **son** père.   That's *her* father. *or* That's *his* father.

  C'est **sa** mère.   That's *her* mother. *or* That's *his* mother.

  Ce sont **ses** parents.   Those are *her* parents. *or* Those are *his* parents.

- **Mon, ton,** and **son** are used before all singular nouns that begin with a vowel sound, whether the noun is masculine or feminine.

  C'est **ton amie** Marianne?

  C'est **mon oncle** Xavier.

- Liaison is always made with **mon, ton,** and **son,** and with all the plural forms.

  mon école   nos amis

- Can you figure out when to use **ton, ta, tes,** and when to use **votre and vos?**[1]

---

9 Ecoute!

Listen to Roland and Odile. Are they talking about their own pets or someone else's? Then, listen again to find out what kind of pets they're talking about.

---

1. Use **ton, ta,** and **tes** with people you would normally address with **tu.** Use **votre** and **vos** with people you would normally address with **vous.**

10 Ma famille française

You're showing a classmate a photo of the family you stayed with in France. Take turns with a partner identifying the people and asking questions about them.

—C'est qui, ça?
—C'est ma sœur.
—Elle joue souvent au tennis?
—Oui. Une fois par semaine.

11 Devine! *Guess!*

Identify the teenagers in the photos below and tell how you think the other people in the photos are related to them. Take turns with a partner.

C'est Nadine et son grand-père.

Hassan

Thierry

Monique et Annie

Nadine

Liliane

COMMENT DIT-ON...?

Introducing people

To introduce someone to a friend:
C'est Jean-Michel.
Je te présente mon ami Jean-Michel.
I'd like you to meet . . .

To introduce someone to an adult:
Je vous présente Jean-Michel.

To respond to an introduction:
Salut, Jean-Michel. Ça va?
Bonjour.
Très heureux (heureuse). *Pleased to meet you.* (FORMAL)

> Mlle Martin, je vous présente mon ami Jean-Michel.
> Bonjour, Jean-Michel!

---

12 Ecoute!

Are the people in these conversations identifying someone or introducing someone?

13 Je te présente...

A new student from France has just arrived at your school and asks you the names and ages of some students in your class. Introduce him or her to those classmates. Act this out in your group, changing roles.

14 Mon journal

Write about your family, giving the names and ages of each person. Tell what each of them likes to do. You may choose to create an imaginary family or you may want to write about a famous family in real life or on TV.

Tu te rappelles?

Do you remember how to ask for and give people's names and ages?
—Elle s'appelle comment?
—Magali.
—Elle a quel âge?
—Seize ans.

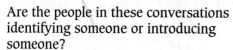

Vocabulaire à la carte

Here are some other words you might need to talk about your family.

une femme	*wife*
un mari	*husband*
une fille	*daughter*
un fils	*son*
un(e) enfant	*child*
des petits-enfants	*grandchildren*
un demi-frère	*stepbrother; half-brother*
une demi-sœur	*stepsister; half-sister*
un(e) enfant unique	*an only child*
une belle-mère	*stepmother*
un beau-père	*stepfather*
un petit-fils	*grandson*
une petite-fille	*granddaughter*

DEUXIEME ETAPE

Describing and characterizing people

VOCABULAIRE

Ils sont comment?

PETITE GRAND

BRUNE BLOND ROUX

JEUNE AGEE

MINCE GROS

You can also use these descriptive words:

mignon(mignonne)(s) *cute*   **ne... ni grand(e)(s) ni petit(e)(s)** . . . *neither tall nor short*

You can use these words to characterize people.

amusant(e)(s)	*funny*	**intelligent(e)(s)**	*smart*	**embêtant(e)(s)**	*annoying*
timide(s)	*shy*	**fort(e)(s)**	*strong*	**pénible(s)**	*a pain in the neck*
gentil(le)(s)	*nice*	**sympa(sympathique(s))**	*nice*	**méchant(e)(s)**	*mean*

De bons conseils

Organizing vocabulary in various ways can help you remember words. Group words by categories, like foods, sports, numbers, colors, and so forth. Try to associate words with a certain context, such as school (school subjects, classroom objects) or a store (items for sale, salesperson). Try to use associations like opposites, such as **petit—grand** or **gros—mince**.

15 Ecoute!

Match the descriptions you hear with the students' names.

Roger   Denise   Julie   Martin   Carmen

COMMENT DIT-ON... ?

Describing and characterizing people

To ask what someone is like:

Il est comment? *What is he like?*
Elle est comment? *What is she like?*
Ils/Elles sont comment? *What are they like?*

To describe someone:

Il n'est ni grand ni petit.
Elle est brune.
Ils/Elles sont âgé(e)s.

To characterize someone:

Il est pénible.
Elle est timide.
Ils/Elles sont amusant(e)s.

16 Ecoute!

Ariane is telling a friend about her cousins. Does she have a favorable or unfavorable opinion of them?

17 Des familles bizarres

Comment sont les membres de ces familles?

*G*rammaire Adjective agreement

As you may remember from Chapter 3, you often change the pronunciation and spelling of adjectives according to the nouns they describe.

- If the adjective describes a feminine noun, you usually add an **e** to the masculine form of the adjective.

- If the adjective describes a plural noun, you usually add an **s** to the singular form, masculine or feminine.

- If an adjective describes both males and females, you always use the masculine plural form.

- Some adjectives have special (irregular) feminine or plural forms. Here are some irregular adjectives that you've seen in this chapter.

Il est **roux**.	Elle est **rousse**.
Ils sont **roux**.	Elles sont **rousses**.
Il est **mignon**.	Elle est **mignonne**.
Ils sont **mignons**.	Elles sont **mignonnes**.
Il est **gentil**.	Elle est **gentille**.
Ils sont **gentils**.	Elles sont **gentilles**.
Il est **gros**.	Elle est **grosse**.
Ils sont **gros**.	Elles sont **grosses**.

- In the masculine forms, the final consonant sound is silent. In the feminine forms, the final consonant sound is pronounced.

- A few adjectives don't ever change. Here are some that you've already seen.

marron　　**orange**　　**cool**　　**super**　　**sympa**

18 On est différents!

Frédéric and Denise are brother and sister. Look at the picture and tell how they're alike and how they're different.

Frédéric est grand, mais Denise est petite.

19 Les meilleurs amis

Take turns with a partner describing your best friends. Tell about your friends' appearance, personality, and interests.

Grammaire   The verb être

Etre is an irregular verb.

être *(to be)*

Je **suis** intelligent(e).	Nous **sommes** intelligent(e)s.
Tu **es** intelligent(e).	Vous **êtes** intelligent(e)(s).
Il/Elle/On **est** intelligent(e).	Ils/Elles **sont** intelligent(e)s.

20 Devine!

Describe a member of the Louvain family to your partner. He or she will try to figure out who it is. Take turns.

M. Louvain — Chantal — Gabrielle — Mme Louvain — M. Louvain — Mme Louvain — Emile — Philou et Chouchou — Luc

21 Qui suis-je?

Pretend you're a famous person and describe yourself to a partner. Your partner will try to guess who you are. Take turns.

—Je suis très grand et très fort. Je joue au basket-ball. Qui suis-je?
—Tu es Shaquille O'Neal?
—Oui. C'est ça! *or* Non. C'est pas ça.

22 Mon journal

Choose your favorite family member. Write a paragraph describing that person and telling what he or she likes to do and where he or she likes to go. If you prefer, choose a member of your favorite TV family and describe and characterize that person.

PANORAMA CULTUREL

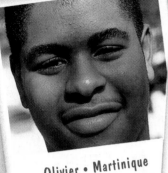

Olivier • Martinique

Onélia • France

Marie-Emmanuelle • France

Do you have pets? What are their names? We talked to some French-speaking people about their pets. Here's what they had to say.

Tu as un animal domestique? Il est comment?

«Oui, j'ai un animal à la maison, un chien. Son nom, c'est Chopine. Il n'est pas trop gros, [il est] vivant. Il aime beaucoup s'amuser et beaucoup manger aussi.»

—Olivier

«J'ai un chat. Il s'appelle Fabécar. Il a trois ans. C'est un mâle. On le voit assez rarement. On le voit seulement quand il veut manger, sinon il se promène dans les jardins. Il est très affectueux.»

—Onélia

«J'ai un cheval. Il est grand. Il fait 1 mètre 78 de garrot. Il est brun. Il s'appelle Viêt. Et on fait des balades à cheval.»

—Marie-Emmanuelle

Qu'en penses-tu?

1. What names do these people give their pets?
2. Do you take your pets out in public? Why or why not? If so, where?
3. What kind of system is used in the United States to identify lost pets?

Savais-tu que...?

More than half of French households have pets. City dwellers often take them along when they shop. In many francophone countries, people sometimes carry small animals in baskets (**paniers**) made just for them! It isn't unusual to see dogs and cats on trains or in subways, restaurants, department stores, and other public places. Most pet owners have their four-legged friends tattooed with a number that allows them to be identified in case they are lost. Various groups in France have launched poster campaigns to encourage dog-owners to teach their pets to use the gutter instead of the sidewalk: **Apprenez-leur le carniveau!**

Asking for, giving, and refusing permission

COMMENT DIT-ON... ?

Asking for, giving, and refusing permission

To ask for permission:
Je voudrais aller au cinéma. **Tu es d'accord?**
Is that OK with you?
(Est-ce que) je peux sortir? *May I . . .*

To give permission:
Oui, si tu veux. *Yes, if you want to.*
Pourquoi pas?
Oui, bien sûr.
D'accord, si tu fais **d'abord** la vaisselle.
OK, if you . . . first.

To refuse permission:
Pas question! *Out of the question!*
Non, c'est impossible. *No, that's impossible.*
Non, tu dois faire tes devoirs.
No, you've got to . . .
Pas ce soir. *Not tonight.*

23 Ecoute!

Listen to these people ask for permission.
Are they given or refused permission?

VOCABULAIRE

débarrasser la table	*to clear the table*
faire les courses	*to do the shopping*
faire le ménage	*to clean house*
faire la vaisselle	*to do the dishes*
garder ta petite sœur	*to look after . . .*
laver la voiture	*to wash the car*
passer l'aspirateur	*to vacuum*
promener le chien	*to walk the dog*
ranger ta chambre	*to pick up your room*
sortir la poubelle	*to take out the trash*
tondre le gazon	*to mow the lawn*

24 Ecoute!

Listen to some French teenagers ask permission to go out with their friends. Which picture represents the outcome of each dialogue?

a.

b.

c.

d.

e.

f.

25 Qui doit le faire?

Ask your partner who does various chores at his or her house. Then, change roles.

—Qui promène le chien?
—Mon frère. Et moi aussi quelquefois.

26 Qu'est-ce qu'ils disent?

1.

2.

3.

4.

27 Et toi?

Give or refuse permission in these situations.

1. Your little sister or brother asks to listen to your cassette.
2. Your friend wants to read your novel.
3. Your little sister or brother wants to go to the movies with you and your friend.

28 Jeu de rôle

Pretend you're a parent. Your partner asks permission to do several activities this weekend. Refuse permission for some, give permission for others, and give reasons. Change roles.

PRONONCIATION

The nasal sounds [õ], [ɛ̃], and [œ̃]

In Chapter 5 you learned about the nasal sound [ã]. Now listen to the other French nasal sounds [õ], [ɛ̃], and [œ̃]. As you repeat the following words, try not to put a trace of the consonant **n** in your nasal sounds.

on   hein   un

How are these nasal sounds represented in writing? The nasal sound [õ] is represented by a combination of **on** or **om**. Several letter combinations can represent the sound [ɛ̃], for example, **in, im, ain, aim, (i)en**. The nasal sound [œ̃] is spelled **un** or **um**. A vowel after these groups of letters or, in some cases, a doubling of the consonants **n** or **m** will result in a non-nasal sound, as in **limonade** and **ennemi**.

A. A prononcer

Repeat the following words.

1. ton   blond   pardon   nombre
2. cousin   impossible   copain   faim
3. un   lundi   brun   humble

B. A lire

Take turns with a partner reading the following sentences aloud.

1. Ils ont très faim. Ils vont prendre des sandwiches au jambon. C'est bon!
2. Allons faire du patin ou bien, allons au concert!
3. Ce garçon est blond et ce garçon-là est brun. Ils sont minces et mignons!
4. Pardon. C'est combien, cette montre? Cent soixante-quinze francs?

C. A écrire

You're going to hear a short dialogue. Write down what you hear.

LISONS!

Have you ever read an article about animals in an American magazine or newspaper? Here are some articles that appeared in the French magazine *Femme Actuelle*.

DE BONS CONSEILS

When you read something, it's important to separate the main idea from the supporting details. Sometimes the main idea is clearly stated at the beginning, other times it's just implied.

A. Which completion best expresses the main idea of these articles?

These articles are about . . .

1. animals that are missing.
2. animals that have performed heroic rescues.
3. animals that are up for adoption.
4. animals that have won prizes at cat and dog shows.

B. Now that you've decided what the main idea of the reading is, make a list of the kinds of details you expect to find in each of the articles.

C. How is Mayo different from the other animals? What is the main idea of the article about him? What other details are given?

D. Each of the articles includes a description of the animal. Look at the articles again and answer these questions.

1. Which animal is the oldest? The youngest?
2. Which animals get along well with children?

EN DIRECT DES REFUGES

IL VOUS ATTEND, ADOPTEZ-LE

CAMEL, 5 ANS

Ce sympathique bobtail blanc et gris est arrivé au refuge à la suite du décès accidentel de son maître. Il est vif, joyeux, a bon caractère et s'entend très bien avec les enfants. En échange de son dévouement et de sa fidélité, ce sportif robuste demande un grand espace afin de pouvoir courir et s'ébattre à son aise.

Cet animal vous attend au refuge de la Société normande de protection aux animaux, 7 bis, avenue Jacques-Chastellain, Ile Lacroix 76000 Rouen. Tél.: (16) 35.70.20.36. Si Camel a été adopté, pensez à ses voisins de cage.

Continuez à nous écrire, et envoyez-nous votre photo avec votre protégé, une surprise vous attend!

ELLE VOUS ATTEND, ADOPTEZ-LA

DADY, 2 ANS

Toute blanche, à l'exception de quelques petites taches et des oreilles noires bien dressées, Dady a un petit air de spitz, opulente fourrure en moins. Gentille, enjouée, très attachante, elle a été abandonnée après la séparation de ses maîtres et attend une famille qui accepterait de s'occuper d'elle un peu, beaucoup, passionnément.

Cet animal vous attend au refuge de l'Eden, Rod A'char, 29430 Lanhouarneau. Tél.: (16) 98.61.64.55. Colette Di Faostino tient seule, sans aucune subvention, ce havre exemplaire mais pauvre. Si Dady avait été adoptée, pensez à ses compagnons de malchance !

Mayo a trouvé une famille

Mayo a été adopté à la SPA de Valenciennes par Françoise Robeaux qui rêvait d'un chat gris ! Il a ainsi rejoint l'autre «fils» de la famille, un superbe siamois âgé de 13 ans.

ELLE VOUS ATTEND, ADOPTEZ-LA

POUPETTE, 3 ANS

Cette jolie chatte stérilisée au regard tendre et étonné a été recueillie à l'âge de quelques semaines par une vieille dame, dont elle a été la dernière compagne. Sa maîtresse est malheureusement décédée après un long séjour à l'hôpital. Poupette, l'orpheline, ne comprend pas ce qui lui arrive et commence à trouver le temps long ! Elle a hâte de retrouver un foyer «sympa», des bras caressants et une paire de genoux pour ronronner.

Cet animal vous attend avec espoir au refuge Grammont de la SPA 30, av. du Général-de-Gaulle 92230 Gennevilliers. Tél.: (1) 47.98.57.40. Rens. sur Minitel: 36.15 SPA. Si Poupette est déjà partie, pensez aux autres!

IL VOUS ATTEND, ADOPTEZ-LE

JUPITER, 7 MOIS

Cet adorable chaton tigré et blanc vient tout juste d'être castré et est dûment tatoué. Très joueur et affectueux, il a été recueilli au refuge parce que, malheureusement, sa maîtresse a dû être hospitalisée pour un séjour de longue durée. Sociable, il s'entend très bien avec les jeunes enfants et accepterait volontiers un chien pour compagnon.

Cet animal vous attend au refuge de la fondation Assistance aux animaux, 8, rue des Plantes 77410 Villevaudé. Tél.: (1) 60.26.20.48 (l'après-midi seulement).

ELLE VOUS ATTEND, ADOPTEZ-LA

FLORA, 3 ANS

C'est une pure braque Saint Germain roux et blanc. Elle ne pense qu'à jouer, s'entend bien avec les enfants et témoigne d'une gentillesse infatigable. Flora a été abandonnée car elle ne s'intéressait pas à la chasse. Son sport passion : la course derrière la «baballe».

Elle vous attend au refuge de l'Eden, Rod A'char, 29430 Lanhouarneau. Tél.: (16) 98.61.64.55. Colette Di Faostino tient seule, sans aucune subvention, ce havre exemplaire mais pauvre. Si Flora est adoptée, pensez à ses compagnons !

Vous avez recueilli un animal par notre intermédiaire ? Envoyez-nous votre photo avec votre protégé, une surprise vous attend!

3. Which animal needs a lot of space?

4. Which animals love to play?

E. Make a list of all the adjectives of physical description that you can find in the articles. Now, list the adjectives that describe the animals' characteristics.

F. Each article also explains why these animals were sent to the animal shelter.

1. Which animal wasn't interested in hunting?

2. Whose owner was involved in an accident?

3. Whose owner had to go to the hospital for a long time?

4. Whose family got separated?

G. A third kind of detail tells where you can go to adopt these animals. Can you find the French word for *animal shelter*?

H. Now, write your own classified ad to try to find a home for a lost pet. Remember to give the animal's name and age, tell what the animal looks like, and describe his or her character.

or

Write a letter to the animal shelter telling them what kind of pet you would like to adopt.

1. First, make a list of all of the characteristics you're looking for in a pet. Will you choose to adopt a cat or a dog? What will he or she look like? Act like? Like to do?

2. Write a short letter, including all the important information about your desired pet.

3. Don't forget to give your address and telephone number!

ouah - ouah

1 Ecoute Nathalie qui va te parler de sa famille. Puis, réponds aux questions.

1. Comment s'appelle le frère de Nathalie?
2. Il a quel âge?

3. Est-ce qu'elle a un chien ou un chat?
4. Comment est son animal?

2 Skim these documents. Then, read them more thoroughly and answer the questions below.

1. What kind of document is this? How do you know?
2. Who is Michel Louis Raymond?
3. Who are Denise Morel-Tissot and Raymond Tissot?
4. What happened on May 20, 1994?

Nous avons la joie de vous annoncer la naissance de notre fils

Michel Louis Raymond
20 Mai 1994

Denise Morel-Tissot
Raymond Tissot

Christelle et Nicolas

ont le plaisir de vous faire part de leur mariage

qui aura lieu le onze février 1995 à 15 heures, en la Mairie de Saint-Cyr-sur-Loire

M. et Mme Lionel Desombre
305 Rue des Marronniers
37540 Saint-Cyr-sur-Loire

5. What kind of document is this? How do you know?
6. Who are Christelle and Nicolas?
7. What happened on February 11, 1995, at three o'clock?
8. Who do you think M. and Mme Lionel Desombre are?

3 Take turns with a partner pointing out and describing someone in the picture below. Give the person's name and age and tell a little bit about him or her.

4 Write a short paragraph describing the family in the picture above. Give French names to all the family members, tell their ages, give a brief physical description, tell something about their personalities, and tell one or two things they like to do.

5 Are the following sentences representative of French culture, American culture, or both?

1. Dogs are not allowed in restaurants or department stores.
2. The government gives money to all families with two or more children.
3. Pets are tattooed with an identification number.
4. Women have a paid maternity leave of 14 weeks.

6

J E U   D E   R O L E

Your friends arrive at your door and suggest that you go out with them. Your parent tells them that you can go out if you finish your chores, so your friends offer to help. As you work around the house, you discuss where to go and what to do. Create a conversation with your classmates. Be prepared to act out the scene, using props.

Can you use what you've learned in this chapter?

Can you identify people? p. 179

1 How would you point out and identify Isabelle Ménard's relatives? How would you give their names and approximate ages? See page 180.

1. her grandparents
2. her uncle
3. her cousin Loïc
4. her brother

Can you introduce people? p. 183

2 How would you introduce your friend to . . .

1. an adult relative?
2. a classmate?

Can you describe and characterize people? p. 185

3 How would you describe these people?

1.

2.

4 How would you . . .

1. tell a friend that he or she is nice?
2. tell several friends that they're annoying?
3. say that you and your friend are intelligent?

Can you ask for, give, and refuse permission? p. 189

5 How would you ask permission to . . .

1. go to the movies?
2. go out with your friends?
3. go shopping?
4. go ice-skating?

6 How would you give someone permission to do something? How would you refuse?

7 What are three things your parents might ask you to do before allowing you to go out with your friends?

VOCABULAIRE

PREMIERE ETAPE

Identifying people

C'est... *This/That is . . .*
Ce sont... *These/those are . . .*
Voici... *Here's . . .*
Voilà... *There's . . .*

Family members

le grand-père *grandfather*
la grand-mère *grandmother*
la mère *mother*
le père *father*
la sœur *sister*
le frère *brother*

l'oncle (m.) *uncle*
la tante *aunt*
la cousine *girl cousin*
le cousin *boy cousin*
le chat *cat*
le chien *dog*
le canari *canary*
le poisson *fish*

Possessive adjectives

mon/ma/mes *my*
ton/ta/tes *your*
son/sa/ses *his, her*

notre/nos *our*
votre/vos *your*
leur/leurs *their*

Introducing people

C'est... *This is . . .*
Je te/vous présente... *I'd like you to meet . . .*
Très heureux (heureuse). *Pleased to meet you.* (FORMAL)

Other useful expressions

de *of (indicates possession)*

DEUXIEME ETAPE

Describing and characterizing people

Il est comment? *What is he like?*
Elle est comment? *What is she like?*
Ils/Elles sont comment? *What are they like?*
Il est... *He is . . .*
Elle est... *She is . . .*
Ils/Elles sont... *They're . . .*
amusant(e) *funny*
embêtant(e) *annoying*

fort(e) *strong*
gentil (gentille) *nice*
intelligent(e) *smart*
méchant(e) *mean*
pénible *annoying; a pain in the neck*
sympa(thique) *nice*
timide *shy*
âgé(e) *older*
blond(e) *blond*
brun(e) *brunette*

grand(e) *tall*
gros (grosse) *fat*
jeune *young*
mince *slender*
mignon (mignonne) *cute*
ne... ni grand(e) ni petit(e) *neither tall nor short*
petit(e) *short*
roux (rousse) *redheaded*
être *to be*

TROISIEME ETAPE

Asking for, giving, and refusing permission

Tu es d'accord? *Is that OK with you?*
(Est-ce que) je peux...? *May I . . . ?*
Oui, si tu veux. *Yes, if you want to.*
Pourquoi pas? *Why not?*
Oui, bien sûr. *Yes, of course.*
D'accord, si tu... d'abord... *OK, if you . . . first.*
Pas question! *Out of the question!*

Non, c'est impossible. *No, that's impossible.*
Non, tu dois... *No. You've got to . . .*
Pas ce soir. *Not tonight.*

Chores

faire les courses *to do the shopping*
faire la vaisselle *to do the dishes*
faire le ménage *to do housework*
ranger ta chambre *to pick up your room*

passer l'aspirateur *to vacuum*
promener le chien *to walk the dog*
garder... *to look after . . .*
sortir la poubelle *to take out the trash*
débarrasser la table *to clear the table*
laver la voiture *to wash the car*
tondre le gazon *to mow the lawn*

CHAPITRE 8

Allez, viens à Abidjan!

La ville d'Abidjan

Abidjan

Ville principale de la République de Côte d'Ivoire

Population : plus de 1.850.000

Points d'intérêt : l'Assemblée nationale, le palais du Président, le parc national du Banco, le Musée national

Abidjanais célèbres : Bernard Dadié, Coffi Gadeau, Amon d'Aby, Abdoulaye Traoré

Ressources et industries : café, cacao, bananes, textiles, bois

Spécialités : foutou, aloco, kedjenou, attiéké, sauce arachide, sauce graine, sauce claire

N

MALI

BURKINA FASO

GUINÉE

Korhogo

CÔTE D'IVOIRE

Bouaké

Yamoussoukro

GHANA

LIBERIA

Abidjan

Océan Atlantique

Abidjan

Abidjan is a modern city that lies on the **baie de Cocody** in Côte d'Ivoire. It is a bustling metropolitan area sometimes called the "Paris of Africa." The office buildings and hotels of **Le Plateau** contrast sharply with the lively and colorful district of **Treichville,** the cultural heart of Abidjan.

① Côte d'Ivoire is famous for its brightly colored fabrics and weavings.

② **Le parc Banco,** a national park since 1953, is a beautiful rain forest reserve.

③ **Le Plateau** is Abidjan's center of commerce and government.

④ The port of **Adjamé** is one of the busiest in West Africa.

⑤ Many different kinds of traditional masks are displayed in the National Museum in Abidjan.

⑥ **Treichville** is the main shopping district of Abidjan. The combination of colors, sounds, and aromas of this lively quarter of town will awaken all the senses.

8 Au marché

① Le marché en Côte d'Ivoire, c'est un plaisir pour les yeux.

Imagine shopping for food in the Republic of Côte d'Ivoire—the tropical fruits, lively market-place, and Ivorian merchants would make it an adventure. You'd also gain experience with the metric system and the currency of francophone Africa, *le franc de la Communauté financière africaine (CFA)*.

In this chapter you will learn

- to express need
- to make, accept, and decline requests; to tell someone what to do
- to offer, accept, or refuse food

And you will

- listen to French-speaking people talk about the foods they like
- read recipes for African dishes
- write about your favorite and least favorite foods
- find out about the metric system of weights and measures

② Tu me rapportes des fruits?

③ Tiens, Djeneba, tu peux m'aider?

Mise en train

Une invitée pour le déjeuner

Where does Djeneba go to do the grocery shopping?
Do you recognize any of the food items she buys?

Le matin chez les Diomandé, à Abidjan. C'est l'heure du petit déjeuner.

2500

BANQUE CENTRALE DES ÉTATS DE L'AFRIQUE DE L'OUEST
1000

1 kilo de riz
250 grammes de pâte d'arachide
1 poisson
7 oignons
1 douzaine de tomates
3 citrons
un paquet de beurre
du pain

1 — Encore du pain, Aminata?

— Non, merci. Je n'ai plus faim.

— Je pense faire du foutou avec de la sauce arachide pour le déjeuner.

2 — Tiens, te voilà, Djeneba. Tu me fais le marché?

— Volontiers! Qu'est-ce qu'il te faut?

3 — Il me faut des légumes, du riz, du poisson... Tu me rapportes aussi du pain... Et prends de la pâte de tomates.

— Bon, d'accord.

Djeneba va au marché...

...puis, elle rentre chez elle.

Voilà le poisson, les 250 grammes de pâte d'arachide, les oignons, les tomates et les citrons. J'ai aussi acheté un paquet de beurre, de la pâte de tomates, du pain et du riz.

Merci, chérie.

Mme Diomandé fait la cuisine.

Viens. Goûte voir. C'est bon?

Oui, très bon.

Toc toc toc!

Ah, j'ai oublié... Devine qui j'ai vu au marché.

Aucune idée... Va voir qui est à la porte.

1 Tu as compris?

1. What time of day is it?
2. What does Mme Diomandé want Djeneba to do? Why?
3. What are some of the things Djeneba buys?
4. What happens at the end of the story?
5. Judging from the title, what do you think Djeneba forgot?

2 Vrai ou faux?

1. Aminata va au marché.
2. Mme Diomandé va faire du foutou avec de la sauce arachide.
3. Djeneba ne veut pas aller au marché.
4. Djeneba achète des bananes au marché.
5. Djeneba oublie le pain.

3 Choisis la photo

Match the foods that Djeneba bought to their pictures.

1. du poisson   2. des tomates   3. des oignons   4. des citrons   5. du pain

a.   b.   c.   d.   e.

4 C'est qui?

1. «Non, merci. Je n'ai plus faim.»
2. «Tu me fais le marché?»
3. «J'ai aussi acheté un paquet de beurre, du riz, de la pâte de tomates et du pain.»
4. «Ah, j'ai oublié... »
5. «Va voir qui est à la porte.»

5 Cherche l'expression

In **Une invitée pour le déjeuner**, how does . . .

1. Mme Diomandé offer more food to Mme Bonfils?
2. Aminata refuse the offer?
3. Mme Diomandé ask Djeneba to do the shopping?
4. Mme Diomandé tell Djeneba what she needs?
5. Djeneba agree to do what Mme Diomandé asks?

6 Et maintenant, à toi

Who does the grocery shopping in your family? Where do they do the shopping?

VOCABULAIRE

Qu'est-ce qu'on trouve **au marché**?

Qu'est-ce qu'on vend **au supermarché**?

du beurre	butter	du gâteau	cake	des fraises (f.)	strawberries
de la confiture	jam	de la tarte	pie	du raisin	grapes
du lait	milk	des pommes (f.)	apples	des petits pois (m.)	peas
du yaourt	yogurt	des poires (f.)	pears	des carottes (f.)	carrots
du riz	rice	des pêches (f.)	peaches	des champignons (m.)	mushrooms
de la farine	flour	des citrons (m.)	lemons		

* **Poule** refers to live chickens, while **poulet** refers to cooked chicken.

7 Ecoute!

Listen to the dialogues and decide if the people are talking about fruit, vegetables, fish, or poultry.

> ### Grammaire The partitive articles du, de la, de l', and des
>
> Use **du**, **de la**, **de l'**, or **des** to indicate *some of* or *part of* something.
>
> > Je voudrais **du** gâteau.
> > Tu veux **de la** salade?
> > Elle va prendre **de l'**eau minérale.
> > Il me faut **des** oranges.
>
> - If you want to talk about a whole item, use the articles **un** and **une**.
>
>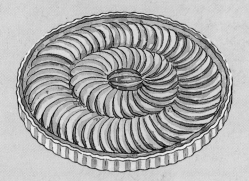
>
> > Il achète **une** tarte.   Il prend **de la** tarte.
>
> - In a negative sentence, **du**, **de la**, **de l'**, and **des** change to **de** *(none or any)*.
>
> > —Tu as **du** pain?   —Tu prends **de la** viande?
> > —Désolée, je n'ai pas **de** pain.   —Merci, je ne prends jamais **de** viande.
>
> - You can't leave out the article in French as you do in English.
>
> > Elle mange **du** fromage. *She's eating cheese.*

8 Qu'est-ce qu'on prend?

Complète ce dialogue avec du, de la, de l' ou des.

ASSIKA	J'ai très faim, maman.
MAMAN	Qu'est-ce que tu veux manger?
ASSIKA	Moi, je voudrais __1__ poisson, __2__ riz et __3__ haricots.
MAMAN	Bon. Tu peux prendre __4__ pain aussi.
ASSIKA	Et comme boisson?
MAMAN	Prends __5__ eau minérale.
ASSIKA	D'accord.
MAMAN	Et comme dessert, prends __6__ bananes ou __7__ oranges.
ASSIKA	C'est tout?
MAMAN	Non, tu peux prendre __8__ yaourt aussi.

9 Qu'est-ce qu'elles ont acheté?

What are Prisca, Clémentine, and Adjoua buying at the market?

1.

2.

3.

NOTE CULTURELLE

Shopping at a market in Côte d'Ivoire can be an exciting and colorful experience. Every city, town, and village has an open-air market where people come to buy and sell food, cloth, housewares, medicine, and herbal remedies. Although French is the official language in Côte d'Ivoire, more than 60 different African languages are spoken there. To make shopping easier for everyone, there is a common market language called **djoula**. Here are a few phrases in **djoula**.

í ní sɔ̀gɔ̀ma	(ee nee so*go*ma)	*Good morning.*
í ní wúla	(ee *nee* woulah)	*Good afternoon./Hello.*
í ká kénɛ wá?	(ee kah keh*neh* wah)	*How are you?/How's it going?*
n ká kénɛ kósobɛ	(nnkah keh*neh* kuh*soh*beh)	*I'm fine.*

ETIENNE NANGBO

10 Qu'est-ce qu'il y a dans le chariot?

Your partner has mixed his or her shopping cart with five others whose contents are listed below. Ask about the contents until you have enough information to guess which cart belongs to your partner. Then, change roles.

— Tu as acheté des tomates?   — Non.
— Tu as acheté du poisson?   — Oui.
— Ton chariot, c'est le numéro... ? — Oui.

1. du poisson
   des tomates
   des bananes
   du fromage
   du lait

2. du pain
   des œufs
   des oignons
   du poisson
   des haricots

3. du sucre
   des ananas
   du lait
   du maïs
   des tomates

4. des tomates
   des haricots
   des œufs
   du sucre
   du maïs

5. des ananas
   des bananes
   du fromage
   des oignons
   des haricots

6. des bananes
   des œufs
   du poisson
   du pain
   des tomates

COMMENT DIT-ON... ?

Expressing need

— Qu'est-ce qu'il te faut?

— **Il me faut** des bananes, du riz et de l'eau minérale.

— **De quoi est-ce que tu as besoin?** *What do you need?*

— **J'ai besoin de** riz pour faire du foutou. *I need . . .*

Note de Grammaire

The expression **avoir besoin de** can be followed by a noun or a verb. The partitive article is not used with this expression.

Tu **as besoin de** tomates?

Nous **avons besoin d'œufs** pour l'omelette.

J'**ai besoin d'**aller au marché.

A la française

Many French expressions involve foods: **On est dans la purée** *(We're in trouble)*; **C'est pas de la tarte** *(It's not easy)*. Can you guess what **C'est du gâteau** means? *

Vocabulaire à la carte

Here are some additional words you may want to know:

du concombre	*cucumber*
des cornichons (m.)	*pickles*
de la moutarde	*mustard*
des noix (f.)	*nuts*
du poivre	*pepper*
du sel	*salt*

---

11 Que faut-il?

Tu as besoin de quoi pour faire...

1. un bon sandwich?
2. une quiche?
3. une salade?
4. une salade de fruits?
5. un banana split?

12 Un repas entre amis

Sandrine is having a party, but she won't tell what she's cooking. Based on what she needs, try to guess what she's preparing.

1. J'ai besoin de salade, de tomates, de carottes, d'oignons...
2. J'ai besoin de fromage, de pain, de jambon...
3. J'ai besoin d'œufs, de champignons, de fromage, de lait...
4. J'ai besoin de bananes, de pommes, d'oranges...

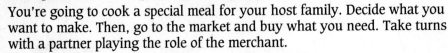

une tarte aux pommes

un banana split   une salade de fruits

une salade   un sandwich

une omelette

13 De quoi est-ce que tu as besoin?

You're going to cook a special meal for your host family. Decide what you want to make. Then, go to the market and buy what you need. Take turns with a partner playing the role of the merchant.

* It means *It's easy; it's a piece of cake.*

PANORAMA CULTUREL

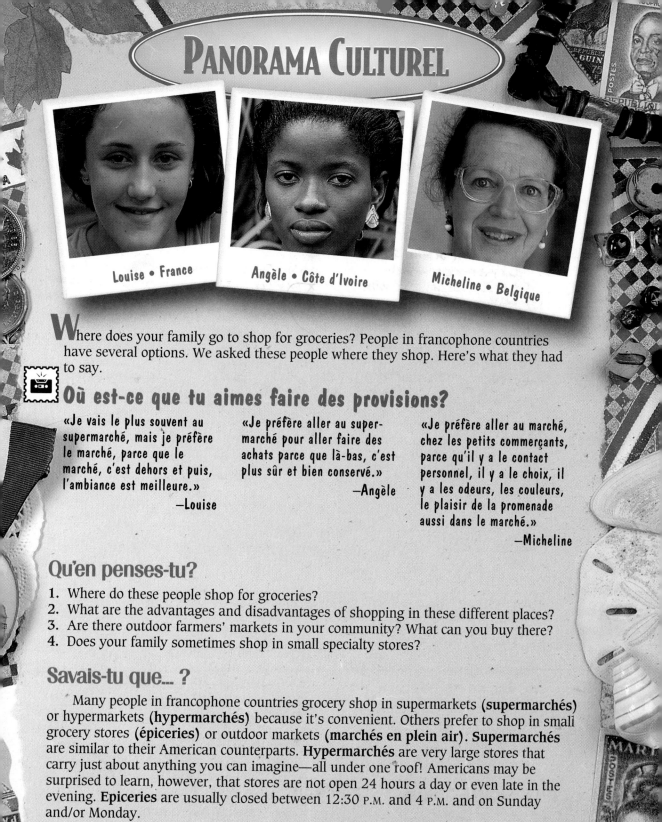

Louise • France

Angèle • Côte d'Ivoire

Micheline • Belgique

Where does your family go to shop for groceries? People in francophone countries have several options. We asked these people where they shop. Here's what they had to say.

Où est-ce que tu aimes faire des provisions?

«Je vais le plus souvent au supermarché, mais je préfère le marché, parce que le marché, c'est dehors et puis, l'ambiance est meilleure.»
—Louise

«Je préfère aller au super-marché pour aller faire des achats parce que là-bas, c'est plus sûr et bien conservé.»
—Angèle

«Je préfère aller au marché, chez les petits commerçants, parce qu'il y a le contact personnel, il y a le choix, il y a les odeurs, les couleurs, le plaisir de la promenade aussi dans le marché.»
—Micheline

Qu'en penses-tu?

1. Where do these people shop for groceries?
2. What are the advantages and disadvantages of shopping in these different places?
3. Are there outdoor farmers' markets in your community? What can you buy there?
4. Does your family sometimes shop in small specialty stores?

Savais-tu que... ?

Many people in francophone countries grocery shop in supermarkets (**supermarchés**) or hypermarkets (**hypermarchés**) because it's convenient. Others prefer to shop in small grocery stores (**épiceries**) or outdoor markets (**marchés en plein air**). **Supermarchés** are similar to their American counterparts. **Hypermarchés** are very large stores that carry just about anything you can imagine—all under one roof! Americans may be surprised to learn, however, that stores are not open 24 hours a day or even late in the evening. **Epiceries** are usually closed between 12:30 P.M. and 4 P.M. and on Sunday and/or Monday.

COMMENT DIT-ON... ?

**Making, accepting, and declining requests; telling
someone what to do**

To make requests:
Tu peux aller faire les courses?
Can you . . . ?
Tu me rapportes des œufs?
Will you bring me . . . ?

To tell someone what to do:
Rapporte(-moi) du beurre.
Bring (me) back . . .
Prends du lait. *Get . . .*
Achète(-moi) du riz. *Buy (me) . . .*
N'oublie pas d'acheter le lait.
Don't forget to . . .

To accept:
Pourquoi pas?
Bon, d'accord.
Je veux bien. *Gladly.*
J'y vais tout de suite.
I'll go right away.

To decline:
Je ne peux pas maintenant.
**Je regrette, mais je n'ai pas le
temps.** *I'm sorry, but I don't
have time.*
J'ai des trucs à faire.
J'ai des tas de choses à faire.

14 Ecoute!

a. Listen to these dialogues. Is the first speaker making a request or telling someone what to do?

b. Now, listen again. Does the second speaker accept or decline the request or command?

ᴬₗₐ française

You already know that the verb **faire** means *to do*. What do you think the verb **refaire** might mean? The prefix **re-** in front of a verb means *to redo* something; to do something again. Use **r-** in front of a verb that begins with a vowel.

Tu dois **re**lire ce livre. *You need to reread this book.*
On va **r**acheter du lait. *We'll buy milk again.*
Rapporte-moi du beurre! *Bring me back some butter!*

Does this same rule apply in English?

---

*G*rammaire   The verb **pouvoir**

Pouvoir is an irregular verb. Notice how similar it is to the verb **vouloir,** which you learned in Chapter 6.

pouvoir *(to be able to, can, may)*

Je **peux**		Nous **pouvons**
Tu **peux** ⎱ faire les courses?		Vous **pouvez** ⎱ promener le chien?
Il/Elle/On **peut**		Ils/Elles **peuvent**

---

15 Tu peux... ?

Ask your classmates to bring something back for you, depending on where they're going. Your classmates will accept or refuse your requests.

— Tu vas à la bibliothèque?
— Oui.
— Tu peux me rapporter un livre?
— Bien sûr!

> au supermarché
> à la librairie   au fast-food
> au marché   aux magasins

16 On peut?

Find out if your classmates can do these things with or for you.

—Vous pouvez écouter de la musique après l'école?
—Non, nous ne pouvons pas.

> regarder la télé après l'école
> aller nager
> faire des courses avec moi
> me rapporter un sandwich
> jouer au foot demain
> sortir ce soir

VOCABULAIRE

Vous en voulez combien?

un kilo(gramme) de
pommes de terre et
une livre d'oignons

**une bouteille
d'**eau minérale

une douzaine d'œufs

une boîte de tomates

un paquet de sucre

une tranche de jambon

un morceau de fromage

un litre de lait

Note de Grammaire

Notice that you always use **de** or **d'** after expressions of quantity.

Une tranche **de** jambon, s'il vous plaît.

Je voudrais un kilo **d'**oranges.

NOTE CULTURELLE

The metric system was created shortly after the French Revolution and has since been adopted by nearly all countries in the world except the United States. Although the United States is officially trying to convert to the metric system, many people aren't yet used to it. In the metric system, distances are measured in centimeters and meters, rather than inches and yards. Large distances are measured in kilometers. Grams and kilograms are the standard measures of weight. **Une livre** is about half a kilo. Liquids, including gasoline, are measured in liters. To convert metric measurements, use the following table:

1 centimeter = .39 inches	1 gram = .035 ounces
1 meter = 39.37 inches	1 kilogram = 2.2 pounds
1 kilometer = .62 miles	1 liter = 1.06 quarts

17 Ecoute!

Listen to Sophie as she does her shopping.
Write down the items and the quantities she asks for.

18 Allons au marché!

You're shopping for groceries. Make sure that you
place your orders in appropriate quantities. Your
partner will be the merchant. Then, change roles.

Vous avez choisi?

Et avec ça?   Voilà.

C'est tout?

Vous désirez?

Je voudrais...   Il me faut...

Je prends...

avocats
tomates
vinaigre
oignons
oeufs
pain
huile d'olive
fromage
riz
haricots
raisin
sucre

19 Essaie!

You're at a market in Côte d'Ivoire and you decide to try some fruits you're unfamiliar with.
Ask the vendor if he or she has the fruits and how much they cost. The vendor will ask
how many you would like. Act out this scene with a partner. Then, change roles.

1.

2.

3.

4.

5.

20 Jeu de rôle

You're working as a volunteer to pick up groceries for senior citizens. Make a list of what
you need to get and the quantity of each item. Take turns with your partner playing the role
of the senior citizen.

◀ **Le foutou,** the national dish of Côte d'Ivoire, is a paste made from boiled plantains, manioc, or yams. It is eaten with various sauces, such as peanut sauce or palm oil nut sauce.

▼ **La sauce arachide** is one of the many sauces eaten in Côte d'Ivoire. It is made from peanut butter with beef, chicken, or fish, hot peppers, peanut oil, garlic, onions, tomato paste, tomatoes, and a variety of other vegetables. It is usually served over rice.

▶ **L'aloco,** a popular snack food in Côte d'Ivoire, is a dish of fried plantain bananas. It is usually eaten with a spicy sauce **(sauce pimentée).**

Qu'en penses-tu?

1. Do these dishes resemble any that are eaten in the United States?
2. Which ingredients in these dishes can you find in your neighborhood grocery store? Which ingredients are unfamiliar?
3. What dishes are typical of your part of the country? Why are they more common than others?

Savais-tu que... ?

Yams (**ignames**) and plantains are abundant in the Republic of Côte d'Ivoire, which explains why **foutou** is a popular dish. A typical lunch consists of one main course — often **foutou**, rice, or **attiéké** (ground manioc root) with a sauce; and a dessert — usually tropical fruits such as guavas, pineapples, or papayas. Lunch is traditionally followed by an hour-long siesta. To accommodate this custom, stores are closed from noon until 3:00 P.M., even in large cities such as Abidjan. Unlike lunch, dinner tends to be a much lighter meal. Heavy foods are rarely eaten in the evening.

VOCABULAIRE

Qu'est-ce qu'on prend pour...

petit déjeuner?

le déjeuner?

goûter?

le dîner?

21 Ecoute!

Listen to these people tell what they have for breakfast. Match each speaker with his or her breakfast.

a.

b.

c.

NOTE CULTURELLE

In the morning, most francophone people have a very light breakfast (**le petit déjeuner**). Coffee with hot steamed milk (**café au lait**) or hot chocolate is the drink of choice. It is usually served with bread or croissants, butter, and jam. Children may eat cereal for breakfast as well, sometimes with warm milk. The largest meal of the day, **le déjeuner**, has traditionally been between noon and 1:00 P.M. Dinner (**le dîner**) is eaten after 7:00 P.M.

---

22 Et comme goûter?

Ton ami(e) et toi, vous rentrez chez toi après l'école.
Qu'est-ce que vous allez prendre comme goûter?

— Qu'est-ce que tu voudrais?
— Tu as une pomme?
— Non, il n'y a pas de pommes. Mais il y a des poires.
— Alors, donne-moi une poire, s'il te plaît.

du lait   une poire   une glace

un sandwich   une banane   une pomme

du gâteau   du fromage

du yaourt   une pêche

de la confiture   du beurre   du pain

23 Quel repas?

Describe one of these meals to your partner. He or she will try to guess which meal you're talking about. Take turns.

Il y a du poulet,...

1.

2.

3.

24 Devine!

Write down what you think you'll have for your meals tomorrow, using the **Vocabulaire** on p. 207. Your partner will do the same. Take turns guessing what each of you will have.

—Au petit déjeuner, tu vas prendre... ?
—Oui, c'est ça. *or* Non, pas de...

COMMENT DIT-ON... ?

Offering, accepting, or refusing food

To offer food to someone:
Tu veux du riz?
Vous voulez de l'eau minérale?
Vous prenez du fromage?
Tu prends du fromage?
Encore du pain? *More . . . ?*

To accept:
Oui, s'il vous/te
  plaît.
Oui, j'en veux bien.
  Yes, I'd like some.
Oui, avec plaisir.
  Yes, with pleasure.

To refuse:
Non, merci.
Je n'en veux
  plus. *I don't
  want any more.*
Non, merci. Je
  n'ai plus faim.
  *No thanks.
  I'm not
  hungry
  anymore.*

---

25 Ecoute!

Is the speaker offering, accepting, or refusing food?

26 Encore du pain?

An Ivorian exchange student is having dinner at your house. Encourage him or her to try some of the foods on the table. Your friend will accept or politely refuse.

Look for opportunities to practice your French wherever you go. Try to meet French-speaking people and talk with them. Ask your teacher to help you find a pen pal in a French-speaking country. Rent videocassettes of French films. See how many French products you can find at the grocery store and the cosmetic counter, and how many French dishes you can find on restaurant menus.

Grammaire   The pronoun en

En takes the place of a phrase beginning with **du, de la, de l', des,** or **de** to avoid repetition. **En** usually means *some (of it/them)* or simply *it/them.*

— Tu veux **des mangues**?

— Oui, j'**en** veux bien.

— Tu manges **des légumes**?

— Oui, j'**en** mange souvent.

In a negative sentence, **en** means *any* or *none.*

— Tu veux **du beurre**?

— Merci, je n'**en** veux pas.

27 Elle en a combien?

What quantity of each of these items would you expect Aïssata to have in her basket?

Des haricots? Elle en a un kilo.

1. Du lait?
2. Du beurre?
3. Des tomates?
4. Du riz?
5. Des œufs?
6. De l'eau minérale?

28 Tu en veux?

Take turns with a partner asking each other if you eat the foods shown in Activity 26. Use the pronoun **en** in your answers.

— Tu manges du poulet?
— Oui, j'en mange souvent.

P R O N O N C I A T I O N

The sounds [o] and [ɔ]

The sound [o] is similar to the vowel sound in the English word *boat.* To make the sound [o], hold your mouth in a whistling position. Keep the lips and tongue steady to avoid the glide heard in *boat.* Repeat each of these words: **trop, kilo, mot.** The spellings **au, eau, ô,** and sometimes **o** represent the sound [o]. Now, repeat these words: **jaune, chaud, beau, rôle.**

The sound [ɔ] is between the vowel sounds in the English words *boat* and *bought.* Usually, this sound is followed by a consonant sound in the same syllable. The sound [ɔ] is more open, so hold your mouth in a semi-whistling position to produce it. This sound is usually spelled with the letter **o.** Now repeat these words: **bof, donne, fort, carotte.**

A. A prononcer

Repeat the following words and phrases.

1. au revoir
2. un gâteau
3. des pommes
4. encore

un stylo jaune
moi aussi
d'abord
dormir

au restaurant
des haricots verts
une promenade
l'école

B. A lire

Take turns with a partner reading each of the following sentences aloud.

1. Elle a une gomme violette et un stylo jaune.
2. Tu aimes les carottes? Moi, j'adore. J'aime bien aussi les escargots et le porc.
3. Elle est occupée aujourd'hui. Elle a informatique et biologie.
4. Il me faut un short parce qu'il fait trop chaud.
5. Tu peux sortir si tu promènes d'abord le chien.

C. A écrire

You're going to hear a short dialogue. Write down what you hear.

LISONS!

la cuisine autour du monde

LA CUISINE AFRICAINE

Skim the titles and photographs. What will you be reading?

DE BONS CONSEILS

Remember to look for cognates to help you figure out what you're reading. Occasionally, you will encounter false cognates, words that look alike in two languages but have different meanings.

Context clues can sometimes help you recognize false cognates. An example of a false cognate is the French phrase **fruits de mer.** **Fruits de mer** may make you think of the English word *fruit*, but it means *seafood*.

A. You already know a few false cognates. Try to figure out the meaning of the false cognates in the sentences below.

1. Je vais à San Francisco à 11h00. Maintenant, il est 10h40, et **j'attends** le train.

   a. I'm attending
   b. I'm late for
   c. I'm waiting for

2. J'adore les sciences. Ce soir, je vais **assister** à une conférence sur l'ozone.

   a. to attend
   b. to assist
   c. to teach

Les desserts

Croissants au coco et au sésame
(Afrique occidentale)

Prép. : 30 mn. - Cuiss. : 10 mn.
Repos : 1 h. - 8 pers.

2 œufs
140 g de sucre
190 g de noix de coco râpée

170 g de farine
Vanille en poudre
Graines de sésame.

Mélanger la noix de coco râpée, le sucre, la vanille et les œufs entiers. Incorporer la farine. Travailler la pâte. Former une boule. Laisser reposer 1 heure au frais.
Etaler la pâte sur 1/2 cm. Découper en croissants. Les rouler dans le sésame. Cuire au four à 200 °C, (th. 6-7), 10 minutes.

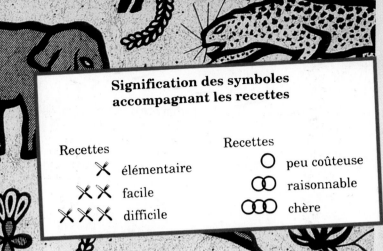

Signification des symboles accompagnant les recettes

Recettes

✗ élémentaire

✗✗ facile

✗✗✗ difficile

Recettes

◯ peu coûteuse

◯◯ raisonnable

◯◯◯ chère

— *Les entrées*

Mousseline africaine de petits légumes

✗ ◯◯

Prép. : 40 mn. - Cuiss. : 15 mn.

(Afrique occidentale - Bénin - Togo)

4 pers.

2 petits concombres
Ail
1 lime
1 radis noir
1/2 papaye

1 avocat
1 épi de maïs
Graines de carvi
4 petites brioches
Sel.

Eplucher les concombres. Les détailler en dés. Faire la même chose avec l'avocat. Débarrasser l'épis de maïs des feuilles et des barbes. Le faire cuire durant 15 minutes à l'eau bouillante. Saler en fin de cuisson.

Egréner le maïs. Débarrasser la papaye de ses graines. La découper en petits dés. Emincer le radis noir. Parfumer de graines de carvi et d'ail haché. Arroser la salade de jus de lime.

Retirer le chapeau des brioches. Les évider. Les garnir de la salade parfumée.

Les brioches ne doivent pas être sucrées. Si on les fabrique, il convient d'ôter le sucre. Ne pas saler l'épi de maïs au début de la cuisson mais à la fin afin d'éviter qu'il durcisse.

B. With a partner, scan the reading and write down all of the cognates you can find in these selections.

C. Did you find any false cognates? Were you able to figure out what they mean? If so, how?

D. Where would you expect to find these reading selections? Where are these dishes from?

E. Which of the dishes would make a good dessert?

F. Are these dishes easy or difficult to make? How do you know? Are they expensive or inexpensive to make? How do you know?

G. To make **croissants**, how long do you need to chill the dough? At what temperature do you bake them? What temperature is that on the Fahrenheit scale? (To convert from Celsius to Fahrenheit, multiply by $\frac{9}{5}$ and add 32.)

H. To make **mousseline**, how long do you have to cook the corn? Do you think this dish would taste sweet or salty? How many people does this dish serve?

I. Now, with a partner, write the instructions for an easy recipe that you know how to make. Include the ingredients, the steps required to prepare the dish, and the cooking and preparation time required.

The background design on the two **Lisons!** pages is from a piece of cloth purchased in Côte d'Ivoire.

MISE EN PRATIQUE

1 Listen to this supermarket advertisement. List four of the foods that are on sale. Then, listen again for the prices of the four items you listed.

2 On the plane to Abidjan, you order dinner. Discuss the menu with your partner and decide what you're both going to have.

AIR AFRIQUE

MENU

Crevettes Sauce Cocktail

Sauté d'Agneau Créole

Pomme Duchesse

Petits Pois à l'Anglaise

OU

Saumon au Gratin

Champignons Sautés aux Fines Herbes

Riz à la Créole

Fromage

Gâteau Coco et Pistache

Café

Il est possible que le plat chaud que vous avez choisi ne soit plus disponible, nous vous remercions de votre compréhension.

MY

3 Choose a food item. Pretend you're the producer of that item and you need to sell it. With a partner, write an ad that encourages people to buy your product. Tell people when they should have it and why it's good. Include pictures or logos as well. Consider your audience, the people who might be likely to buy your product.

4

LES GROUPES D'ALIMENTS

Les aliments sont regroupés en 6 catégories selon leurs caractéristiques nutritionnelles :

- **Le lait et les produits laitiers** sont nos principaux fournisseurs de calcium.
- **Viandes, poissons et œufs** sont nos sources essentielles de protéines de bonne qualité.
- **Le groupe du pain, des féculents et des légumes secs** apporte les «glucides lents» libérant progressivement l'énergie nécessaire à notre organisme.
- **Légumes et fruits** sont nos sources de fibres, vitamines et minéraux.
- **Les matières grasses** sont les sources énergétiques les plus importantes pour notre corps.
- **Le sucre et ses dérivés** apportent les «glucides rapides» nécessaires au bon fonctionnement cérébral et musculaire.

Groupe	Lait Produits Laitiers	Viandes Poissons Œufs	Pains Féculents	Fruits Légumes	Matières Grasses	Sucre Dérivés
Intérêt Principal	Calcium	Protéines	Glucides	Fibres Vitamines A et B	Lipides	Glucides
Intérêt Secondaire	Protéines Vitamines A, B, D	Fer Vitamine B	Fibres	Glucides	Vitamines (A, E, selon mat. grasses)	

L'ensemble de ces catégories permet, au sein d'une alimentation diversifiée, de couvrir tous nos besoins.

1. What kind of chart is this?
2. What do the six categories listed mean?
3. According to the chart, what are some of the nutrients found in . . .
   - **a.** produits laitiers?
   - **b.** viandes?
   - **c.** pain?
   - **d.** fruits et légumes?
   - **e.** matières grasses?
   - **f.** sucre et ses dérivés?
4. Give some examples of foods you know in French that fall into each category.
5. Name three foods that are high in protein and three that are high in calcium.

5 What are some differences between meals in Africa, France, and the United States?

6

JEU DE ROLE

- **a.** Make a list in French of everything you've eaten for the last two days. Use the food vocabulary that you've learned in this chapter.
- **b.** Now, you go to a nutrition counselor. The counselor will evaluate your diet, telling you what you need to eat more of and what you shouldn't eat anymore. Act out this scene with a partner. Then, change roles.

Can you use what you've learned in this chapter?

Can you express need? p. 210

1 How would you tell someone that you need these things?

1.

2.

3.

4.

5.

Can you make, accept, and decline requests or tell someone what to do? p. 212

2 How would you . . .

1. ask someone to go grocery shopping for you?
2. tell someone to bring back some groceries for you?

3 How would you accept the requests in number 2? How would you refuse?

4 How would you ask for a specific quantity of these foods?

1. œufs
2. lait
3. oranges
4. beurre
5. jambon
6. eau minérale

Can you offer, accept, or refuse food? p. 219

5 How would you offer someone these foods?

1. some rice
2. some oranges
3. some milk

6 How would you accept the foods listed in number 5 if they were offered? How would you refuse them?

7 How would you tell someone what you have for . . .

1. breakfast?
2. lunch?
3. an afternoon snack?
4. dinner?

PREMIERE ETAPE

Expressing need

Qu'est-ce qu'il te faut? *What do you need?*
Il me faut... *I need . . .*
De quoi est-ce que tu as besoin? *What do you need?*
J'ai besoin de... *I need . . .*
du, de la, de l', des *some*

Foods; Shopping

des ananas (m.) *pineapples*
des avocats (m.) *avocados*
des bananes (f.) *bananas*
du beurre *butter*
du bifteck *steak*
des carottes (f.) *carrots*
des champignons (m.) *mushrooms*

des citrons (m.) *lemons*
de la confiture *jam*
de la farine *flour*
des fraises (f.) *strawberries*
du fromage *cheese*
des gâteaux (m.) *cakes*
des gombos (m.) *okra*
des goyaves (f.) *guavas*
des haricots (m.) *beans*
du lait *milk*
du maïs *corn*
des mangues (f.) *mangoes*
des noix de coco (f.) *coconuts*
des œufs (m.) *eggs*
des oranges (f.) *oranges*
du pain *bread*
des papayes (f.) *papayas*
des pêches (f.) *peaches*

des petits pois (m.) *peas*
des poires (f.) *pears*
du poisson *fish*
des pommes (f.) *apples*
des pommes de terre (f.) *potatoes*
du porc *pork*
des poules (f.) *live chickens*
du poulet *cooked chicken*
du raisin *grapes*
du riz *rice*
de la salade *salad, lettuce*
des tartes (f.) *pies*
des tomates (f.) *tomatoes*
de la viande *meat*
des yaourts (m.) *yogurt*
le marché *the market*
le supermarché *the supermarket*

DEUXIEME ETAPE

Making, accepting, and declining requests

Tu peux...? *Can you . . . ?*
Tu me rapportes... ? *Will you bring me . . . ?*
Bon, d'accord. *Well, OK.*
Je veux bien. *Gladly.*
J'y vais tout de suite. *I'll go right away.*
Je regrette, mais je n'ai pas le temps. *I'm sorry, but I don't have time.*

Je ne peux pas maintenant. *I can't right now.*

Telling someone what to do

Rapporte(-moi...) *Bring (me) back . . .*
Prends... *Get . . .*
Achète(-moi)... *Buy (me) . . .*
N'oublie pas de... *Don't forget . . .*
pouvoir *to be able to, can, may*

Quantities

une boîte de *a can of*
une bouteille de *a bottle of*
une douzaine de *a dozen*
un kilo(gramme) de *a kilogram of*
un litre de *a liter of*
une livre de *a pound of*
un morceau de *a piece of*
un paquet de *a carton/box of*
une tranche de *a slice of*

TROISIEME ETAPE

Offering, accepting, or refusing food

Tu veux... ? *Do you want . . . ?*
Vous voulez... ? *Do you want . . . ?*
Vous prenez... ? *Will you have . . . ?*
Tu prends... ? *Will you have . . . ?*

Encore de... ? *More . . . ?*
Oui, s'il vous/te plaît. *Yes, please.*
Oui, j'en veux bien. *Yes, I'd like some.*
Oui, avec plaisir. *Yes, with pleasure.*
Non, merci. *No, thank you.*
Je n'en veux plus. *I don't want any more.*

Non, merci. Je n'ai plus faim. *No thanks. I'm not hungry anymore.*
en *some, of it, of them, any*

Meals

le petit déjeuner *breakfast*
le déjeuner *lunch*
le goûter *afternoon snack*
le dîner *dinner*

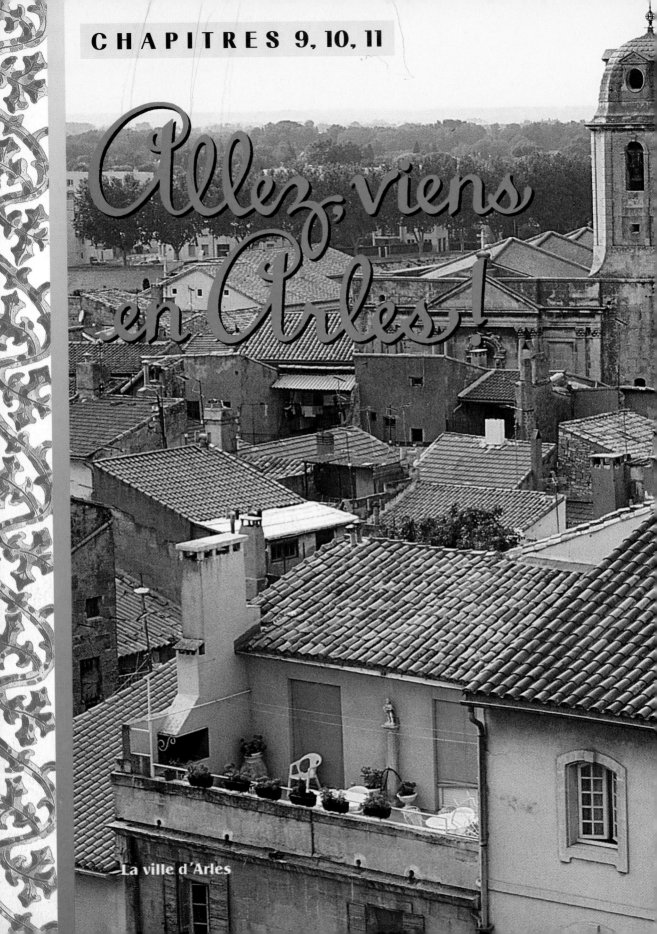

Allez, viens en Arles !

La ville d'Arles

Arles

Population : plus de 50.000

Points d'intérêt : la place Richelme, la place du Forum, les arènes romaines, les thermes de Constantin, les Alyscamps, le théâtre antique

Aux environs d'Arles : les Baux-de-Provence, les Antiques à St-Rémy-de-Provence, le moulin d'Alphonse Daudet

Personnages célèbres : Alphonse Daudet, Vincent Van Gogh, Frédéric Mistral

Musées : le musée Réattu, le musée Lapidaire d'Art païen, le Museon Arlaten, le musée d'Art chrétien

Industries : riz, papier, industries chimiques et métalliques

ANGLETERRE
Lille • BELGIQUE ALLEMAGNE
LUXEMBOURG
Chartres • ★ Paris • Strasbourg
Tours •
• Poitiers SUISSE
Océan Atlantique F R A N C E
• Bordeaux • Lyon ITALIE
Arles • Nice
• Aix-en-Provence
CORSE
N
ESPAGNE Mer Méditerranée

Arles

Founded by the Greeks in the fifth century B.C., Arles later prospered for hundreds of years under Roman rule. It was the largest city in Provence and the capital of ancient Gaul. In the Middle Ages, Arles was an important religious center. It did not became a part of France until 1481. In 1888, Vincent Van Gogh moved to Arles and painted some of his most famous works. Today, Arles still attracts artists, as well as historians and archeologists. But Arles is not only famous for its past. Festivals, the many museums, and the beautiful countryside draw thousands of visitors every year to this very special place known to some as "the soul of Provence."

① **Les arènes romaines,** one of the most ancient Roman amphitheaters, dates back to the first century B.C. Measuring 136 meters long and 107 meters wide, it is also one of the largest, holding 12,000 spectators..

② **Les Alyscamps is** well-known as an ancient Christian burial site. Both Vincent van Gogh and Paul Gauguin immortalized it in their paintings.

③ The marshland known as **la Camargue**, is a stunningly beautiful nature reserve. It is particularly known for its pink flamingos and wild horses.

④ Arles is home to several festivals that feature dancers from all over Provence dressed in their traditional costumes.

⑤ **Le théâtre antique**, constructed in the first century B.C., is still in use. It is here that the Festival d'Arles, the Rencontres Internationales de la Photographie, and numerous shows are staged.

CHAPITRE 9
Au téléphone

① Allô? C'est Hélène à l'appareil.

Messo

Communication reçu

le _____

de M _____

pour M _____

☐ a téléphoné san
message.

Teenagers in francophone countries like to talk to their friends about the good things that are happening to them, as well as their problems, just as teenagers do in the United States.

In this chapter you will learn

- to ask for and express opinions; to inquire about and relate past events
- to make and answer a telephone call
- to share confidences and console others; to ask for and give advice

And you will

- listen to French-speaking students talk about what they did during the weekend
- read letters from French teenagers
- write about what you did over the weekend
- learn about the French telephone system

② Tu as passé un bon week-end?

③ J'ai un petit problème.

Mise en train

Un week-end spécial

What is the subject of Hélène and Magali's telephone conversation? How do you know?

Hélène

Magali

Florent

Ahmed

Hélène et Magali sont au téléphone et racontent ce qu'elles ont fait pendant le week-end. Magali a fait beaucoup de choses. La conversation dure...

① **Allô?**

Bof, ça a été. Je n'ai rien fait de spécial.

Hélène? C'est Magali à l'appareil. Tu as passé un bon week-end?

② Samedi, j'ai fait mes devoirs.

③ Dimanche, j'ai regardé la télévision...

④ ...et j'ai lu un peu.

1 Tu as compris?

Answer the following questions about **Un week-end spécial.**

1. How was Hélène's weekend?
2. Did Magali have a good weekend? Why? Why not?
3. Do you think Magali likes Ahmed? How can you tell?
4. Why does Magali have to hang up?

2 Magali ou Hélène?

Qui a fait ça, Magali ou Hélène?

1. aller aux Baux
2. faire ses devoirs
3. lire
4. aller au théâtre antique
5. regarder la télévision
6. ne rien faire de spécial

3 Mets en ordre

Put Magali's activities in order according to **Un week-end spécial.**

1. Elle est allée au théâtre antique avec un copain.
2. Elle est allée aux Baux-de-Provence.
3. Elle a parlé avec Hélène au téléphone.
4. Elle a rencontré un garçon sympa.

4 C'est qui?

Match the photos of these people with the sentences that refer to them.

Magali

Hélène

Ahmed

le père de Magali

1. Cette personne veut téléphoner.
2. Cette personne a passé un très bon week-end.
3. Cette personne est super gentille.
4. Pendant le week-end, cette personne n'a rien fait de spécial.
5. Cette personne va téléphoner plus tard.

5 Cherche les expressions

According to **Un week-end spécial,** what do you say in French . . .

1. to answer the phone?
2. to identify yourself on the phone?
3. to ask if someone had a good weekend?
4. to ask what someone did?
5. to tell someone to hold?
6. to ask what happened?

6 Et maintenant, à toi

What do you think happened to Magali at les Baux?

Asking for and expressing opinions; inquiring about and relating past events

COMMENT DIT-ON... ?
Asking for and expressing opinions

To ask for someone's opinion:
Tu as passé un bon week-end?
Did you have a good weekend?

To express indifference:
Oui, ça a été. *Yes, it was OK.*
Oh, pas mauvais.

To express satisfaction:
Oui, très chouette. *Yes, super.*
Oui, excellent.
Oui, très bon.

To express dissatisfaction:
Très mauvais.
C'était épouvantable.
It was horrible.

7 Ecoute!
Listen to these people talk about their weekend. Tell if they had a really good time, a mildly good time, or no fun at all.

8 Tu as passé un bon week-end?
Find out if some of your classmates had a good or bad weekend. Then, tell them how your weekend was.

COMMENT DIT-ON... ?
Inquiring about and relating past events

To inquire about past events:

Qu'est-ce qui s'est passé?
What happened?

Qu'est-ce que tu as fait vendredi
soir? *What did you do . . . ?*

Et après? *And then?*

Tu es allé(e) où? *Where did you go?*

To relate past events:

Nous avons parlé. *We talked.*

D'abord, j'ai fait mes devoirs.
First, . . .

Ensuite, j'ai téléphoné à un copain.
Then, . . .

Après, je suis sorti(e).
Afterwards, I went out.

Enfin, je suis allé(e) chez Paul.
Finally, . . .

Et après ça, j'ai parlé au téléphone.
And after that, . . .

Je suis allé(e) au cinéma. *I went . . .*

9 Méli-mélo!

Remets la conversation entre Albert et Marcel dans le bon ordre.

—Salut, Marcel! Ça va?

—Vendredi et samedi, rien de spécial.

—Et après ça?

—Pas mal. Dis, qu'est-ce que tu as fait ce week-end?

—Vous êtes allés où?

—Après, nous sommes allés au café et nous avons parlé jusqu'à minuit.

—Dimanche, j'ai téléphoné à Gisèle et nous avons décidé de sortir.

—Et dimanche?

—D'abord, nous avons fait un pique-nique. Ensuite, nous sommes allés au cinéma.

—Oui, ça va bien. Et toi?

*G*rammaire   The **passé composé** with **avoir**

To tell what happened in the past, use the **passé composé** of the verb. The **passé composé** is composed of two parts: *(a)* a present-tense form of the helping verb **avoir** or **être**—which you've already learned—and *(b)* the past participle of the verb you want to use. You use **avoir** as the helping verb with most verbs. Only with a small number of French verbs, like **aller**, do you use **être** as the helping verb. You'll learn more about these later.

Helping Verb +	Past Participle
J' **ai**	
Tu **as**	
Il/Elle/On **a**	**parlé** au téléphone.
Nous **avons**	
Vous **avez**	
Ils/Elles **ont**	

- To form the past participle of a verb that ends in **-er**, drop the **-er** and add **-é**.
- To make a verb in the **passé composé** negative, put **ne (n')... pas** around the helping verb.

Je n'ai pas étudié.

- Some French verbs have irregular past participles, that is, they don't follow a regular pattern. You'll have to memorize them when you learn the verb. Here are the past participles of some irregular verbs that you've already seen.

faire	**fait**	J'ai **fait** mes devoirs.
prendre	**pris**	Ils ont **pris** un taxi.
voir	**vu**	Il a **vu** sa grand-mère.
lire	**lu**	Elle a **lu** un roman français.

10   Ecoute!

Listen to these conversations and decide whether the speakers are talking about what they did last weekend or what they're going to do next weekend.

11   Une journée à la plage

Qu'est-ce que Claire et ses amis ont fait à la plage?

1.

2.

3.

12 Jeu de rôle

You ask permission to go out. Your parent wants to know if all the chores have been done. Act out this scene with a partner. Then, change roles.

(Est-ce que) je peux... ?

Tu es d'accord?   C'est impossible.

Pas question! Est-ce que tu as... ?

Oui, si tu... d'abord...

faire tes devoirs   laver la voiture

acheter le pain   sortir la poubelle

faire la vaisselle   ranger ta chambre

promener le chien

13 Une carte postale

Write a postcard to your classmates telling them what you did during your first weekend in Arles.

EN PROVENCE....
ARLES (Bouches-du-Rhône).
10.033-Z. - Les arènes, amphithéâtre bâti par les premiers empereurs de Rome, pouvaient contenir 26.000 spectateurs; au fond, le Rhône.

Editions ESTEL, 63 rue de la Mare, BLOIS (L&C.)
Imprimé en Hollande. Reproduction Interdite.

Salut !

Aujourd'hui, on a visité les arènes. Après, le théâtre antique... et le palais Constantin pour voir les thermes. Oh là là ! Que j'ai mal aux pieds !
— Marie-Claire —

Véronique BOUCHER

8, rue de Liège

75009 PARIS

Production LECONTE.

manger un croque-monsieur

aller au musée   aller au café

voir un film français

faire les vitrines

visiter les arènes

parler français   aller au restaurant

faire une promenade

NOTE CULTURELLE

In the first centuries A.D., its location on the Rhône river made Arles the most important port and trading center in the Roman province of Southern Gaul, called Provincia. The Roman influence can still be seen today in Arles. You can visit the Roman amphitheater that is still in use, an ancient theater, and the largest existing thermal baths in Provence.

J'ai raté le bus.

J'ai trouvé cinquante francs.

J'ai oublié mes devoirs.

J'ai déjeuné à la cantine.

J'ai rencontré une fille sympa.

J'ai chanté dans la chorale.

J'ai acheté un CD.

J'ai travaillé au fast-food.

Here are some other activities you may have done during your day.

apporter	*to bring*	**gagner**	*to win, to earn*	**répéter**	*to rehearse, to practice music*
chercher	*to look for*	**montrer**	*to show*		
commencer	*to begin, to start*	**passer un examen**	*to take an exam*	**retrouver**	*to meet with*
dîner	*to have dinner*	**rater une interro**	*to fail a quiz*	**visiter**	*to visit (a place)*

14 Qu'est-ce qu'ils ont fait le week-end dernier?

1.

2.

3.

15 Pierre a fait quoi?

Pierre spent a week at a sports camp. Which of the activities below do you think he did and which do you think he didn't do?

chanter avec des copains

jouer au volley-ball

gagner un match

faire du ski nautique

rater un examen   nager

faire une promenade

manger des escargots

rater le bus   faire de l'équitation

faire les courses   acheter un CD

manger un hot-dog

De bons conseils

French words that look similar are often related in meaning, so you can use words you already know to guess the meanings of new words. If you already know what **chanter** means, you can probably guess the meaning of **une chanteuse.** You know what **commencer** means, so what do you think **le commencement** means? Likewise, you should be able to figure out **le visiteur** from the verb **visiter.**

voir la tour Eiffel

faire du deltaplane

étudier le japonais   manger des escargots

lire un poème français   jouer au hockey

nager dans la mer des Caraïbes

acheter une montre   travailler en été

rencontrer une fille francophone

oublier les devoirs   visiter le Louvre

16 Tu as déjà fait ça?

Try to find classmates who've already done some of the activities in the box to the right and write down their names.

—Tu as déjà visité le Louvre?
—Oui, j'ai visité le Louvre.

  or

— Non, je n'ai jamais visité le Louvre.

17 Mon journal

Write down five things you did last weekend. Be sure to tell when you did each activity, with whom, and as many other details as you can think of.

Making and answering a telephone call

—Allô, Anita?
—Oui. C'est moi.
—Salut. C'est François.

—Allô? C'est Michel. Véronique est là,
s'il vous plaît?
—Une seconde.
—Merci.

—Allô? Est-ce que Xuan est là, s'il vous plaît?
—Non, il est chez Robert.
—Est-ce que je peux laisser un message?
—Bien sûr.
—Vous pouvez lui dire qu'Emmanuel
a téléphoné?
—D'accord.
—Merci.

18 Au téléphone

Answer the questions as you read the
conversations.

1. What does each of these people say
   to answer the phone?
2. Who has to wait a few seconds to
   speak to his or her friend?
3. Who gets to talk right away to the
   person he or she is calling?
4. Who isn't home?

COMMENT DIT-ON... ?

Making and answering a telephone call

To make a phone call:

Bonjour.

Je suis bien chez Véronique?
Is this . . . 's house?

C'est Michel.

(Est-ce que) Véronique **est là,
s'il vous plaît?**

Je peux parler à Véronique?

Je peux laisser un message?
May I leave a message?

**Vous pouvez lui dire que j'ai
téléphoné?**
Can you tell her/him that I called?

To answer a phone call:

Allô?

Qui est à l'appareil?
Who's calling?

Vous pouvez rappeler plus tard?
Can you call back later?

Une seconde, s'il vous plaît.

D'accord.

Bien sûr.

Here are some additional phrases you may need:

Ne quittez pas. *Hold on.*

Ça ne répond pas.
There's no answer.

C'est occupé.
It's busy.

19 Ecoute!

Ecoute ces conversations téléphoniques. Qui téléphone? A qui voudrait-il/-elle parler?

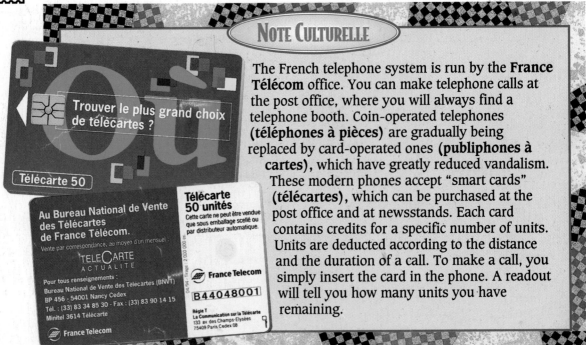

NOTE CULTURELLE

The French telephone system is run by the **France Télécom** office. You can make telephone calls at the post office, where you will always find a telephone booth. Coin-operated telephones **(téléphones à pièces)** are gradually being replaced by card-operated ones **(publiphones à cartes)**, which have greatly reduced vandalism. These modern phones accept "smart cards" **(télécartes)**, which can be purchased at the post office and at newsstands. Each card contains credits for a specific number of units. Units are deducted according to the distance and the duration of a call. To make a call, you simply insert the card in the phone. A readout will tell you how many units you have remaining.

20 Méli-mélo!

Ecris cette conversation dans le bon ordre.

—D'accord.

—Salut, Aurélie. Désolée, elle n'est pas là. Tu peux rappeler plus tard?

—Allô?

—Bien sûr.

—Qui est à l'appareil?

—Tu peux lui dire que j'ai téléphoné?

—Bonjour. Je peux parler à Nicole?

—Est-ce que je peux laisser un message?

—C'est Aurélie.

21 Ecoute!

During your exchange visit to France, you stay with a French family, **les Tissot.** You're the only one at home today. Several of their friends call and leave messages. Write down the messages and compare your notes with a classmate's.

22 On fait quoi ce week-end?

Phone a classmate and discuss three things you're planning to do this weekend. Don't forget to arrange the times and decide with whom you're going to do these things.

> —Allô. Philippe?
> —Oui, c'est moi.
> —Dis, tu vas faire quoi ce week-end?
> —Samedi, je vais...

23 Jeu de rôle

The friend you're phoning isn't home, so you leave a message. Take turns playing the role of the friend's parent.

Note de Grammaire

You've learned about -er verbs, like **aimer,** the largest group of regular French verbs. Other regular verbs, with infinitives ending in -re, follow a slightly different pattern.

répondre *(to answer)*

Je **réponds**
Tu **réponds**
Il/Elle/On **répond**
Nous **répondons**
Vous **répondez**
Ils/Elles **répondent** } au téléphone.

- **Réponds** and **répond** are pronounced alike. **Répondre** is followed by a form of **à**.
- Another regular -re verb you've seen is **attendre** *(to wait for).*
- The past participle of regular -re verbs ends in -u: j'ai répo... as attendu.

PANORAMA CULTUREL

Nicole • Martinique

Virgile • France

Marie • France

How often do you call your friends? We asked some francophone teenagers about their telephone habits. Here's what they told us.

Tu aimes téléphoner?

«Oui, j'aime beaucoup télé-phoner. Mes parents rous-pètent souvent parce que je reste longtemps au télé-phone, parce que ça coûte cher, le téléphone, et donc ils me demandent d'éviter de parler trop souvent au télé-phone, de rester moins longtemps. Le plus souvent, je téléphone à peu près une heure de temps.»

—Nicole

«Ah oui, j'aime beaucoup téléphoner. Ça permet de discuter, de prendre des nouvelles un peu partout. C'est pratique.»

—Virgile

«Ben, j'aime bien télé-phoner... Ça dépend à qui, mes copines, mes copains. J'aime bien parce que j'aime bien leur parler, surtout à ma meilleure amie Caroline. J'aime beaucoup lui parler. On reste très longtemps. Mais sinon, téléphoner aux gens que je connais pas, j'aime pas trop.»

—Marie

Qu'en penses-tu?

1. How are your phone habits different from those of these people?
2. How might your life be different if you did or didn't have a phone in your room?
3. What restrictions on the use of the phone do you have at your house?

Savais-tu que... ?

The French telecommunications network is one of the best in the world. However, talking on the telephone in France and other francophone countries is still expensive, even when calling locally. For this reason, teenagers are not usually allowed to spend long periods of time on the phone, and most do not have a phone in their room.

TROISIEME ETAPE

Sharing confidences and consoling others; asking for and giving advice

COMMENT DIT-ON... ?

Sharing confidences and consoling others; asking for and giving advice

To share a confidence:

J'ai un petit problème.
I've got a little problem.

Je peux te parler?
Can I talk to you?

Tu as une minute?
Do you have a minute?

To ask for advice:

A ton avis, qu'est-ce que je fais?
In your opinion, what do I do?

Qu'est-ce que tu me conseilles?
What do you advise me to do?

To console someone:

Je t'écoute. *I'm listening.*

Qu'est-ce que je peux faire?
What can I do?

Ne t'en fais pas! *Don't worry!*

Ça va aller mieux!
It's going to get better!

To give advice:

Oublie-le/-la/-les!
Forget him/her/it/them!

Téléphone-lui/-leur!
Call him/her/them!

Tu devrais lui/leur parler.
You should talk to him/her/them.

Pourquoi tu ne téléphones pas?
Why don't you . . . ?

Note de Grammaire

In the expressions above, **le, la,** and **les** are object pronouns that refer to people or things. The pronouns **lui** and **leur** only refer to people. You will learn more about these pronouns later. For now, translate them as: *him, her, them,* or *to him, to her, to them.*

De bons conseils

Study at regular intervals. It's best to learn language in small chunks and to review frequently. Cramming will not usually work for French. Study at least a little bit every day, whether you have an assignment or not. The more often you review words and structures, the easier it will be for you to understand and speak in class. And don't forget to talk to yourself or to a classmate in French!

---

24 Ecoute!

Are these people giving advice or asking for advice?

25 Ecoute!

Ecoute cette conversation entre Mireille et Simone. Simone a un problème. Quel est son problème?

26 J'ai un petit problème

Match each of the following problems with a logical solution.

1. Mon frère ne me parle plus depuis *(for)* cinq jours.
2. Je veux acheter un vélo, mais je n'ai pas d'argent.
3. J'ai oublié mes devoirs.
4. Je vais rater l'interro d'anglais.

a. Tu devrais étudier plus souvent.
b. Pourquoi tu ne travailles pas?
c. Refais-les!
d. Parle-lui!

27 Pauvre Hervé!

Console Hervé.

1.   2.   3.

28 Et à ton avis?

Your friend phones and asks to speak to you. He or she is having a lot of problems and wants to ask your advice about some of them. Console your friend and offer some advice. Then, change roles.

Il/Elle...

veut rencontrer de nouveaux copains.

n'a pas acheté de cadeau pour l'anniversaire de sa sœur.

veut faire une boum, mais ses parents ne sont pas d'accord.

n'a pas d'argent pour acheter des baskets.

a raté un examen.

ne peut pas trouver de travail pour l'été.

n'aime pas le prof de biologie.

n'a pas parlé avec son petit ami (sa petite amie) depuis *(for)* 3 jours.

n'a pas gagné son match de tennis.

a oublié ses devoirs.

29 Ne t'en fais pas!

Your friend asks you to listen to his or her account of a very bad day. Console your friend. Act this out with a partner. Then, change roles.

The vowel sounds [e] and [ɛ]

Listen to the vowels in the word **préfère.** How are they different? The first one is pronounced [e], and the second one [ɛ]. To make the vowel sound [e], hold your mouth in a closed smiling position. Keep your lips and tongue steady to avoid the glide as in the English word *day.* Repeat these words.

été	désolé	occupé	répondre

Now, take a smiling position once again, but this time open your mouth wider. This will produce the vowel sound [ɛ]. Repeat these words.

règle	algèbre	achète	frère

In the examples, you can see that **é** represents the sound [e], while **è** represents the sound [ɛ] in writing. You've probably noticed that **e** with no accent and some other letter combinations can represent these sounds as well. Repeat these words.

apportez	trouver

You see that the spellings **ez** and **er** normally represent the sound [e]. This is true of all infinitives ending in **-er.** Now repeat these words.

fait	français	neige	bête
elle	cassette	examen	cherche

Some spellings of the vowel sound [ɛ] are **ait, ais, ei,** and **ê.** An unaccented **e** is pronounced as open [ɛ] when it is followed by a double consonant, such as **ll** or **tt,** when followed by **x,** and, in most cases, when followed by **r,** or by any pronounced consonant.

A. A prononcer

Repeat the following words.

1. délicieux	méchant	théâtre	vélo
2. après-midi	père	mère	très
3. février	chanter	chez	prenez
4. cette	française	treize	pêches

B. A lire

Take turns with a partner reading each of the following sentences aloud.

1. Ne quittez pas! Je vais chercher mon frère.
2. Marcel a visité Arles en mai. Il est allé au musée, à la cathédrale et aux arènes.
3. Elle n'aime pas trop l'algèbre et la géométrie, mais elle aime bien l'espagnol.
4. Tu ne peux pas aller au cinéma. Tu n'as pas fait la vaisselle.

C. A écrire

You're going to hear a short dialogue. Write down what you hear.

$\mathcal{H}$ow will the "information superhighway" affect your life? How will you be able to use your computer and TV set in the future? As you look at the illustrations, what do you expect this reading will be about?

DE BONS CONSEILS

As you read, you use many different reading strategies at the same time. You may start by looking at illustrations, then move on to the titles and subtitles. You may need to skim the passage to get the general idea, then scan for specific details, and finally read the passage for more complete comprehension.

A. According to the illustrations, titles, and subtitles, you should be able to tell that **Minitel** is a kind of computer. It links your home computer screen and keyboard to the outside world. Using **Minitel,** you can connect to various services that allow you to shop, get entertainment information, weather reports, travel information, and so on. Do we have anything similar in the United States?

B. Now, skim the information in the three major sections. What is the purpose of each section?

1. To explain how to disconnect Minitel
2. To explain how to hook up Minitel
3. To introduce the reader to all of Minitel's advantages
4. To tell how to purchase Minitel

Minitel 2
Mode d'emploi modèle Alcatel

Présentation

Votre Minitel 2 qui appartient à la nouvelle gamme des Minitel de FRANCE TELECOM est conçu pour une utilisation tant privée que professionnelle. Bi-standard, Télétel et ASCII, compatible avec tous les autres Minitel, votre Minitel 2 est en plus :

Simple
pour obtenir un service Télétel, composez le n° d'appel directement sur le clavier de votre Minitel 2, un haut-parleur permet de suivre l'établissement de votre appel ; la présence d'un poste téléphonique associé n'est donc pas nécessaire.

Efficace
pour vous faciliter l'accès aux services fréquemment consultés, le répertoire télématique du Minitel 2 garde en mémoire jusqu'à 10 numéros d'appel avec les codes de service Télétel associés.

Sûr
le verrouillage du Minitel 2 vous protège contre les utilisations abusives ou indésirables. Détenteur du mot de passe, vous pouvez laisser libre l'utilisation des seuls services inscrits dans le répertoire ou vous réserver totalement l'utilisation de votre Minitel 2.

Disponible
à tout moment, votre Minitel 2 en état de veille est prêt à fonctionner sur votre demande ou celle d'un dispositif branché sur la prise péri-informatique (télécommande, domotique, télésurveillance, ...).

Performant
le Minitel 2 dispose de plusieurs jeux de caractères dont un téléchargeable (DRCS*) par les serveurs et qui permet des présentations graphiques précises.

*DRCS : Dynamically Redefinable Character Set (Jeu de caractères dynamiquement redéfinissable).

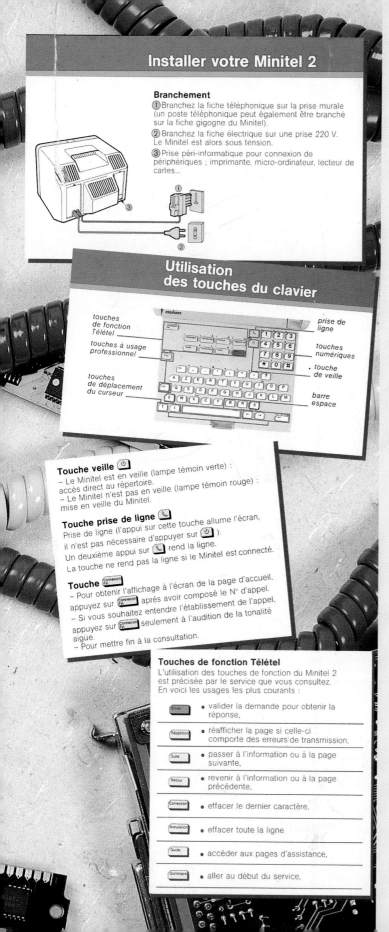

Installer votre Minitel 2

Branchement

① Branchez la fiche téléphonique sur la prise murale (un poste téléphonique peut également être branché sur la fiche gigogne du Minitel).

② Branchez la fiche électrique sur une prise 220 V. Le Minitel est alors sous tension.

③ Prise péri-informatique pour connexion de périphériques ; imprimante, micro-ordinateur, lecteur de cartes...

Utilisation des touches du clavier

touches de fonction Télétel

touches à usage professionnel

touches de déplacement du curseur

prise de ligne

touches numériques

touche de veille

barre espace

Touche veille ⏻
– Le Minitel est en veille (lampe témoin verte) : accès direct au répertoire.
– Le Minitel n'est pas en veille (lampe témoin rouge) : mise en veille du Minitel.

Touche prise de ligne 📞
Prise de ligne (l'appui sur cette touche allume l'écran, il n'est pas nécessaire d'appuyer sur ⏻).
Un deuxième appui sur 📞 rend la ligne.
La touche ne rend pas la ligne si le Minitel est connecté.

Touche [Connexion Fin]
– Pour obtenir l'affichage à l'écran de la page d'accueil, appuyez sur [Connexion Fin] après avoir composé le N° d'appel.
– Si vous souhaitez entendre l'établissement de l'appel, appuyez sur [Connexion Fin] seulement à l'audition de la tonalité aiguë.
– Pour mettre fin à la consultation.

Touches de fonction Télétel
L'utilisation des touches de fonction du Minitel 2 est précisée par le service que vous consultez. En voici les usages les plus courants :

[Envoi]	• valider la demande pour obtenir la réponse,
[Répétition]	• réafficher la page si celle-ci comporte des erreurs de transmission,
[Suite]	• passer à l'information ou à la page suivante,
[Retour]	• revenir à l'information ou à la page précédente,
[Correction]	• effacer le dernier caractère,
[Annulation]	• effacer toute la ligne,
[Guide]	• accéder aux pages d'assistance,
[Sommaire]	• aller au début du service.

5. To explain how to use the Minitel keyboard

6. To discourage people from using Minitel

C. Présentation

Skim the section entitled **Présentation**. Then, try to match each subtitle with its English equivalent.

1. **Simple**   a. *efficient*
2. **Efficace**   b. *always available*
3. **Sûr**   c. *safe*
4. **Disponible**   d. *easy to use*
5. **Performant**   e. *high performance*

D. Installer votre Minitel 2

1. What do you think **branchement** means?

2. How many steps are involved in hooking up **Minitel**?

E. Utilisation des touches du clavier

Match each of the following cognates with the appropriate English equivalent.

1. **précédante**   a. *key*
2. **touche**   b. *beginning screen*
3. **caractère**   c. *line*
4. **accéder**   d. *preceding*
5. **début**   e. *to access*
6. **ligne**   f. *character*

F. Which button do you press . . .

1. to get help?

2. to return to the preceding page?

3. to go back to the opening screen?

4. to erase the last character that you typed?

G. If **Minitel** became widely available in the United States, how would it change your life? What kinds of things would you like to be able to do through the computer?

MISE EN PRATIQUE

1 A friend has left a message on your answering machine telling you what he did over the weekend. Listen, then decide if these sentences are true or false.

1. Martin a passé un mauvais week-end.
2. Il est allé à la plage.
3. Il a fait beau pendant le week-end.
4. Il a joué au football samedi.
5. Il n'a pas joué au tennis.
6. Dimanche, il a fait de l'aérobic.

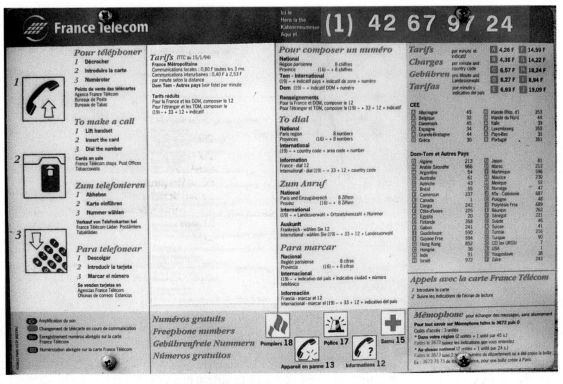

2 Answer the following questions based on the document above.

1. What kind of information is this? Where would you expect to find it?
2. What number could you call to find someone else's number in France?
3. What emergency numbers are provided?

3 Based on what you know about the French telephone system, tell whether the statements below are true or false.

1. The only way to make a call from a public phone in France is to use coins.
2. You can generally find a public phone at the post office.
3. You can't buy phone cards at the post office.
4. Card-operated phones are being replaced by coin-operated ones.
5. If you make a call using a phone card, you will be charged based on the distance and duration of the call.

4 You're going to have a party! "Phone" your classmates and invite them to come. Be sure to tell them when and where the party will be. If you can't reach them, leave a message. Act out this scene with your group.

5 You just had the best (or worst) weekend in your life.

1. Make a list of six things that happened to you.

2. Using the list of what happened, write a note to a friend, telling about your weekend. Be sure to include details such as where you went, who was with you, in what order things happened, and so on.

6 Scan these letters first and then read them more carefully. What are they about? Who is Agnès?

1. What is Monique's problem?

2. How does Agnès respond?

3. Who is S having difficulties with?

4. What does Agnès advise her to do?

Chère Agnès

Agnès vous comprend. Vous pouvez lui confier tous vos problèmes. Elle trouve toujours une solution!

Il me dit qu'il veut sortir avec moi. Est-ce vrai?

Chère Agnès,

J'aime beaucoup un garçon, Pierre, qui me dit, dans une lettre très tendre, qu'il veut sortir avec moi. Mais il ne m'appelle jamais. Se moque-t-il de moi? Aide-moi car je suis dingue de lui!

--Monique..

Ne sois pas découragée! Tu aimes ce garçon et il t'aime également. Tu t'imagines qu'il se moque de toi, mais lui aussi doit se demander s'il a ses chances. A toi d'aller vers lui. Bonne chance!

Toute ma famille me déteste

Chère Agnès,

J'ai 14 ans et j'ai un problème: tout le monde dans ma famille me déteste, sauf ma mémé. Mes parents et ma sœur se moquent toujours de moi et me disent que je suis laide. Je suis très déprimée. Au secours!

--S

Ah S...! N'écoute pas ce que ta famille te dit. Et puis, il y a toujours ta mémé qui t'aime. Tu as 14 ans et tes parents ont sûrement peur de perdre leur petite fille. Parle-leur de tes sentiments et tu verras, tout ira mieux.

7

1. Make up an imaginary problem. Describe your problem in a brief letter to Agnès, sign a fictitious name, and place your letter in a pile together with your classmates' letters.

2. Choose a letter from the pile and write a response, offering advice. Place your response together with your classmates' responses.

3. Now, find and read the response to your own letter. What do you think of the advice?

8

JEU DE ROLE

You haven't seen your friend in a while. You want to find out what he or she has been doing. Phone and ask to speak to your friend. Talk about what you both did last weekend. Find out also what your friend is planning to do next summer. Act this out with a partner.

Can you use what you've learned in this chapter?

Can you ask for and express opinions? p. 237

1 How would you ask a friend how his or her weekend went?

2 How would you tell someone that your weekend was . . .
1. great?
2. OK?
3. horrible?

Can you inquire about and relate past events? p. 238

3 If you were inquiring about your friend's weekend, how would you ask . . .
1. what your friend did?
2. where your friend went?
3. what happened?

4 How would you tell someone that you did these things?

1.   2.   3.

Can you make and answer a telephone call? p. 244

5 If you were making a telephone call, how would you . . .
1. tell who you are?
2. ask if it's the right house?
3. ask to speak to someone?
4. ask to leave a message?
5. ask someone to say you called?
6. tell someone the line's busy?

6 If you were answering a telephone call, how would you . . .
1. ask who's calling?
2. ask someone to hold?
3. ask someone to call back later?

Can you share confidences, console others, and ask for and give advice? p. 247

7 How would you approach a friend about a problem you have?

8 What would you say to console a friend?

9 How would you ask a friend for advice?

10 How would you tell a friend what you think he or she should do?

PREMIERE ETAPE

Asking for and expressing opinions

Tu as passé un bon week-end?
Did you have a good weekend?
Oui, très chouette. *Yes, super.*
Oui, excellent. *Yes, excellent.*
Oui, très bon. *Yes, very good.*
Oui, ça a été. *Yes, it was OK.*
Oh, pas mauvais. *Oh, not bad.*
Très mauvais. *Very bad.*
C'était épouvantable. *It was horrible.*

Inquiring about and relating past events

Qu'est-ce qui s'est passé? *What happened?*
Nous avons parlé. *We talked.*
Qu'est-ce que tu as fait... ? *What did you do . . . ?*

D'abord,... *First, . . .*
Ensuite,... *Then, . . .*
Après, je suis sorti(e).
Afterwards, I went out.
Enfin,... *Finally, . . .*
Et après (ça)? *And after (that)?*
Tu es allé(e) où? *Where did you go?*
Je suis allé(e)... *I went . . .*
fait (faire) *done, made*
pris (prendre) *taken*
vu (voir) *seen*
lu (lire) *read*
déjà *already*
bien *well*
mal *badly*
ne... pas encore *not yet*
acheter *to buy*
apporter *to bring*
chanter *to sing*
chercher *to look for*

commencer *to begin, to start*
déjeuner *to have lunch*
à la cantine *at the cafeteria*
dîner *to have dinner*
gagner *to win, to earn*
montrer *to show*
oublier *to forget*
rater le bus *to miss the bus*
passer un examen *to take an exam*
rater une interro *to fail a quiz*
rencontrer *to meet for the first time*
répéter *to rehearse, to practice music*
retrouver *to meet with*
travailler au fast-food *to work at a fast-food restaurant*
trouver *to find*
visiter *to visit (a place)*

DEUXIEME ETAPE

Making and answering a telephone call

Allô? *Hello?*
Je suis bien chez... ? *Is this . . . 's house?*
Qui est à l'appareil? *Who's calling?*
(Est-ce que)... est là, s'il vous plaît? *Is . . . there, please?*

Une seconde, s'il vous plaît. *One second, please.*
(Est-ce que) je peux parler à... ? *May I speak to . . . ?*
Bien sûr. *Certainly.*
Vous pouvez rappeler plus tard? *Can you call back later?*
Je peux laisser un message? *May I leave a message?*

Vous pouvez lui dire que j'ai téléphoné? *Can you tell her/him that I called?*
Ne quittez pas. *Hold on.*
Ça ne répond pas. *There's no answer.*
C'est occupé. *It's busy.*
attendre *to wait for*
répondre (à) *to answer*

TROISIEME ETAPE

Sharing confidences and consoling others

J'ai un petit problème. *I've got a little problem.*
Je peux te parler? *Can we talk?*
Tu as une minute? *Do you have a minute?*
Je t'écoute. *I'm listening.*
Qu'est-ce que je peux faire? *What can I do?*
Ne t'en fais pas! *Don't worry!*

Ça va aller mieux! *It's going to get better!*

Asking for and giving advice

A ton avis, qu'est-ce que je fais? *In your opinion, what do I do?*
Qu'est-ce que tu me conseilles? *What do you advise me to do?*
Oublie-le/-la/-les! *Forget him/her/it/them!*

Téléphone-lui/-leur! *Call him/her/them!*
Tu devrais lui/leur parler. *You should talk to him/her/them.*
Pourquoi tu ne... pas? *Why don't you . . . ?*
le *him, it*
la *her, it*
les *them*
lui *to him, to her*
leur *to them*

10
Dans un magasin de vêtements

① Je ne sais pas quoi mettre pour aller à la boum.

It's not easy to decide what to wear on a special occasion. It's often a welcome excuse to buy something new. But what? It depends on the statement you want to make. Chic? Casual? How do you create just the right look?

In this chapter you will learn

- to ask for and give advice
- to express need; to inquire
- to ask for an opinion; to pay a compliment; to criticize; to hesitate; to make a decision

And you will

- listen to French-speaking students talk about what they like to wear on different occasions
- read about the clothing styles French-speaking teenagers like
- write about what you wear on different occasions
- find out how francophone teenagers feel about fashion

② J'aimerais un foulard pour aller avec cette jupe.

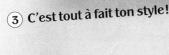

③ C'est tout à fait ton style!

Mise en train

Chacun ses goûts

What event are Hélène and Magali discussing at the beginning of the story? Where does Magali go? Why do you think Hélène doesn't go with her?

Oh là là! Je ne sais pas quoi mettre demain. C'est l'anniversaire de Sophie. J'ai envie d'acheter quelque chose de joli. Et toi, qu'est-ce que tu vas mettre?

Oh, je ne sais pas. Sans doute un jean et un tee-shirt.

Pourquoi est-ce que tu ne trouves pas quelque chose d'original? De mignon?

Ecoute, Magali. Moi, j'aime bien être en jean et en tee-shirt. C'est simple et agréable à porter. Chacun ses goûts.

Bonjour. Je peux vous aider?

Je cherche quelque chose pour aller à une fête. J'aimerais quelque chose d'original et pas trop cher.

Qu'est-ce que vous faites comme taille?

Je fais du 38.

Au magasin...

1 Tu as compris?

1. Why does Magali want to buy something new?
2. What is Hélène going to wear? Why?
3. What type of clothing is Magali looking for?
4. What outfit does Magali like?
5. What does she think of the price?

2 C'est qui?

Qui parle? C'est Magali, Hélène ou la vendeuse?

1. «J'aimerais quelque chose d'original et pas trop cher.»
2. «Je peux vous aider?»
3. «Moi, j'aime bien être en jean et en tee-shirt. C'est simple et agréable à porter.»
4. «Qu'est-ce que vous faites comme taille?»
5. «Chacun ses goûts.»
6. «Est-ce que vous l'avez en vert?»
7. «C'est tout à fait votre style.»
8. «Ce n'est pas tellement mon style.»

3 Chacun ses goûts

What does Magali say about these things?

1. le jean et le tee-shirt d'Hélène
2. la jupe verte en 38
3. le prix de l'ensemble

4 Qu'est-ce qu'elle répond?

Qu'est-ce que Magali répond à la vendeuse?

1. Qu'est-ce que vous faites comme taille?
2. Comment la trouvez-vous?
3. Je peux vous aider?
4. Ça vous fait 670 francs.

a. C'est cher!
b. Je fais du 38.
c. Je cherche quelque chose pour aller à une fête.
d. Bof. Ce n'est pas tellement mon style.

5 Cherche les expressions

Look back at **Chacun ses goûts** to find how you would . . .

1. express indecision.
2. express satisfaction with your clothes.
3. tell a salesperson what you want.
4. tell what size you wear.
5. express dissatisfaction with clothes.
6. ask for a certain color or size.
7. ask what all of your purchases cost.

6 Et maintenant, à toi

Do you prefer Magali's style or Hélène's? What sort of clothes do you like to wear?

VOCABULAIRE

PRINTEMPS

La mode décontractée

blouson noir **1290 F**

chaussettes noires, blanches, pêche ou bleues **9,90 F** la paire

chaussures noires **279 F**

chemise bleue ou blanche **69 F**

chemisier blanc **89 F**

maillot de bain bleu, rouge et vert **99 F**

Le style chic

bottes noires **399 F**

manteau bleu ou noir **845 F**

jupe grise **299 F**

robe noire à fleurs **349 F**

veste bleue **690 F**

Les accessoires

écharpe blanche ou noire **99,50 F**

casquette blanche **159 F**

cravate bleue **79 F**

ceinture noire ou marron **99,50 F**

chapeau noir **249 F**

boucles d'oreilles **249 F**

montre noire **259 F**

lunettes de soleil **59,50 F**

Here are some other words you may want to use to talk about what you're wearing.

des baskets (f.)	**un jean**	**des sandales** (f.)
un bracelet	**un pantalon**	**un short**
un cardigan	**un pull (-over)**	**un sweat-shirt**

7 Ecoute!

Listen as Armelle tells her friend about her big shopping trip. Then, choose the illustration that represents her purchases.

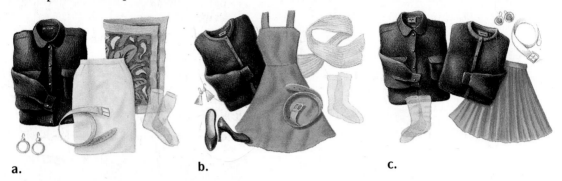

a.   b.   c.

8 Des cadeaux

Look at the picture and tell what Lise bought for her family.

Elle a acheté... pour...

9 Pas de chance!

On your way to France, the airline lost your luggage. Fortunately, the airline is paying you $500 for new clothes. Make a list of the clothes you'll buy.

—D'abord, je vais acheter...

10 La fête

Imagine that you've been invited to a party. Of the clothes you listed in Activity 9, which would you choose to wear? What clothes would you need that aren't on your list?

11 Qu'est-ce qu'on met?

Ces gens vont sortir. Qu'est-ce qu'ils mettent?

1.

2.

3.

4.

12 Qu'est-ce que tu as mis hier?

Ask your partner what he or she wore yesterday and tell what you wore.

De bons conseils

Although it's common to feel a little uncomfortable when speaking a new language, the best way to overcome it is to talk and talk and talk. Whenever you answer a question or have a conversation with a partner, try to keep the conversation going as long as possible. Don't worry about making a mistake. The more you think about making mistakes, the less likely you will be to talk.

COMMENT DIT-ON...?
Asking for and giving advice

To ask for advice:

Je ne sais pas quoi mettre pour aller à la boum. *I don't know what to wear for (to) . . .*

Qu'est-ce que je mets? *What shall I wear?*

To give advice:

Pourquoi est-ce que tu ne mets pas ta robe? *Why don't you wear . . . ?*

Mets ton jean. *Wear . . .*

13 **Ecoute!**

Are these people asking for or giving advice?

14 **Harmonie de couleurs**

Ask your partner's advice on what you should wear with the following items. Take turns.

—Qu'est-ce que je mets avec ma jupe noire?
—Pourquoi tu ne mets pas ton pull gris?

1. Avec mon pantalon bleu?
2. Avec ma chemise rouge?
3. Avec mes baskets violettes?

4. Avec mon pull gris?
5. Avec mon short orange?

15 **Qu'est-ce que je mets?**

Tell your partner where you'll go and what you'll do during your stay as an exchange student in France. Ask for advice about what you should wear. Then, change roles.

—Je vais aller au café. Qu'est-ce que je mets?
—Pour aller au café? Mets un jean et un sweat-shirt.

pour aller à une boum

pour aller à la plage

pour aller au café

pour dîner dans un restaurant élégant

pour jouer au football

pour aller au parc

pour aller au théâtre

pour faire du patin à glace

pour aller au musée

pour faire du ski

16 **Mon journal**

Write about what you normally wear to school, to parties, to go out with friends, or what you wear to dress up for a special occasion.

Expressing need; inquiring

COMMENT DIT-ON... ?

Expressing need; inquiring

To express need:
When the salesperson asks you:
  Vous désirez?
  (Est-ce que) je peux vous aider?
    May I help you?

You might answer:
  Oui, il me faut un chemisier vert.
  Oui, vous avez des chapeaux?
  Je cherche quelque chose pour
    aller à une boum.
    I'm looking for something to . . .
  J'aimerais un chemisier **pour aller**
    avec ma jupe.
    I'd like . . . to go with . . .
  Non, merci, je regarde.
    No, thanks, I'm just looking.
  Je peux l'/les essayer?
    Can I try it/them on?
  Je peux essayer le/la/les
    bleu(e)(s)?
    Can I try on the . . . ?

To inquire about prices:
  C'est combien,... ?
  Ça fait combien?

To ask about sizes, color, and fabric:
  Vous avez ça en 36?
    Do you have that in . . . ?
    en bleu?
    en coton? *cotton?*
    en jean? *denim?*
    en cuir? *leather?*

Speech bubbles: BONJOUR, J'AIMERAIS UN PANTALON POUR ALLER AVEC MON TEE-SHIRT! — VOUS AVEZ CES CHAUSSURES EN 43?

Note de *Grammaire*

You can use colors and other adjectives as nouns by putting **le**, **la**, or **les** before them. Change their spelling according to the things they refer to: **le bleu, la bleue** = *the blue one;* **les verts, les vertes** = *the green ones.*

17 Ecoute!

Listen and decide whether a customer or salesperson is speaking.

18 Ecoute!

Listen and decide whether these people are talking about the color, price, or size of the items they're looking at.

19 Méli-mélo!

Mets cette conversation en ordre.

—Oui. Nous les avons en bleu, en rouge et en orange.

—C'est combien?

3 Voilà, ces maillots de bain sont très chic.

—Oh là là! C'est trop cher, ça!

—C'est 450 F.

1 Je peux vous aider?

—Euh, je n'aime pas trop la couleur. Vous les avez en bleu?

2 Oui, je cherche un maillot de bain.

20 Préférences

You and a partner are looking at some clothes in the **Trois Suisses** catalogue. Talk about which items you both like and in which colors.

—J'aimerais un pull pour aller avec mon pantalon marron. J'aime bien ce polo en beige. Et toi?

—Moi, j'aime mieux le vert.

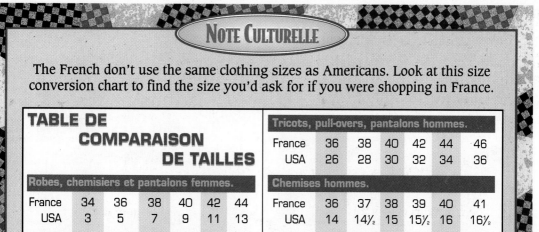

The French don't use the same clothing sizes as Americans. Look at this size conversion chart to find the size you'd ask for if you were shopping in France.

TABLE DE COMPARAISON DE TAILLES

Robes, chemisiers et pantalons femmes.

France	34	36	38	40	42	44
USA	3	5	7	9	11	13

Chaussures femmes.

France	36	37	38	38½	39	40
USA	5-5½	6-6½	7-7½	8	8½	9

Tricots, pull-overs, pantalons hommes.

France	36	38	40	42	44	46
USA	26	28	30	32	34	36

Chemises hommes.

France	36	37	38	39	40	41
USA	14	14½	15	15½	16	16½

Chaussures hommes.

France	39	40	41	42	43	44
USA	6½-7	7½	8	8½	9-9½	10-10½

21 Jeu de rôle

You need something to go with some of the items below. Tell the salesperson what you need and ask about prices and sizes. Act out this scene with a partner. Then, change roles.

un jean
un blouson en jean
une veste en cuir noir
un pull jaune
un short noir
une chemise en coton

Vocabulaire à la carte

à rayures	striped	en laine	wool
à carreaux	checked	en nylon	nylon
à pois	polka dot	en lin	linen
à fleurs	flowered	en soie	silk
bleu clair	light blue	bleu foncé	dark blue

Grammaire -ir verbs

You've already learned the forms of regular -er and -re verbs. There is one more regular verb pattern for you to learn. Here are the forms of regular -ir verbs.

choisir *(to choose, to pick)*

Je **choisis**	Nous **choisissons**
Tu **choisis** — un manteau noir.	Vous **choisissez** — ce jean-là.
Il/Elle/On **choisit**	Ils/Elles **choisissent**

- The past participle of regular -ir verbs ends in -i: Elle a choisi une belle robe.
- Other regular -ir verbs you might want to use when talking about clothes are: **grandir** *(to grow)*, **maigrir** *(to lose weight)*, and **grossir** *(to gain weight)*.

22 Qu'est-ce qu'ils choisissent?

Qu'est-ce qu'ils choisissent pour aller avec leurs ensembles?

1.　　　　　2.　　　　　3.　　　　　4.

23 Ça ne me va plus!

Why can't these people wear these clothes anymore? Remember to use the **passé composé** in your answer.

1.　　　　　2.　　　　　3.　　　　　4.

24 En vacances!

You're going to Montreal for a winter vacation and you need some new clothes for the trip. Go shopping, tell the salesperson what you need, and inquire about prices, sizes, and colors. Act out this scene with a partner. Then, change roles.

25 Dans un grand magasin

With a partner, act out a scene in a department store between a customer and salesperson. The customer should tell what he or she is looking for, ask about size, colors, styles, fabrics, and prices, and ask to try things on. The salesperson should respond appropriately. Change roles.

PANORAMA CULTUREL

Marie-Emmanuelle • France

Thomas • France

Aminata • Côte d'Ivoire

We asked some francophone people what they like to wear. Here's what they said.

Qu'est-ce que tu aimes comme vêtements?

«J'aime bien mettre des jeans, des tee-shirts, des affaires simples, mais de temps en temps, j'aime bien être originale et porter des jupes longues, ou euh... quelque chose de plus classique ou plus moderne.»

—Marie-Emmanuelle

«J'aime les jeans, les chemises, les grosses chaussures et les casquettes aussi.»

—Thomas

«J'adore beaucoup les jupes droites, les robes, les pagnes. J'aime beaucoup me mettre aussi en tissu.»

—Aminata

Qu'en penses-tu?

1. How do you and your friends like to dress? How is this different from the way these people like to dress?
2. Which of these people share your tastes in clothing?

Savais-tu que...?

   In France and other francophone countries, it is common to see people dressed quite well on the streets, on trains, at work, and in restaurants, even fast-food restaurants. In Africa, women commonly drape themselves in brightly-colored fabrics called **pagnes**. Martinique is famous for its **madras** patterns, and southern France is known for its pretty **provençal** prints. Although Paris has the reputation of being a fashion capital, only the rich can afford fashions created by well-known designers. Most young people like to wear jeans, just like American teenagers.

Asking for an opinion; paying a compliment; criticizing; hesitating; making a decision

COMMENT DIT-ON... ?

Asking for an opinion, paying a compliment, and criticizing

To ask for an opinion:

Comment tu trouves... ?

Elle me va, cette robe?
Does this dress suit me?

Il te/vous plaît, ce jean?
Do you like these jeans?

Tu aimes mieux le bleu ou le noir?

> IL ME VA, CE JEAN?
>
> IL VOUS VA TRÈS BIEN. C'EST TOUT À FAIT VOTRE STYLE!

To pay a compliment:

C'est parfait. *It's perfect.*

C'est tout à fait ton/ votre style. *It looks great on you!*

Elle te/vous va très bien, cette jupe. *That skirt suits you really well.*

Il/Elle va très bien avec ta chemise. *It goes very well with . . .*

Je le/la/les trouve... *I think it's/they're . . .*
        à la mode. *in style.*
        chic. *chic.*
        mignon(mignonne)(s). *cute.*
        sensas. *fantastic.*

To criticize:

Il/Elle ne te/vous va pas du tout. *That doesn't look good on you at all.*

Il/Elle est (Ils/Elles sont) trop serré(e)(s). *It's/They're too tight.*
        large(s). *baggy.*
        petit(e)(s). *small.*
        grand(e)(s). *big.*
        court(e)(s). *short.*

Il/Elle ne va pas du tout avec tes chaussures. *That doesn't go at all with . . .*

Je le/la/les trouve moche(s). *I think it's/they're tacky.*
        démodé(e)(s). *old-fashioned.*
        horrible(s). *terrible.*
        rétro. *the style of the Forties or Fifties.*

branché- trendy
nule- useless

26 Ecoute!

Listen to the following conversations and decide if the speakers are complimenting or criticizing each other's clothing.

27 Un après-midi au grand magasin

You and a friend are spending the afternoon shopping at **Printemps.** If these people asked you for advice, what would you say?

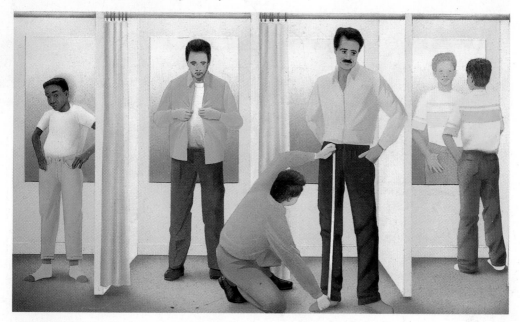

28 Sondage

Complete this survey from a French fashion magazine. How many points did you get? Which category do you fall into? Compare your answers with your partner's.

ENQUETE: LA MODE

Es-tu à la mode?

Fais notre petit test pour savoir si tu es vraiment à la dernière mode.

En général, quelle sorte de vêtements est-ce que tu portes?
a. Des vêtements super chic. (3 points)
b. Ça dépend de l'occasion. (2 points)
c. Des jeans, des tee-shirts et des baskets. (1 point)

Tu achètes de nouveaux vêtements...
a. très souvent. (3 points)
b. quelquefois. (2 points)
c. presque jamais. (1 point)

Quand tu achètes des vêtements, en général, tu...
a. achètes ce qui est à la dernière mode. (3 points)
b. achètes quelque chose que tu aimes. (2 points)
c. achètes ce qui est en solde. (1 point)

Dans un magazine de mode, tu vois que les chemises en plastique fluorescentes sont très populaires. Tu...
a. achètes 4 chemises de 4 couleurs différentes. (3 points)
b. attends patiemment pour voir si les autres en portent. (2 points)
c. tu refuses d'en acheter! Tu ne veux pas être ridicule! (1 point)

Réponses :
10 -12 points : Tu es vraiment à la mode! Attention! Tu risques de perdre ton originalité.
5 - 9 points : Parfaitement raisonnable! Tu es à la mode tout en gardant ton propre style.
0 - 4 points : Tu ne t'intéresses pas à la mode! Tu sais, il y a quelquefois des styles uniques. Essaie de les trouver.

NE PRENDS PAS CE TEST TROP AU SERIEUX!

RENCONTRE CULTURELLE

Read the following dialogues to find out how French people compliment one another.

—J'aime bien ta chemise.
—Ah oui?
—Oui, elle est pas mal.
—Tu trouves? Tu sais, c'est une vieille chemise.

—Il est super, ce chapeau!
—Tu crois?
—Oui, il te va très bien.
—C'est gentil.

—Tu es ravissante aujourd'hui!
—Vraiment? Je n'ai rien fait de spécial.

Qu'en penses-tu?

1. How do these people react to a compliment?
2. How do you usually react to a compliment? How is that different from the French reactions you've just read?

Savais-tu que...?

The French do not compliment freely and generally do so only in exceptional cases. They rarely respond to compliments with **Merci**, since that could be viewed as conceited. French people are much more likely to respond with a modest expression of disbelief, such as **Vraiment? Tu crois? Tu trouves? Ah oui?** or a comment downplaying the importance of the item complimented, such as **Oh, c'est vieux; Ce n'est rien.**

29 Fais des compliments!

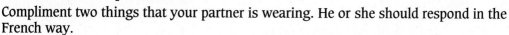

Compliment two things that your partner is wearing. He or she should respond in the French way.

> —Elles sont sensas, tes baskets!
> —Vraiment?
> —Oui, elles sont très à la mode!

---

*G*rammaire   The direct object pronouns **le, la,** and **les**

The pronouns **le,** *him* or *it,* **la,** *her* or *it,* and **les,** *them,* refer to people or things. In the sentences below, what do the pronouns **le, la,** and **les** refer to?*

— Ce pull, il te plaît?	— Oui, je **le** trouve assez chic.
— Comment tu trouves cette robe?	— Je **la** trouve démodée.
— Vous aimez ces chaussures?	— Oui, je vais **les** prendre.

- You normally place the direct object pronouns before the conjugated verb.

   Je **le** prends.   Je l'ai pris.

   Je ne **la** prends pas.   Ne **les** prends pas!

- There are two exceptions to this rule. You place the direct object pronoun after the conjugated verb in a positive command and when an infinitive follows.

   Prends-**le**!

   Je vais **la** prendre.

- When **le** or **la** comes before a verb that starts with a vowel, it changes to **l'**.

   Je vais essayer **le pull**. Je vais **l'**essayer.

30 Prends-le!

Imagine you and a friend are shopping. Tell what you think of the items you see. If your friend likes something, encourage him or her to buy it. Take turns.

> —Ce pantalon est très chic.
> —Tu trouves?
> —Oui, j'aime bien.
> —Il me va?
> —Oui, il te va très bien. Prends-le!

---

* the pullover, the dress, the shoes

COMMENT DIT-ON... ?

Hesitating; making a decision

When the salesperson asks you:

Vous avez choisi?

Vous avez décidé de prendre ce pantalon? *Have you decided to take . . . ?*

Vous le/la/les prenez? *Are you going to take it/them?*

To hesitate, say:

Je ne sais pas.

Euh... J'hésite.
Oh, I'm not sure.

Il/Elle me plaît, mais il/elle est cher/chère.
I like it, but it's expensive.

To make a decision, say:

Je le/la/les prends.
I'll take it/them.

C'est trop cher.
It's too expensive.

Note de *Grammaire*

- Use **il/elle/ils/elles** when you are referring to a specific item.
  Comment tu trouves cette robe? Elle est chouette, n'est-ce pas?

- Use **ce (ça)** when you are speaking in general.
  J'aime porter des pantalons parce que c'est pratique.

In the sentence above, **ce (c'est)** refers to the general idea of wearing pants.

- Here, **c'est** refers to the idea of passing a test.
  —**J'ai réussi à mon examen d'anglais!**
  —**C'est super!**

31 Ecoute!

Listen to these exchanges between a customer and a salesperson. Tell whether the customer takes the item, doesn't take it, or can't decide.

32 Qu'est-ce qu'ils disent?

Write down what you think these people are saying. Then, get together with a partner and compare what you both have written.

1.

2.

3.

4.

33 J'hésite

You're shopping for something new to wear to a party. The salesperson helps you find something. You're unsure, but your friend offers you advice. Take turns.

The glides [j], [w], and [ɥ]

As you listen to people speak French, you may notice a sound that reminds you of the first sound in the English word *yes*. This sound is called a *glide,* because one sound glides into another. Now, try making the sound [j] in these common French words: **mieux, chemisier, bien.** Did you notice that this gliding sound often occurs when the letter **i** is followed by **e?** The sound is also represented by the letters **ill** in words such as **maillot** and **gentille.**

There are two more glides in French. [w] sounds similar to the *w* sound you hear in *west wind.* Listen to these French words: **moi, Louis, jouer.**

The last glide sound is the one you hear in the French word **lui.** It sounds like the French vowel sounds [y] and [i] together. This sound is often written as **ui.** Listen to the glide [ɥ] in these words: **cuir, huit, juillet.**

A. A prononcer

Repeat the following words.

1. travailler   monsieur   combien   conseiller
2. pouvoir   soif   poires   moins
3. suis   minuit   suite   juillet

B. A lire

Take turns with a partner reading each of the following sentences aloud.

1. J'aime bien tes boucles d'oreilles. Elles sont géniales!
2. Il me faut des feuilles de papier, un taille-crayon et un cahier.
3. Elle a choisi un blouson en cuir et une écharpe en soie. C'est chouette!
4. Tu as quoi aujourd'hui? Moi, j'ai histoire et ensuite, je vais faire mes devoirs.
5. —Tu veux promener le chien avec moi?
   —Pourquoi pas?

C. A écrire

You're going to hear a short dialogue. Write down what you hear.

LISONS!

LA MODE AU LYCÉE

$\mathcal{H}$ow important is fashion to you? Do you generally favor one style or do you like to vary the look of what you wear?

A. Think for a moment about the role fashion plays in your life.
1. Do you follow trends you see in magazines or at school?
2. How much influence do your parents have on your wardrobe?
3. Do you think clothing is a reflection of a person's personality or lifestyle?

B. How would you categorize styles that are popular at your school or in your town? What words would you use to describe them?

C. What can you tell about the people who wrote these essays?

D. Which of the students consider fashion important? Which consider it unimportant?

Mélanie

• 15 ans. En seconde au lycée Théodore Aubanel, Avignon.

Ce que je trouve dommage aujourd'hui, c'est que les filles ressemblent de plus en plus à des garçons. Au lycée, presque toutes mes copines portent des jeans ou des pantalons avec des sweat-shirts. Moi aussi, j'aime bien les jeans, mais de temps en temps, je préfère m'habiller «en fille» avec des robes ou des jupes. Je porte aussi beaucoup de bijoux, surtout des boucles d'oreilles; j'adore ça. Et puis en même temps, ça fait plaisir à mes parents quand je suis habillée comme ça; ils préfèrent ça au look garçon manqué.

Christophe

• 17 ans. En terminale au lycée Henri IV, Paris.

Moi, ce qui m'énerve avec la mode, c'est que si tu ne la suis pas, tout le monde te regarde d'un air bizarre au lycée. Moi, par exemple, le retour de la mode des années 70, les pattes d'eph et le look grunge, c'est vraiment pas mon truc. Je trouve ça horrible. Alors, je ne vois pas pourquoi je devrais m'habiller comme ça, simplement parce que c'est la mode. Je préfère porter des pantalons à pinces, des blazers et des chemises avec des cravates. Mes copains trouvent que ça fait trop sérieux, trop fils-à-papa, mais ça m'est égal. Je suis sûr que dans quelques années, quand ils travailleront, ils seront tous habillés comme moi et quand ils regarderont des photos de terminale, ils rigoleront bien en voyant les habits qu'ils portaient à 18 ans!

Serge

- 16 ans. En première au lycée Ampère de Lyon.

Pour moi, ce qui est vraiment important, c'est d'avoir des vêtements confortables. Je suis très sportif et j'aime pouvoir bouger dans mes habits. Mais, je veux aussi des trucs cool. Pas question de porter des vêtements très serrés ou très chers, par exemple. Je ne vois pas l'intérêt d'avoir un blouson qui coûte 4 000 F. Je préfère un blouson bon marché dans lequel je peux jouer au foot avec les copains. Comme ça, si je tombe ou si je l'abîme, c'est pas tragique. En général, je mets des jeans parce que c'est pratique et sympa. En été, je porte des tee-shirts très simples et en hiver, des sweat-shirts. Et comme chaussures, je préfère les baskets.

Emmanuelle

- 17 ans et demi. Lycée Mas de Tesse, Montpellier.

Pour moi, la façon dont quelqu'un s'habille est un reflet de sa personnalité. Au lycée, j'étudie les arts plastiques, et comme on le dit souvent, les artistes sont des gens originaux et créatifs. Je n'aime pas dépenser beaucoup pour mes vêtements. Je n'achète jamais de choses très chères, mais j'utilise mon imagination pour les rendre plus originales. Par exemple, j'ajoute toujours des accessoires sympa : bijoux fantaisie que je fabrique souvent moi-même, foulards, ceintures, sacs... Parfois, je fais même certains de mes vêtements, surtout les jupes car c'est facile. Et comme ça, je suis sûre que personne ne portera la même chose que moi!

E. Although many people consider France a fashion capital, America also influences fashion. What English words can you find in the essays?

F. Look for the words in the box below in the essays. Then, try to match them with their English equivalents.

1. bijoux	a. fashion
2. la mode	b. things
3. pattes d'eph	c. ruin
4. bouger	d. jewelry
5. abîme	e. to move
6. les trucs	f. bell-bottoms

G. Which student . . .
1. likes clothes that are practical and comfortable?
2. Makes some of his or her clothing and jewelry?
3. doesn't buy expensive clothes?
4. thinks girls should wear feminine clothes sometimes?

H. Which of the following sentences are facts and which are opinions?
1. En été, je porte des tee-shirts.
2. Les artistes sont des gens originaux et créatifs.
3. Les filles ressemblent de plus en plus à des garçons.
4. Je n'achète jamais de choses très chères.
5. La façon dont on s'habille est un reflet de sa personnalité.

I. Write a short paragraph in French telling what you like to wear. Mention colors and any other details you feel are important.

MISE EN PRATIQUE

1 Listen to this conversation between Philippe and a saleswoman at a French department store. Then, answer these questions.

1. What does Philippe want to buy?
2. What colors does he prefer?
3. What does the salesperson say about the first item Philippe tries on?
4. How does Philippe feel about the way the item fits?
5. Does he end up buying it?

2 You've been invited to a party. What should you wear? Ask your partner's advice and advise him or her what to wear.

3 You've been hired by a French magazine to write about fashion trends among American teenagers today. Interview two or three classmates about their tastes in clothing. Find out what clothes they like to wear, what they wear to parties (**les boums**), what colors they like to wear, and their favorite article of clothing. Take notes and write a short article in French based on your interviews.

4 From what you know about French culture, are these statements true or false?

1. The French are famous for giving lots of compliments.
2. The French tend to downplay the compliments they receive.
3. If you say **merci** in response to a compliment, you could be considered conceited.
4. A common French way to respond to a compliment on something you're wearing is to say **Tu trouves?**

5 You and your friend are watching a fashion show. Ask each other how you like the clothes you see.

—Comment tu trouves ce pantalon?
—Je le trouve moche!

1.

2.

3.

NOUVELLE COLLECTION CLAUDE SAINT GENEST

FEMME : Pantalon imprimé bleu, 100 % viscose. Du 36 au 44, **199 F**. Existe en rouge. **Pull** tunique, maille brillante, sable, 50 % coton 50 % acrylique. Du 38/40 au 42/44, **189 F**. Existe en indigo. **HOMME : Chemise** à carreaux, manches longues, indigo, 100 % coton. Du 2 au 6, **139 F**. **Pantalon** pinces, micro-sablé, chiné beige, 50 % polyester 50 % viscose. Du 38 au 52, **239 F**. Existe en tilleul et anthracite. **Pull** maille anglaise indigo, 50 % coton 50 % acrylique. Du 2 au 6, **149 F**. Existe en lichen et beige. **ENFANT : Tee-shirt** uni rouge, broderie poitrine, 100 % coton peigné. Du 2 au 5 ans, **29 F**. Existe en 17 coloris. **Jean** western marine, 100 % coton. Du 2 au 5 ans, **79 F**. Existe en sable, bleu et blanc.

VENDUE EXCLUSIVEMENT DANS LES HYPERMARCHES GEANT CASINO ET RALLYE

6 Look over the advertisement above. Then, answer these questions.

1. Who does **Claude Saint Genest** make clothes for?
2. How many colors does the child's T-shirt come in?
3. The women's pants are available in what sizes?
4. What material is the men's shirt made of?
5. What's the most expensive item on the page? The least expensive?

7

JEU DE ROLE

Choose one of the items from the advertisement and ask the salesperson about it. Do they have it in your size? Can you try it on? The salesperson should compliment the way it looks, and you should decide whether to buy it or not. Take turns playing the role of salesperson.

Can you use what you've learned in this chapter?

1 How would you ask a friend what you should wear to a party?

2 How would you advise a friend to wear these clothes, using the verb **mettre**?

1.

2.

3 How would you tell a salesperson . . .
   1. that you're just looking?   2. what you would like?

4 How would you ask a salesperson . . .
   1. if you can try something on?
   2. if they have what you want in a different size?
   3. if they have what you want in a particular color?
   4. how much something costs?

5 How would you tell what these people are choosing?

Charles   **Jean-Marc et Farid**   **Astrid**   **Delphine et Camille**

6 If you were shopping with a friend, how would you ask . . .
   1. if your friend likes what you have on?
   2. if something fits?
   3. if it's too short?

7 How would you compliment a friend's clothing? How would you criticize it?

8 How can you express your hesitation?

9 How would you tell a salesperson what you've decided to do?

PREMIERE ETAPE

Clothes

un blouson   *a jacket*
des bottes (f.)   *boots*
des boucles d'oreilles (f.)
   earrings
un bracelet   *a bracelet*
un cardigan   *a cardigan*
une casquette   *a cap*
une ceinture   *a belt*
un chapeau   *a hat*
des chaussettes (f.)   *socks*
des chaussures (f.)   *shoes*
une chemise   *a shirt (men's)*

un chemisier   *a shirt (women's)*
une cravate   *a tie*
une écharpe   *a scarf*
une jupe   *a skirt*
des lunettes (f.) de soleil
   sunglasses
un manteau   *a coat*
un pantalon   *(a pair of) pants*
une robe   *a dress*
des sandales (f.)   *sandals*
un maillot de bain   *a bathing suit*
une veste   *a suit jacket, a blazer*

Asking for and giving advice

Je ne sais pas quoi mettre pour...
   *I don't know what to wear for
   (to) . . .*
Qu'est-ce que je mets?   *What
   shall I wear?*
Pourquoi est-ce que tu ne mets
   pas...?   *Why don't you wear...?*
Mets...   *Wear . . .*
mettre   *to put, to put on, to wear*
porter   *to wear*

DEUXIEME ETAPE

Expressing need; inquiring

Vous désirez?   *What would you
   like?*
(Est-ce que) je peux vous aider?
   May I help you?
Je cherche quelque chose pour...
   I'm looking for something to . . .
J'aimerais... pour aller avec...   *I'd
   like . . . to go with . . .*

Non, merci, je regarde.   *No,
   thanks, I'm just looking.*
Je peux l'/les essayer?   *Can I try
   it/them on?*
Je peux essayer le/la/les... ?   *Can
   I try on the . . . one(s)?*
Vous avez ça... ?   *Do you have
   that . . . ? (size, fabric, color)*
   en bleu   *in blue*

en coton   *cotton*
en jean   *denim*
en cuir   *leather*

Other useful expressions

choisir   *to choose, to pick*
grandir   *to grow*
maigrir   *to lose weight*
grossir   *to gain weight*

TROISIEME ETAPE

Asking for an opinion; paying a compliment; criticizing

Comment tu trouves... ?   *How do
   you like . . . ?*
Il/Elle me va?   *Does . . . suit me?*
Il/Elle te (vous) plaît?   *Do you
   like it?*
C'est parfait.   *It's perfect.*
C'est tout à fait ton style.   *It
   looks great on you!*
Il/Elle te/vous va très bien.   *It
   suits you really well.*
Il/Elle va très bien avec...   *It goes
   very well with . . .*
Je le/la/les trouve...   *I think it's/
   they're . . .*
   à la mode   *in style*

chic   *chic*
mignon (mignonne)   *cute*
sensas   *fantastic*
serré(e)(s)   *tight*
large(s)   *baggy*
petit(e)(s)   *small*
grand(e)(s)   *big*
court(e)(s)   *short*
moche(s)   *tacky*
démodé(e)(s)   *old-fashioned*
horrible(s)   *terrible*
rétro   *the style of the Forties or
   Fifties*
Il/Elle ne te/vous va pas du tout.
   *It doesn't look good on you
   at all.*
Il/Elle ne va pas du tout avec...
   It doesn't go at all with . . .

Hesitating; making a decision

Vous avez choisi?   *Have you
   decided?*
Vous avez décidé de prendre...?
   Have you decided to take . . . ?
Vous le/la/les prenez?   *Are you
   taking it/them?*
Je ne sais pas.   *I don't know.*
Euh... J'hésite.   *Well, I'm not sure.*
Il/Elle me plaît, mais il/elle est
   cher (chère).   *I like it, but it's
   expensive.*
Je le/la/les prends.   *I'll take it/
   them.*
C'est trop cher.   *It's too expensive.*

11
Vive les vacances!

① Pourquoi tu ne vas pas à la plage?

How do you spend your vacation? Do you work? Do you do things in your hometown with your friends? Do you travel to other places and meet new people?

In this chapter you will learn

- to inquire about and share future plans; to express indecision; to express wishes; to ask for advice; to make, accept, and refuse suggestions
- to remind; to reassure; to see someone off
- to ask for and express opinions; to inquire about and relate past events

And you will

- listen to francophone students talk about their vacation plans
- read about tourist attractions in Provence
- write about your ideal vacation
- find out where French-speaking people go and what they do during their vacations

② Tu n'as pas oublié ton dictionnaire?

③ C'était formidable, les vacances en Provence!

Mise en train

Bientôt les vacances!

What are these teenagers discussing? What clues do you have? What is Florent's dilemma?

1 Tu as compris?

Answer the following questions about **Bientôt les vacances!** Don't be afraid to guess.

1. What time of year is it? How do you know?
2. Who is planning to travel during the vacation? Where?
3. Who is going to work during the vacation? Why?
4. What is Florent going to do?

2 C'est qui?

D'après **Bientôt les vacances!** qui a l'intention de (d')...

Florent

Ahmed

Magali

aller dans les Alpes?

travailler en Arles?

rester en Arles?

partir en colonie de vacances?

aller voir ses cousins?

aller à la montagne?

faire du camping?

3 Vrai ou faux?

1. Tous les jeunes restent en France pendant les vacances.
2. Les cousins de Magali habitent à la montagne.
3. Ahmed va faire du camping dans les Alpes.
4. Ahmed va travailler dans un café.
5. Ahmed veut aller au Festival de la photographie.
6. Florent part en colonie de vacances.

4 Cherche les expressions

According to **Bientôt les vacances!**, what can you say in French...

1. to ask what someone is going to do?
2. to tell what a place looks like?
3. to express an opinion?
4. to express indecision?
5. to make a suggestion?
6. to express a preference?

5 Et maintenant, à toi

Whose vacation plans are the most interesting to you? Why?

PREMIERE ETAPE

Inquiring about and sharing future plans; expressing indecision; expressing wishes; asking for advice; making, accepting, and refusing suggestions

VOCABULAIRE

Où est-ce que tu vas aller pendant tes vacances?

à la montagne

à la campagne

au bord de la mer

en forêt

en colonie de vacances

chez les grands-parents

Qu'est-ce qu'on peut y faire?

faire du camping

faire de la randonnée

faire du bateau

faire de la plongée

faire de la planche à voile

faire de la voile

6 Ecoute!

Listen as Nathalie, Bruno, Pauline, and Emile tell about their vacation plans. What is each teenager going to do?

Although there are few hard-and-fast rules to help you remember if a noun is masculine or feminine, you can often predict the gender of a word by its ending. Some of the endings that usually indicate a feminine word are **-tion, -sion, -ie, -ette, -elle, -ine, -ude,** and **-ure.** Endings that often signal a masculine word are **-ment, -age, -oir, -ier, -et,** and **-eau.** But be careful! There are exceptions.

Tu te rappelles?

Do you remember how to tell what is going to happen? Use a form of the verb **aller** *(to go)* plus the infinitive of another verb.

Demain, je **vais faire** du bateau.

Si tu as oublié the verb *aller* va à la page 154.

7 Dans une colonie de vacances

Qu'est-ce que Vincent et Roland vont faire en colonie de vacances?

1.

2.

3.

4.

5.

6.

NOTE CULTURELLE

In francophone countries, many children and teenagers attend summer camps **(colonies de vacances),** where they learn folklore, folk dances, arts and crafts, foreign languages, and many other subjects. Of course, they also participate in sports. The camps are usually run by young adults called **animateurs.** In France alone there are hundreds of **colonies de vacances.**

COMMENT DIT-ON... ?

Inquiring about and sharing future plans; expressing indecision; expressing wishes

To inquire about someone's plans:

Qu'est-ce que tu vas faire cet été?

Où est-ce que tu vas aller pendant les vacances?

To express indecision:

J'hésite.

Je ne sais pas.

Je n'en sais rien. *I have no idea.*

Je n'ai rien de prévu. *I don't have any plans.*

To share your plans:

En juillet, **je vais** travailler.

En août, **j'ai l'intention d'**aller en Algérie. . . . *I intend to . . .*

To express wishes:

Je voudrais bien aller chez mes cousins.

J'ai envie de travailler.

I feel like . . .

8 Ecoute!

Listen to these speakers talk about their vacations. Do they have definite plans or are they undecided?

9 Les vacances en France

Imagine you're going to France on vacation next summer. Your partner will ask about your vacation plans. Tell what you feel like doing or plan to do there. Then, change roles.

visiter le Louvre

faire des photos

faire du ski

rencontrer des jeunes français

voir la tour Eiffel

parler français

aller à un concert de rock français

aller au café

Note de Grammaire

- To say *to* or *in* before the names of most cities, use the preposition **à**.

    Tu vas **à** Paris pendant les vacances?

- Names of countries are either masculine or feminine. Use **au** *(to, in)* before all masculine names and **en** *(to, in)* before all feminine names. Use **en** before the names of all countries that begin with a vowel. Before any plural name, use **aux**.

    Vous allez **au** Canada?

    Hélène va **en** Allemagne.

    Nous allons **aux** Etats-Unis.

- States and provinces follow slightly different rules.

Vocabulaire à la carte

en Angleterre	en Floride
en Allemagne	en Italie
en Australie	au Maroc
en Belgique	au Mexique
au Brésil	en Russie
en Californie	au Sénégal
en Chine	en Suisse
en Egypte	au Texas
en Espagne	au Viêt-Nam

10 Où vont-ils?

Dans quel pays vont-ils passer leurs vacances?

au Canada   au Maroc
aux Etats-Unis
en Russie   en Angleterre
en Egypte   en France

1. Murielle va prendre des photos de la tour Eiffel.
2. Monique va visiter le château Frontenac.
3. Joseph va visiter la tour de Londres.
4. Mathieu va voir les pyramides.
5. Than et Laure vont visiter le Texas.
6. Dominique va voir le Kremlin.
7. Paul et Gilles vont aller à Casablanca.

11 On y fait quoi?

Select two of the countries from Activity 10 and discuss with your group at least three activities you would like to do on vacation in each one.

12 Un voyage gratuit

You've won a trip from an airline to anywhere you want. Where will you go? Why? What will you do there? Discuss this with a partner. Take turns.

Tu te rappelles ?

Do you remember how to ask for advice? Make, accept, and refuse suggestions?

To ask for advice:
Je ne sais pas quoi faire (où aller).
Tu as une idée?
Qu'est-ce que tu me conseilles?

To make suggestions:
Je te conseille de…
Tu devrais…

To accept suggestions:
C'est une bonne idée!
Pourquoi pas?
D'accord!
Allons-y!

To refuse suggestions:
Non, ce n'est pas possible.
Non, je ne peux pas.
Ça ne me dit rien.
C'est trop cher.

13 Ecoute!

Ecoute Alain et Valérie qui parlent de leurs vacances. Est-ce que ces phrases sont vraies ou fausses?

1. Alain ne sait pas quoi faire.
2. Valérie n'a pas d'idées.
3. Valérie est déjà allée à la Martinique.
4. Alain ne veut pas aller à la Martinique.

14 Des conseils

Ces élèves rêvent *(are dreaming)* de ce qu'ils aiment. Ils ne savent pas où aller pendant les vacances. Tu as une idée?

Malika

Marion

Hai

Christian

Adrienne

Ali

15 Où aller?

Tell your partner what you like to do on vacation. Your partner will then make some suggestions about where you might want to go. Accept your partner's suggestions, or refuse them and give an excuse. Then, change roles.

16 Mon journal

Décris un voyage que tu vas faire ou que tu voudrais faire. Où veux-tu aller? Quand? Avec qui? Qu'est-ce que tu vas y faire?

PANORAMA CULTUREL

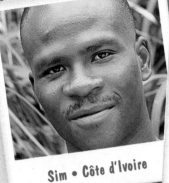

Sim • Côte d'Ivoire

Nicole • Martinique

Céline • France

We asked some francophone people where they go and what they do on vacation. Here are their responses.

Qu'est-ce que tu fais pendant les vacances?

«Pendant les vacances, d'habitude je vais au village chez les parents qui sont restés au village. Et après une année scolaire, il faut aller les voir parce que ça... il y a longtemps qu'on se voit pas. Donc, ça fait plaisir aux parents de revoir les enfants quand ils vont au village. Voilà. Ça fait changer de climat. On va se reposer un peu.»

—Sim

«Pendant les vacances, alors, je vais généralement à la plage, au cinéma. Le soir, je sors, enfin je vais dans des fêtes, chez des amis. On danse. On s'amuse. On rigole. On joue aux cartes. Les vacances se passent comme ça.»

Quand est-ce que tu as des vacances?

«J'ai des vacances en juillet, à partir de juillet. Les vacances durent deux mois et nous reprenons l'école en septembre.»

—Nicole

«Ben, pendant les vacances, bon, des fois je pars. L'année dernière, je suis partie en Espagne, cette année je pars en Corse. Je pars souvent avec des copains ou... sinon, je reste à Aix.»

—Céline

Qu'en penses-tu?

1. Where do these people like to go and what do they like to do during their vacations?
2. Where do you go and what do you do on vacation? How does this differ from what these people do?

Savais-tu que...?

Salaried employees in France are guaranteed five weeks of vacation time per year. Most people take a month off in July or August, and take the fifth week at some other time of the year, often in winter.

VOCABULAIRE

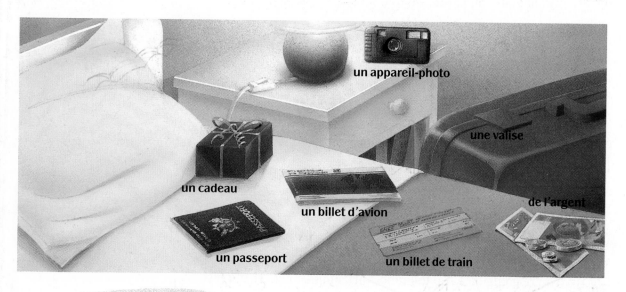

un appareil-photo

une valise

un cadeau

un billet d'avion

de l'argent

un passeport

un billet de train

17 Qu'est-ce qu'il te faut?

1. Qu'est-ce qu'il faut pour entrer dans un pays étranger?
2. Qu'est-ce qu'il faut pour prendre le train?
3. Qu'est-ce qu'il faut pour acheter des souvenirs?
4. Qu'est-ce qu'on offre à des amis?

COMMENT DIT-ON... ?

Reminding; reassuring

To remind someone of something:

N'oublie pas ton passeport!

Tu n'as pas oublié ton billet d'avion? *You didn't forget . . . ?*

Tu ne peux pas partir sans ton écharpe! *You can't leave without . . . !*

Tu prends ton manteau? *Are you taking . . . ?*

To reassure someone:

Ne t'en fais pas.

J'ai pensé à tout. *I've thought of everything.*

Je n'ai rien oublié. *I didn't forget anything.*

18 Ecoute!

Listen to these speakers. Are they reminding or reassuring someone?

19 Qu'est-ce qu'il a oublié?

Read the list of things Jean-Paul needs for his trip. Make a list of what he's forgotten to pack. Next, play the role of Jean-Paul's parent and remind him what to take. Then, change roles.

Si tu as oublié
clothing
va à la page 261.

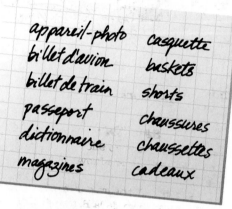

appareil-photo   casquette
billet d'avion   baskets
billet de train   shorts
passeport   chaussures
dictionnaire   chaussettes
magazines   cadeaux

20 Jeu de rôle

You're going on a trip to France this summer with the French Club. Ask your friend, who went last year, what you should take. He or she will remind you of some things you'll need. Act this out with a partner and then change roles.

Grammaire   The verb partir

A small group of verbs whose infinitives end in -ir follow a pattern different than the one you learned in Chapter 10.

partir *(to leave)*

Je **pars**	Nous **partons**
Tu **pars** } à dix heures.	Vous **partez** } à dix heures.
Il/Elle/On **part**	Ils/Elles **partent**

- Don't pronounce the **s** or **t** in **pars** or **part**.
- **Sortir** *(to go out)* and **dormir** *(to sleep)* also follow this pattern.

À la française

French speakers often use the present tense to talk about the future.

Je **pars** à neuf heures. *I'm leaving (or) I'm going to/will leave . . .*
Je **vais** à la plage samedi. *I'm going (or) I'm going to/will go . . .*

21 On part à quelle heure?

Ces jeunes vont aller en vacances. Ils partent à quelle heure?

1. 18h15

2. 21h30

3. 22h15

22 Vacances en Provence

Regarde l'itinéraire de Marianne. Ensuite, réponds aux questions.

1. D'où part Marianne?
2. Où est-ce qu'elle va?
3. Son voyage va durer combien de temps?
4. Qu'est-ce qu'elle a l'intention de faire?

23 Jeu de rôle

You're going to take the same trip as Marianne. Your partner will ask you questions about the trip and remind you what to take.

24 Bonjour de Provence!

Pendant ton voyage en Provence, écris une carte postale à ton ami(e), à tes camarades de classe ou à ton professeur.

Bienvenue en Provence!

SAMEDI :

départ Arles, bus de 9h35;
arrivée aux Baux-de-Provence à 10h10;
* visite de la Cathédrale d'Images;
   dîner : Auberge de la Benvengudo

DIMANCHE :

départ pour Saint-Rémy de Provence,
bus de 9h15;
arrivée à 9h45;
* visite du musée Van Gogh; déjeuner :
   pique-nique à Fontvieille;

* visite du moulin de Daudet;
   retour aux Baux-de-Provence;
   départ pour Avignon, bus de 18h16;
   arrivée à 19h10 Hôtel le Midi;
   dîner

LUNDI :

* visite de la Cité des Papes, le Pont
   St-Bénézet, promenade du Rocher des
   Doms, le musée du Petit-Palais;
* spectacle folklorique;
   départ pour Grasse 20h15;
   arrivée à 22h10 Hôtel les Aromes

MARDI :

* visite de la Parfumerie
   Fragonard;
* Musée d'Art et d'Histoire de
   Provence; retour en Arles
   17h42;
   arrivée à 19h20

COMMENT DIT-ON... ?
Seeing someone off

To wish someone a good trip:

Bon voyage! *Have a good trip!*
Bonnes vacances! *Have a good vacation!*
Amuse-toi bien! *Have fun!*
Bonne chance! *Good luck!*

---

25 Ecoute!

Ecoute ces conversations.
On arrive ou on part?

26 Au revoir!

It's time for your French exchange student to return home. See him or her off at the airport. Act this out with your partner.

27 Un grand voyage

You and a friend have decided to take a trip together to a foreign country. Decide where you will go and what you will do there. Talk about the weather conditions and when you will go. Discuss what clothes and other items you each plan to pack and what you will wear on the plane.

28 Un petit mot

Your friend is leaving on a trip tomorrow. Write a note wishing him or her well and suggesting things he or she might like to see and do while on vacation.

Tu te rappelles ?

Do you remember how to give commands? Use the **tu** or **vous** form of the verb without a subject.

Attends! Allez!

When you use an **-er** verb, remember to drop the final **s** of the **tu** form.

Ecoute!

When you use an object pronoun with a positive command, place it after the verb, separated by a hyphen in writing.

Donnez-moi votre billet, s'il vous plaît.

Si tu as oublié *weather* va à la page 106.

COMMENT DIT-ON... ?

Asking for and expressing opinions

To ask someone's opinion:

Tu as passé un bon été?

Ça s'est bien passé?
Did it go well?

Tu t'es bien amusé(e)?
Did you have fun?

To express an opinion:

Oui, très chouette.
Oui, c'était formidable!
Yes, it was great!
Oui, ça a été.
Oh, pas mauvais.
C'était épouvantable.
Non, pas vraiment. *No, not really.*
C'était un véritable cauchemar!
It was a real nightmare!
C'était ennuyeux. *It was boring.*

29 Ecoute!

Listen to these conversations and then tell whether these people had a good, fair, or bad vacation.

Tu te rappelles ?

Do you remember how to inquire about and relate events that happened in the past?

Tu es allé(e) où?
Qu'est-ce que tu as fait?
D'abord,... Ensuite,... Après,... Enfin,...

30 Méli-mélo!

Remets la conversation entre Thierry et Hervé dans l'ordre.

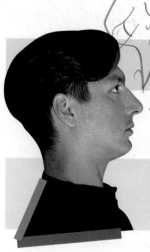

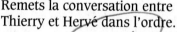
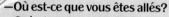

—Où est-ce que vous êtes allés?
—Qu'est-ce que tu as fait?
—Et ensuite?
—Salut, Hervé! Ça s'est bien passé, l'été?

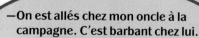

—On est allés chez mon oncle à la campagne. C'est barbant chez lui.
—Ah non, alors! C'était ennuyeux!
—Après ça, on est rentrés à la maison.
—Je suis allé en vacances avec mes parents.

Do you remember how to form the **passé composé?** Use a form of **avoir** as a helping verb with the past participle of the main verb. The past participles of regular **-er**, **-re**, and **-ir** verbs end in **é**, **u**, and **i**.

Nous **avons** beaucoup **mangé.**   J'**ai répondu** à leur lettre.   Ils **ont fini.**

You have to memorize the past participles of irregular verbs.

J'**ai fait** du camping.   Ils **ont vu** un film.

To make a verb in the **passé composé** negative, you place **ne… pas** around the helping verb.

Il **n'a pas** fait ses devoirs.

With **aller**, you use **être** as the helping verb instead of **avoir.**

31 Qu'est-ce qu'elle a fait?

Mets ces activités en ordre d'après l'itinéraire de Marianne à la page 295.

D'abord, elle...

visiter le musée Van Gogh

voir un spectacle folklorique

visiter la Parfumerie Fragonard

visiter la Cité des Papes

voir le moulin de Daudet

faire la promenade du Rocher des Doms

faire un pique-nique

32 On fait la même chose?

You and your partner took these photographs on a trip to France last year. Take turns telling where you went, what you did, and what you thought of each place or activity.

Un café sur le cours Mirabeau

Le palais des Papes, c'est formidable.

La mer Méditerranée

Les arènes à Arles

La Côte d'Azur

Tu reviens d'un voyage. Ton ami(e) te demande où tu es allé(e), avec qui, ce que tu as fait et comment ça s'est passé.

PRONONCIATION

Aspirated h, th, ch, and gn

You've learned that you don't pronounce the letter **h** in French. Some words begin with an aspirated **h** (**h aspiré**). This means that you don't make elision and liaison with the word that comes before. Repeat these phrases: **le haut-parleur; le houx; les halls; les haricots.**

Haut and **houx** begin with an aspirated **h**, so you can't drop the **e** from the article **le**. **Halls** and **haricots** also begin with an aspirated **h**, so you don't pronounce the **s** in the article **les**. How will you know which words begin with an aspirated h? If you look the words up in the dictionary, you may find an asterisk (*) before an aspirated **h**.

How do you pronounce the combination **th**? Just ignore the letter **h** and pronounce the **t**. Repeat these words: **mathématiques, théâtre, athlète.**

What about the combination **ch**? In French, **ch** is pronounced like the English *sh*, as in the word *show*. Compare these English and French words: *change/***change**, *chocolate/***chocolat**, *chance/***chance**. In some words, **ch** is pronounced like *k*. Listen to these words and repeat them: **chorale, Christine, archéologie.**

Finally, how do you pronounce the combination **gn**? The English sound /ny/, as in the word *onion* is similar. Pronounce these words: **oignon, montagne, magnifique.**

A. A prononcer

Repeat the following words.

1. le héros   la harpe   le hippie   le hockey
2. thème   maths   mythe   bibliothèque
3. Chine   choisir   tranche   pêches
4. espagnol   champignon   montagne   magnifique

B. A lire

Take turns with a partner reading each of the following sentences aloud.

1. J'aime la Hollande, mais je veux aller à la montagne en Allemagne.
2. Je cherche une chemise, des chaussures et un chapeau.
3. Il n'a pas fait ses devoirs de maths et de chimie à la bibliothèque dimanche.
4. Charles a gagné trois hamsters. Ils sont dans ma chambre! Quel cauchemar!

C. A écrire

You're going to hear a short dialogue. Write down what you hear.

LISONS!

𝒲hat would you like to do if you were visiting Provence?

DE BONS CONSEILS

When you read for a purpose, it's a good idea to decide beforehand what kind of information you want. If you're looking for an overview, a quick, general reading may be all that is required. If you're looking for specific details, you'll have to read more carefully.

A. The information at the top of both pages is from a book entitled *Le Guide du Routard.* Do you think this is
   1. a history book?
   2. a travel guide?
   3. a geography book?

B. You usually read a book like this to gather general information about what is going on, or to find details about a certain place or event. What general categories of information can you find? Under what titles?

C. Where should you stay if . . .
   1. you plan to visit Provence in November?
   2. you want a balcony?
   3. you want the least expensive room you can get?
   4. you have a tent and a sleeping bag?

D. Which restaurant should you try if . . .
   1. you want the most expensive meal available?
   2. you love salad?
   3. you want to go out on Sunday night?

ARLES (13200)

Où dormir?

🛏 **Très bon marché**
   Auberge de jeunesse : 20, av. Foch. ☎ 90-96-18-25. Fax : 90-96-31-26. Fermée pendant les vacances de Noël. 100 lits. 75 F la nuit, draps et petit déjeuner compris. Fait aussi restaurant. Repas à 45 F.

🛏 **Prix modérés**
   Hôtel Gauguin : 5, place Voltaire. ☎ 90-96-14-35. Fermé du 15 novembre au 20 décembre et du 10 janvier au 15 février. De 130 à 190 F la double. Sur trois étages. Chambres simples, bien aménagées. Celles qui donnent sur la place ont un balcon. Peu de charme cependant dans ce quartier de l'après-guerre.

🛏 **Plus chic**
   Hôtel Diderot : 5, rue Diderot. ☎ 90-96-10-30. Fermé du 6 janvier au 31 mars. 14 chambres. De 140 F la double avec cabinet de toilette, à 220 et 290 F avec douche ou bains, et w.-c. Chambres sobres et bien meublées.

🛏 **Camping**
   Camping City : 67, route de Crau. ☎ 90-93-08-86. Fermé du 30 octobre au 1er mars. En allant vers Raphèle-lès-Arles. Assez ombragé. Piscine, épicerie, plats à emporter, restaurant-pizzeria, animations en été.

BATEAU «MIREIO»

Bateau restaurant de 250 places, chauffé, climatisé. Croisières déjeuner sans escale vers Chateauneuf-du-Pape ou avec escale en Arles – visite de la capitale de la Camargue –, à Roquemaure avec dégustation des vins de Côtes du Rhône, à Villeneuve avec visite du village et de ses monuments. Croisières dîner et soirées spectacle devant Avignon et Villeneuve. Animation dansante et commentaires sur toutes les croisières.

84000 AVIGNON -
Tél. : 90 85 62 25 - Fax : 90 85 61 14

BATEAU « MIREIO »

CATHEDRALES D'IMAGES

Aux Baux-de-Provence, dans les anciennes carrières du Val-d'Enfer, CATHEDRALE D'IMAGES propose un spectacle permanent en IMAGE TOTALE.
4.000m² d'écrans naturels, 40 sources de projection, 2 500 diapos créent une féerie visuelle et sonore où déambule le spectateur.
–Couvrez-vous car les carrières sont fraîches!–

13520 LES BAUX-DE-PROVENCE -
Tél. : 90 54 38 65 - Fax : 90 54 42 65

CATHÉDRALE D'IMAGES

Où manger?

Bon marché

Vitamine : 16, rue du Docteur-Fanton. ☎ 90-93-77-36. Fermé le dimanche. Une carte de 50 salades différentes, de 16 à 45 F, et 15 spécialités de pâtes de 28 à 42 F, le tout dans une salle agréablement décorée (expos photos) et avec un accueil décontracté.

Hôtel-restaurant-d'Arlaten : 7, rue de la Cavalerie. ☎ 90-96-24-85. Fermé le dimanche soir. Intérieur très simple. Menu intéressant à 68 F, avec une entrée, un plat, légumes et dessert. Trois autres menus à 88, 105 et 135 F. Réserver.

Le Poisson Banane : 6, rue du Forum. ☎ 90-96-02-58. Ouvert uniquement le soir. Fermé le mercredi. Avec sa grande terrasse couverte de verdure, ce petit resto caché derrière la place du Forum passe facilement inaperçu et c'est dommage. Il est agréable de venir y goûter une cuisine sucrée-salée inventive avec un menu à 125 F, et une spécialité antillaise : le «poisson-banane», bien sûr. Plat du jour à 70 F environ.

CHATEAU MUSEE DE L'EMPERI

CHATEAU MUSEE DE L'EMPERI

Le CHATEAU DE L'EMPERI, la plus importante forteresse médiévale en Provence, abrite une des plus somptueuses collections d'art et d'uniformes militaires qui soit en Europe.
Cette collection unique illustre l'évolution des uniformes et de l'art militaire de Louis XIV à 1914. La période napoléonienne est la plus présente.
Le Château de l'Emperi est situé en plein cœur de la ville ancienne.

13300 SALON DE PROVENCE -
Tél : 90 56 22 36

GROTTES DE THOUZON

GROTTES DE THOUZON

Les décors de stalactites qui parent « le ciel » de ce réseau naturel forment des paysages souterrains merveilleux.
(Photo : M. CROTET)
Grotte réputée pour la finesse de ses stalactites (fistuleuses). Parcours aisé pour les personnes âgées et les enfants. Seule grotte naturelle aménagée pour le tourisme en Provence. Ouvert du 1/04 au 31/10. Groupe toute l'année sur rendez-vous.

84250 LE THOR - Tél. : 90 33 93 65
- Fax : 90 33 74 90

E. Do you think the descriptions of the hotels were written by the hotel management? How do you know?

F. At the bottom of both pages, you will find descriptions of several tourist attractions in Provence. After you've read them, match the items listed below with the sites where you would find them.

1. a dinner cruise
2. stalactites
3. thousands of projection screens
4. a collection of military art and uniforms

a. Cathédrale d'images
b. Bateau «Mireio»
c. Grottes de Thouzon
d. Château Musée de l'Emperi

G. Are there similar tourist attractions in your area? What are they?

H. If you were working at a tourist information office, what would you recommend to someone who . . .

1. wants a comfortable cruise package?
2. would like to visit a medieval castle?
3. likes to explore caves?
4. is interested in military art?

I. You and your friend have three days to spend in Arles. You're on a very tight budget, but you still want to enjoy your trip. Where will you stay? Where will you eat your lunches and dinners? How much will you spend for these three days?

MISE EN PRATIQUE

1 Listen to this radio advertisement and then answer these questions.

1. What is being advertised?
2. Can you name two places that are mentioned in the advertisement?
3. What activities are mentioned in the advertisement?
4. For whom do they offer discounts?

2 Read the brochure and then answer the questions that follow.

Le rêve américain devient réalité, en séjour Immersion avec EF

Vivre à l'américaine

Qui n'a rêvé un jour de vivre une autre vie ? Ce rêve devient réalité, grâce à la formule EF Immersion : pendant quelques semaines, vous devenez totalement américain. Parce que les familles d'accueil sont soigneusement séléctionnées par EF, votre intégration est immédiate, et vos progrès linguistiques sont aussi spectaculaires que durables. C'est, sans nul doute, la formule qui vous assure la connaissance la plus directe et la plus profonde du mode de vie américain.

Vacances de Printemps

N° de séjour	Date de départ	Date de retour	Durée du séjour	Région	Frais de séjour*
550	11 avril	25 avril	2 sem.	Côte Est	7.730
551	18 avril	2 mai	2 sem.	Côte Est	7.730
552	18 avril	2 mai	2 sem.	Sud-Est	8.170

*Voyage inclus (départ Paris)

1. Where do students go if they sign up for this trip?
2. Where do they stay?
3. What do they learn?
4. In what months can students make this trip?
5. How long does it last?
6. To what regions of the country can students go?
7. How much does this trip cost?

3 Imagine that an exchange student is coming to stay with your family. Write a letter telling him or her about the weather where you live, what there is to do and see there, and what he or she should bring.

4 Using what you've learned about French culture, decide whether the statements below are true or false.

1. Only a few French children attend summer camp.
2. French children can study foreign languages at summer camp.
3. Most French people take a one week summer vacation.
4. Small businesses may close in the summer when the owners go on vacation.

5

J E U   D E   R O L E

a. You want to take a trip for your vacation, but you're not sure where. Tell your travel agent what you like to do and what you'd like to see. The travel agent will make some suggestions about where you might go and what there is to do there. He or she will also describe the weather conditions and tell you what clothes to take, where you can stay, and when and from where you can leave. The travel agent will also remind you of things you shouldn't forget to take. Act this out with your partner. Then, change roles.

b. You've returned from your trip and your friend wants to know how it went. Tell your friend about your trip and answer any questions he or she has about what you did. Act this out with your partner and then change roles.

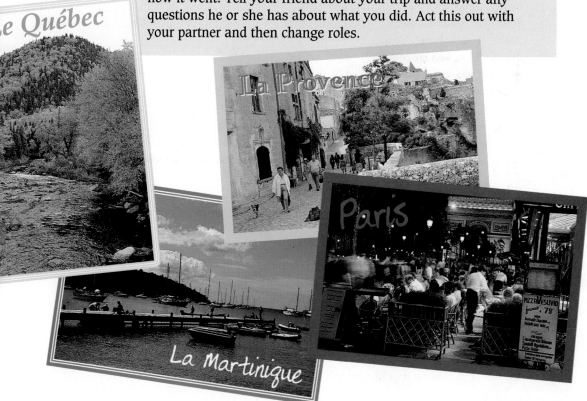

Le Québec

La Provence

Paris

La Martinique

MISE EN PRATIQUE

Can you use what you've learned in this chapter?

Can you inquire about and share future plans? Express indecision and wishes? p. 289

1 How would you ask where a friend is going on vacation and what he or she is going to do? How would you answer these questions?

2 How would you tell someone . . .
1. you're not sure what to do?   2. where you'd really like to go?

3 How would you ask a friend for advice about your vacation?

Can you ask for advice? Make, accept, and refuse suggestions? p. 290

4 How would you suggest to a friend that he or she . . .
1. go to the country?   3. work?
2. go camping?   4. go to Canada?

5 How would you accept and refuse the suggestions in number 4?

Can you remind and reassure someone? p. 293

6 How would you remind a friend to take these things on a trip?

1.   2.   3.

7 How would you reassure someone you haven't forgotten these things?

1.   2.   3.

Can you see someone off? p. 296

8 How would you tell when these people are leaving, using the verb **partir**?
1. Didier / 14h28   3. Nous / 11h15
2. Désirée et Annie / 20h46   4. Tu / 23h59

9 How would you wish someone a good trip?

Can you ask for and express opinions? p. 297

10 How would you ask a friend how his or her vacation went?

11 How would you tell how your vacation went?

Can you inquire about and relate past events? p. 297

12 How would you find out what a friend did on vacation?

13 How would you tell what you did on vacation?

PREMIERE ETAPE

Inquiring about and sharing future plans

Qu'est-ce que tu vas faire...?
What are you going to do . . . ?
Où est-ce que tu vas aller... ?
Where are you going to go . . . ?
Je vais... *I'm going to . . .*
J'ai l'intention de... *I intend to . . .*

Expressing indecision

J'hésite. *I'm not sure.*
Je ne sais pas. *I don't know.*
Je n'en sais rien. *I have no idea.*
Je n'ai rien de prévu. *I don't have any plans.*

Expressing wishes

Je voudrais bien... *I'd really like to . . .*

J'ai envie de... *I feel like . . .*

Vacation places and activities

à la montagne *to/in the mountains*
en forêt *to/in the forest*
à la campagne *to/in the countryside*
en colonie de vacances *to/at a summer camp*
au bord de la mer *to/on the coast*
chez... *to/at . . . 's house*
faire du camping *to go camping*
faire de la randonnée *to go hiking*
faire du bateau *to go sailing*

faire de la plongée *to go scuba diving*
faire de la planche à voile *to go windsurfing*
faire de la voile *to go sailing*
à *to, in (a city or place)*
en *to, in (before a feminine noun)*
au *to, in (before a masculine noun)*
aux *to, in (before a plural noun)*

Asking for advice; making, accepting, and refusing suggestions

See **Tu te rappelles?** on page 290.

DEUXIEME ETAPE

Travel items

un passeport *passport*
un billet de train *train ticket*
un billet d'avion *plane ticket*
une valise *suitcase*
de l'argent *money*
un appareil-photo *camera*
un cadeau *gift*

Reminding, reassuring

N'oublie pas... *Don't forget . . .*

Tu n'as pas oublié... ? *You didn't forget . . . ?*
Tu ne peux pas partir sans... *You can't leave without . . .*
Tu prends... ? *Are you taking . . . ?*
Ne t'en fais pas. *Don't worry.*
J'ai pensé à tout. *I've thought of everything.*
Je n'ai rien oublié. *I didn't forget anything.*
partir *to leave*

Seeing someone off

Bon voyage! *Have a good trip!*
Bonnes vacances! *Have a good vacation!*
Amuse-toi bien! *Have fun!*
Bonne chance! *Good luck!*

TROISIEME ETAPE

Asking for and expressing opinions

Tu as passé un bon... ? *Did you have a good . . . ?*
Ça s'est bien passé? *Did it go well?*
Tu t'es bien amusé(e)? *Did you have fun?*

Oui, très chouette. *Yes, very cool.*
C'était formidable! *It was great!*
Oui, ça a été. *Yes, it was OK.*
Oh, pas mauvais. *Oh, not bad.*
C'était épouvantable. *It was horrible.*
Non, pas vraiment. *No, not really.*

C'était un véritable cauchemar! *It was a real nightmare!*
C'était ennuyeux. *It was boring.*

Inquiring about and relating past events

See **Tu te rappelles?** on page 297.

Allez, viens à Fort-de-France !

La ville de Fort-de-France

Fort-de-France

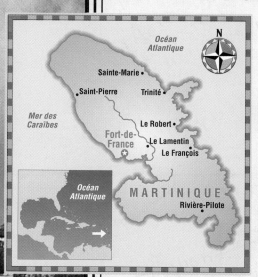

Ville principale de la Martinique

Population : plus de 100.000

Langues : français, créole

Points d'intérêt : la bibliothèque Schœlcher, le Musée Départemental, le fort Saint-Louis, la cathédrale Saint-Louis

Parcs et jardins : la Savane, le Parc floral et culturel

Spécialités : crabes farcis, blanc manger, boudin créole, accras de morue

Evénements : Carnaval, le Festival de Fort-de-France, les Tours des yoles rondes de la Martinique

Fort-de-France

Clinging to the mountains overlooking the Caribbean coast of Martinique, the city of Fort-de-France lies on the **baie des Flamands**. Nearly one-third of the population of Martinique lives in or near the city. Here you will see a blending of cultures. Although Martinique is 4,261 miles from Paris, it is a **département** of France. While its character is decidedly French, the pastel-colored buildings and wrought-iron balconies may remind you of New Orleans, and the sounds of the **créole** language and **zouk** music are purely West Indian.

① **La bibliothèque Schœlcher** is a very elaborate building constructed in a blend of byzantine, Egyptian, and romanesque styles. Like the Eiffel Tower, it was built in 1889 for the Paris Exposition. It was later dismantled and rebuilt among the palm tree Fort-de-France.

② **La Savane** is a 12½-acre landscaped park filled with tropical trees, fountains, benches, and gardens. This is the place to go to meet with friends, take a walk, or play a casual game of soccer.

③ Built on a rocky peninsula, **le fort Saint-Louis** overlooks the port of Fort-de-France.

④ Martinique is known for its colorfully printed fabrics, called **madras.**

⑤ Fresh fruits and vegetables are sold daily in the colorful **marché.**

⑥ The steeple of **la cathédrale Saint-Louis** towers over downtown Fort-de-France.

1 Regarde, c'est la cathédrale Saint-Louis!

Getting around in a new place can be difficult. Knowing where things are and how to get there makes it much easier.

② Tu pourrais passer chez le disquaire?

In this chapter you will review and practice

- pointing out places and things
- making and responding to requests; asking for advice and making suggestions
- asking for and giving directions

And you will

- listen to people giving directions
- read a story from Martinique
- write about your hometown
- find out about getting a driver's license in francophone countries

③ Pardon, monsieur. Nous cherchons le Hit Parade, s'il vous plaît.

Mise en train

Lucien

Lisette

La mère

Un petit service

Do you ever run errands for your family? What kinds of things do you have to do? Look at the pictures below and see if you can figure out what Lucien's mother, father, and sister are asking him to do.

Le père   Une voisine

1 Maman, je vais en ville. J'ai rendez-vous avec Mireille. On va passer la journée à Fort-de-France. Je vais lui faire visiter le fort Saint-Louis.

2 Avant de rentrer, passe au marché et prends de l'ananas, des oranges et des caramboles.

3 Ah, tu peux rendre ces livres à la bibliothèque aussi, s'il te plaît? Et en échange, tu me prends trois autres livres. Voilà ma carte.

Est-ce que tu peux aller à la poste et envoyer ce paquet?

Je ne sais pas si je vais avoir le temps.

BIBLIOTHÈQUE SCHŒLCHER

N° 1075
NOM LAPIQUONNE
Prénom Lisette
Né le 17 décembre 19
Adresse 29, rue Damas
Fort-de-Faam
Profession étudiante

1 Tu as compris?

Answer the following questions about **Un petit service.**

1. What are Lucien's plans for the day?
2. What are Lucien and his family talking about?
3. Is Lucien happy with the situation? Why or why not?
4. What happens at the end?

2 Qui dit quoi?

Lucien

Lisette

M. Lapiquonne

Mme Lapiquonne

1. «Tu peux aller à la boulangerie?»
2. «Tu peux rendre ces livres à la bibliothèque aussi, s'il te plaît?»
3. «Est-ce que tu peux aller à la poste et envoyer ce paquet?»
4. «Tu peux passer chez le disquaire?»
5. «Passe au marché et prends de l'ananas, des oranges et des caramboles.»
6. «Prends-moi aussi le journal.»

3 Où va-t-il?

Où est-ce que Lucien va aller pour...

1. acheter des caramboles?
2. envoyer le paquet?
3. rendre des livres?
4. acheter le disque compact?
5. acheter des baguettes?

> à la boulangerie
> à la poste
> chez le disquaire
> au marché
> à la bibliothèque

4 Vrai ou faux?

1. Lucien va acheter des caramboles, des pêches et des pommes.
2. Il va rendre des livres à la bibliothèque.
3. Lucien va à la boulangerie.
4. Lisette lui donne de l'argent pour acheter un livre.
5. Lucien va chez le disquaire pour son père.
6. Il va acheter le journal pour la voisine.

5 Cherche les expressions

According to **Un petit service,** how do you . . .

1. say you're meeting someone?
2. say you don't know if you'll have time?
3. ask someone to do something for you?
4. express your annoyance?
5. call for help?

6 Et maintenant, à toi

What errands do you do? Do you go to the same places as Lucien?

PREMIERE ETAPE

Pointing out places and things

VOCABULAIRE

Où est-ce qu'on va pour faire les courses?

à **la boulangerie** pour acheter du pain

à **la pâtisserie** pour acheter **des pâtisseries**

à **l'épicerie** pour acheter de la confiture

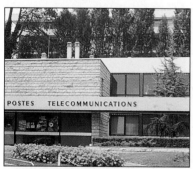

à **la poste** pour acheter **des timbres** et **envoyer des lettres**

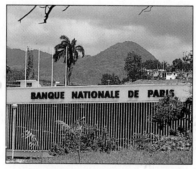

à **la banque** pour **retirer** ou **déposer** de l'argent

à **la librairie-papeterie** pour acheter des livres ou **des enveloppes**

à **la pharmacie** pour acheter **des médicaments**

chez le disquaire pour acheter des disques compacts ou des cassettes

à **la bibliothèque** pour **emprunter** ou **rendre** des livres

7 Ecoute!

Listen to these conversations and tell where the people are.

8 Un petit mot

Read this note that Frédéric wrote to his friend. Then, list three places he went and tell what he did there.

Tu te rappelles ?

Remember, **au**, **à la**, **à l'**, and **aux** mean *to the* or *at the*. Use **au** before a masculine singular noun, **à la** before a feminine singular noun, **à l'** before any singular noun beginning with a vowel sound, and **aux** before any plural noun.

Je vais
{
au musée.
à la boulangerie.
à l' épicerie.
}

Je vais
{
à l' hôtel.
aux Etats-Unis.
}

Cher Pierre,

Ici, rien de bien nouveau. Hier, mes parents sont allés passer la journée chez leurs amis, alors j'étais tout seul. J'en ai profité pour faire des courses. D'abord, je suis allé à la boulangerie acheter du pain. Ensuite, je suis allé à la poste parce que je n'avais plus de timbres, et j'en ai profité pour envoyer une lettre à Jules, mon correspondant québécois. Puis, je suis allé à la bibliothèque emprunter quelques livres parce que j'ai fini de lire toute ma collection. Je n'ai pas trouvé le dernier livre de Stephen King à la bibliothèque (il paraît qu'il est super!), alors je suis allé à la librairie pour l'acheter. Finalement, je suis passé à l'épicerie acheter des légumes et du fromage pour mon déjeuner. Voilà, c'est tout. Ecris-moi vite pour me dire comment tu trouves ton nouveau lycée. Salut.

Frédéric

9 Des courses en ville

Yvette fait des courses en ville. Où est-elle?

1. «Je voudrais ce gâteau au chocolat, s'il vous plaît.»
2. «Je voudrais emprunter ces trois livres, s'il vous plaît.»
3. «Eh bien, je voudrais des médicaments pour ma mère.»
4. «C'est combien pour envoyer cette lettre aux Etats-Unis?»
5. «Zut, alors! Elle est fermée. Je ne peux pas déposer de l'argent!»

NOTE CULTURELLE

Stores in France and Martinique don't stay open 24 hours a day. Between 12:30 P.M. and 3:30 P.M., very few small businesses are open; however, they usually remain open until 7 P.M. By law, businesses must close one day a week, usually Sunday. Only grocery stores, restaurants, and certain places related to culture and entertainment, such as museums and movie theaters, may stay open on Sunday.

10 Il va où?

a. Regarde la liste d'Armand. Où va-t-il?

b. Qu'est-ce qu'il peut acheter d'autre là où il va?

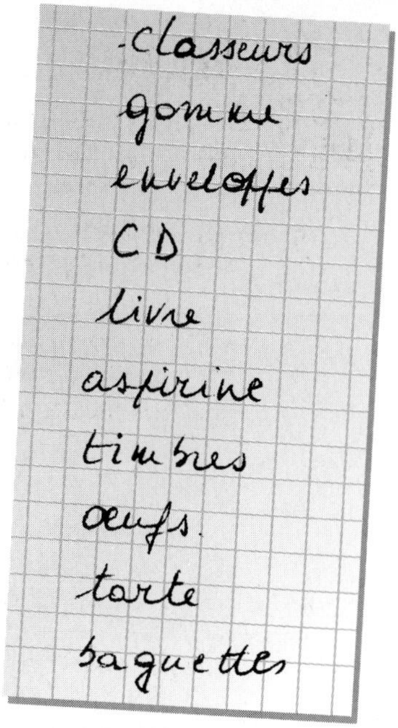

You've already learned that an ending can often help you guess the gender of a word. An ending can also help you guess the meaning of a word. For example, the ending **-erie** often indicates a place where something is sold or made. Look at these words: **poissonnerie, fromagerie, chocolaterie, croissanterie.** What do you think they mean? Another common ending that carries a particular meaning is **-eur (-euse).** It indicates a person who performs a certain activity. In French, **chasser** means *to hunt.* A person who hunts is a **chasseur.** Since **chanter** means *to sing,* how do you think you would say *singer* in French? If **danser** means *to dance,* how would you say *dancer?**

Armand's list (handwritten):
- classeurs
- gomme
- enveloppes
- CD
- livre
- aspirine
- timbres
- oeufs
- tarte
- baguettes

11 Devine!

Think of something that you bought. Then, tell your partner where you went to buy it. Your partner will try to guess what you bought there. Take turns.

Si tu as oublié le passé composé va à la page 239.

— Je suis allé(e) à la boulangerie.
— Tu as acheté des croissants?
— Non.

COMMENT DIT-ON... ?
Pointing out places and things

Voici tes timbres.
Regarde, voilà ma maison.
Look, here/there is/are . . .

Ça, c'est la banque.
This/That is . . .

Là, c'est mon disquaire préféré.
There, that is . . .

Là, tu vois, c'est la maison de mes grands-parents.
There, you see, this/that is . . .

*chanteur, danseur

12 A la Martinique

During your trip to Martinique you took the photos below. Take turns with your partner pointing out and identifying the places and objects in the photos.

le disquaire   la statue de Joséphine de Beauharnais

la pharmacie   la boulangerie

la bibliothèque Schœlcher   le marché

1.

2.

3.

4.

5.

6.

ᴬla française

When you try to communicate in a foreign language, there will always be times when you can't remember or don't know the exact word you need. One way to get around this problem is to use *circumlocution*. Circumlocution means substituting words and expressions you <u>do</u> know to explain what you mean. For example, if you can't think of the French word for *pharmacy*, you might say **l'endroit où on peut acheter des médicaments** *(the place where you can buy medicine)*. Other expressions you can use are **la personne qui/que** *(the person who/whom)*, and **le truc qui/que** *(the thing that)*.

13 Mon quartier

For an exchange student who is coming to stay with your family for a semester, draw a map of your neighborhood and label the school, post office, grocery store, and so on.

14 Jeu de rôle

As your exchange student asks where various places are, point them out on the map you made for Activity 13. Tell what you buy or do there. Take turns playing the role of the exchange student.

RENCONTRE CULTURELLE

Look at the illustrations below. Where are these people? What are they talking about?

— Bonjour, Madame Perrot. Vous avez passé de bonnes vacances?
— Très bonnes. On est allés en Guadeloupe. Vous savez, ma sœur habite là-bas, et…

— Et votre père, il va bien?
— Oui, merci. Il va beaucoup mieux depuis…

— Qu'est-ce que vous allez faire avec ça?
— Ma voisine m'a donné une très bonne recette. C'est très simple. Tout ce qu'il faut faire, c'est…

Qu'en penses-tu?

1. What are the topics of these conversations? What does this tell you about the culture of Martinique?
2. What kind of relationships do you or your family have with the people who work in your town? Do you know them? Do you often make "small talk" with them?

Savais-tu que... ?

In Martinique, as in many parts of France, people like to take the time to say hello, ask how others are doing, and find out what's going on in one another's lives. Of course, the smaller the town, the more likely this is to occur. While it may be frustrating to Americans in a hurry, especially when they are conducting business, in West Indian culture it is considered rude not to take a few minutes to engage in some polite conversation before talking business.

Making and responding to requests; asking for advice and making suggestions

COMMENT DIT-ON... ?
Making and responding to requests

To make a request:
(Est-ce que) tu peux aller au
    marché?
Tu me rapportes des timbres?
Tu pourrais passer à la poste acheter
des timbres?
    Could you go by . . . ?

To accept requests:
D'accord.
Je veux bien.
J'y vais tout de suite.
Si tu veux. *If you want.*

To decline requests:
Je ne peux pas maintenant.
**Je suis désolé(e), mais je n'ai pas le
temps.**

15 Ecoute!

Listen to the following
conversations and decide if
the person agrees to or
refuses the request.

Tu te rappelles ?

Use the partitive articles **du, de la,** and **de l'** when you
mean *some* of an item. If you mean a whole item instead of
a part of it, use the indefinite articles **un, une,** and **des. Du,
de la, de l', des, un,** and **une** usually become **de/d'** in
negative sentences.

16 Un petit service

What would these people say to ask you a favor?

1.

2.

3.

4.

17 Il me faut....

Decide which of these items you need and ask your partner to go to the appropriate store. Your partner will accept or decline your request. Take turns.

Si tu as oublié expressing need va à la page 210.

1.

2.

3.

4.

5.

6.

18 Tu pourrais me rendre un service?

Ask your classmates to do these favors for you. They will either accept or decline and make an excuse.

chercher un livre à la bibliothèque

acheter un dictionnaire de français à la librairie

acheter un CD chez le disquaire

acheter un sandwich au fast-food

acheter une règle à la papeterie

acheter des timbres à la poste

Si tu as oublié making an excuse va à la page 129.

COMMENT DIT-ON... ?

Asking for advice and making suggestions

To ask for advice on how to get somewhere:

Comment est-ce qu'on y va? *How can we get there?*

To suggest how to get somewhere:

On peut y aller en train. *We can go . . .*
On peut prendre le bus. *We can take . . .*

VOCABULAIRE

Comment est-ce qu'on y va?

en bus (m.)

à pied (m.)

à vélo (m.)

en voiture (f.)

en taxi (m.)

en bateau (m.)

en avion (m.)

en train (m.)

en métro (m.)

19 Ecoute!

Listen to these conversations. Where are these people going and how are they going to get there?

20 Comment vont-ils voyager?

1.   2.   3.   4.

*G*rammaire   The pronoun y

You've already seen the pronoun **y** *(there)* several times. Can you figure out how to use it?

> —Je vais **à la bibliothèque.** Tu y vas aussi?
> —Non, je n'y vais pas.

> —Je vais **chez le disquaire.** Tu veux y aller?
> —Non, j'y suis allé hier.

It can replace an entire phrase meaning *to, at,* or *in* any place that has already been mentioned. Place it before the conjugated verb, or, if there is an infinitive, place **y** before the infinitive: Je vais y aller demain.

21 On va en ville

How do you and your friends get to these places?

> Au cinéma? Nous y allons en bus.

au cinéma	au supermarché	à la poste	à la bibliothèque
à la piscine	au centre commercial		au stade
au parc	à la librairie	au lycée	au concert

22 Qu'est-ce qu'on fait vendredi soir?

You call your friend and invite him or her to do something Friday night. When you've decided where you want to go, talk about how to get there.

Si tu as oublié inviting *va à la page 159.*

PANORAMA CULTUREL

Lily-Christine • Québec

Emmanuel • France

Charlotte • France

Here's what some francophone people told us about obtaining a driver's license where they live.

Qu'est-ce qu'il faut faire pour avoir un permis de conduire?

«J'ai mon permis probatoire, temporaire. Je n'ai pas encore mon permis de conduire. Premièrement, pour avoir ton permis, tu suis les cours théoriques. Après ça, tu passes ton examen. Si tu passes l'examen, tu as ton permis temporaire. Après, tu suis des cours pratiques. Tu passes un examen sur route. Et puis, si tu as l'examen sur route, eh bien, tu as ton permis.»

—Lily-Christine

«Non, je n'ai pas encore de permis de conduire parce que je n'ai pas encore 16 ans. Je l'aurai peut-être, [mon] permis accompagné, à 16 ans. Autrement, [pour avoir] un permis de conduire normal, il faut attendre 18 ans en France. Pour avoir un permis de conduire, il faut passer le code. C'est un examen, quoi, c'est le code de la route. Et [il] faut passer la conduite. On est avec un moniteur. On doit faire un trajet qu'il nous indique et puis, suivant si on le fait bien ou pas, on a notre permis.»

—Emmanuel

«Il faut sans doute bien savoir ses signes, son code de la route. [Il ne faut] pas avoir la tête ailleurs souvent, enfin... [Il] faut être bien dans sa tête. Voilà.»

—Charlotte

Qu'en penses-tu?

1. What are the requirements for a driver's license in your state?
2. What means of public transportation are available in your area? Do you use them? Why or why not?
3. How does transportation influence your lifestyle? How would your lifestyle change if you lived where these people do?

Asking for and giving directions

VOCABULAIRE

le lycée   la bibliothèque   la banque

A v e n u e   Lamartine

Chez Ana   le restaurant

la papeterie   la pharmacie

V i c t o r   H u g o   le marché

A v e n u e

le cinéma   Café   le café   la poste

la boulangerie

La bibliothèque est **entre** le lycée et la banque.
La poste est **à droite du** café.
Le cinéma est **à gauche du** café.

La boulangerie est **au coin de** la rue.
Le café est **en face de** la bibliothèque.

Here are some other prepositions you may want to use to give directions:

à côté de	*next to*	**loin de**	*far from*
devant	*in front of*	**près de**	*near*
derrière	*behind*		

23   Ecoute!

Listen to the following statements and tell whether they are true or false, according to the **Vocabulaire**.

24   Qui est-ce?

Tell where a classmate is seated in your classroom. The others in your group will try to guess who it is.

> Cette personne est derrière David et à côté d'Isabelle.

Tu te rappelles ?

Do you remember how to use the preposition **de** *(of, from)*? **De** and **le** become **du**. **De** and **les** become **des**. **De** doesn't change before **la** or **l'**.

C'est près **du** musée.
C'est près **des** vélos.
C'est au coin **de la** rue Mouffetard.
La bibliothèque est à côté **de l'**école.

25 Il est perdu!

Your friend, Hervé, has a poor sense of direction. Everything is in just the opposite direction or location from what he thinks. Help him out by answering his questions.

—La poste est loin de la bibliothèque?
—Mais non, elle est près de la bibliothèque.

1. Est-ce que la papeterie est près de la pharmacie?
2. Le cinéma est devant le centre commercial?
3. La bibliothèque est à droite?
4. Est-ce que le café est derrière le stade?

26 La visite d'Arianne

Arianne a pris des photos pendant sa visite chez son oncle et sa tante. Complète les descriptions des photos avec des prépositions.

1. C'est mon oncle et ma tante dans le jardin _____ leur maison.

2. Là, _____ ma tante, c'est mon cousin Daniel.

3. Et voilà ma cousine Adeline, _____ mon oncle.

4. Il y a une boulangerie _____ leur maison. Les croissants sont délicieux le matin!

5. Leur maison est _____ une autre maison et une épicerie.

6. Il y a un parc au coin de la rue, _____ leur maison.

COMMENT DIT-ON... ?
Asking for and giving directions

To ask for directions:

Pardon, madame. La poste, **s'il vous plaît?**

Pardon, mademoiselle. Où est la banque, **s'il vous plaît?**

Pardon, monsieur. Je cherche le musée, **s'il vous plaît.** *Excuse me, sir. I'm looking for . . . please.*

To give directions:

Vous continuez jusqu'au prochain feu rouge. *You keep going until the next light.*

Vous allez tout droit jusqu'au lycée. *You go straight ahead until you get to . . .*

Vous tournez à droite. *You turn . . .*

Prenez la rue Lamartine, **puis traversez la rue** Isambert. *Take . . . Street, then cross . . . Street.*

Vous passez devant la boulangerie. *You'll pass . . .*

C'est tout de suite à gauche. *It's right there on the . . .*

27 Ecoute!

Guy is at the bus station **(la gare routière)** in Fort-de-France. Follow M. Robinet's directions, using the map on page 328. Where does Guy want to go?

NOTE CULTURELLE

In many French towns, intersections have a traffic circle at the center, which is often decorated with flowers, fountains, or statues. Vehicles enter and continue around the center island, turning off at the various streets that open into the circle. Most towns have at least one public square, often located in front of a public building or a church. Numerous cities have closed off some of the tiny streets in the **centre-ville** and made pedestrian areas where people can stroll freely, without having to worry about traffic.

28 Où est-ce?

Give directions from school to your favorite fast-food restaurant or record store. Your partner will try to guess the name of the place. Take turns.

29 Quel monument est-ce?

Your pen pal from Martinique wrote directions for you to a site that he thinks you should visit. Follow his directions on the map of Fort-de-France to find out which of these sites it is.

la bibliothèque Schœlcher

la cathédrale Saint-Louis

Quand tu sors de la gare routière, va à droite sur le boulevard du Général de Gaulle. Prends la première à droite – c'est la rue Félix Eboué – et continue tout droit. Tu vas passer devant la préfecture. Traverse l'avenue des Caraïbes et va tout droit dans la rue de la liberté jusqu'à la poste. Ensuite, tourne à droite rue Blénac et continue tout droit. Ça sera à droite, tout de suite après la rue Schœlcher.

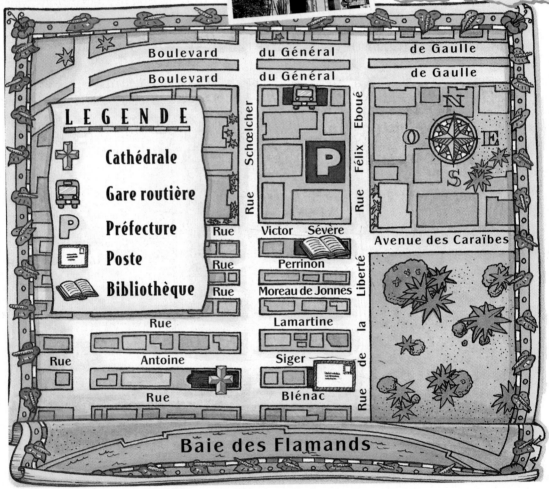

30 Mon journal

Write a description of your city or neighborhood. What does it look like? Where are things located? Draw a small map to accompany your description.

Prononciation

Do you remember what you've learned about French pronunciation? Here is a quick pronunciation review. If you've forgotten how to produce any of these sounds, check the Pronunciation Index at the back of the book and go back to the chapters where they were introduced. Repeat these words.

[y]	du	étude	[u]	rouge	voudrais
[o]	escargots	gâteau	[ɔ]	pomme	carottes
[ø]	veut	heureux	[œ]	sœur	beurre
[e]	cinéma	trouver	[ɛ]	frère	anglaise
[ã]	anglais	il prend	[ɔ̃]	allons	poisson
[ɛ]	quinze	pain	[œ̃]	lundi	emprunter
[j]	papier	viande	[w]	moi	pouvoir
[ɥ]	lui	ensuite	[t]	maths	théâtre
[r]	très	roux	[ʃ]	chat	chercher
[']	le héros	le hockey	[ɲ]	montagne	Allemagne

A. A prononcer

Repeat the following words.

1. nourriture   boutique   bateau   poste
2. feu   déposer   près   derrière
3. devant   avion   timbre   emprunter
4. pied   voiture   envoyer   tout de suite
5. rue   gauche   prochain   bibliothèque

B. A lire

Take turns with a partner reading each of the following sentences aloud.

1. Quand le chat n'est pas là, les souris dansent.
2. Il est mieux de travailler que de s'amuser.
3. Beaucoup de bruit pour rien.
4. Un poisson n'est jamais trop petit pour être frit.
5. On n'attrape pas les mouches avec du vinaigre.

C. A écrire

You're going to hear a short dialogue. Write down what you hear.

Ⓦhat kinds of stories do you like to read? Stories about the past? About the future? About exotic places?

DE BONS CONSEILS
When you read stories, newspaper and magazine articles, or novels that were written for native French speakers, you're bound to come across many unfamiliar words. Just remember to use all the reading tips that you know to try to understand what you're reading.

A. Look at the title and illustrations that accompany the text. What is this story going to be about? Where does the story take place?

B. Scan the story to see if you can find the answers to these questions.
 1. Who are the main characters in the story?
 2. What is going on when the story starts?
 3. Why does Congo come to help the horse?
 4. How does Congo help the horse?

C. Read the story carefully and then see if you can put these events in the correct order.
 1. Congo burns the blue horse.
 2. A child is frightened by the blue horse.
 3. Congo first comes to see the blue horse.
 4. M. Quinquina and his sons play music.
 5. The blue bird is freed.
 6. The mayor goes to see Congo.

Cheval de bois

Ⓒette année, la ville de Saint-Pierre accueille le manège de la famille Quinquina pour sa fête patronale. Le manège s'est

installé sur la place du marché, face à la mer. Madame Quinquina tient une buvette où elle sert des limonades multicolores.

Monsieur Quinquina et ses deux fils jouent de la flûte de bambou et du "ti-bwa". Au rythme de cette musique, le manège de chevaux de bois, poussé par de robustes jeunes gens, tourne, tourne, tourne.

Cheval bleu, bleu comme l'océan.
Cheval noir, noir comme la nuit.
Cheval blanc, blanc comme les nuages.
Cheval vert, vert comme les bambous.
Cheval rouge, rouge comme le flamboyant.
Cheval jaune, jaune comme l'allamanda.

Ⓛes chevaux de bois tournent, tournent et, sur leur dos, tous les enfants sont heureux.

Mais quand la nuit parfumée caresse l'île, les chevaux de bois rêvent. Le cheval bleu, bleu comme l'océan, rêve de partir, partir loin, visiter les îles, visiter le monde. Il a entendu dire que la terre est ronde. Vrai ou faux? Il aimerait bien savoir ! Cela fait si longtemps qu'il porte ce rêve dans sa carcasse de bois que cette nuit-là, son rêve devient oiseau. L'oiseau bat des ailes dans le corps du cheval bleu, bleu comme l'océan.

Au matin, un enfant monte sur le cheval bleu.
Tout à coup, il commence à hurler :
— Maman, maman, il y a une bête dans le cheval. J'ai peur! Je veux descendre.

On arrête la musique, on arrête le manège. C'est un tollé général : les mères rassemblent leurs enfants. En quelques secondes, la place est vide. Le maire et ses conseillers décident d'aller chercher le sage Congo.

...Congo s'approche du manège et caresse les flancs du cheval bleu, bleu comme l'océan :

— Je vais te délivrer ! cheval bleu, bleu comme l'océan, car ton rêve est vivant, il s'est métamorphosé en oiseau.

Congo s'assied près du cheval bleu, bleu comme l'océan. Quand le maire voit Congo tranquillement assis, il sort de la mairie en courant et hurle :

— Que faites-vous?

— J'attends, dit doucement Congo.

— Vous attendez quoi? demande le maire.

— J'attends que la nuit mette son manteau étoilé et ouvre son œil d'or. Je ferai alors un grand feu.

Quand la nuit met son manteau étoilé et ouvre son œil d'or, Congo prend tendrement dans ses bras le cheval bleu, bleu comme l'océan, et le dépose dans les flammes. Le feu crépite, chante, et l'or des flammes devient bleu, bleu comme l'océan. Les habitants de Saint-Pierre voient un immense oiseau bleu, bleu comme l'océan, s'élever dans la nuit étoilée et s'envoler vers l'horizon. Congo, heureux, murmure :

-Bon vent, oiseau-rêve !

RAPPEL As you read the story, you probably came across some unfamiliar words. Remember, you don't have to understand every word to get a sense of what you're reading. If you decide that the meaning of a particular word is necessary to help you understand the story, there are two techniques you've learned that can help: using the context to figure out the meaning of the word, and trying to see a cognate in the word.

D. Below are some cognates that appear in *Cheval de bois.* See if you can match them with their English equivalents.

1. habitants	a. counselors
2. fête	b. to descend; to get down
3. flammes	c. island
4. conseillers	d. festival
5. île	e. flames
6. descendre	f. inhabitants, people who live in a certain area

E. Make a list of all of the other cognates you can find in *Cheval de bois.* You should be able to find at least six more. Watch out for false cognates!

F. How can you tell this story was written for a young audience?

G. What stories, fairy tales, or myths have you read or heard that are similar to this story? In what ways are they similar? In what ways are they different?

H. Do you think there really was a bird inside the horse? What do you think the bird represents?

I. Compose a fairy tale of your own. Write it out or record it on tape in French. Keep it simple so that your teacher can use it in the future with students who are beginning to learn French! Illustrate your story to make it easier to understand.

MISE EN PRATIQUE

1   **a.**   Brigitte et Cara ont fait des courses. Qu'est-ce qu'elles ont acheté?

      b.   Qui a écrit le petit mot? La mère de Brigitte ou la mère de Cara?

Salut, chérie! Ça va aujourd'hui? Est-ce que tu pourrais faire des courses pour moi? Il me faut des timbres et des enveloppes. Tu peux passer à la poste? Le livre qu'il me faut est enfin à la bibliothèque. Tu peux aller le chercher? Tu pourrais aussi passer à la pharmacie pour prendre de l'aspirine? Merci

2   Write the dialogue that is taking place in the situation shown here.

3   Listen to Didier tell his family about his trip to Martinique. Put the pictures in order according to Didier's description.

a.   b.   c.   d.

4 You're planning a trip to Martinique and you'll need some transportation. Look at these ads. What kinds of transportation are available?

LOCATION TROIS-ILETS
Anse à l'Ane - 97229 Trois-Ilets

68.40.37
Lundi à Vendredi
8 H - 13 H
et 15 H - 18 H
Week-end :
à la demande

Avec Location TROIS-ILETS, la moto que vous avez louée par téléphone, 48 heures plus tôt, vient à vous. Chez vous. Si vous vous trouvez dans la commune des Trois-Ilets. Location possible pour une semaine au moins.

TAXI
FORT-DE-FRANCE
102 Rue de la République -
97200 Fort-de-France

70.44.08 Tous les jours : 5 H - 20 H

Nos taxis répondent sans délais quand vous téléphonez à Taxi Fort-de-France. Déplacement dans toute l'île.

LOCA CENTER
3 Km Route de Schœlcher -
97200 Fort-de-France

Livraison de voiture (Renault Super-cinq) à domicile (Nord Caraïbe, Schœlcher, Fort-de-France) pour une durée minimum de trois jours. Pas de frais de déplacement. Pendant la haute saison, pour une location de 10 jours au moins, réserver un mois à l'avance. Pour une location d'une durée de 3 à 7 jours, réserver 48 heures à l'avance. Pendant la basse saison, réserver la veille ou le jour même.

61.05.95
61.40.12
Lundi à
Vendredi
7 H 30 -
16 H 30
Week-end :
à la
demande

---

1. Where can you call if you want a taxi? When is the latest you can call?
2. Where can you call if you want to rent a Renault? What about a motorcycle?
3. What's the minimum length of time you can rent these vehicles?
4. How long in advance do you need to make a reservation?
5. Are these places open on weekends?

5

JEU DE ROLE

a. While visiting Fort-de-France, you stop at the tourist office to ask for directions to **la Savane, le Musée départemental, le Grand Marché, la cathédrale Saint-Louis,** and **le parc floral.** The employee is new, so write down the directions and ask questions if the directions aren't clear.

b. Now, pick some other sites on the island you would like to visit. Ask the employee how you can get there.

Can you use what you've learned in this chapter?

Can you point out places and things?
p. 317

1 How would you identify . . .
1. a certain building?
2. a certain store?
3. a certain person?

Can you make and respond to requests?
p. 320

2 How would you ask someone to . . .
1. buy some stamps?
2. go to the bookstore?
3. deposit some money?

3 How would you agree to do the favors you asked in number 2? How would you refuse?

4 How would you ask a friend which means of transportation you should use to get to a certain store?

Can you ask for advice and make suggestions?
p. 322

5 How would you suggest these means of transportation?

1.
2.
3.
4.

Can you ask for and give directions?
p. 327

6 How would you tell someone that you're looking for a certain place?

7 How would you ask someone where a certain place in town is?

8 How would you give someone directions to your house from . . .
1. your school?
2. your favorite fast-food restaurant?

PREMIERE ETAPE

Pointing out places and things

Voici... *Here is/are . . .*
Regarde, voilà... *Look, here/there is/are . . .*
Ça, c'est... *This/That is . . .*
Là, c'est... *There, that is . . .*
Là, tu vois, c'est... *There, you see, this/that is . . .*

Buildings

la banque *bank*

la boulangerie *bakery*
chez le disquaire *at the record store*
l'épicerie (f.) *small grocery store*
la librairie *bookstore*
la papeterie *stationery store*
la pâtisserie *pastry shop*
la pharmacie *drugstore*
la poste *post office*

Things to do or buy in town

envoyer des lettres *to send letters*

un timbre *a stamp*
retirer de l'argent (m.) *to withdraw money*
déposer de l'argent *to deposit money*
rendre *to return something*
emprunter *to borrow*
des médicaments (m.) *medicine*
une enveloppe *envelope*
une pâtisserie *pastry*

DEUXIEME ETAPE

Making and responding to requests

Tu peux... ? *Can you . . . ?*
Tu me rapportes... ? *Will you bring me . . . ?*
Tu pourrais passer à... ? *Could you go by . . . ?*
D'accord. *OK.*
Je veux bien. *Gladly.*
J'y vais tout de suite. *I'll go right away.*
Si tu veux. *If you want.*
Je ne peux pas maintenant. *I can't right now.*

Je suis désolé(e), mais je n'ai pas le temps. *I'm sorry, but I don't have time.*

Asking for advice and making suggestions

Comment est-ce qu'on y va? *How can we get there?*
On peut y aller... *We can go . . .*
On peut prendre... *We can take . . .*
y *there*

Means of transportation

en bus (m.) *by bus*
à pied (m.) *on foot*
à vélo (m.) *by bike*
en voiture (f.) *by car*
en taxi (m.) *by taxi*
en bateau (m.) *by boat*
en avion (m.) *by plane*
en train (m.) *by train*
en métro (m.) *by subway*

TROISIEME ETAPE

Asking for and giving directions

Pardon, ..., s'il vous plaît? *Excuse me, . . . please?*
Pardon, ... Où est..., s'il vous plaît? *Excuse me, . . . Where is . . . , please?*
Pardon, ... Je cherche..., s'il vous plaît. *Excuse me, . . . I'm looking for . . . , please.*
Vous continuez jusqu'au prochain feu rouge. *You keep going until the next light.*

Vous allez tout droit jusqu'à... *You go straight ahead until you get to . . .*
Vous tournez... *You turn . . .*
Prenez la rue..., puis traversez la rue... *Take . . . Street, then cross . . . Street.*
Vous passez... *You'll pass . . .*
C'est tout de suite à... *It's right there on the . . .*

Locations

à côté de *next to*
loin de *far from*
près de *close to*
au coin de *on the corner of*
en face de *across from*
derrière *behind*
devant *in front of*
entre *between*
à droite(de) *to the right*
à gauche(de) *to the left*

SUMMARY OF FUNCTIONS

Function is another word for the way in which you use language for a specific purpose. When you find yourself in specific situations, such as in a restaurant, in a grocery store, or at school, you'll want to communicate with those around you. In order to communicate in French, you have to "function" in the language.

Each chapter in this book focuses on language functions. You can easily find them in boxes labeled **Comment dit-on... ?** The other features in the chapter—grammar, vocabulary, culture notes—support the functions you're learning.

Here is a list of the functions presented in this book and their French expressions. You'll need them in order to communicate in a wide range of situations. Following each function are the numbers of the chapter and page where it was presented.

SOCIALIZING

Greeting people   **Ch. 1, p. 22**

> Bonjour.
> Salut.

Saying goodbye   **Ch. 1, p. 22**

> Salut.   A bientôt.
> Au revoir.   A demain.
> A tout à l'heure.   Tchao.

Asking how people are and telling how you are
Ch. 1, p. 23

> (Comment) ça va?   Bof.
> Ça va.   Pas mal.
> Super!   Pas terrible.
> Très bien.   Et toi?
> Comme ci, comme ça.

Extending invitations   **Ch. 6, p. 159**

> Allons... !
> Tu veux... ?
> Tu viens?
> On peut...

Accepting invitations   **Ch. 6, p. 159**

> Je veux bien.   D'accord.
> Pourquoi pas?   Bonne idée.

Refusing invitations   **Ch. 6, p. 159**

> Désolé(e), je suis occupé(e).
> Ça ne me dit rien.
> J'ai des trucs à faire.
> Desolé(e), je ne peux pas.

Identifying people   **Ch. 7, p. 179**

> C'est...
> Ce sont...
> Voici...
> Voilà...

Introducing people   **Ch. 7, p. 183**

> C'est...
> Je te/vous présente...
> Très heureux (heureuse).   (FORMAL)

Inquiring about past events   **Ch. 9, p. 238**

> Qu'est-ce que tu as fait... ?
> Tu es allé(e) où?
> Et après?
> Qu'est-ce qui s'est passé?

Relating past events   **Ch. 9, p. 238**

> D'abord,...
> Ensuite,...
> Après,...
> Je suis allé(e)...
> Et après ça,...
> Enfin,...

Inquiring about future plans   **Ch. 11, p. 289**

> Qu'est-ce que tu vas faire... ?
> Où est-ce que tu vas aller... ?

Sharing future plans   **Ch. 11, p. 289**

> J'ai l'intention de...
> Je vais...

Seeing someone off   **Ch. 11, p. 296**

> Bon voyage!
> Bonnes vacances!
> Amuse-toi bien!
> Bonne chance!

EXCHANGING INFORMATION

Asking someone's name and giving yours
Ch. 1, p. 24

> Tu t'appelles comment?
> Je m'appelle...

Asking and giving someone else's name
Ch. 1, p. 24

Il/Elle s'appelle comment?
Il/Elle s'appelle...

Asking someone's age and giving yours
Ch. 1, p. 25

Tu as quel âge?
J'ai... ans.

Asking for information   Ch. 2, pp. 51, 54

Tu as quels cours... ?
Tu as quoi... ?
Vous avez... ?
Tu as... à quelle heure?

Giving information   Ch. 2, pp. 51, 54

Nous avons...
J'ai...

Telling when you have class   Ch. 2, p. 54

à... heures
à... heures quinze
à... heures trente
à... heures quarante-cinq

Making requests   Ch. 3, p. 72

Tu as... ?
Vous avez... ?

Responding to requests   Ch. 3, p. 72

Voilà.
Je regrette.
Je n'ai pas de...

Asking others what they need and telling what you need   Ch. 3, p. 74

Qu'est-ce qu'il te faut pour... ?
Qu'est-ce qu'il vous faut pour... ?
Il me faut...

Expressing need   Ch. 8, p. 210; Ch. 10, p. 265

Qu'est-ce qu'il te faut?
Il me faut...
De quoi est-ce que tu as besoin?
J'ai besoin de...
Oui, il me faut...
Oui, vous avez... ?
Je cherche quelque chose pour...
J'aimerais... pour aller avec...
Non, merci, je regarde.

Asking for information   Ch. 3, p. 82

C'est combien?

Expressing thanks   Ch. 3, p. 82

Merci.
A votre service.

Getting someone's attention
Ch. 3, p. 82; Ch. 5, p. 135

Pardon
Excusez-moi.
... , s'il vous plaît.
Monsieur!
Madame!
Mademoiselle!

Exchanging information   Ch. 4, p. 104

Qu'est-ce que tu fais comme sport?
Qu'est-ce que tu fais pour t'amuser?
Je fais...
Je ne fais pas de...
Je (ne) joue (pas)...

Ordering food and beverages   Ch. 5, p. 135

Vous avez choisi?
Vous prenez?
Je voudrais...
Je vais prendre... , s'il vous plaît.
... , s'il vous plaît.
Donnez-moi... , s'il vous plaît.
Apportez-moi... , s'il vous plaît.
Vous avez... ?
Qu'est-ce que vous avez comme... ?
Qu'est-ce que vous avez comme boissons?

Paying the check   Ch. 5, p. 139

L'addition, s'il vous plaît.
Oui, tout de suite.
Un moment, s'il vous plaît.
Ça fait combien, s'il vous plaît?
Ça fait... francs.
C'est combien,... ?
C'est... francs.

Making plans   Ch. 6, p. 153

Qu'est-ce que tu vas faire... ?
Tu vas faire quoi... ?
Je vais...
Pas grand-chose.
Rien de spécial.

Arranging to meet someone   Ch. 6, p. 163

Quand (ça)?   et quart
tout de suite   moins le quart
Où (ça)?   moins cinq
devant   midi (et demi)
au métro...   minuit (et demi)
chez...   vers
dans...   Quelle heure est-il?
Avec qui?   Il est...
A quelle heure?   On se retrouve...
A cinq heures...   Rendez-vous...
et demie   Entendu.

Describing and characterizing people
Ch. 7, p. 185

Il est comment?
Elle est comment?

SUMMARY OF FUNCTIONS

Ils/Elles sont comment?
Il est...
Elle est...
Ils/Elles sont...

Making a telephone call Ch. 9, p. 244

Bonjour.
Je suis bien chez... ?
C'est...
(Est-ce que)... est là, s'il vous plaît?
(Est-ce que) je peux parler à... ?
Je peux laisser un message?
Vous pouvez lui dire que j'ai téléphoné?
Ça ne répond pas.
C'est occupé.

Answering a telephone call Ch. 9, p. 244

Allô?
Bonjour.
Qui est à l'appareil?
Une seconde, s'il vous plaît.
D'accord.
Bien sûr.
Vous pouvez rappeler plus tard?
Ne quittez pas.

Inquiring Ch. 10, p. 265

(Est-ce que) je peux vous aider?
Vous désirez?
Je peux l'(les) essayer?
Je peux essayer... ?
C'est combien,... ?
Ça fait combien?
Vous avez ça en... ?

Pointing out places and things Ch. 12, p. 317

Là, tu vois, c'est...
Ça, c'est...
Regarde, voilà...
Là, c'est...
Voici...

Asking for advice Ch. 12, p. 322

Comment est-ce qu'on y va?

Making suggestions Ch. 12, p. 322

On peut y aller...
On peut prendre...

Asking for directions Ch. 12, p. 327

Pardon, ..., s'il vous plaît?
Pardon, ... Où est..., s'il vous plaît?
Pardon, ... Je cherche..., s'il vous plaît.

Giving directions Ch. 12, p. 327

Vous continuez jusqu'au prochain feu rouge.
Vous tournez...
Vous allez tout droit jusqu'à...
Prenez la rue... puis traversez la rue...
Vous passez devant...
C'est tout de suite à...

EXPRESSING FEELINGS AND EMOTIONS

Expressing likes, dislikes, and preferences about things Ch. 1, pp. 26; 32

J'aime (bien)...
Je n'aime pas...
Je préfère...

J'aime mieux...
J'adore...

Ch. 5, p. 138

C'est...
  bon!
  excellent!
  délicieux!
  pas bon!
  pas terrible!
  dégoûtant!

Telling what you'd like and what you'd like to do Ch. 3, p. 77

Je voudrais...
Je voudrais acheter...

Telling how much you like or dislike something Ch. 4, p. 102

Beaucoup.
Pas beaucoup.
Pas tellement.
Pas du tout.
surtout

Inquiring about likes and dislikes Ch. 1, p. 26

Tu aimes... ?

Ch. 5, p. 138

Comment tu trouves ça?

Sharing confidences Ch. 9, p. 247

J'ai un petit problème.
Je peux te parler?
Tu as une minute?

Consoling others Ch. 9, p. 247

Je t'écoute.
Ne t'en fais pas!
Ça va aller mieux!
Qu'est-ce que je peux faire?

Making a decision Ch. 10, p. 274

Vous avez décidé de prendre... ?
Vous avez choisi?
Vous le/la/les prenez?
Je le/la/les prends.
Non, c'est trop cher.

Hesitating Ch. 10, p. 274

Euh... J'hésite.
Je ne sais pas.
Il/Elle me plaît, mais il/elle est...

Expressing indecision   Ch. 11, p. 289

J'hésite.
Je ne sais pas.
Je n'en sais rien.
Je n'ai rien de prévu.

Expressing wishes   Ch. 11, p. 289

J'ai envie de...
Je voudrais bien...

EXPRESSING ATTITUDES AND OPINIONS

Agreeing   Ch. 2, p. 50

Oui, beaucoup.
Moi aussi.
Moi non plus.

Disagreeing   Ch. 2, p. 50

Moi, non.
Non, pas trop.
Moi, si.
Pas moi.

Asking for opinions   Ch. 2, p. 57

Comment tu trouves... ?
Comment tu trouves ça?

Ch. 9, p. 237
Tu as passé un bon week-end?

Ch. 10, p. 270
Il/Elle me va?
Il/Elle te/vous plaît?
Tu aimes mieux... ou... ?

Ch. 11, p. 297
Tu as passé un bon... ?
Tu t'es bien amusé(e)?
Ça s'est bien passé?

Expressing opinions   Ch. 2, p. 57

C'est...

facile	pas terrible
génial	pas super
super	zéro
cool	barbant
intéressant	nul
passionnant	pas mal
difficile	

Ça va.

Ch. 9, p. 237
Oui, très chouette.
Oui, excellent.
Oui, très bon.
Oui, ça a été.
Ça va.
Oh, pas mauvais.

C'était épouvantable.
Très mauvais.

Ch. 11, p. 297
Oui, très chouette.
C'était formidable!
Non, pas vraiment.
C'était ennuyeux.
C'était un véritable cauchemar!

Paying a compliment   Ch. 10, p. 270

C'est tout à fait ton style.
Il/Elle te/vous va très bien.
Il/Elle va très bien avec...
Je le/la/les trouve...
C'est...

Criticizing   Ch. 10, p. 270

Il/Elle ne te/vous va pas du tout.
Il/Elle ne va pas du tout avec...
Il/Elle est (Ils/Elles sont) trop...
Je le/la/les trouve...

PERSUADING

Making suggestions   Ch. 4, p. 110

On... ?
On fait... ?
On joue... ?

Ch. 5, p. 129
On va... ?

Accepting suggestions   Ch. 4, p. 110

D'accord.
Bonne idée.
Oui, c'est...
Allons-y!

Turning down suggestions; making excuses
Ch. 4, p. 110

Non, c'est...
Ça ne me dit rien.
Désolé(e), mais je ne peux pas.

Ch. 5. p. 129
Désolé(e). J'ai des devoirs à faire.
J'ai des courses à faire.
J'ai des trucs à faire.
J'ai des tas de choses à faire.

Making a recommendation   Ch. 5, p. 132

Prends...
Prenez...
prendre

Asking for permission   Ch. 7, p. 189

Tu es d'accord?
(Est-ce que) je peux... ?

Giving permission   Ch. 7, p. 189

Oui, si tu veux.
Pourquoi pas?
D'accord, si tu... d'abord...
Oui, bien sûr.

Refusing permission   Ch. 7, p. 189

Pas question!
Non, c'est impossible.
Non, tu dois...
Pas ce soir.

Making requests   Ch. 8, p. 212

Tu peux aller faire les courses?
Tu me rapportes... ?

Ch. 12, p. 320
Est-ce que tu peux... ?
Tu pourrais passer à... ?

Accepting requests   Ch. 8, p. 212

Pourquoi pas?
Bon, d'accord.
Je veux bien.
J'y vais tout de suite.

Ch. 12, p. 320
D'accord.
Si tu veux.

Declining requests   Ch. 8, p. 212

Je ne peux pas maintenant.
Je regrette, mais je n'ai pas le temps.
J'ai des tas de choses (trucs) à faire.

Ch. 12, p. 320
Non, je ne peux pas.
Je suis désolé(e), mais je n'ai pas le temps.

Telling someone what to do   Ch. 8, p. 212

Rapporte(-moi)...
Prends...
Achète(-moi)...
N'oublie pas de...

Offering food   Ch. 8, p. 219

Tu veux... ?
Vous voulez... ?
Vous prenez ... ?
Tu prends... ?
Encore de... ?

Accepting food   Ch. 8, p. 219

Oui, s'il vous/te plaît.
Oui, avec plaisir.
Oui, j'en veux bien.

Refusing food   Ch. 8, p. 219

Non, merci.
Non, merci. Je n'ai plus faim.
Je n'en veux plus.

Asking for advice   Ch. 9, p. 247

A ton avis, qu'est-ce que je fais?
Qu'est-ce que tu me conseilles?

Ch. 10, p. 264
Je ne sais pas quoi mettre pour...
Qu'est-ce que je mets?

Giving advice   Ch. 9, p. 247

Oublie-le/-la/-les!
Téléphone-lui/-leur!
Tu devrais...
Pourquoi tu ne... pas?

Ch. 10, p. 264
Pourquoi est-ce que tu ne mets pas... ?
Mets...

Reminding   Ch. 11, p. 293

N'oublie pas...
Tu n'as pas oublié... ?
Tu ne peux pas partir sans...
Tu prends... ?

Reassuring   Ch. 11, p. 293

Ne t'en fais pas.
J'ai pensé à tout.
Je n'ai rien oublié.

SUPPLEMENTARY VOCABULARY

This list presents additional vocabulary you may want to use when you're working on the activities in the textbook and workbook. It also includes the optional vocabulary labeled **Vocabulaire à la carte** that appears in several chapters. If you can't find the words you need here, try the English-French and French-English vocabulary lists beginning on page 352.

ADJECTIVES

absurd *absurde*
awesome (impressive) *impressionnant(e)*
boring *ennuyeux (ennuyeuse)*
chilly *froid(e), frais* (m.)/*fraîche* (f.)
colorful (thing) *vif (vive)*
despicable *méprisable*
eccentric *excentrique*
incredible *incroyable*
tasteless (flavor) *insipide;* (remark, object) *de mauvais goût*
tasteful (remark, object) *de bon goût*
terrifying *terrifiant(e)*
threatening *menaçant(e)*
tremendous (excellent) *formidable*
unforgettable *inoubliable*
unique *unique*

CLOTHING

blazer *un blazer*
button *un bouton*
coat *un manteau*
collar *le col*
eyeglasses *des lunettes* (f.)
gloves *des gants* (m.)
handkerchief *un mouchoir*
high-heeled shoes *des chaussures* (f.) *à talons*
lace *de la dentelle*
linen *le lin*
nylon *le nylon*
pajamas *un pyjama*
polyester *le polyester*
raincoat *un imperméable*
rayon *la rayonne*
sale (discount) *les soldes* (m.)
silk *la soie*
sleeve *une manche*
slippers *des pantoufles* (f.)
suit (man's) *un costume;* (woman's) *un tailleur*
suspenders *des bretelles* (f.)
velvet *le velours*
vest *un gilet*
wool *la laine*
zipper *une fermeture éclair*

COLORS AND PATTERNS

beige *beige*

checked *à carreaux*
colorful *coloré(e), vif/vive*
dark blue *bleu foncé*
dark-colored *foncé*
flowered *à fleurs*
gold (adj.) *d'or, doré*
light blue *bleu clair*
light-colored *clair*
patterned *à motifs*
polka-dotted *à pois*
striped *à rayures*
turquoise *turquoise*

ENTERTAINMENT

blues *le blues*
CD player *un lecteur de CD*
flash *un flash*
folk music *la musique folklorique*
headphones *les écouteurs*
hit (song) *un tube*
lens *l'objectif* (m.)
microphone *un micro(phone)*
opera *l'opéra* (m.)
pop music *la musique pop*
reggae *le reggae*
roll of film *une pellicule (photo)*
screen *l'écran* (m.)
speakers *des enceintes* (f.), *des baffles* (m.)
to turn off *éteindre*
to turn on *allumer*
turntable *une platine*
walkman *un walkman*

FAMILY

adopted *adopté(e), adoptif (adoptive)*
brother-in-law *le beau-frère*
child *un(e) enfant*
couple *un couple*
daughter-in-law *la belle-fille*
divorced *divorcé(e)*
engaged *fiancé(e)*
godfather *le parrain*
godmother *la marraine*
grandchildren *les petits-enfants*
granddaughter *la petite-fille*
grandson *le petit-fils*
great-granddaughter *l'arrière-petite-fille* (f.)

great-grandfather   *l'arrière-grand-père* (m.)
great-grandmother   *l'arrière-grand-mère* (f.)
great-grandson   *l'arrière-petit-fils* (m.)
half-brother   *un demi-frère*
half-sister   *une demi-sœur*
husband   *le mari*
mother-in-law   *la belle-mère*
only child   *un/une enfant unique*
single   *célibataire*
sister-in-law   *la belle-sœur*
son-in-law   *le gendre; le beau-fils*
stepbrother   *le demi-frère*
stepdaughter   *la belle-fille*
stepfather   *le beau-père*
stepmother   *la belle-mère*
stepsister   *une demi-sœur*
stepson   *le beau-fils*
widow   *une veuve*
widower   *un veuf*
wife   *la femme*

FOODS AND BEVERAGES

appetizer   *une entrée*
apricot   *un abricot*
asparagus   *des asperges* (f.)
bacon   *du bacon*
beef   *du bœuf*
bowl   *un bol*

Brussels sprouts   *des choux* (m.) *de Bruxelles*
cabbage   *du chou*
cauliflower   *du chou-fleur*
cereal   *des céréales* (f.)
chestnut   *un marron*
cookie   *un biscuit*
cucumber   *un concombre*
cutlet   *une escalope*
fried eggs   *des œufs au plat;* **hard-boiled egg**   *un œuf dur;* **scrambled eggs**   *des œufs brouillés;* **soft-boiled egg**   *un œuf à la coque*
eggplant   *une aubergine*
French bread   *une baguette*
fruit   *un fruit*
garlic   *de l'ail* (m.)
grapefruit   *un pamplemousse*
honey   *du miel*
liver   *du foie*
margarine   *de la margarine*
marshmallows   *des guimauves* (f.)
mayonnaise   *de la mayonnaise*
medium (cooked)   *à point*
melon   *un melon*
mustard   *de la moutarde*
nuts   *des noix*
onion   *un oignon*
peanut butter   *du beurre de cacahouètes*
popcorn   *du pop-corn*
potato chips   *des chips* (f.)
raspberry   *une framboise*
salmon   *du saumon*
salt   *du sel*
pepper (spice)   *du poivre;* (vegetable) *un poivron*

shellfish   *des fruits* (m.) *de mer*
soup   *de la soupe*
spinach   *des épinards* (m.)
spoon   *une cuillère*
syrup   *du sirop*
veal   *du veau*
watermelon   *une pastèque*
zucchini   *une courgette*
bland   *doux (douce)*
hot (spicy)   *épicé(e)*
juicy (fruit)   *juteux (juteuse);* (meat)   *tendre*
rare (cooked)   *saignant*
medium (cooked)   *à point*
spicy   *épicé(e)*
well-done (cooked)   *bien cuit(e)*
tasty   *savoureux (savoureuse)*

HOUSEWORK

to clean   *nettoyer*
to dry   *faire sécher*
to dust   *faire la poussière*
to fold   *plier*
to hang   *pendre*
to iron   *repasser*
to put away   *ranger*
to rake   *ratisser*
to shovel   *enlever à la pelle*
to sweep   *balayer*

PETS

bird   *un oiseau*
cow   *une vache*
frog   *une grenouille*
goldfish   *un poisson rouge*
guinea-pig   *un cochon d'Inde*
hamster   *un hamster*
horse   *un cheval*
kitten   *un chaton*
lizard   *un lézard*
mouse   *une souris*
parrot   *un perroquet*
pig   *un cochon*
puppy   *un chiot*
rabbit   *un lapin*
turtle   *une tortue*

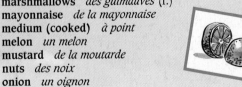

PLACES AROUND TOWN

airport   *un aéroport*
beauty shop   *le salon de coiffure*
bridge   *un pont*
church   *l'église* (f.)
consulate   *le consulat*
hospital   *l'hôpital* (m.)
mosque   *la mosquée*
police station   *le commissariat de police*

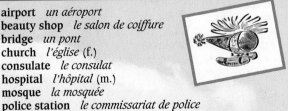

synagogue   *la synagogue*
tourist office   *l'office du tourisme* (m.)
town hall   *l'hôtel* (m.) *de ville*

PROFESSIONS

Note: If only one form is given, that form is used for both men and women. Note that you can also say **une femme banquier, une femme médecin,** and so forth.

archaeologist   *un(e) archéologue*
architect   *un(e) architecte*
athlete   *un(e) athlète*
banker   *un banquier*
businessman/businesswoman   *un homme d'affaires (une femme d'affaires)*
danser   *un danseur (une danseuse)*
dentist   *un(e) dentiste*
doctor   *un médecin*
editor   *un rédacteur (une rédactrice)*
engineer   *un ingénieur*
fashion designer   *un(e) styliste de mode*
fashion model   *un mannequin*
hairdresser   *un coiffeur, une coiffeuse*
homemaker   *un homme au foyer/une femme au foyer*
lawyer   *un(e) avocat(e)*
manager   (company)   *le directeur (la directrice);* (store, restaurant)   *le gérant (la gérante)*
mechanic   *un mécanicien*
painter   (art)   *un peintre;* (buildings)   *un peintre en bâtiment*
pilot   *un pilote*
plumber   *un plombier*
scientist   *un(e) scientifique*
secretary   *un(e) secrétaire*
social worker   *un assistant social (une assistante sociale)*
taxi driver   *un chauffeur de taxi*
technician   *un technicien (une technicienne)*
truck driver   *un routier*
veterinarian   *un(e) vétérinaire*
worker   *un ouvrier (une ouvrière)*
writer   *un écrivain*

SCHOOL SUBJECTS

accounting   *la comptabilité*
business   *le commerce*
home economics   *les arts ménagers* (m.)
languages   *les langues* (f.)
marching band   *la fanfare*
orchestra   *l'orchestre* (m.)
shorthand   *la sténographie*
social studies   *les sciences sociales* (f.)
typing   *la dactylographie*
woodworking   *la menuiserie*
world history   *l'histoire mondiale* (f.)

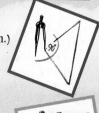

SCHOOL SUPPLIES

calendar   *un calendrier*
colored pencils   *des crayons* (m.) *de couleur*
compass   *un compas*
correction fluid   *du liquide correcteur*
glue   *de la colle*
gym suit   *une tenue de gymnastique*
marker   *un feutre*
rubber band   *un élastique*
scissors   *des ciseaux* (m.)
staple   *une agrafe*
stapler   *une agrafeuse*
transparent tape   *du ruban adhésif* (m.)

SPORTS AND INTERESTS

badminton   *le badminton*
boxing   *la boxe*
fishing rod   *une canne à pêche*
foot race   *une course à pied*
to go for a ride   (by bike, car, motorcycle, moped)   *faire une promenade, faire un tour (à bicyclette, en voiture, à moto, à vélomoteur)*
to do gymnastics   *faire de la gymnastique*
hunting   *la chasse*
to lift weights   *soulever des haltères*
mountain climbing   *l'alpinisme* (m.)
to play cards   *jouer aux cartes*
to play checkers   *jouer aux dames*
to play chess   *jouer aux échecs*
to ride a skateboard   *faire de la planche à roulettes*
to sew   *coudre; faire de la couture*
speed skating   *le patinage de vitesse*
to surf   *faire du surf*

WEATHER

barometer   *le baromètre*
blizzard   *une tempête de neige*
cloudy   *nuageux*
drizzle   *la bruine*
fog   *le brouillard*
It's sleeting.   *Il tombe de la neige fondue.*
frost   *la gelée*
hail   *la grêle* to hail   *grêler*
heat wave   *la canicule*
hurricane   *un ouragan*
ice   (on the road)   *le verglas*
It's pouring.   *Il pleut à verse.*
lightning bolt   *un éclair*
mist   *la brume*
shower   (rain)   *une averse*
storm   *une tempête*
sunny   *Il fait du soleil.*
thermometer   *un thermomètre*
thunder   *le tonnerre*
thunderstorm   *un orage*
tornado   *une tornade*

CITIES

Algiers *Alger*
Brussels *Bruxelles*
Cairo *Le Caire*
Geneva *Genève*
Lisbon *Lisbonne*
London *Londres*
Montreal *Montréal*
Moscow *Moscou*
New Orleans *La Nouvelle-Orléans*
Quebec City *Québec*
Tangier *Tanger*
Venice *Venise*
Vienna *Vienne*

THE CONTINENTS

Africa *l'Afrique* (f.)
Antarctica *l'Antarctique* (f.)
Asia *l'Asie* (f.)
Australia *l'Océanie* (f.)
Europe *l'Europe* (f.)
North America *l'Amérique* (f.) *(du Nord)*
South America *l'Amérique* (f.) *(du Sud)*

COUNTRIES

Algeria *l'Algérie* (f.)
Argentina *l'Argentine* (f.)
Australia *l'Australie* (f.)
Austria *l'Autriche* (f.)
Belgium *la Belgique*
Brazil *le Brésil*
Canada *le Canada*
China *la Chine*
Egypt *l'Egypte* (f.)
England *l'Angleterre* (f.)
France *la France*
Germany *l'Allemagne* (f.)
Greece *la Grèce*
Holland *la Hollande*
India *l'Inde* (f.)
Ireland *l'Irlande* (f.)
Israel *Israël* (m.) *(no article)*
Italy *l'Italie* (f.)
Ivory Coast *la République de Côte d'Ivoire*
Jamaica *la Jamaïque*
Japan *le Japon*
Jordan *la Jordanie*
Lebanon *le Liban*
Libya *la Libye*
Luxembourg *le Luxembourg*
Mexico *le Mexique*
Monaco *Monaco* (f.) *(no article)*
Morocco *le Maroc*
Netherlands *les Pays-Bas* (m.)
North Korea *la Corée du Nord*
Peru *le Pérou*
Philippines *les Philippines* (f.)

Poland *la Pologne*
Portugal *le Portugal*
Russia *la Russie*
Senegal *le Sénégal*
South Korea *la Corée du Sud*
Spain *l'Espagne* (f.)
Switzerland *la Suisse*
Syria *la Syrie*
Tunisia *la Tunisie*
Turkey *la Turquie*
United States *les Etats-Unis* (m.)
Vietnam *le Viêt-Nam*

STATES

California *la Californie*
Florida *la Floride*
Georgia *la Géorgie*
Louisiana *la Louisiane*
New Mexico *le Nouveau Mexique*
North Carolina *la Caroline du Nord*
Pennsylvania *la Pennsylvanie*
South Carolina *la Caroline du Sud*
Virginia *la Virginie*

OCEANS AND SEAS

Atlantic Ocean *l'Atlantique* (m.), *l'océan* (m.)
   Atlantique
Caribbean Sea *la mer des Caraïbes*
English Channel *la Manche*
Indian Ocean *l'océan* (m.) *Indien*
Mediterranean Sea *la mer Méditerranée*
Pacific Ocean *le Pacifique, l'océan* (m.) *Pacifique*

OTHER GEOGRAPHICAL TERMS

Alps *les Alpes* (f.)
border *la frontière*
capital *la capitale*
continent *un continent*
country *un pays*
hill *une colline*
lake *un lac*
latitude *la latitude*
longitude *la longitude*
mountain *une montagne*
North Africa *l'Afrique* (f.) *du Nord*
ocean *l'océan* (m.)
plain *une plaine*
Pyrenees *les Pyrénées* (f.)
river *une rivière, un fleuve*
sea *la mer*
state *un état*
the North Pole *le pôle Nord*
the South Pole *le pôle Sud*
valley *une vallée*

GRAMMAR SUMMARY

ARTICLES

SINGULAR		PLURAL	
MASCULINE	FEMININE	MASCULINE	FEMININE
un frère un ami	une sœur une amie	des frères des amis	des sœurs des amies
le frère l'ami	la sœur l'amie	les frères les amis	les sœurs les amies
ce frère cet ami	cette sœur cette amie	ces frères ces amis	ces sœurs ces amies

ADJECTIVES: FORMATION OF FEMININE

	MASCULINE	FEMININE
Most adjectives (add -**e**)	Il est brun.	Elle est brune.
Most adjectives ending in -**é** (add -**e**)	Il est démodé.	Elle est démodée.
All adjectives ending in an unaccented -**e** (no change)	Il est jeune.	Elle est jeune.
Most adjectives ending in -**eux** (-**eux** → -**euse**)	Il est délicieux.	Elle est délicieuse.
All adjectives ending in -**ien** (-**ien** → -**ienne**)	Il est ivoirien.	Elle est ivoirienne.

ADJECTIVES AND NOUNS: FORMATION OF PLURAL

		MASCULINE	FEMININE
Most noun and adjective forms	SING. PL.	un pantalon vert des pantalons verts	une jupe verte des jupes vertes
All noun and masculine adjective forms ending in **-eau**	SING. PL.	le nouveau manteau les nouveaux manteaux	la nouvelle robe les nouvelles robes
All noun and masculine adjective forms ending in **-s**	SING. PL.	un bus gris des bus gris	une maison grise des maisons grises
All masculine adjective forms ending in **-x**	SING. PL.	un garçon heureux des garçons heureux	une fille heureuse des filles heureuses

POSSESSIVE ADJECTIVES

SINGULAR		PLURAL		SINGULAR		PLURAL	
MASCULINE	FEMININE	MASCULINE	FEMININE	MASCULINE	FEMININE	MASCULINE	FEMININE
mon frère	ma sœur	mes frères	mes sœurs	notre frère	notre sœur	nos frères	nos sœurs
mon ami	mon amie	mes amis	mes amies			nos amis	nos amies
ton frère	ta sœur	tes frères	tes sœurs	votre frère	votre sœur	vos frères	vos sœurs
ton ami	ton amie	tes amis	tes amies			vos amis	vos amies
son frère	sa sœur	ses frères	ses sœurs	leur frère	leur sœur	leurs frères	leurs sœurs
son ami	son amie	ses amis	ses amies			leurs amis	leurs amies

CONTRACTIONS WITH à AND de

à or **de** + article =	CONTRACTION
à + le =	**au**
à + la =	à la (no contraction)
à + l' =	à l' (no contraction)
à + les =	**aux**
de + le =	**du**
de + la =	de la (no contraction)
de + l' =	de l' (no contraction)
de + les =	**des**

PRONOUNS

INDEPENDENT PRONOUNS	SUBJECT PRONOUNS	DIRECT OBJECT PRONOUNS	INDIRECT OBJECT PRONOUNS	PRONOUN REPLACING à, dans, sur... + noun phrase	PRONOUN REPLACING de + noun phrase
moi toi lui elle	je (j') tu il elle on	le la	lui lui		
	nous vous ils elles	les les	leur leur	y	en

REGULAR VERBS

	STEM	ENDING	STEM	ENDING	STEM	ENDING	STEM	ENDING
INFINITIVE	aim	-er	sort	-ir	chois	-ir	répond	-re
PRESENT	aim	-e -es -e -ons -ez -ent	sor sort	-s -s -t -ons -ez -ent	chois	-is -is -it -issons -issez -issent	répond	-s -s — -ons -ez -ent
REQUESTS COMMANDS SUGGESTIONS	aim	-e -ons -ez	sor sort	-s -ons -ez	chois	-is -issons -issez	répond	-s -ons -ez

Verbs like **sortir: dormir, partir**

		AUXILIARY	PAST PARTICIPLE
PASSE COMPOSE	with **avoir**	ai as a avons avez ont	aim -é chois -i répond -u

VERB INDEX

VERBS WITH STEM AND SPELLING CHANGES

Verbs listed in this section are not irregular, but they do show some stem and spelling changes. The forms in which the changes occur are printed in boldface type.

Acheter	(to buy)
Present	**achète, achètes, achète,** achetons, achetez, **achètent**
Commands	**achète,** achetons, achetez
Passé Composé	Auxiliary: avoir
	Past Participle: acheté

Essayer	(to try)
Present	**essaie, essaies, essaie,** essayons, essayez, **essaient**
Commands	**essaie,** essayons, essayez
Passé Composé	Auxiliary: avoir
	Past Participle: essayé

Appeler	(to call)
Present	**appelle, appelles, appelle,** appelons, appelez, **appellent**
Commands	**appelle,** appelons, appelez

Manger	(to eat)
Present	mange, manges, mange, **mangeons,** mangez, mangent
Commands	mange, **mangeons,** mangez

Commencer	(to start)
Present	commence, commences, commence, **commençons,** commencez, commencent
Commands	commence, **commençons,** commencez
Passé Composé	Auxiliary: avoir
	Past Participle: commencé

Préférer	(to prefer)
Present	**préfère, préfères, préfère,** préférons, préférez, **préfèrent**
Commands	**préfère,** préférons, préférez
Passé Composé	Auxiliary: avoir
	Past Participle: préféré

VERBS WITH IRREGULAR FORMS

Verbs listed in this section are those that do not follow the pattern of verbs like **aimer,** verbs like **choisir,** verbs like **sortir,** or verbs like **répondre.**

Aller	(to go)
Present	vais, vas, va, allons, allez, vont
Commands	va, allons, allez
Passé Composé	Auxiliary: être
	Past Participle: allé

Devoir	(to have to)
Present	dois, dois, doit, devons, devez, doivent
Commands	dois, devons, devez
Passé Composé	Auxiliary: avoir
	Past Participle: dû

Avoir	(to have)
Present	ai, as, a, avons, avez, ont
Commands	aie, ayons, ayez
Passé Composé	Auxiliary: avoir
	Past Participle: eu

Dire	(to say, tell)
Present	dis, dis, dit, disons, dites, disent
Commands	dis, disons, dites
Passé Composé	Auxiliary: avoir
	Past Participle: dit

Ecrire	*(to write)*		**Pouvoir**	*(to be able, can)*

Ecrire *(to write)*
Present écris, écris, écrit, écrivons, écrivez, écrivent
Commands écris, écrivons, écrivez
Passé Composé *Auxiliary:* avoir
Past Participle: écrit

Etre *(to be)*
Present suis, es, est, sommes, êtes, sont
Commands sois, soyons, soyez
Passé Composé *Auxiliary:* avoir
Past Participle: été

Faire *(to make, to do)*
Present fais, fais, fait, faisons, faites, font
Commands fais, faisons, faites
Passé Composé *Auxiliary:* avoir
Past Participle: fait

Lire *(to read)*
Present lis, lis, lit, lisons, lisez, lisent
Commands lis, lisons, lisez
Passé Composé *Auxiliary:* avoir
Past Participle: lu

Mettre *(to put, to put on)*
Present mets, mets, met, mettons, mettez, mettent
Commands mets, mettons, mettez
Passé Composé *Auxiliary:* avoir
Past Participle: mis

Pouvoir *(to be able, can)*
Present peux, peux, peut, pouvons, pouvez, peuvent
Passé Composé *Auxiliary:* avoir
Past Participle: pu

Prendre *(to take)*
Present prends, prends, prend, prenons, prenez, prennent
Commands prends, prenons, prenez
Passé Composé *Auxiliary:* avoir
Past Participle: pris

Venir *(to come)*
Present viens, viens, vient, venons, venez, viennent
Commands viens, venons, venez
Passé Composé *Auxiliary:* être
Past Participle: venu

Voir *(to see)*
Present vois, vois, voit, voyons, voyez, voient
Commands vois, voyons, voyez
Passé Composé *Auxiliary:* avoir
Past Participle: vu

Vouloir *(to want)*
Present veux, veux, veut, voulons, voulez, veulent
Passé Composé *Auxiliary:* avoir
Past Participle: voulu

PRONUNCIATION INDEX

CHAPTER	LETTER COMBINATION	IPA SYMBOL	EXAMPLE
Ch. 1, p. 35 Intonation			
Ch. 2, p. 59 Liaison			vous_avez des_amis
Ch. 3, p. 83 The r sound	the letter r	/ʀ/	rouge vert
Ch. 4, p. 113 The sounds [y] and [u]	the letter u the letter combination ou	/y/ /u/	une nous
Ch. 5, p. 141 The nasal sound [ã]	the letter combination an the letter combination am the letter combination en the letter combination em	/ã/	anglais jambon comment temps
Ch. 6, p. 167 The vowel sounds [ø] and [œ]	the letter combination eu the letter combination eu	/ø/ /œ/	deux heure
Ch. 7, p. 191 The nasal sounds [ɔ̃], [ɛ̃], and [œ̃]	the letter combination on the letter combination om the letter combination in the letter combination im the letter combination ain the letter combination aim the letter combination (i)en the letter combination un the letter combination um	/ɔ̃/ /ɛ̃/ /œ̃/	pardon nombre cousin impossible copain faim bien lundi humble
Ch. 8, p. 221 The sounds [o] and [ɔ]	the letter combination au the letter combination eau the letter ô the letter o	/o/ /ɔ/	jaune beau rôle carotte
Ch. 9, p. 249 The vowel sounds [e] and [ɛ]	the letter combination ez the letter combination er the letter combination ait the letter combination ais the letter combination ei the letter ê	/e/ /ɛ/	apportez trouver fait français neige bête
Ch. 10, p. 275 The glides [j], [w], and [ɥ]	the letter i the letter combination ill the letter combination oi the letter combination oui the letter combination ui	/j/ /w/ /ɥ/	mieux maillot moi Louis huit
Ch. 11, p. 299 h, th, ch, and gn	the letter h the letter combination th the letter combination ch the letter combination gn	/'/ /t/ /ʃ/ /ɲ/	les halls théâtre chocolat oignon
Ch. 12, p. 329 Review			

NUMBERS

LES NOMBRES CARDINAUX

0	zéro	20	vingt	80	quatre-vingts
1	un(e)	21	vingt et un(e)	81	quatre-vingt-un(e)
2	deux	22	vingt-deux	82	quatre-vingt-deux
3	trois	23	vingt-trois	90	quatre-vingt-dix
4	quatre	24	vingt-quatre	91	quatre-vingt-onze
5	cinq	25	vingt-cinq	92	quatre-vingt-douze
6	six	26	vingt-six	100	cent
7	sept	27	vingt-sept	101	cent un
8	huit	28	vingt-huit	200	deux cents
9	neuf	29	vingt-neuf	300	trois cents
10	dix	30	trente	800	huit cents
11	onze	31	trente et un(e)	900	neuf cents
12	douze	32	trente-deux	1.000	mille
13	treize	40	quarante	2.000	deux mille
14	quatorze	50	cinquante	3.000	trois mille
15	quinze	60	soixante	10.000	dix mille
16	seize	70	soixante-dix	19.000	dix-neuf mille
17	dix-sept	71	soixante et onze	40.000	quarante mille
18	dix-huit	72	soixante-douze	500.000	cinq cent mille
19	dix-neuf	73	soxiante-treize	1.000.000	un million

- The word **et** is used only in 21, 31, 41, 51, 61, and 71.
- **Vingt (trente, quarante,** and so on) **et une** is used when the number refers to a feminine noun: **trente et une cassettes.**
- The **s** is dropped from **quatre-vingts** and is not added to multiples of **cent** when these numbers are followed by another number: **quatre-vingt-cinq; deux cents,** *but* **deux cent six.** The number **mille** never takes an **s: deux mille insectes.**
- **Un million** is followed by **de** + a noun: **un million de francs.**
- In writing numbers, a period is used in French where a comma is used in English.

LES NOMBRES ORDINAUX

1er, 1ère	premier, première	9e	neuvième	17e	dix-septième
2e	deuxième	10e	dixième	18e	dix-huitième
3e	troisième	11e	onzième	19e	dix-neuvième
4e	quatrième	12e	douzième	20e	vingtième
5e	cinquième	13e	treizième	21e	vingt et unième
6e	sixième	14e	quatorzième	22e	vingt-deuxième
7e	septième	15e	quinzième	30e	trentième
8e	huitième	16e	seizième	40e	quarantième

FRENCH-ENGLISH VOCABULARY

This list includes both active and passive vocabulary in this textbook. Active words and phrases are those listed in the **Vocabulaire** section at the end of each chapter. You are expected to know and be able to use active vocabulary. All entries in black heavy type in this list are active. All other words are passive. Passive vocabulary is for recognition only.

The number after each entry refers to the chapter where the word or phrase is introduced. Verbs are given in the infinitive. Nouns are always given with an article. If it is not clear whether the noun is masculine or feminine, *m.* (masculine) or *f.* (feminine) follow the noun. Irregular plurals are also given, indicated by *pl.* An asterisk (*) before a word beginning with *h* indicates an aspirate *h*. Phrases are alphabetized by the key word(s) in the phrase.

The following abbreviations are used in this vocabulary: pl. (plural), pp. (past participle), and inv. (invariable).

A

à *to, in (a city or place)*, 11; à côté de *next to*, 3; **à la** *to, at*, 6; **A bientôt.** *See you soon.* 1; **A demain.** *See you tomorrow.* 1; à la carte *pick and choose*, 3; à la française *French-style*, 1; **à la mode** *in style*, 10; **A quelle heure?** *At what time?* 6; **A tout à l'heure!** *See you later!* 1; **A votre service.** *At your service; You're welcome*, 3; de 0 à 20 *from 0 to 20*, 0; Et maintenant, à toi. *And now, it's your turn*, 1

l' **abbaye** (f.) *abbey*, 6
abîmer *to ruin*, 10
abonnez: abonnez-vous à... *subscribe to . . .* , 3
l' **abricot** (m.) *apricot*, 5
absent *absent*, 2
accompagner *to accompany*, 4
accueille (accueillir) *to welcome*
l' **accueil** (m.) *reception, welcome*, 4
acheter *to buy*, 9; **Achète (-moi)...** *Buy me . . .* , 8; Je n'achète pas... *I won't buy . . .* , 3
l' **activité** (f.) *activity*, 4
l' **addition** (f.): **L'addition, s'il vous plaît.** *The check please.* 5
adorer *to adore*, 1; **J'adore...** *I adore . . .* 1
adorerais: J'adorerais *I would adore*, 1
l' **aérobic: faire de l'aérobic** *to do aerobics*, 4
afin de *in order to*, 7
âgé(e) *older*, 7
l' **âge** (m.): **Tu as quel âge?** *How old are you?* 1

l' **agenda** (m.) *planner*, 4
agit: il s'agit de *it's concerned with; it's about*, 6
agréable *pleasant*, 4
ai: J'ai... *I have . . .* , 2
aider: (Est-ce que) je peux vous aider? *May I help you?* 10
aimé(e) (pp.) *loved*, 1
aimer *to like*, 1; **aimer mieux: J'aime mieux...** *I prefer . . .* 1; aimerais: J'aimerais... pour aller avec... *I'd like . . . to go with . . .* , 10; Je n'aime pas... *I don't like . . .* 1; **Moi, j'aime (bien)...** *I (really) like . . .* 1; **Tu aimes... ?** *Do you like . . . ?* 1
ainsi que *as well as*, 4
l' **algèbre** (f.) *algebra*, 2
l' **Algérie** (f.) *Algeria*, 0
l' **alimentation** (f.) *food*, 12
les **aliments** (m.) *nutrients*, 8
l' **allemand** (m.) *German*, 2
aller *to go*, 6; Ça va aller mieux! *It's going to get better!* 9; **On peut y aller...** *We can go there . . .* , 12
allez: Allez au tableau! *Go to the blackboard!* 0; *Allez, viens!* *Come along!* 0
allons: Allons-y! *Let's go!*, 4; Allons... *Let's go . . .* 6
allé(e) (pp.): Je suis allé(e)... *I went . . .* , 9; Tu es allé(e) où? *Where did you go?* 9
l' **aise** (f.) *ease*, 7
Allô? *Hello?* 9
alors *well, then*, 3
l' **alphabet** (m.) *alphabet*, 0
aménagé(e) *newly equipped*, 6
américain(e) *American*, 0
l' **ami(e)** *friend*, 1

amical (e) (pl. amicaux) *friendly*, 2
amicalement (to close a letter) *best wishes*, 2
l' **amitié** (f.) *friendship*, 1
l' **amour** (m.) *love*, 1
amusant(e) *funny*, 7
amuser (s'amuser): Amuse-toi bien! *Have fun!* 11; **Qu'est-ce que tu fais pour t'amuser?** *What do you do to have fun?* 4; **Tu t'es bien amusé(e)?** *Did you have fun?* 11
les **ananas** (m.) *pineapples*, 8
ancien (ancienne): l'ancienne gare *the former train station*, 6
Andorre (no article) *Andorra*, 0
l' **anglais** (m.) English, 1
les **annonces** (f.): petites annonces *personal or business ads*, 1
ans: J'ai... ans. *I am . . . years old.* 1
les **antiquités** (f.) *antiquities, antiques*, 6
août *August*, 4
l' **appareil-photo** (m.) *camera*, 11
l' **appareil** (m.): **Qui est à l'appareil?** *Who's calling?* 9
appartient (appartenir) à *to belong to*, 9
appeler: s'appeler *to call oneself, to be called*, 1; **Il/Elle s'appelle comment?** *What's his/her name?* 1; **Il/Elle s'appelle...** *His/Her name is . . .* 1; **Je m'appelle...** *My name is . . .* 1; **Tu t'appelles comment?** *What's your name?* 1
appel: composez le numéro d'appel *dial the telephone number*, 9
apporter *to bring*, 9; **Apportez-**

moi... , s'il vous plaît. *Please bring me . . .* 5

apprendre *to learn,* 0

aprèm: cet aprèm *this afternoon,* 2

après-guerre *post-war,* 11

l' **après-midi** *in the afternoon,* 2; l'**après-midi libre** *afternoon off,* 2

après: Après, je suis sorti(e). *Afterwards, I went out.* 9; Et **après?** *And afterwards?* 9

l' ardoise (f.) *writing slate,* 3

argent: de l'argent *money,* 11

l' arrivée (f.) *arrival,* 6

arroser *to sprinkle,* 8

l' artiste (f.) *artist,* 0

les **arts** (m.) **plastiques** *art class,* 2

as: Tu as... ? *Do you have . . . ?* 3; Tu as... à quelle heure? *At what time do you have . . . ?* 2

l' ascenseur (m.) *elevator,* 6

l' ascension (f.): ascension en haut de la tour *ascent/climb to the top of the tower,* 6

Asseyez: Asseyez-vous! *Sit down!* 0

assez *enough, fairly,* 2

assidu *regular (punctual),* 2

l' **assiette** (f.) *plate,* 5

l' **athlétisme** (m.): **faire de l'athlétisme** *to do track and field,* 4

attachant(e) *loving,* 7

attendre *to wait for,* 9

au *to, at,* 6; *to, in (before a masculine noun),* 11; **au métro...** *at the . . . metro stop,* 6; **Au revoir!** *Goodbye!* 1

l' auberge de jeunesse *youth hostel,* 11

aucun(e) *none,* 7

aujourd'hui *today,* 2

aussi *also,* 1; **Moi aussi.** *Me too.* 2

autant *as much, equally,* 4

l' **automne** (m.) *autumn, fall,* 4; **en automne** *in the fall,* 4

autre *other,* 4

aux *to, in (before a plural noun),* 11

Av. (abbrev. of avenue) *avenue,* 6

avant *before,* 1

avec *with,* 1; avec moi *with me,* 6; Avec qui? *With whom?* 6

avez: Qu'est-ce que vous avez **comme... ?** *What kind of . . . do you have?* 5; Vous avez... ? *Do you have . . . ?* 2

l' avion (m.): *plane;* en avion *by plane,* 12

avis: A ton avis, qu'est-ce que je fais? *In your opinion, what do I do?* 9

les avocats (m.) *avocados,* 8

avons: Nous avons... *We have . . . ,* 2

avoir *to have* 2; avoir faim *to be hungry,* 5; avoir soif *to be thirsty,* 5

avril *April,* 4

ayant: ayant pu donner *having been able to give,* 2

B

le baby (foot) *an arcade soccer game,* 5

le bac(calauréat) *The secondary school exam for entering a university,* 2

le bachelier *someone who has passed the bac exam,* 2

se balader *to stroll,* 6

les **bananes** (f.) *bananas,* 8

les bandes dessinées (f.) *comic strips,* 2

la **banque** *bank,* 12

barbant *boring,* 2

la barre espace *space-bar,* 9

le **base-ball** *baseball,* 4

le basilic *basil,* 5

le **basket(ball): jouer au basket** *to play basketball,* 4

les **baskets** (f.) *sneakers,* 3

le **bateau** *boat,* 11; **en bateau** *by boat,* 12; **faire du bateau** *to go sailing,* 11

Bd (abbrev. of boulevard) *boulevard,* 6

beau: Il fait beau. *It's nice weather,* 4

Beaucoup. *A lot.* 4; **Oui, beaucoup.** *Yes, very much.,* 2; **Pas beaucoup.** *Not very much.* 4

belge *Belgian,* 1

la Belgique *Belgium,* 0

belle maille jersey *jersey knit,* 10

le besoin *need,* 8; De quoi est-ce que tu as besoin? *What do you need?* 8; J'ai besoin de... *I need . . . ,* 8

le beurre *butter,* 8

la bibliothèque *the library,* 6

bien: Je veux bien. *Gladly.* 8; **Je veux bien.** *I'd really like to.* 6; **J'en veux bien.** *I'd like some.* 8; **Moi, j'aime (bien)...** *I (really) like . . .* 1; **Très bien.** *Very well.* 1

Bien sûr. *Of course,* 3; *Certainly,* 9; **Oui, bien sûr.** *Yes, of course.* 7

le **bien-vivre** *good living, the good life,* 6

bientôt: A bientôt. *See you soon.* 1

Bienvenue! *Welcome!* 0

le **bifteck** *steak,* 8

les bijoux (m.) *jewelry,* 10

le **billet** *ticket,* 11; **d'avion** *plane ticket,* 11; **billet de train** *train ticket,* 11

la biologie *biology,* 2

blanc(he) *white,* 3

bleu(e) *blue,* 3

blond(e) *blond,* 7

le **blouson** *jacket,* 10

Bof! *(expression of indifference),* 1

la **boisson** *drink, beverage* 5; **Qu'est-ce que vous avez comme boissons?** *What do you have to drink?* 5

la **boîte: une boîte de** *a can of,* 8

le **bon** *coupon,* 6

bon *good,* 5; Bon courage! *Good luck!* 2; Bon voyage! *Have a good trip!* 11; Bon, d'accord. *Well, OK.* 8; de bons conseils *good advice,* 1; Oui, très bon. *Yes, very good.* 9; pas bon *not very good,* 5; bon marché *inexpensive,* 10

Bonjour *Hello,* 1

bonne: Bonne chance! 11; Bonne idée. *Good idea.* 4; Bonnes vacances! *Have a good vacation!* 11

le **bord: au bord de la mer** *to/at the coast,* 11

les **bottes** (f.) *boots,* 10

les **boucles d'oreilles** (f.) *earrings,* 10

bouger *to move,* 10

la **boulangerie** *bakery,* 12

la boule *ball,* 8

la **bouteille** *bottle,* 8; **une bouteille de** *a bottle of,* 8

la boutique *store, shop,* 3; une boutique de souvenirs *a souvenir shop,* 3

le **bracelet** *a bracelet,* 3

branché *plugged in,* 9

le branchement *hookup,* 9

la brochure *brochure,* 4

brun(e) *brunette,* 7

le **bus** *bus,* 12; **en bus** *by bus,* 12

la buvette *refreshment stand,* 12

C

ça fait: Ça fait combien, s'il vous plaît? *How much is it,*

please? 5; **Ça fait... francs.**
It's . . . francs. 5

ça: **Ça boume** *How's it going?* 2;
Ça va. *Fine.* 1; **Ça va?** *How
are things going?* 1; **Ça,
c'est...** *This/That is . . . ,* 12;
Et après ça... *And after that,
. . . ,* 9; **Oui, ça a été.** *Yes, it
was fine.* 9

le cadeau *gift,* 11

le café *coffee, café* 5

le cahier *notebook,* 0

la calculatrice *calculator,* 3; une
calculatrice-traductrice
translating calculator, 3

la Californie *California,* 4

le caméscope *a camcorder,* 4

la campagne *countryside,* 11; **à la
campagne** *to/at the countryside,* 11

le camping *camping,* 11; **faire du
camping** *to go camping,* 11

le canal *channel,* 3

le canari *canary,* 7

la cantine: à la cantine *at the
school cafeteria,* 9

le cardigan *a sweater,* 10

la carrière *quarry,* 11

la carte *map,* 0; à la carte *pick
and choose,* 3; **La carte,
s'il vous plaît.** *The menu,
please.* 5

la cartouche: cartouche d'encre *ink
cartridge,* 3

carvi: graines de carvi *cumin
seeds,* 8

la casquette *cap,* 10

la cassette *cassette tape,* 3

la cassette vidéo *videocassette,* 4

la cathédrale *cathedral,* 1

le cauchemar *nightmare,* 11;
**C'était un véritable
cauchemar!** *It was a real
nightmare!* 11

ce *this; that,* 3; **Ce sont . . .**
These (those) are . . . , 7

C'est... *It's . . . ,* 2; **C'est...**
This is . . . , 7; **C'est qui?** *Who
is it?* 2; **Ça, c'est...** *This/That
is . . . ,* 12

la ceinture *a belt,* 10

le centre commercial *the mall,* 6

le cercle *circle, group,* 6; au cercle
français *at French Club,* 4

ces *these; those,* 3

cet *this; that,* 3

cette *this; that,* 3

chacun: Chacun ses goûts! *To
each his own!,* 1

chacun *each (person),* 5

la chambre *room,* 7; **ranger ta
chambre** *to pick up your
room,* 7

les champignons (m.) *mushrooms,* 8

la chance *luck,* 11; **Bonne
chance!** *Good luck!* 11

chanter *to sing,* 9

chantilly: la crème Chantilly
sweetened whipped cream, 5

le chapeau *hat,* 10

chaque *each,* 4

chargé(e) *busy,* 2

chasse: une chasse au trésor
treasure hunt, 3

le chat *cat,* 7

chaud: Il fait chaud. *It's hot.* 4

chauffé(e) *heated,* 11

les chaussettes (f.) *socks,* 10

les chaussures (f.) *shoes,* 10

le chef-d'œuvre *masterpiece,* 6

la chemise *a shirt (men's),* 10

la chemise *folder,* 3

le chemisier *a shirt (women's),*
10

cher (chère) *dear,* 1 *expensive,*
3; **C'est trop cher.** *It's too
expensive.* 10

chercher *to look for,* 9; **Je
cherche quelque chose pour...**
*I'm looking for something
for . . . ,* 10

le cheval *horse,* 12

chez... *to/at . . . 's house,* 11;
chez le disquaire *at the
record store,* 12; **Je suis bien
chez... ?** *Is this . . . 's house?*
9; chez: chez les garçons *with
boys, according to boys,* 4

chic *chic,* 10

le chien *dog,* 7; **promener le
chien** *to walk the dog,* 7

les chiffres (m.) *numbers,* 0

la chimie *chemistry,* 2

le chocolat *chocolate,* 1; **un
chocolat** *hot chocolate,* 5

choisir *to choose, to pick,* 10

la chorale *choir,* 2

la chose *thing,* 4

**choses: J'ai des tas de choses
(trucs) à faire.** *I have lots of
things to do.* 5

chou: mon chou *my darling,
dear,* 1

chouette: Oui, très chouette.
Yes, very cool. 9

le cinéma *the movie theater,* 6; *the
movies,* 1

le clavier *keyboard,* 9

le classeur *loose-leaf binder,* 3

classique *classical,* 4

climatisé(e) *air-conditioned,* 11

le coca *cola,* 5

le coin: au coin de *on the corner
of,* 12

au col montant *turtleneck,* 10

le collant *hose,* 10

la colle: un pot de colle *container
of glue,* 3

la colonie: en colonie de vacances
to/at a summer camp, 11

le coloris *color, shade,* 3

combien *how much, how many,*
3; **C'est combien,... ?** *How
much is . . . ?* 5; **C'est combien?** *How much is it?* 3; **Ça
fait combien, s'il vous plaît?**
How much is it, please? 5

comme: Comme ci, comme ça.
So-so. 1; **Qu'est-ce qu'ils
aiment comme cours?** *What
subjects do they like?* 2;
**Qu'est-ce que tu fais comme
sport?** *What sports do you
play?* 4; **Qu'est-ce que vous
avez comme boissons?** *What
do you have to drink?* 5;
**Qu'est-ce que vous avez
comme... ?** *What kind of . . .
do you have?* 5

commencer *to begin, to start,* 9

comment *what,* 0; **(Comment)
ça va?** *How's it going?* 1;
Comment dit-on? *How do you
say it?* 1; Comment le dire?
How should you say it? 1;
Comment tu trouves ça?
What do you think of that/it?,
2; **Comment tu trouves... ?**
What do you think of . . . ?, 2;
Elle est comment? *What is
she like?* 7; **Il est comment?**
What is he like? 7; **Ils/Elles
sont comment?** *What are
they like?* 7; **Tu t'appelles
comment?** *What is your
name?* 0

le compagnon *companion,* 7

le compas *a compass,* 3

compétent(e) *competent,* 2

compléter *to complete,* 4

composez: composez le numéro
d'appel *dial the telephone
number,* 9

compris *included,* 5

compris: Tu as compris? *Did you
understand?* 1

les concerts (m.) *concerts,* 1

conçu(e) (pp.) *conceived,* 9

la confiture *jam,* 8

connaissance: Faisons connaissance! *Let's get acquainted.* 1

connais: Tu les connais? *Do you
know them?* 0

connu: le plus connu *the best-
known (adj.),* 6

le conseil *advice,* 1; de bons conseils *good advice,* 1

conseiller: Qu'est-ce que tu me conseilles? *What do you advise me to do?* 9

conservé: ce bulletin doit être conservé *this report card must be kept,* 2

content(e), *happy, pleased,* 1

consultés: services fréquemment consultés *frequently-used services,* 9

continuer *to continue,* 12; **Vous continuez jusqu'au prochain feu rouge.** *You keep going until the next light.* 12

contre *against,* 2

cool *cool,* 2

le cordon: le cordon de serrage *drawstring,* 10

le corps *body,* 8

le correspondant (la correspondante) *pen pal,* 1

côté: à côté de *next to,* 12

le coton: en coton *cotton,* 10

la coupe *dish (ful),* 5

courir *to run,* 7

le cours *course,* 2; **cours de développement personnel et social (DPS)** *health,* 2; **Tu as quels cours... ?** *What classes do you have . . . ?,* 2

les courses *shopping, errands,* 7; **faire les courses** *to do the shopping* 7

court(e) *short* (things), 10

le cousin *male cousin,* 7

la cousine *female cousin,* 7

coûteuse *expensive,* 8

la cravate *tie,* 10

le crayon *pencil,* 3; des crayons de couleur *colored pencils,* 3

la croisère *cruise,* 11

le croque-monsieur *toasted cheese and ham sandwich,* 5

cru *uncooked,* 5

le cuir: en cuir *leather,* 10

culturel (culturelle) *cultural,* 0

D

d'abord: D'abord, ... *First, . . . ,* 9

D'accord. *OK.* 4; **D'accord, si tu... d'abord...** *OK, if you . . . , first.* 7

d'habitude *usually,* 4

dans *in,* 6

danser *to dance,* 1; **la danse** *dance,* 2

de *from,* 0; *of,* 0; **de l'** *some,* 8; **de la** *some,* 8; **Je n'ai pas de...** *I don't have . . . ,* 3; **Je ne fais pas de...** *I don't play/do . . .* 4

déambuler *to stroll,* 11

débarrasser la table *to clear the table,* 7

décédé(e) *deceased,* 7

décembre *December,* 4

le décès *death,* 7

décider *to decide,* 5; **Vous avez décidé de prendre... ?** *Have you decided to take . . . ?* 10

la découverte *discovery,* 3

dedans *inside,* 3

dégoûtant *gross,* 5

dehors *outside,* 8

déjà *already,* 9

déjeuner *to have lunch,* 9; **le déjeuner** *lunch,* 2

délicieux (délicieuse) *delicious,* 5

délirer: La techno me fait délirer *I'm wild about techno.* 1

délivré: il n'en sera pas délivré de duplicata *duplicates will not be issued,* 2

demain *tomorrow,* 6

demain: A demain. *See you tomorrow.* 1

demande: sur votre demande *on your command,* 9

demi: et demi *half past (after midi and minuit),* 6; **et demie** *half past,* 6

démodé(e) *old-fashioned,* 10

dépêchez: dépêchez-vous de... *hurry up and . . . ,* 1

déposer *to deposit,* 12

le déplacement *movement,* 9

derrière *behind,* 12

des *some,* 8

dés: découper en dés *to dice,* 8

désagréable *unpleasant,* 4

désirer: Vous désirez? *What would you like?* 10

désolé: Désolé(e), je suis occupé(e). *Sorry, I'm busy.* 6; **Désolé(e), mais je ne peux pas.** *Sorry, but I can't.* 4

le dessin *drawing,* 3

détailler *to slice,* 8

le détenteur: détenteur du mot de passe *holder of the password,* 9

devant *in front of,* 6

deviennent: Que deviennent... ? *What happened to . . . ?* 7

Devine! *Guess!* 0

les devoirs *homework,* 2; **J'ai des devoirs à faire.** *I've got homework to do,* 5

le dévouement *devotion,* 7

devrais: Tu devrais... *You should . . . ,* 9

la dictée *dictation,* 0

le dictionnaire *dictionary,* 3

difficile *hard,* 2

dimanche *Sunday,* 2; **le dimanche** *on Sundays,* 2

dîner *to have dinner,* 9; **le dîner** *dinner,* 8

dingue: Je suis dingue de... *I'm crazy about . . . ,* 1

dire: Comment le dire? *How should you say it?* 1; Dis,... Say, . . . , 2; **Ça ne me dit rien.** *That doesn't interest me.* 4; Comment dit-on... ? *How do you say . . . ?* 1; Jacques a dit... Simon says . . . , 0; Qu'est-ce qu'on se dit? *What are they saying to themselves?* 2; **Vous pouvez lui dire que j'ai téléphoné?** *Can you tell her/him that I called?* 9

direct: en direct *live,* 7

discute: Ne discute pas! *Don't argue!* 3

discuter *to discuss,* 7

disponible *available,* 8

le dispositif *device,* 9

le disquaire: chez le disquaire *at the record store,* 12

le disque compact/CD, *compact disc/CD,* 3

distant *distant,* 2

la distribution: une distribution étincelante *a brilliant cast,* 1

divers *various,* 3

le domicile *place of residence,* 4

donne sur *overlooks,* 11

donner *to give,* 5; **Donnez-moi... , s'il vout plaît.** *Please give me . . .* 5

dormir *to sleep,* 1

dos: un sac à dos, *backpack,* 3

la douche: avec douche ou bains *with shower or bath,* 11

la douzaine: une douzaine de *a dozen,* 8

les draps (m.) *linens, sheets,* 11

dressé *pointed,* 7

droite: à droite *to the right,* 12

du *some,* 8

le duplicata: il n'en sera pas délivré de duplicata *duplicates will not be issued,* 2

E

l' eau (f.) **minérale** *mineral water,* 5

ébattre: s'ébattre *to frolic,* 7

échange: en échange de *in exchange for,* 7

l' échantillon (m.) *sample,* 2

l' écharpe (f.) *a scarf,* 10

l' école (f.) *school,* 1; A l'école *At school,* 0

écouter *to listen*, 1; Ecoute! *Listen!* 0; écouter de la musique *to listen to music*, 1; Ecoutez! *Listen!* 0; Je t'écoute. *I'm listening.* 9

l' écran (m.) *screen*, 11

l' écrin (m.) *case*, 6

écrire *to write*, 2; Ecris-moi. *Write me.* 1

l' édifice (m.) *edifice, building*, 6

l' éducation (f.) physique et sportive (EPS) *physical education*, 2

efficace *efficient*, 9

égrener *to shell*, 8

égyptien (égyptienne) *Egyptian*, 6

élastique *elastic* (adj.), 3

l' éléphant (m.) *elephant* 0

l' élève (m./f.) *student*, 2

embêtant(e) *annoying*, 7

l' émission (f.) *TV program*, 4

empêche (empêcher) *to prevent, to keep from doing*, 2

emploi: un emploi du temps *schedule*, 2

emprunter *to borrow*, 12

en *in*, 1; en *some, of it, of them, any, none*, 8; en *to, in (before a feminine noun)*, 11; en coton *cotton*, 10; en cuir *leather*, 10; en français *in French*, 1; en jean *denim*, 10; en retard *late*, 2; Je n'en veux plus. *I don't want anymore*, 8; Qu'en penses-tu? *What do you think (about it)?* 1; Vous avez ça en... ? *Do you have that in . . . ? (size, fabric, color)*, 10

encore: Encore de... ? *More . . . ,?* 8

les enfants (m.) *children*, 7

enfin *finally*, 9

enjoué(e) *playful*, 7

ennuyeux: C'etait ennuyeux. *It was boring*, 5

l'enquête (f.) *survey*, 1

ensemble *together*, 4

l' ensemble (m.) *collection, emsemble*, 3

ensuite *next*, 2

ensuite: Ensuite, ... *Then, . . .* 9

entendre: s'entendre avec *to get along with*, 7

Entendu. *Agreed.* 6

entendu dire que: Il a entendu dire que... *He heard that . . . ,* 12

l' enthousiasme (m.) *enthusiasm*, 2

entrant *entering*, 2

entre *between*, 12

l' enveloppe (f.) *envelope*, 12

envie: J'ai envie de... *I feel like . . . ,* 11

envoyer: envoyer des lettres *to send letters*, 12

épi: l'épi (m.) de maïs *ear of corn*, 8

l' épicerie (f.) *grocery store*, 12

éplucher *to clean, to peel*, 8

l' éponge (f.) *sponge*, 3

épouvantable: C'était épouvantable. *It was horrible.* 9

l' équitation (f.): faire de l'équitation *to go horseback riding*, 1

l' escale *docking (of a boat)*, 11

l' escalier (m.) *staircase*, 6

les escargots (m.) *snails*, 1

l' espace (m.) *space, area*, 7

espace: une barre espace *space-bar*, 9

l' espagnol (m.) *Spanish*, 2

espère: J'espère que oui. *I hope so.* 1

l' espoir (m.) *hope*, 7

essayer: Je peux essayer... ? *Can I try on . . . ?* 10; Je peux l'/les essayer? *Can I try it/them on ?* 10

Est-ce que *(Introduces a yes-or-no question)*, 4; (Est-ce que) je peux... ? *May I . . . ?* 7

et: *and*, 1; Et après ça... *And after that, . . . ,* 9; Et toi? *And you?* 1

l' établissement (m.): l'établissement de votre appel *the connection of your call*, 9

l' étage (m.) *floor, story (of a building)*, 6

etaler *to spread*, 8

l' étape (f.) *part*, 1; première étape *first part*, 1; deuxième étape *second part*, 1; troisième étape *third part*, 1

l' état (m.) *state* 0

les Etats-Unis (m.) *United States*, 0

l' été (f.) *summer*, 4; en été *in the summer*, 4

été (pp.) *was*, 9

être *to be*, 7; C'est... *This is . . . ,* 7; Ce sont . . . *These (those) are . . . ,* 7; Elle est... *She is . . . ,* 7; Il est... *He is . . . ,* 7; Il est... *It is . . .* (time), 6; Ils/Elles sont . . . *They're . . . ,* 7; Oui, ça a été. *Yes, it was fine.* 9

l' étude (f.) *study hall*, 2

étudier *to study*, 1

l' Europe (f.) *Europe*, 0

évider *to scoop out*, 8

éviter *to avoid*, 9

les examens (m.) *exams*, 1

excellente *excellent*, 5; Oui, excellent. *Yes, excellent.* 9

excusez: Excusez-moi. *Excuse me*, 3

exemplaire *exemplary*, 7

F

face: en face de *across from*, 12

facile *easy*, 2

faim: avoir faim *to be hungry*, 5; Non, merci. Je n'ai plus faim. *No thanks. I'm not hungry anymore.* 8

faire *to do, to make, to play*, 4; Désolé(e), j'ai des devoirs à faire. *Sorry, I have homework to do.* 5; J'ai des courses à faire. *I have errands to do.* 5; J'ai des tas de choses à faire. *I have lots of things to do.* 5; J'ai des trucs à faire. *I have some things to do.* 5; Qu'est-ce que tu vas faire... ? *What are you going to do . . . ?* 6; Tu vas faire quoi... ? *What are you going to do . . . ?* 6; faire les courses *to do the shopping*, 7

fais: A ton avis, qu'est-ce que je fais? *In your opinion, what do I do?* 9; Fais-moi... *Make me . . . ,* 3; Je fais... *I play/do . . .* 4; Ne t'en fais pas! *Don't worry!* 9; Qu'est-ce que tu fais comme sport? *What sports do you play?* 4; Qu'est-ce que tu fais pour t'amuser? *What do you do to have fun?* 4; Qu'est-ce que tu fais... ? *What do you do . . . ?,* 4; Qu'est-ce que tu fais quand... ? *What do you do when . . . ?,* 4

faisons: Faisons connaissance!. *Let's get acquainted.* 1

fait: Il fait beau. *It's nice weather.* 4; Il fait chaud. *It's hot.* 4; Il fait frais. *It's cool.* 4; Il fait froid. *It's cold.*, 4; Qu'est-ce que tu as fait... ? *What did you do . . . , ?* 9

ferai: je me ferai une joie de... *I'll gladly . . . ,* 1

ferais: Je ferais le bac... *I would take bac . . . ,* 2

faut: Il me faut... *I need . . . ,* 3; Qu'est-ce qu'il te faut pour... ? *What do you need for . . . ? (informal)*, 3; Qu'est-ce qu'il te faut? *What do you need?* 8; Qu'est-ce qu'il vous faut

pour... ? *What do you need for . . . ? (formal),* 3
la farine *flour,* 8
faux *false,* 2
les féculents (m.) *starches,* 8
la fenêtre *window,* 0
fermez: Fermez la porte. *Close the door.* 0
la fête *party,* 1; faire la fête *to live it up,* 1
la feuille: une feuille de papier *a sheet of paper,* 0
le feutre *a marker,* 3
février *February,* 4
la fiche: la fiche électrique *power plug,* 9; la fiche téléphonique *telephone plug,* 9
la fidélité *loyalty,* 7
la fille *girl,* 0
le film *movie,* 6; **voir un film** *to see a movie,* 6; un film d'aventures *adventure film,* 1
la fin *end,* 4
le flipper *pinball,* 5
fois: une fois par semaine *once a week,* 4
follement *madly,* 1
fonctionner *to function,* 9
le foot *soccer,* 4
le football *soccer,* 1; **le football américain** *football,* 4
la forêt *forest,* 0; **en forêt** *to the forest,* 11
formidable: C'était formidable! *It was great!* 11
fort(e) *strong,* 7
les fournitures scolaires (f.) *school supplies,* 3
fraîche *cool, cold,* 5
frais: Il fait frais. *It's cool.* 4
les fraises (f.) *strawberries,* 8
franc (the French monetary unit) 3; **C'est... francs.** *It's . . . francs.* 5
le français *French (language),* 1; français(e) *French (adj.)* 0; A la française *French-style,* 2
francophone *French-speaking,* 0
fréquemment *frequently,* 9
le frère *brother,* 7
les friandises (f.) *sweets,* 6
les frites (f.) *French fries,* 1
froid: Il fait froid. *It's cold.* 4
le fromage *cheese,* 5
fuit (pp.) *fled,* 1
le fun: C'est le fun! (in Canada) *It's fun!* 4

G

gagner *to win, to earn,* 9
la gamme: la nouvelle gamme de *the new line of,* 9

le garçon *boy,* 0
garde: garde en mémoire *stores in memory,* 9
garder *to look after,* 7
le gâteau *cake,* 8
gauche: à gauche *to the left,* 12
génial(e) *great,* 2
le génie *genius,* 6
genoux: une paire de genoux *pair of knees, a lap,* 7
gentil (gentille) *nice,* 7
la géographie *geography,* 2
la géométrie *geometry,* 2
la glace *ice cream,* 1
glace: faire du patin à glace *to ice skate,* 4
le golf *golf,* 4; **jouer au golf** *to play golf,* 4
les gombos (m.) *okra,* 8
la gomme *eraser,* 3
la gosse: être traité comme une gosse *to be treated like a kid,* 2
le gouache *paint,* 3
le goûter *afternoon snack,* 8
les goûts (m.) *tastes,* 4
les goyaves (m.) *guavas,* 8
les graines (f.) *seeds,* 8
la grammaire *grammar,* 1
grand(e) *tall,* 7; *big,* 10
grand-chose: Pas grand-chose. *Not much.* 6
la grand-mère *grandmother,* 7
le grand-père *grandfather,* 7
grandir *to grow,* 10
gratuit(e) *free,* 6
grec *Greek (adj.),* 6
gris(e) *grey,* 3
gros (grosse) *fat,* 7
grossir *to gain weight,* 10
les groupes (f.) *music groups,* 2
la Guadeloupe *Guadeloupe,* 0
le guichet *ticket window,* 6
la Guyane *Guiana,* 0

H

habitant: habitant le monde entier *living all over the world,* 1
habite: J'habite à... *I live in . . . ,* 1
les habitudes (f.) *habits,* 4; **d'habitude** *usually,* 4
habituellement *usually,* 2
Haïti (no article) *Haiti,* 0
*****les hamburgers** (m.) *hamburgers,* 1
*****la harpe** *harp,* 11
*****les haricots** (m.) *beans,* 8; les haricots verts (m.) *green beans,* 8
*****hâte: Elle a hâte de...** *She can't wait to . . . ,* 7
*****haut(e)** *tall, high,* 6
*le haut-parleur *loudspeaker,* 11

*le havre *haven,* 7
l' hébergement (m.) *lodging,* 6
*****le héros** *hero,* 11
hésite: Euh... J'hésite. *Oh, I'm not sure.* 10
l' heure: à l'heure de *at the time of,* 1; **A quelle heure?** *At what time?* 6; **A tout à l'heure!** *See you later!* 1; **Quelle heure est-il?** *What time is it?* 6; **Tu as . . . à quelle heure?** *At what time do you have . . . ?,* 2
heures: à... heures *at . . . o'clock,* 2; **à... heures quarante-cinq** *at . . . forty-five,* 2; **à... heures quinze** *at . . . fifteen,* 2; **à... heures trente** *at . . . thirty,* 2
heureusement *luckily, fortunately,* 4
heureux: Très heureux (heureuse). *Pleased to meet you.* 7
l' histoire (f.) *history,* 2
l' hiver (m.) *winter,* 4; **en hiver** *in the winter,* 4
*****le hockey** *hockey,* 4; **jouer au hockey** *to play hockey,* 4
l' hôpital (pl. -aux) *hospital,* 0
horrible *terrible,* 10
*****le hot-dog** *hot dog,* 5
l' hôtel (m.) *hotel,* 0
*le houx *holly,* 11

I

l' idée (f.) *idea,* 4; **Bonne idée.** *Good idea.* 4
l' identité: une photo d'identité *a photo ID,* 1
il y a *there is, there are,* 4; il y a du soleil/du vent *it's sunny/ windy,* 4
l' île (f.) *island,* 0
imagines: Tu imagines? *Can you imagine?* 4
l' imprimante (f.) *printer,* 9
inclus *included,* 6
incompétent *incompetent,* 2
l' informatique (f.) *computer science,* 2
inscrit(e) *written,* 9
intelligent(e) *smart,* 7
intention: J'ai l'intention de... *I intend to . . . ,* 11
intéressant *interesting,* 2
l'interro (f.) *quiz,* 9
international *international,* 5
les interviewés *interviewees,* 2
intime *personal,* 1
ivoirien, -ne, *from the Republic of Côte d'Ivoire,* 1

J

jamais: ne...jamais *never*, 4
le jambon *ham*, 5
janvier *January*, 4
le jardin *garden*, 0
jaune *yellow*, 3
le jazz *jazz*, 4
je *I*, 0
le jean *(a pair of) jeans*, 3; en jean *denim*, 10
le jeu: un jeu de rôle *role-playing exercise*, 1; jouer à des jeux vidéo *to play video games*, 4
jeudi *Thursday* 2; le jeudi *on Thursdays*, 2
jeune *young*, 7; les jeunes *youths*, 4
le jogging: faire du jogging *to jog*, 4
joignant (joigner) *to attach*, 1
joli(e) *pretty*, 4
jouer *to play*, 4; Je joue... *I play . . .*, 4; jouer à . . . *to play (a game) . . .* 4
le jour *day*, 2
le journal *journal*, 1
la journée *day*, 2
juillet *July*, 4
juin *June*, 4
la jupe *a skirt*, 10
le jus d'orange *orange juice*, 5
le jus de pomme *apple juice*, 5
jusqu'à: jusqu'à dix numéros *up to ten numbers*, 9; Vous allez tout droit jusqu'à... *You go straight ahead until you get to . . .*, 12
juste *just*, 4

K

le kilo: un kilo de *a kilogram of*, 8

L

la *her, it*, 9
là *there*, 3; -là *there (noun suffix)*, 3; (Est-ce que) . . . est là, s'il vous plaît? *Is . . . , there, please?* 9
laisser: Je peux laisser un message? *Can I leave a message?* 9
le lait *milk*, 8
laitiers: les produits laitiers (m.) *dairy products*, 8
large *baggy*, 10
le latin *Latin*, 2
laver: laver la voiture *to wash the car*, 7
la légèreté *lightness*, 6
le *him, it*, 9

les *them*, 9
leur *to them*, 9
leur/leur(s) *their*, 7
levez: Levez la main! *Raise your hand!* 0; Levez-vous! *Stand up!* 0
la librairie *bookstore*, 12
la librairie-papeterie *bookstore*, 3
liégeois: café ou chocolat liégeois *coffee or chocolate ice cream with whipped cream*, 5
la limonade *lemon soda*, 5
lire *to read*, 1
lisons: Lisons! *Let's read!* 1
la litote *understatement*, 5
litre: un litre de *a liter of*, 8
la livre: une livre de *a pound of*, 8
le livre *book*, 0
la location *rental*, 4
loin: loin de *far from*, 12
le loisir *pastime*, 4
la longeur *length*, 10
la Louisiane *Louisiana*, 0
lu (pp. of lire) *read*, 9
lui *to him, to her*, 9
lundi *Monday* 2; le lundi *on Mondays*, 2
les lunettes (f.) de soleil *sunglasses*, 10
le Luxembourg *Luxembourg*, 0
le lycée *high school*, 2

M

ma *my*, 7
madame (Mme) *ma'am; Mrs*, 1; Madame! *Waitress!* 5
mademoiselle (Mlle) *miss; Miss*, 1; Mademoiselle! *Waitress!* 5
les magasins (m.) *stores*, 1; faire les magasins *to go shopping*, 1
le magazine *magazine*, 3
le magnétoscope *videocassette recorder, VCR*, 0
mai *May*, 4
maigrir *to lose weight*, 10
le maillot de bain *a bathing suit*, 10
la main *hand*, 0
maintenant *now*, 2
mais *but*, 1
le maïs *corn*, 8
la Maison des jeunes et de la culture (MJC) *the recreation center*, 6
le maître *master, owner*, 7
mal: Pas mal. *Not bad.* 1
la malchance *misfortune*, 7
malheureusement *unfortunately*, 7

le Mali *Mali*, 0
la manche *sleeve*, 10
le manchot *penguin*, 6
le manège *carousel*, 12
manger *to eat*, 6
les mangues (f.) *mangoes*, 8
manque: Qu'est-ce qui manque? *What's missing?* 2
manqué: garçon manqué *tomboy*, 10
le manteau *coat*, 10
mardi *Tuesday* 2; le mardi *on Tuesdays*, 2
le Maroc *Morocco*, 0
marocain(e) *Moroccan*, 1
marron (inv.) *brown*, 3
mars *March*, 4
martiniquais(e) *from Martinique*, 1
la Martinique *Martinique*, 0
le match: regarder un match *to watch a game (on TV)*, 6; voir un match *to see a game (in person)*, 6
les maths (f.) *math*, 1
les matières grasses (f.) *fat*, 8
le matin *in the morning*, 2
mauvais: Oh, pas mauvais. Oh, not bad. 9; Très mauvais. Very bad. 9
méchant(e) *mean*, 7
mécontent(e) *unhappy*, 2
les médicaments (m.) *medicine*, 12
meilleurs: les meilleurs amis *best friends*, 7
méli-mélo! *mishmash*, 1
le ménage: faire le ménage *to do housework*, 1
méprisant *contemptuous*, 2
la mer: au bord de la mer *to/at the coast*, 11
Merci. *Thank you*, 3; Non, merci. *No, thank you.* 8
mercredi *Wednesday*, 2; le mercredi *on Wednesdays*, 2
la mère *mother*, 7
mes *my*, 7
le métro: au métro... *at the . . . metro stop*, 6; en métro *by subway*, 12
mets: mets en ordre *put into order*, 6
mettre *to put, to put on, to wear*, 10; Je ne sais pas quoi mettre pour . . . *I don't know what to wear for (to) . . .*, 10; Mets... *Wear . . .*, 10; Qu'est-ce que je mets? *What shall I wear?* 10
meublé(e) *furnished*, 11
miam, miam *yum-yum*, 5
midi *noon*, 6
mieux: Ça va aller mieux! *It's*

going to get better! 9; **J'aime mieux... ?** *I prefer . . . ?*, 10

mignon (mignonne) *cute*, 7

mince *slender*, 7

minuit *midnight*, 6

la minute: Tu as une minute? *Do you have a minute?* 9

mise: mise en pratique *putting into practice*, 1; mise en train *getting started*, 1

mixte *mixed*, 5

le mobilier *furniture*, 6

moche: Je le/la/les trouve moche(s). *I think it's/they're tacky.* 10

la mode: à la mode *in style*, 10

le mode d'emploi *instructions*, 9

modéré(e) *moderate*, 11

moi *me*, 2

moins (with numbers) *lower*, 0; **moins cinq** *five to*, 6; **moins le quart** *quarter to*, 6

le moment: Un moment, s'il vous plaît. *One moment, please.* 5

mon *my*, 7

Monaco *Monaco*, 0

le monde *world*, 0

monsieur (M.) *sir; Mr.* 1; **Monsieur!** *Waiter!* 5

la montagne *mountain*, 4; **à la montagne** *to/at the mountains*, 11

la montée *ascent*, 6

la montre *watch*, 3

montrer *to show*, 9

le monument *monument*, 6

le moral *morale*, 2

le morceau: un morceau de *a piece of*, 8

la mousseline *chiffon*, 8

murale: la prise murale *wall outlet*, 9

le musée *museum*, 6

la musique *music*, 2; écouter de la musique *to listen to music*, 1; la musique classique *classical music*, 4

le mystère *mystery*, 5

les niveaux (m.) *levels*, 6

le nocturne *late-night opening*, 6

le Noël *Christmas*, 0

noir(e) *black*, 3

la noisette *hazelnut*, 5

les noix (f.) *nuts*, 5

les noix de coco (f.) *coconuts*, 8

le nom *(last) name*, 1

non *no*, 1; **Moi non plus.** *Neither do I.* 2; **Moi, non.** *I don't.* 2; **Non, pas trop.** *No, not too much.* 2

nos *our*, 7

notre *our*, 7

la Nouvelle-Angleterre *New England*, 0

novembre *November*, 4

les nuages (m.) *clouds*, 12

nul *useless*, 2

le numéro *number*, 0; un numéro de téléphone *telephone number*, 3; les numéros *issues (for magazines, etc.)*, 3

ouvrez: Ouvrez vos livres à la page... *Open your books to page . . . ,* 0

it go well? 9; **passé: Qu'est-ce qui s'est passé?** *What happened?* 9; **Tu as passé un bon week-end?** *Did you have a good weekend?* 9

le passeport *passport,* 11

passer: Tu pourrais passer à...? *Could you go by...,?* 12; **Vous passez...** *You'll pass...,* 12; **passer un examen** *to take a test,* 9

passionnant *fascinating,* 2

la **pastille** *tablet,* 3

le **pâté** *pâté,* 0

les **pâtes** (f.) *pasta,* 11

le **patin** *ice skating,* 1; **faire du patin à glace** *to ice skate,* 4

la **pâtisserie** *pastry shop, pastry,* 12

les **pattes d'eph** (f.) *bell-bottoms,* 10

pauvre *poor,* 7

le **pays** *country,* 6

les **pêches** (f.) *peaches,* 8

la **peinture** *painting,* 6

pendant *during,* 1

pénible *annoying,* 7

penser: J'ai pensé à tout. *I've thought of everything.* 11; **Qu'en penses-tu?** *What do you think (about it)?* 1

le **père** *father,* 7

performant *high-performance,* 9

le **permis de conduire** *driver's license,* 12

personnel (personnelle) *personal,* 4

le **petit déjeuner** *breakfast,* 8

petit(e) *short (height),* 7; *small (size),* 10; **petites annonces** *classified ads,* 1

les **petits pois** (m.) *peas,* 8

peu *not very,* 2; **peu content** *not very happy,* 2

la **pharmacie** *drugstore,* 12

la **philosophie** *philosophy,* 2

la **photo: faire des photos** *to take pictures,* 4

les **photographies** (f.) *photographs,* 6

la **phrase** *sentence,* 4

la **physique** *physics,* 2

la **pièce** *play,* 6; **voir une pièce** *to see a play,* 6

le **pied** *foot,* 12; **à pied** *on foot,* 12

le **pinceau** *paintbrush,* 3

pinces: des pantalons à pinces *pleated pants,* 10

le **pingouin** *penguin,* 0

le **pique-nique: faire un piquenique** *to have a picnic,* 6

la **piscine** *the swimming pool,* 6

la **pizza** *pizza,* 1

la **plage** *beach,* 1

plaît: Il/Elle me plaît, mais il/elle est cher. *I like it, but it's expensive.* 10; **Il/Elle te/vous plaît?** *Do you like it?* 10; **Ça te plaît?** *Do you like it?* 2; **s'il vous (te) plaît** *please,* 3

le **plaisir** *pleasure, enjoyment,* 4; **Oui, avec plaisir.** *Yes, with pleasure.* 8

la **planche: faire de la planche à voile** *to go windsurfing,* 11

plaque: les plaques d'immatriculation (f.) *license plates,* 0

pleut: Il pleut. *It's raining.* 4

la **plongée: faire de la plongée** *to go scuba diving,* 11

plus *plus (math),* 2; (with numbers) *higher,* 0; **Je n'en veux plus.** *I don't want any more,* 8; **Moi non plus.** *Neither do I.* 2; **Non, merci. Je n'ai plus faim.** *No thanks. I'm not hungry anymore.* 8

la **poche** *pocket,* 10

le **poème** *poem,* 0

les **poires** (f.) *pears,* 8

le **poisson** *fish,* 7

la **poitrine** *chest,* 10

les **pommes** (f.) *apples,* 8; **les pommes de terre** (f.) *potatoes,* 8

le **porc** *pork,* 8

la **porte** *door,* 0

porter *to wear,* 10

le **portefeuille** *wallet,* 3

la **poste** *post office,* 12

le **poste: un poste téléphonique** *telephone subscriber,* 9

le **poster** *poster,* 0

le **pot: pot de colle** *container of glue,* 3

la **poubelle** *trashcan,* 7; **sortir la poubelle** *to take out the trash,* 7

la **poudre** *powder,* 8

les **poules** *chickens,* 8

le **poulet** *chicken meat,* 8

pour *for,* 2; **Qu'est-ce qu'il te faut pour...** *What do you need for...? (informal),* 3; **Qu'est-ce que tu fais pour t'amuser?** *What do you do to have fun?* 4

pourquoi *why,* 0; **Pourquoi est-ce que tu ne mets pas...?** *Why don't you wear...?,* 10; **Pourquoi pas?** *Why not?* 6; **Pourquoi tu ne... pas?** *Why don't you...?,* 9

pouvoir *to be able to, can,* 8; **(Est-ce que) je peux...?** *May I...?,* 7; **Tu peux...?** *Can you...?,* 8; **Je ne peux pas**

maintenant. *I can't right now.* 8; **Je peux te parler?** *Can I talk to you?,* 9; **Non, je ne peux pas.** *No, I can't.* 12; **Qu'est-ce que je peux faire?** *What can I do?* 9; **(Est-ce que) tu pourrais me rendre un petit service?** *Could you do me a favor?* 12; **Tu pourrais passer à...?** *Could you go by...?,* 12

précieusement *carefully,* 2

précisant: en précisant *specifying,* 1

préféré(e) *favorite,* 4

la **préférence** *preference,* 3

premier (première) *first,* 1

prendre *to take or to have (food or drink),* 5; **Je vais prendre...,s'il vous plaît.** *I'm going to have..., please.* 5; **On peut prendre...** *We can take...,* 12; **Prends...** *Get...,* 8; **Prends...** *Have...,* 5; **Je le/la/les prends.** *I'll take it/them.* 10; **Tu prends...?** *Are you taking...?,* 11; **Tu prends...?** *Will you have...?,* 8; **Prenez une feuille de papier.** *Take out a sheet of paper.* 0; **Vous prenez...?** *Will you have...?,* 8; **Prenez la rue... puis traversez la rue...** *You take..., Street, then cross... Street,* 12; **Vous prenez?** *What are you having?* 5; **Vous avez décidé de prendre...?** *Have you decided to take...?* 10; **Vous le/la/les prenez?** *Are you going to take it/them?* 10

le **prénom** *first name,* 1

près: près de *close to,* 12

présenter: Je te (vous) présente... *I'd like you to meet...,* 7; **Présente-toi!** *Introduce yourself!* 0

prêt (prête) *ready,* 9

prévu: Je n'ai rien de prévu. *I don't have any plans.* 11

le **printemps** *spring,* 4; **au printemps** *in the spring,* 4

pris (pp. of prendre) *took, taken,* 9

la **prise** *plug, outlet,* 9; **la prise murale** *wall outlet,* 9

le **prix** *price,* 6

le **problème: J'ai un petit problème.** *I've got a problem.* 9

prochain(e): Vous continuez jusqu'au prochain feu rouge. *You go down this street to the next light.* 12

le prof(esseur) *teacher*, 0
la promenade: faire une promenade *to go for a walk*, 6
promener: promener le chien *to walk the dog*, 7
promets (promettre) *to promise*, 1
prononcer *to pronounce*, 1; **prononcent: ne se prononcent pas** *no response*, 2
la prononciation *pronunciation*, 2
protège: protège contre *protects against*, 9
puis: Prenez la rue... puis traversez la rue... *Take . . . Street, then cross . . . Street*, 12
le pull(-over) *a pullover sweater*, 3

Q

qu'est-ce que *what*, 1; **Qu'est-ce qu'il y a dans...?** *What's in the . . . ?*, 3; **Qu'est-ce qu'il y a?** *What's wrong?* 2; **Qu'est-ce qu'on fait?** *What are we/they doing?* 4; **Qu'est-ce que je peux faire?** *What can I do?* 9; **Qu'est-ce que tu as fait... ?** *What did you do . . . ?* 9; **Qu'est-ce que tu fais... ?** *What do you do . . . ?* 4; **Qu'est-ce que tu vas faire... ?** *What are you going to do . . . ?* 6; **Qu'est-ce que vous avez comme boissons?** *What do you have to drink?* 5; **Qu'est-ce que vous avez comme... ?** *What kind of . . . do you have?* 5; **Qu'est-ce qui manque?** *What's missing?* 2
Qu'est-ce qui: Qu'est-ce qui s'est passé? *What happened?* 9
quand: Quand (ça)? *When?* 6
quart: et quart *quarter past*, 6; **moins le quart** *quarter to*, 6
que: Que sais-je? *Self-check (What do I know?)*, 1
le Québec *Quebec*, 0
québécois(e) *from Quebec*, 1
quel(le) *which*, 1; **Ils ont quels cours?** *What classes do they have?* 2; **Tu as quel âge?** *How old are you?* 1; **Tu as quels cours... ?** *What classes do you have . . . ?*, 2; **Tu as... à quelle heure?** *At what time do you have . . . ?*, 2; **Quelle heure est-il?** *What time is it?* 6
quelqu'un *someone*, 1
quelque chose: Je cherche quelque chose pour... *I'm looking for something for . . . *, 10

quelquefois *sometimes*, 4
la question *question*, 0
le questionnaire *questionnaire, survey*, 4
qui *who*, 0; **Avec qui?** *With whom?* 6; **C'est qui?** *Who is it?*, 2; **Qui suis-je?** *Who am I?* 0
quittez: Ne quittez pas. *Hold on.* 9
quoi: Je ne sais pas quoi mettre pour... *I don't know what to wear for . . . *, 10; **Tu as quoi... ?** *What do you have . . .?*, 2

R

le rabat *flap*, 3
le raccourci *short cut*, 2
la radio *radio*, 3
le radis *radish*, 8
le raisin *grapes*, 8
la randonnée: faire de la randonnée *to go hiking*, 11
ranger: ranger ta chambre *to pick up your room*, 7
rappeler: Vous pouvez rappeler plus tard? *Can you call back later?* 9; **Tu te rappelles?** *Do you remember?* 3
rapporter: rapporte: Rapporte-moi... *Bring me back . . . *, 8; **Tu me rapportes... ?** *Will you bring me . . . ,?* 8
rater: rater le bus *to miss the bus*, 9; **rater une interro**, *to fail a quiz*, 9
le rayon *department*, 3; **au rayon de musique** *in the music department*, 3
la récréation *break*, 2
recueilli (pp. of recueillir) *to take in*, 7
réfléchir: Réfléchissez. *Think about it.* 2
le refuge *animal shelter*, 7
le réfugié *refugee*, 1
les refus (m.) *refusals*, 6
le regard *look*, 7
regarder: Non, merci, je regarde. *No, thanks, I'm just looking.* 10; **Regarde, voilà...** *Look, here's (there's) (it's) . . . *, 12; **regarder la télé** *to watch TV*, 1; **regarder un match** *to watch a game (on TV)*, 6; **Regardez la carte!** *Look at the map!* 0
la règle *ruler*, 3
regroupé(e) *rearranged*, 6
rejoint (pp. of rejoindre) *to rejoin*, 7

Je regrette. *Sorry*, 3; **Je regrette, mais je n'ai pas le temps.** *I'm sorry, but I don't have time.* 8
la rencontre *encounter*, 1
rencontrer *to meet*, 9
rendre *to return something*, 12; **Rendez-vous...** *We'll meet . . .* 6
renfort: renforts aux épaules *reinforced shoulder seams*, 10
la rentrée *back to school*, 2
le répertoire *index*, 9
répéter *to rehearse, to practice*, 9; **Répétez!** *Repeat!* 0
le répondant *respondent*, 4
répondre *to answer*, 9; **Ça ne répond pas.** *There's no answer.* 9
la réponse *response, answer*, 2
reposer: laisser reposer *to let stand*, 8; **se reposer** *to relax*, 11
la République de Côte d'Ivoire *the Republic of Côte d'Ivoire*, 0
respectueux (respectueuse) *respectful*, 2
ressemblez: si vous me ressemblez *if you're like me*, 1
le restaurant *restaurant*, 6
la restauration *dining*, 6
retard: en retard *late*, 2
retirer: retirer de l'argent (m.) *withdraw money*, 12
le retour *return*, 6
rétro (inv.) *style of the Forties or Fifties*, 10
retrouve: Bon, on se retrouve... *We'll meet . . .* 6
retrouver *to find again*, 6
la Réunion *the island of Réunion*, 0
rêvait (imp. of rêver) *to dream*, 7
rien: Ça ne me dit rien. *That doesn't interest me.* 4; **Je n'ai rien oublié.** *I didn't forget anything.* 11; **Rien de spécial.** *Nothing special.* 6
le riz *rice*, 8
la robe *dress*, 10
le rock *rock (music)*, 4
le roller: faire du roller en ligne *to in-line skate*, 4
romain(e) *Roman (adj.)*, 6
le roman *novel*, 3
ronronner *to purr*, 7
le rosbif *roast beef*, 5
rose *pink*, 3; **la rose** (flower) *rose*, 0
le rôti *roast*, 5
rouge *red*, 3
le rouleau: un rouleau protège livres *a roll of plastic material to protect books*, 3

roux (rousse) *redhead,* 7
rouspètent (rouspéter) *to complain,* 9
le **ruban: ruban adhésif transparent** *transparent adhesive tape,* 3

S

sa *his, her,* 7
le **sac (à dos)** *bag; backpack,* 3
sage *wise,* 12
Je n'en sais rien. *I have no idea.* 11; **Je ne sais pas.** *I don't know.* 10; **Que sais-je?** *Self-check (What do I know?),* 1; **savais: Savais-tu que... ?** *Did you know . . . ? 2*
la **saison** *season,* 4
la **salade** *salad, lettuce,* 8
la **salle** *room,* 2; **la salle de classe** *classroom,* 2
Salut *Hi! or Goodbye!* 1
samedi *Saturday* 2; **le samedi** *on Saturdays,* 2
les **sandales** (f.) *sandals,* 10
le **sandwich** *sandwich,* 5
sans *without,* 3
le **saucisson** *salami,* 5
savoir *to know,* 1
les **sciences** (f.) **naturelles** *natural science,* 2
scolaire: la vie scolaire *school life,* 2
la **séance** *showing* (at the movies), 6
seconde: Une seconde, s'il vous plaît. *One second, please.* 9
secours: poste de secours *first-aid station,* 6
le **séjour** *stay, residence,* 7
la **semaine: une fois par semaine** *once a week,* 4
le **Sénégal** *Senegal,* 0
sensas (sensationnel) *fantastic,* 10
septembre *September,* 4
sera: ce sera *it will be,* 6
le **serpent** *snake,* 0
serré(e) *tight,* 10
service: A votre service. *At your service; You're welcome,* 3
ses *his, her,* 7
sévère *severe, harsh,* 0
le **short** *(a pair of) shorts,* 3
si: Moi, si. *I do.* 2
le **siècle** *century,* 6
s'il vous plaît *please,* 5
le **ski** *skiing,* 1; **faire du ski** *to ski,* 4; **faire du ski nautique** *to water-ski,* 4
la **sœur** *sister,* 7
soif: avoir soif *to be thirsty,* 5

soigné(e) *with attention to detail,* 10
le **soir** *evening, in the evening,* 4; **Pas ce soir.** *Not tonight.* 7
le **soleil** *sun, sunshine,* 4
son *his, her,* 7
le **sondage** *poll,* 1
la **sortie** *dismissal,* 2
sortir: sortir avec les copains *to go out with friends,* 1; **sortir la poubelle** *to take out the trash,* 7
souvent *often,* 4
spécial: Rien de spécial. *Nothing special.* 6
le **sport** *gym,* 2; *sports,* 1; **faire du sport** *to play sports,* 1; **Qu'est-ce que tu fais comme sport?** *What sports do you play?* 4
le **sportif (la sportive)** *sportsman, sportswoman,* 4
le **stade** *the stadium,* 6
le **steak-frites** *steak and French fries,* 5
le **style: C'est tout à fait ton style.** *It looks great on you!* 10
le **stylo** *pen,* 0; **un stylo plume** *fountain pen,* 3
la **subvention** *subsidy,* 7
suis: Qui suis-je? *Who am I?* 0
suisse *Swiss,* 1; **la Suisse** *Switzerland,* 0
suite: tout de suite *right away,* 6; **C'est tout de suite à...** *It's right there on the . . . ,* 12; **J'y vais tout de suite.** *I'll go right away.* 8
suivre *to follow,* 9
super *super,* 2; **Super!** *Great!* 1; **pas super** *not so hot,* 2
supportez (supporter) *to put up with,* 2
sur: sur place *on-site,* 4; **sur un total de** *out of a total of,* 4
sûr(e) *safe,* 9
surtout *especially,* 1
le **sweat-shirt** *a sweatshirt,* 3
sympa (abbrev. of **sympathique**) (inv.) *nice,* 7
sympathique *nice,* 7

T

ta *your,* 7
le **tableau** *blackboard,* 0
la **tache** *spot,* 7
la **taille elastiquée** *elastic waist,* 10
le **taille-crayon** *pencil sharpener,* 3
tant: tant privée que professionelle *more private than professional,* 9

la **tante** *aunt,* 7
la **tarte** *pie,* 8
tas: J'ai des tas de choses à faire. *I have lots of things to do.* 5
le **taux de réussite** *rate of success,* 7
le **taxi: en taxi** *by taxi,* 12
le **Tchad** *Chad,* 0
Tchao! *Bye!* 1
le **tee-shirt** *T-shirt,* 3
le **téléphone** *telephone,* 0; **téléphone: parler au téléphone** *to talk on the phone,* 1; **téléphoner: Téléphone-lui/ -leur!** *Call him/her/them!* 9
la **télévision** *television,* 0; **regarder la télé(vision)** *to watch TV,* 1
tellement: Pas tellement. *Not too much.* 4
temps: de temps en temps *from time to time,* 4; **Je suis désolé(e), mais je n'ai pas le temps.** *Sorry, but I don't have time.* 12; **Quel temps est-ce qu'il fait à... ?** *How's the weather in . . . ? 4*
le **tennis** *tennis,* 4
la **tenue: une tenue de gymnastique** *a gym suit,* 3
termine (terminer) *to finish,* 2
terrible: Pas terrible. *Not so great.* 1
tes *your,* 7
le **théâtre** *the theater,* 6; **faire du théâtre** *to do drama,* 4
le **thon** *tuna,* 5
Tiens! *Hey!* 3
tient (tenir) *to hold,* 12
le **timbre** *stamp,* 12
timide *shy,* 7
toi: Et toi? *And you?* 1
les **tomates** (f.) *tomatoes,* 8
ton *your,* 7
la **touche** *button, key,* 9
tour: tour de poitrine *chest size,* 10
tournez: Vous tournez... *You turn . . . ,* 12
le **tournoi** *tournament,* 4
tous *all,* 7
tout: A tout à l'heure! *See you later!* 1; **J'ai pensé à tout.** *I've thought of everything.* 11; **pas du tout** *not at all,* 2; **Il/Elle ne va pas du tout avec...** *It doesn't go at all with . . .* 10; **tout à fait: C'est tout à fait ton style.** *It looks great on you!* 10; **tout de suite** *right away,* 6; **C'est tout de suite à...** *It's right there on*

the . . . , 12; **Oui, tout de suite.** *Yes, right away.* 5; **tout droit: Vous allez tout droit jusqu'à...** *You go straight ahead until you get to . . . ,* 12

le train: en train *by train,* 12

traité: être traité comme une gosse *to be treated like a kid,* 2

la tranche: une tranche de *a slice of,* 8

le travail scolaire *school work,* 2

travailler *to work,* 9; travailler la pâte *to knead the dough,* 8

les travaux (m.) **pratiques** *lab,* 2

très: Très bien. *Very well.* 1

le trésor *treasure,* 3; chasse au trésor *treasure hunt,* 3

la trompette *trumpet,* 0

trop *too (much),* 10; **Il/Elle est trop cher.** *It's too expensive.* 10; **Non, pas trop.** *No, not too much.,* 2

la trousse *pencil case,* 3

trouver *to find,* 9; **Comment tu trouves ça?** *What do you think of that/it?,* 2; **Comment tu trouves... ?** *What do you think of . . . ?,* 2; **Je le/la/les trouve...** *I think it's/they're . . . ,* 10

les trucs: J'ai des trucs à faire. *I have some things to do.* 5

tu *you,* 0

la Tunisie *Tunisia,* 0

U

un *a, an,* 3

une *a, an,* 3

l' utilisation (f.) *the use of,* 9

utiliser *to use,* 10

V

va: Ça va. *Fine.* 1 (Comment) ça va? *How's it going?* 1; **Comment est-ce qu'on y va?** *How can we get there?* 12; **Il/Elle me va?** *Does . . . suit me?* 10; **Il/Elle ne te/vous va pas du tout.** *It doesn't look good on you at all.* 10; **Il/Elle ne va pas du tout avec...** *It doesn't go at all with . . . ,* 10; **Il/Elle te/vous va très bien.**

It suits you really well. 10; **Il/Elle va très bien avec...** *It goes very well with . . . ,* 10

les vacances (f.) *vacation,* 4; **Bonnes vacances!** *Have a good vacation!* 11; **en colonie de vacances** *to/at a summer camp,* 11; **en vacances** *on vacation,* 4

vais: Je vais... *I'm going . . .* 6; *I'm going (to) . . . ,* 11

la vaisselle: faire la vaisselle *to do the dishes,* 7

valable *valid,* 6

la valise *suitcase,* 11

la vedette *celebrity,* 1

veille: en état de veille *ready,* 9

le vélo *biking,* 1; **à vélo** *by bike,* 12; **faire du vélo** *to bike,* 4

vendredi *Friday* 2; **le vendredi** *on Fridays,* 2

la vente *sales,* 6

la verdure *vegetation,* 11

véritable *veritable,* 6; **C'était un véritable cauchemar!** *It was a real nightmare!* 11

le verre *glass,* 6

viens: Tu viens? *Will you come?* 6

le verrouillage *lock,* 9

vers *about,* 6

vert(e) *green,* 3

la veste *a suit jacket, a blazer,* 10

la viande *meat,* 8

la vidéo: faire de la vidéo *to make videos,* 4; **faire des jeux vidéo** *to play video games,* 4

la vidéocassette *a videotape,* 3

viennois(e) *Viennese* (adj), 5

vietnamien(ne) *Vietnamese,* 1

vieux *old,* 4

violet(violette) *purple,* 3

la virgule *comma,* 3

visiter *to visit (a place),* 9

vite *fast, quickly,* 2

vitrines: faire les vitrines *to window-shop,* 6

vivant *living,* 7

Vive... ! *Hurray for . . . !* 3

vivre *to live,* 2

le vocabulaire *vocabulary,* 1

Voici... *Here's . . . ,* 7

Voilà. *Here,* 3; **Voilà...** *There's . . . ,* 7

la voile *sailing,* 11; **faire de la planche à voile** *to go wind-surfing,* 11; **faire de la voile** *to go sailing,* 11

voir: voir un film *to see a movie,* 6; **voir un match** *to see a game (in person),* 6; **voir une pièce** *to see a play,* 6

le voisin *neighbor,* 1

la voiture *car,* 7; **en voiture** *by car,* 12; **laver la voiture** *to wash the car,* 7

la voix *voice,* 3

le volley (-ball) *volleyball,* 4

vos *your,* 7

votre *your,* 7

vouloir *to want,* 6; **Je veux bien.** *Gladly,* 12; **Je veux bien.** *I'd really like to.* 6; **Oui, si tu veux.** *Yes, if you want to.* 7; **Tu veux... ?** *Do you want . . . ?* 6; **Je voudrais acheter...** *I'd like to buy . . . ,* 3; **Je voudrais bien...** *I'd really like to . . . ,* 11; **Je voudrais...** *I'd like . . . ,* 3; **voulez: Vous voulez... ?** *Do you want . . . ?* 8

vous *you,* 0

voyager *to travel,* 1; **un voyage** *trip,* 0; **Bon voyage!** *Have a good trip!* 11

vrai *true,* 2

vraiment: Non, pas vraiment. *No, not really.* 11

vu (voir) *seen,* 9

la vue *view,* 6

W

le week-end: ce week-end *this weekend,* 6

le western *western (movie),* 0

Y

y *there,* 12; **Allons-y!** *Let's go!,* 4; **Comment est-ce qu'on y va?** *How can we get there?* 12; **On peut y aller...** *We can go there . . . ,* 12

le yaourt *yogurt,* 8

Z

le zèbre *zebra,* 0

zéro *a waste of time,* 2

le zoo *the zoo,* 6

Zut! *Darn!,* 3

ENGLISH-FRENCH VOCABULARY

In this vocabulary, the English definitions of all active French words in the book have been listed, followed by the French. The number after each entry refers to the chapter in which the entry is introduced. It is important to use a French word in its correct context. The use of a word can be checked easily by referring to the chapter where it appears.

French words and phrases are presented in the same way as in the French-English vocabulary.

A

a *un, une*, 3
about *vers*, 6
across from *en face de*, 12
adore: I adore . . . *J'adore...* 1
advise: What do you advise me to do? *Qu'est-ce que tu me conseilles?* 9
aerobics: to do aerobics *faire de l'aérobic*, 4
after: And after that, . . . *Et après ça...* 9
afternoon: afternoon off *l'après-midi libre*, 2; **in the afternoon** *l'après-midi* (m.), 2
afterwards: Afterwards, I went out. *Après, je suis sorti(e).* 9; **And afterwards?** *Et après?* 9
Agreed. *Entendu.* 6
algebra *l'algèbre* (f.), 2
all: Not at all. *Pas du tout.* 4
already *déjà*, 9
also *aussi*, 1
am: I am . . . years old. *J'ai... ans.* 1
an *un, une*, 3
and *et*, 1
annoying *embêtant(e)*, 7; *pénible*, 7
answer *répondre*, 9; **There's no answer.** *Ça ne répond pas.* 9
any (of it) *en* 8; **any more: I don't want any more** *Je n'en veux plus.* 8
anything: I didn't forget anything. *Je n'ai rien oublié.* 11
apple juice *le jus de pomme*, 5
apples *les pommes* (f.), 8
April *avril*, 4
are: These/those are . . . *Ce sont...* 7; **They're . . .** *Ils/Elles sont...* 7
art class *les arts* (m.) *plastiques*, 2
at *à la*, 6; *au*, 6; **at . . . fifteen** *à... heure(s) quinze*, 2; **at . . . forty-five** *à... heure(s) quarante-cinq*, 2; **at . . . thirty** *à... heure(s) trente*, 2; **at . . . (s) house** *chez...* , 6; **at the record store** *chez le disquaire*, 12; **At what time?** *A quelle heure?* 6

August *août*, 4
aunt *la tante*, 7
avocados *les avocats* (m.), 8

B

backpack *le sac à dos*, 3
bad: Not bad. *Pas mal.* 1; **Very bad.** *Tres mauvais.*
bag *le sac*, 3
baggy *large(s)*, 10
bakery *la boulangerie*, 12
bananas *les bananes* (f.), 8
bank *la banque*, 12
baseball: to play baseball *jouer au base-ball*, 4
basketball: to play basketball *jouer au basket(-ball)*, 4
bathing suit *le maillot de bain*, 10
be *être*, 7
be able to, can: *pouvoir*, 8; **Can you . . . ?** *Tu peux... ?* 12
beach *la plage*, 1
beans *les haricots* (m.), 8
begin *commencer*, 9
behind *derrière*, 12
belt *la ceinture*, 10
better: It's going to get better! *Ça va aller mieux!* 9
between *entre*, 12
big *grand(e)*, 10
bike: le vélo; *faire du vélo*, 4; **by bike** *à vélo*, 12
biking *le vélo*, 1
binder: loose-leaf binder *le classeur*, 3
biology *la biologie*, 2
black *noir(e)*, 3
blackboard *le tableau*, 0; **Go to the blackboard!** *Allez au tableau!* 0
blazer *la veste*, 10
blond *blond(e)*, 7
blue *bleu(e)*, 3
boat: by boat *en bateau*, 12
book *le livre*, 0
bookstore *la librairie*, 12
boots *les bottes* (f.), 10

boring *barbant*, 2; *C'etait ennuyeux.* **It was boring.** 5
borrow *emprunter*, 12
bottle: a bottle of *une bouteille de*, 8
box: a carton/box of *un paquet de*, 8
boy *le garçon*, 8
bracelet *le bracelet*, 3
bread *le pain*, 8
break *la récréation*, 2
breakfast *le petit déjeuner*, 8
bring *apporter*, 9; **Bring me back . . .** *Rapporte-moi...* 8; **Please bring me . . .** *Apportez-moi... , s'il vous plaît.* 5; **Will you bring me . . . ?** *Tu me rapportes... ?* 8
brother *le frère*, 7
brown *marron* (inv.), 3
brunette *brun(e)*, 7
bus: by bus *en bus*, 12
busy: It's busy. *C'est occupé.* 9; **Sorry, I'm busy.** *Désolé(e), je suis occupé(e).* 6
but *mais*, 1
butter *le beurre*, 8
buy *acheter*, 9; **Buy me . . .** *Achète(-moi)...* 8
Bye! *Tchao!* 1

C

cafeteria: at the school cafeteria *à la cantine*, 9
cake *le gâteau*, 8
calculator *la calculatrice*, 3
call: Call him/her/them! *Téléphone-lui/-leur!* 9; **Can you call back later?** *Vous pouvez rappeler plus tard?* 9; **Who's calling?** *Qui est à l'appareil?*, 9
camera *l'appareil-photo* (m.), 11
camp: to/at a summer camp *en colonie de vacances*, 11
camping: to go camping *faire du camping*, 11
can: to be able to, can *pouvoir*, 8; **Can you . . . ?** *Est-ce que tu peux... ?* 12; **Can you . . . ?** *Tu*

peux aller... ? 8; **Can I try on . . . ?** *Je peux l'/les essayer... ?* 10

can't: I can't right now. *Je ne peux pas maintenant.* 8

can: a can of *une boîte de,* 8

canary *le canari,* 7

cap *la casquette,* 10

car: by car *en voiture,* 12; **to wash the car** *laver la voiture,* 7

carrots *les carottes* (f.), 8

carton: a carton/box of *un paquet de,* 8

cassette tape *la cassette,* 3

cat *le chat,* 7

CD/compact disc *le disque compact/le CD,* 3

Certainly. *Bien sûr.* 9

chair *la chaise,* 0

check: The check please. *L'addition, s'il vous plaît.* 5

cheese *le fromage,* 5; **toasted cheese and ham sandwich** *le croque-monsieur,* 5

chemistry *la chimie,* 2

chic *chic,* 10

chicken: chickens *les poules,* 8; **chicken meat** *le poulet,* 8

chocolate *le chocolat,* 1

choir *la chorale,* 2

choose *choisir,* 10

class: What classes do you have . . . ? *Tu as quels cours... ?* 2

clean: to clean house *faire le ménage,* 7

clear: to clear the table *débarrasser la table,* 7

Close the door! *Fermez la porte!* 0

close to *près de,* 12

coast: to/at the coast *au bord de la mer,* 11

coat *le manteau,* 10

coconuts *les noix de coco* (f.), 8

coffee *le café,* 5

cola *le coca,* 5

cold: It's cold. *Il fait froid.* 4

come: to come: Will you come? *Tu viens?* 6

compact disc/CD *le disque compact/le CD,* 3

computer *l'ordinateur* (m.), 3

computer science *l'informatique* (f.), 2

concerts *les concerts* (m.), 1

cool *cool,* 2; **It's cool out.** *Il fait frais.* 4; **Yes, very cool.** *Oui, très chouette.* 9

corn *le maïs,* 8

corner: on the corner of *au coin de,* 12

cotton (adj.) *en coton,* 10

could: Could you go by . . . ? *Tu pourrais passer à... ?* 12

country: to/at the countryside *à la campagne,* 11

course *le cours,* 2

course: Of course. *Bien sûr.* 3

cousin *le cousin (la cousine),* 7

cute *mignon (mignonne),* 7

D

dance *danser,* 1; **dance (subject)** *la danse,* 2

Darn! *Zut!* 3

December *décembre,* 4

decide: Have you decided? *Vous avez choisi?* 5; **decide: Have you decided to take . . . ?** *Vous avez décidé de prendre... ?* 10

delicious *délicieux,* 5

denim: in denim *en jean,* 10

deposit: to deposit money *déposer de l'argent,* 12

dictionary *le dictionnaire,* 3

dinner *le dîner,* 8; **to have dinner** *dîner,* 9

dishes: to do the dishes *faire la vaisselle,* 7

dismissal (when school gets out) *la sortie,* 2

do *faire,* 4; **Do you play/do . . . ?** *Qu'est-ce que tu fais...? 4; I do. Moi, si.* 2; **to do homework** *faire les devoirs,* 7; **to do the dishes** *faire la vaisselle,* 7; **I don't play/do . . .** *Je ne fais pas de...* 4; **I have errands to do.** *J'ai des courses à faire.* 5; **I play/do . . .** *Je fais...* 4; **In your opinion, what do I do?** *A ton avis, qu'est-ce que je fais?* 9; **Sorry. I have homework to do.** *Désolé(e). J'ai des devoirs à faire.* 5; **What are you going to do . . . ?** *Qu'est-ce que tu vas faire... ?* 6; *Tu vas faire quoi... ?* 6; **What can I do?** *Qu'est-ce que je peux faire?* 9; **What did you do . . . ?** *Qu'est-ce que tu as fait... ?* 9; **What do you advise me to do?** *Qu'est-ce que tu me conseilles?* 9; **What do you do . . . ?** *Qu'est-ce que tu fais...?* 4; **What do you do when . . . ?** *Qu'est-ce que tu fais quand...?* 4

dog *le chien,* 7; **to walk the dog** *promener le chien,* 7

done, made *fait* (pp.), 9

door *la porte,* 0

down: You go down this street to the next light. *Vous continuez jusqu'au prochain feu rouge.* 12

dozen: a dozen *une douzaine de,* 8

drama: to do drama *faire du théâtre,* 4

dress *la robe,* 10

drink: What do you have to drink? *Qu'est-ce que vous avez comme boissons?* 5

drugstore *la pharmacie,* 12

E

earrings *les boucles* (f.), *d'oreilles* 10

easy *facile,* 2

eat *manger,* 6

eggs *les œufs* (m.), 8

English *l'anglais* (m.), 1

envelope *l'enveloppe* (f.) 12

eraser *la gomme,* 3

especially *surtout,* 1

everything: I've thought of everything. *J'ai pensé à tout.* 11

exam *l'examen* (m.), 1

excellent *excellent,* 5

excuse: Excuse me. *Excusez-moi.* 3; **Excuse me, ma'am . . . , please?** *Pardon,... s'il vous plaît?* 12

F

fail: to fail a test *rater un examen,* 9

fall: in the fall *en automne,* 4

fantastic *sensas (sensationnel),* 10

far from *loin de,* 12

fascinating *passionnant,* 2

fat *gros (grosse),* 7

father *le père,* 7

February *février,* 4

feel: I feel like . . . *J'ai envie de...* 11

finally *enfin,* 9

find *trouver,* 9

Fine. *Ça va.* 1

first *d'abord* 9; **OK, if you . . . first.** *D'accord, si tu... d'abord...* 7

fish *le poisson,* 7

flour *la farine,* 8

foot: on foot *à pied,* 12

football: to play football *jouer au football américain,* 4

forest: to the forest *en forêt,* 11

forget *oublier,* 9; **Don't forget.** *N'oublie pas de...* , 8; **Forget him/her/them!** *Oublie-le/-la/-les!* 9; **I didn't forget anything.** *Je n'ai rien oublié.* 11; **You didn't forget your . . . ?** *Tu n'as pas oublié... ?* 11

franc (the French monetary unit) *le franc,* 3

French *le français,* 1; **French fries** *les frites* (f.), 1

Friday: on Fridays *le vendredi,* 2

friends *les amis* (m.), 1; **to go out with friends** *sortir avec les copains,* 1

front: in front of *devant*, 6
fun: Did you have fun? *Tu t'es bien amusé(e)?* 11; Have fun! *Amuse-toi bien!* 11; What do you do to have fun? *Qu'est-ce que tu fais pour t'amuser?* 4
funny *amusant(e)*, 7

G

gain: to gain weight *grossir*, 10
game: to watch a game (on TV) *regarder un match*, 6
geography *la géographie*, 2
geometry *la géométrie*, 2
German *l'allemand* (m.), 2
get: Get . . . *Prends...* 8; How can we get there? *Comment est-ce qu'on y va?* 12
gift *le cadeau*, 11
girl *la fille,* 0
give: to give: Please give me . . . *Donnez-moi... , s'il vous plaît.* 5
Gladly. *Je veux bien.* 8
go *aller*, 6; Go to the blackboard! *Allez au tableau!* 0; I'm going . . . *Je vais...* 6; What are you going to do . . . ? *Tu vas faire quoi... ?* 6; It doesn't go at all with . . . *Il/Elle ne va pas du tout avec...* 10; It goes very well with . . . *Il/Elle va très bien avec...* 10; to go out with friends *sortir avec les copains*, 1; I'd like . . . to go with . . . *J'aimerais... pour aller avec...* 10; Afterwards, I went out. *Après, je suis sorti(e).* 9; Could you go by . . . ? *Tu pourrais passer à... ?* 12; Did it go well? *Ça s'est bien passé?* 11; I'm going to have . . . , please. *Je vais prendre... , s'il vous plaît.* 5; What are you going to do . . . ? *Qu'est-ce que tu vas faire... ?* 6; I went . . . *Je suis allé(e)...* 9; I'm going to . . . *Je vais...* 11; Let's go . . . *Allons...* 6; to go for a walk *faire une promenade*, 6; We can go there . . . *On peut y aller...* 12; Where are you going to go . . . ? *Où est-ce que tu vas aller... ?* 11; Where did you go? *Tu es allé(e) où?* 9; You keep going until the next light. *Vous continuez jusqu'au prochain feu rouge.* 12; How's it going? *(Comment) ça va?* 1
golf: to play golf *jouer au golf*, 4
good *bon*, 5; Did you have a good . . . ? *Tu as passé un bon... ?* 11; not very good *pas bon*, 5; Yes, very good. *Oui, très bon.* 9

Goodbye! *Au revoir!* 1; *Salut!* 1
got: No, you've got . . . to . . . *Non, tu dois...* 7
grandfather *le grand-père*, 7
grandmother *la grand-mère*, 7
grapes *le raisin*, 8
great *génial*, 2; Great! *Super!* 1; It was great! *C'était formidable!* 11; not so great *pas terrible*, 2
green *vert(e)*, 3
green beans *les *haricots verts* (m.), 8
grey *gris(e)*, 3
(small) grocery store *l'épicerie* (f.), 12
gross *dégoûtant*, 5
grow *grandir*, 10
guavas *les goyaves* (m.), 8
gym *le sport*, 2

H

half: half past *et demie*, 6; half past (after midi and minuit) *et demi*, 6
ham *le jambon*, 5; toasted cheese and ham sandwich *le croque-monsieur*, 5
hamburgers *les hamburgers* (m.), 1
hand *la main*, 0
happened: What happened? *Qu'est-ce qui s'est passé?* 9
hard *difficile*, 2
hat *le chapeau*, 10
have *avoir*, 2; At what time do you have . . . ? *Tu as... à quelle heure?* 2; Do you have . . . ? *Vous avez... ?* 2; *Tu as... ?* 3; Do you have that in . . . ? (size, fabric, color) *Vous avez ça en... ?* 10; Have . . . *Prends/Prenez...* 5; What are you having? *Vous prenez?* 5; I don't have . . . *Je n'ai pas de...* 3; I have some things to do. *J'ai des trucs à faire.* 5; I have . . . *J'ai...* 2; I'll have . . . , please. *Je vais prendre... , s'il vous plaît.* 5; to take or to have (food or drink) *prendre*, 5; We have . . . *Nous avons...* 2; What classes do you have . . . ? *Tu as quels cours... ?* 2; What do you have . . . ? *Tu as quoi... ?* 2; What kind of . . . do you have? *Qu'est-ce que vous avez comme... ?* 5; Will you have . . . ? *Tu prends... ?* 8; Will you have . . . ? *Vous prenez... ?* 8
health *le cours de développement personnel et social (DPS)*, 2
Hello *Bonjour*, 1; Hello? (on the phone) *Allô?* 9
help: May I help you? *(Est-ce que) je peux vous aider?* 10

her *la*, 9; *son/sa/ses*, 7
Here. *Voilà.* 3
Hi! *Salut!* 1
hiking: to go hiking *faire de la randonnée*, 11
him *le*, 9
his *son/sa/ses*, 7
history *l'histoire* (f.), 2
hockey: to play hockey *jouer au hockey*, 4
Hold on. *Ne quittez pas.* 9
homework *les devoirs*, 2; to do homework *faire les devoirs*, 7
horrible: It was horrible. *C'était épouvantable.* 9
horse: to go horseback riding *faire de l'équitation*, 1
hose *le collant*, 10
hot chocolate *le chocolat*, 5
hot dog *le hot-dog*, 5
hot: It's hot. *Il fait chaud.* 4; not so hot *pas super*, 2
house: at my house *chez moi*, 6; Is this . . . 's house? *Je suis bien chez... ?* 9; to/at . . . 's house *chez...* 11;
housework: to do housework *faire le ménage*, 7
how much: How much is . . . ? *C'est combien,... ?* 3; How much is it? (total) *Ça fait combien, s'il vous plaît?* 5
how: How old are you? *Tu as quel âge?* 1; How about . . . ? *On . . . ?* 4; How do you like it? *Comment tu trouves ça?* 5; How much is . . . ? *C'est combien... ?* 5; How much is it, please? (total) *Ça fait combien, s'il vous plaît?* 5; How's it going? *(Comment) ça va?* 1
hungry: to be hungry *avoir faim*, 5; No thanks. I'm not hungry anymore. *Non, merci. Je n'ai plus faim.* 8

I

I *je*, 1; I *do.* *Moi, si.* 2; I don't. *Moi, non.* 2
ice cream *la glace*, 1
ice-skate *faire du patin à glace*, 4
idea: Good idea. *Bonne idée.* 4; I have no idea. *Je n'en sais rien.* 11
if: OK, if you . . . first. *D'accord, si tu... d'abord...* 7
in *dans*, 6; in (a city or place) *à*, 11; in (before a feminine country) *en*, 11; in (before a masculine country) *au*, 11; in (before a plural country) *aux*, 11; in front of *devant*, 6; in the afternoon

l'après-midi, 2; **in the evening** *le soir*, 4; **in the morning** *le matin*, 2

indifference: (expression of indifference) *Bof!* 1

intend: I intend to . . . *J'ai l'intention de. . .* 11

interest: That doesn't interest me. *Ça ne me dit rien.* 4

interesting *intéressant*, 2

is: He is . . . *Il est... ,* 7; **It's . . .** *C'est... ,* 2; **She is . . .** *Elle est... ,* 7; **There's . . .** *Voilà... ,* 7; **This is . . .** *C'est... ; Voici... ,* 7

it *le, la,* 9

It's . . . *C'est...* 2; **It's . . .** *Il est...* (time), 6; **It's . . . francs.** *Ça fait... francs.* 5; **No, it's . . .** *Non, c'est...* 4; **Yes, it's . . .** *Oui, c'est...* 4

J

jacket *le blouson,* 10

jam *la confiture,* 8

January *janvier,* 4

jeans *le jean,* 3

jog *faire du jogging,* 4

July *juillet,* 4

June *juin,* 4

K

kilogram: a kilogram of *un kilo de,* 8

kind: What kind of . . . do you have? *Qu'est-ce que vous avez comme... ?* 5

know: I don't know. *Je ne sais pas.* 10

L

lab *les travaux* (m.) *pratiques,* 2

later: Can you call back later? *Vous pouvez rappeler plus tard?* 9; **See you later!** *A tout à l'heure!* 1

Latin *le latin,* 2

leather: in leather *en cuir,* 10

leave *partir,* 11; **Can I leave a message?** *Je peux laisser un message?* 9; **You can't leave without . . .** *Tu ne peux pas partir sans...* 11

left: to the left *à gauche,* 12

lemon soda *la limonade,* 5

let's: Let's go . . . *Allons...* 6; **Let's go!** *Allons-y!* 4

letter: to send letters *envoyer des lettres,* 12

library *la bibliothèque,* 6

like *aimer,* 1; **I'd really like . . .** *Je voudrais bien...* 11; **Do you like . . . ?** *Tu aimes... ?* 1; **Do you like it?** *Il/Elle te (vous) plaît?* 10; **How do you like . . . ?** *Comment tu trouves... ?* 10; **How do you like it?** *Comment tu trouves ça?* 5; **I (really) like . . .** *Moi, j'aime (bien)...* 1; **I don't like . . .** *Je n'aime pas...* 1; **I like it, but it's expensive.** *Il/Elle me plaît, mais il/elle est cher (chère).* 10; **I'd like . . .** *Je voudrais...* 3; **I'd like . . . go with . . .** *J'aimerais... pour aller avec...* 10; **I'd really like to.** *Je veux bien.* 6; **I'd like to buy . . .** *Je voudrais acheter...* 3; **What would you like?** *Vous désirez?* 10;

like: What are they like? *Ils/Elles sont comment?* 7; **What is he like?** *Il est comment?* 7; **What is she like?** *Elle est comment?* 7

Listen! *Ecoutez!* 0; **I'm listening.** *Je t'écoute.* 9; **to listen to music** *écouter de la musique,* 1

liter: a liter of *un litre de,* 8

look after: to look after . . . *garder... ,* 7

look: Look at the map! *Regardez la carte!* 0; **That doesn't look good on you.** *Il/Elle ne te vous va pas du tout.* 10; **I'm looking for something for . . .** *Je cherche quelque chose pour...* 10; **It looks great on you!** *C'est tout à fait ton style.* 10; **Look, here's (there's) (it's) . . .** *Regarde, voilà...* 12; **No, thanks, I'm just looking.** *Non, merci, je regarde.* 10; **to look for** *chercher,* 9;

looks: It looks great on you! *C'est tout à fait ton style.* 10

lose: to lose weight *maigrir,* 10

lot: A lot. *Beaucoup.* 4

lots: I have lots of things to do. *J'ai des tas de choses à faire.* 5; **I have lots of things to do.** *J'ai des trucs à faire.* 6

luck: Good luck! *Bonne chance!* 11

lunch *le déjeuner,* 2; **to have lunch** *déjeuner,* 9

M

ma'am *madame (Mme),* 1

made *fait (faire),* 9

magazine *le magazine,* 3

make *faire,* 4

mall *le centre commercial,* 6

mangoes *les mangues* (f.), 8

map *la carte,* 0

March *mars,* 4

math *les maths* (f.), *les mathématiques,* 1

May *mai,* 4

may: May I . . . ? *(Est-ce que) je peux . . . ?* 7; **May I help you?** *(Est-ce que) je peux vous aider?* 10

mean *méchant(e),* 7

meat *la viande,* 8

medicine *les médicaments* (m.), 12

meet *rencontrer,* 9; **I'd like you to meet . . .** *Je te (vous) présente...* 7; **Pleased to meet you.** *Très heureux (heureuse).* 7; **OK, we'll meet . . .** *Bon, se retrouve...* 6; **We'll meet. . .** *Rendez-vous...* 6

menu: The menu, please. *La carte, s'il vous plaît.* 5

message: Can I leave a message? *Je peux laisser un message?* 9

metro: at the . . . metro stop *au métro ... ,* 6

midnight *minuit,* 6

milk *le lait,* 8

mineral water *l'eau minérale* (f.), 5

minute: Do you have a minute? *Tu as une minute?* 9

miss, Miss *mademoiselle (Mlle),* 1

miss: to miss the bus *rater le bus,* 9

moment: One moment, please. *Un moment, s'il vous plaît.* 5

Monday: on Mondays *le lundi,* 2

money *l'argent* (m.), 11

More . . . ? *Encore de... ?* 8

morning: in the morning *le matin,* 2

mother *la mère,* 7

mountain: to/at the mountains *à la montagne,* 11

movie theater *le cinéma,* 6; **the movies** *le cinéma,* 1

Mr. *monsieur (M.),* 1

Mrs. *madame (Mme),* 1

much: How much is . . . ? *C'est combien,... ?* 5; **How much is it, please?** *Ça fait combien, s'il vous plaît?* 5; **How much is it?** *C'est combien?* 3; **No, not too much.** *Non, pas trop.* 2; **Not much.** *Pas grand-chose.* 6; **Not too much.** *Pas tellement.* 4; **Not very much.** *Pas beaucoup.* 4; **Yes, very much.** *Oui, beaucoup.* 2

museum *le musée,* 6

mushrooms *les champignons* (m.), 8

music *la musique,* 2

my *mon/ma/mes,* 7

N

name: His/Her name is . . . *Il/Elle s'appelle...* 1; **My name is . . .** *Je m'appelle...* 0; **What is your name?**

Tu t'appelles comment? 0

natural science *les sciences* (f.) *naturelles*, 2

need: I need . . . *Il me faut...* 3; **I need . . .** *J'ai besoin de...* 8; **What do you need for . . . ? (formal)** *Qu'est-ce qu'il vous faut pour...* 3; **What do you need for . . . ? (informal)** *Qu'est-ce qu'il te faut pour ... ?* 3; **What do you need?** *De quoi est-ce que tu as besoin?* 8

neither: Neither do I. *Moi non plus.* 2

never *ne... jamais*, 4

next to *à côté de*, 12

nice *gentil, gentille*, 7: **It's nice weather.** *Il fait beau.* 4

nightmare: It was a real nightmare! *C'était un véritable cauchemar!* 11

no *non*, 1

none (of it) *en*, 8

noon *midi*, 6

not: Oh, not bad. *Oh, pas mauvais.* 9; **not yet** *ne... pas encore*, 9; **Not at all.** *Pas du tout.* 4; **Not me.** *Pas moi.* 2; **not so great** *pas terrible*, 5; **not very good** *pas bon*, 5;

notebook *le cahier*, 0

nothing: Nothing special. *Rien de spécial.* 6

novel *le roman*, 3

November *novembre*, 4

O

o'clock: at . . . o'clock *à... heure(s)*, 2

October *octobre*, 4

of *de*, 0; **of it** *en*, 8; **of them** *en*, 8

off: afternoon off *l'après-midi libre*, 2

often *souvent*, 4

OK. *D'accord.* 4; **Is that OK with you?** *Tu es d'accord?* 7; **Well, OK.** *Bon, d'accord.* 8; **Yes it was OK.** *Oui, ça a été.*

okra *les gombos* (m.), 8

old: old-fashioned *démodé(e)(s)*, 10; **How old are you?** *Tu as quel âge?* 1; **I am . . . years old.** *J'ai... ans.* 1; **older** *âgé(e)*, 7

on: Can I try on . . . ? *Je peux essayer le/la/les... ?* 10; **on foot** *à pied*, 12; **on Fridays** *le vendredi*, 2; **on Mondays** *le lundi*, 2; **on Saturdays** *le samedi*, 2; **on Sundays** *le dimanche*, 2; **on Thursdays** *le jeudi*, 2; **on Tuesdays** *le mardi*, 2; **on Wednesdays** *le mercredi*, 2; **once: once a week** *une fois par semaine*, 4

open: Open your books to page . . . *Ouvrez vos livres à la page...*, 0

opinion: In your opinion, what do I do? *A ton avis, qu'est-ce que je fais?* 9

orange *orange*, (inv.), 3; **orange juice** *le jus d'orange*, 5; **oranges** *les oranges* (f.), 8

our *notre/nos*, 7

out: Out of the question! *Pas question!* 7

P

page *la page*, 0

pair: pair of pants *le pantalon*, 10; **(a pair of) jeans** *le jean*, 3; **(a pair of) shorts** *le short*, 3

papayas *les papayes* (f.), 8

paper *le papier*, 0; **sheets of paper** *les feuilles* (f.) *de papier*, 3

pardon: Pardon me. *Pardon*, 3

park *le parc*, 6

pass: You'll pass . . . *Vous passez devant...* 12

passport *le passeport*, 11

pastry *la pâtisserie*, 12; **pastry shop** *la pâtisserie*, 12

peaches *les pêches* (f.), 8

pears *les poires* (f.), 8

peas *les petits pois* (m.), 8

pen *le stylo*, 0

pencil *le crayon*, 3; **pencil case** *la trousse*, 3; **pencil sharpener** *le taille-crayon*, 3

perfect: It's perfect. *C'est parfait.* 10

phone: to talk on the phone *parler au téléphone*, 1

physical education *l'éducation* (f.) *physique et sportive (EPS)*, 2

physics *la physique*, 2

pick *choisir*, 10; **to pick up your room** *ranger ta chambre*, 7

picnic: to have a picnic *faire un pique-nique*, 6

picture: to take pictures *faire des photos*, 4

pie *la tarte*, 8

piece: a piece of *un morceau de*, 8

pineapple *les ananas* (m.), 8

pink *rose*, 3

pizza *la pizza*, 1

plane ticket *le billet d'avion*, 11

plane: by plane *en avion*, 12

plans: I don't have any plans. *Je n'ai rien de prévu.* 11

play *jouer*, 4; *faire*, 4; **I don't play/do . . .** *Je ne fais pas de...* 4; **I play . . .** *Je joue...* , 4; **I play/do . . .** *Je fais...* , 4; **to play baseball** *jouer au base-ball*, 4; **to play bas-**

ketball *jouer au basket(-ball)*, 4; **to play football** *jouer au football américain*, 4; **to play golf** *jouer au golf*, 4; **to play hockey** *jouer au hockey*, 4; **to play soccer** *jouer au foot(ball)*, 4; **to play sports** *faire du sport*, 1; **to play tennis** *jouer au tennis*, 4; **to play volleyball** *jouer au volley(-ball)*, 4; **What sports do you play?** *Qu'est-ce que tu fais comme sport?* 4; **What do you do to have fun?** *Qu'est-ce que tu fais pour t'amuser?* 4

please *s'il vous/te plaît*, 3

pleased: Pleased to meet you. *Très heureux (heureuse).* 7

pleasure: Yes, with pleasure. *Oui, avec plaisir.* 8

pork *le porc*, 8

post office *la poste*, 12

poster *le poster*, 0

potatoes *les pommes de terre* (f.), 8

pound: a pound of *une livre de*, 8

practice *répéter*, 9

prefer: I prefer . . . *Je préfère...* 1; *J'aime mieux...* 1

problem: I've got a problem. *J'ai un petit problème.* 9

pullover (sweater) *le pull-over*, 3

purple *violet(te)*, 3

put *mettre*, 10; **to put on** *mettre*, 10

Q

quarter: quarter past *et quart*, 6; **quarter to** *moins le quart*, 6

question: Out of the question! *Pas question!* 7

quiz *l'interro* (f.), 9

R

radio *la radio*, 3

rain: It's raining. *Il pleut.* 4

Raise your hand! *Levez la main!* 0

read *lire*, 1; **read (p. p.)** *lu (lire)*, 9

really: I (really) like . . . *Moi, j'aime (bien)...* 1; **I'd really like to . . .** *Je voudrais bien...* 11; **I'd really like to.** *Je veux bien.* 6; **No, not really.** *Non, pas vraiment.* 11

record: at the record store *chez le disquaire*, 12

recreation center *la Maison des jeunes et de la culture (MJC)*, 6

red *rouge*, 3; **redhead** *roux (rousse)*, 7

rehearse *répéter*, 9

Repeat! *Répétez!* 0

restaurant   *le restaurant*, 6
return: to return something   *rendre*, 12
rice   *le riz*, 8
ride: to ride: to go horseback riding   *faire de l'équitation*, 1
right: to the right   *à droite*, 12
right away: *Oui, tout de suite.* Yes, right away. 5; I'll go right away. *J'y vais tout de suite.* 8
right now: I can't right now. *Je ne peux pas maintenant.* 8
right there: It's right there on the . . .   *C'est tout de suite à...* 12
room: to pick up your room   *ranger ta chambre*, 7
ruler   *la règle*, 3

S

sailing: to go sailing   *faire de la voile*, 11; *faire du bateau*, 11
salad, lettuce   *la salade*, 8
salami   *le saucisson*, 5
sandals   *les sandales* (f.), 10
sandwich   *le sandwich*, 5
Saturday: on Saturdays   *le samedi*, 2
scarf   *l'écharpe* (f.), 10
school   *l'école* (f.), 1
scuba diving: to go scuba diving   *faire de la plongée*, 11
second: One second, please.   *Une seconde, s'il vous plaît.* 9
see: See you later!   *A tout à l'heure!* 1; See you soon.   *A bientôt.* 1; See you tomorrow.   *A demain.* 1; to see a game (in person)   *voir un match*, 6; to see a movie   *voir un film*, 6; to see a play   *voir une pièce*, 6
seen   *vu* (pp.), 9
send: to send letters   *envoyer des lettres*, 12
study   *étudier*, 1
September   *septembre*, 4
service: At your service; You're welcome.   *A votre service.* 3
shall: Shall we go to the café?   *On va au café?* 5
sheet: a sheet of paper   *la feuille de papier*, 0
shirt (men's)   *la chemise*, 10; (women's)   *le chemisier*, 10
shoes   *les chaussures* (f.), 10
shop: to go shopping   *faire les magasins*, 1; to window-shop   *faire les vitrines*, 6; Can you do the shopping?   *Tu peux aller faire les courses?* 8
short (height)   *petit(e)*, 7; (length)   *court(e)*, 10

shorts: (a pair of) shorts   *le short*, 3
should: You should talk to him/her/them.   *Tu devrais lui/leur parler.* 9
show   *montrer*, 9
shy   *timide*, 7
sing   *chanter*, 9
sir   *monsieur* (M.), 1
sister   *la sœur*, 7
Sit down!   *Asseyez-vous!* 0
skate: ice-skate   *faire du patin à glace*, 4; to in-line skate   *faire du roller en ligne*, 4
ski   *faire du ski*, 4; to water-ski   *faire du ski nautique*, 4; skiing   *le ski*, 1
skirt   *la jupe*, 10
sleep   *dormir*, 1
slender   *mince*, 7
slice: a slice of   *une tranche de*, 8
small   *petit(e)(s)*, 10
smart   *intelligent(e)*, 7
snack: afternoon snack   *le goûter*, 8
snails   *les escargots* (m.), 1
sneakers   *les baskets* (f.), 3
snow: It's snowing.   *Il neige.* 4
so: not so great   *pas terrible*, 5; So-so.   *Comme ci, comme ça.* 1
soccer   *le football*, 1; to play soccer   *jouer au foot(ball)*, 4
socks   *les chaussettes* (f.), 10
some   *des*, 3; some   *du, de la, de l', des*, 8; some (of it)   *en*, 8
sometimes   *quelquefois*, 4
soon: See you soon.   *A bientôt.* 1
Sorry.   *Je regrette.* 3; *Désolé(e).* 5
Spanish   *l'espagnol* (m.), 2
speak: Could I speak to . . . ?   *(Est-ce que) je peux parler à... ?* 9
special: Nothing special.   *Rien de spécial.* 6
sports   *le sport*, 1; to play sports   *faire du sport*, 1; What sports do you play?   *Qu'est-ce que tu fais comme sport?* 4
spring: in the spring   *au printemps*, 4
stadium   *le stade*, 6
stamp   *le timbre*, 12
Stand up!   *Levez-vous!* 0
start   *commencer*, 9
stationery store   *la papeterie*, 12
steak   *le bifteck*, 8; steak and French fries   *le steak-frites*, 5
stop: at the . . . metro stop   *au métro ...* , 6
stores   *les magasins* (m.), 1
straight ahead: You go straight ahead until you get to . . .   *Vous allez tout droit jusqu'à...* , 12
strawberries   *les fraises* (f.), 8
street: You keep going until the next light.   *Vous continuez jusqu'au*

prochain feu rouge. 12; Take . . . Street, then cross . . . Street. *Prenez la rue... , puis traversez la rue...* 12
strong   *fort(e)*, 7
student   *l'élève* (m./f.), 2
study hall   *l'étude* (f.), 2
style: in style   *à la mode*, 10; style of the Forties or Fifties   *rétro* (inv.) 10
subway: by subway   *en métro*, 12
suit jacket   *la veste*, 10
suit: Does it suit me?   *Il/Elle me va?* 10; It suits you really well.   *Il/Elle te/vous va très bien.* 10
suitcase   *la valise*, 11
summer: in the summer   *en été*, 4
Sunday: on Sundays   *le dimanche*, 2
sunglasses   *les lunettes* (f.) de soleil, 10
super   *super*, 2
sure: I'm not sure.   *J'hésite.* 10
sweater   *le cardigan*, 10
sweatshirt   *le sweat-shirt*, 3
swim   *nager*, 1; *faire de la natation*, 4
swimming pool   *la piscine*, 6

T

T-shirt   *le tee-shirt*, 3
table: to clear the table   *débarrasser la table*, 7
tacky: I think it's (they're) really tacky.   *Je le/la/les trouve moche(s).* 10
take out: Take out a sheet of paper.   *Prenez une feuille de papier.* 0; to take out the trash   *sortir la poubelle*, 7
take or have (food or drink)   *prendre*, 5; Are you going to take it/them?   *Vous le/la/les prenez?* 10; Are you taking . . . ?   *Tu prends...?* 11; Have you decided to take . . . ?   *Vous avez décidé de prendre... ?* 10; I'll take it/them. *Je le/la/les prends.* 10; to take a test   *passer un examen* (9); to take pictures   *faire des photos*, 4; We can take . . .   *On peut prendre...* 12; Take . . . Street, then . . . Street. *Prenez la rue... , puis la rue...* 12
taken   *pris (prendre)*, 9
talk: Can I talk to you?   *Je peux te parler?* 9; to talk on the phone   *parler au téléphone*, 1; We talked.   *Nous avons parlé.* 9;
tall   *grand(e)*, 7
taxi: by taxi   *en taxi*, 12
teacher   *le professeur*, 0

television *la télévision*, 0

tell: to tell: Can you tell her/him that I called? *Vous pouvez lui dire que j'ai téléphoné?* 9

tennis: to play tennis *jouer au tennis*, 4

terrible *horrible(s)*, 10

tests *les examens* (m.), 1

Thank you. *Merci.* 3; No thanks. I'm not hungry anymore. *Non, merci. Je n'ai plus faim.* 8

that *ce, cet, cette*, 3; This/That is . . . *Ça, c'est...* 12

theater *le théâtre*, 6

their *leur/leurs*, 7

them *les*, 9

then *ensuite* 9

there: there *-là (noun suffix)*, 3; there *y*, 12; Is. . . there, please? *(Est-ce que)... est là, s'il vous plaît?* 9; There's . . . *Voilà...* 7

these *ces*, 3; These/those are . . . *Ce sont...* 7

things: I have lots of things to do. *J'ai des tas de choses à faire.* 5; I have some things to do. *J'ai des trucs à faire.* 5

think: I think it's/they're . . . *Je le/la/les trouve...* 10; I've thought of everything. *J'ai pensé à tout.* 11; What do you think of . . . ? *Comment tu trouves...* ? 2; What do you think of that/it? *Comment tu trouves ça?* 2

thirsty: to be thirsty *avoir soif*, 5

this *ce, cet, cette*, 3; This is . . . *C'est...* 7; This is . . . *Voici...* 7; This/That is . . . *Ça, c'est...* 12

those *ces*, 3; These (those) are . . . *Ce sont...* 7

Thursday: on Thursdays *le jeudi*, 2

ticket: plane ticket *le billet d'avion*, 11; train ticket *le billet de train*, 11

tie *la cravate*, 10

tight *serré(e)(s)*, 10

time: a waste of time *zéro*, 2; At what time do you have . . . ? *Tu as... à quelle heure?* 2; At what time? *A quelle heure?* 6; from time to time *de temps en temps*, 4; I'm sorry, but I don't have time. *Je regrette, mais je n'ai pas le temps.* 8; I'm sorry, but I don't have time. *Je suis désolé(e), mais je n'ai pas le temps.* 12; What time is it? *Quelle heure est-il?* 6

to *à la*, 6; *au*, 6; to (a city or place) *à*, 11; to (before a feminine noun) *en*, 11; to (before a masculine noun) *au*, 11; to (before a plural noun) *aux*, 11; to her *lui*, 9; to him *lui*, 9; to them *leur*, 9; five

to *moins cinq*, 6

today *aujourd'hui*, 2

tomatoes *les tomates* (f.), 8

tomorrow *demain*, 2; See you tomorrow. *A demain.* 1

tonight: Not tonight. *Pas ce soir.* 7

too: It's/They're too . . . *Il/Elle est (Ils/Elles sont) trop...* 10; Me too. *Moi aussi.* 2; No, it's too expensive. *Non, c'est trop cher.* 10; No, not too much. *Non, pas trop.* 2; Not too much. *Pas tellement.* 4

track: to do track and field *faire de l'athlétisme*, 4

train: by train *en train*, 12; train ticket *le billet de train*, 11

trash: to take out the trash *sortir la poubelle*, 7

travel *voyager*, 1

trip: Have a good trip! *Bon voyage!* 11

try: Can I try it (them) on ? *Je peux l'(les) essayer?* 10

Tuesday: on Tuesdays *le mardi*, 2

turn: You turn . . . *Vous tournez...* 12

TV: to watch TV *regarder la télé(vision)*, 1

U

uncle *l'oncle* (m.), 7

useless *nul*, 2

usually *d'habitude*, 4

V

vacation *les vacances* (f.), 1; Have a good vacation! *Bonnes vacances!* 11; on vacation *en vacances*, 4

VCR (videocassette recorder) *le magnétoscope*, 0

very: not very good *pas bon*, 5; Yes, very much. *Oui, beaucoup.* 2

video: to make videos *faire de la vidéo*, 4; video games *des jeux vidéo*, 4

videocassette recorder, VCR *le magnétoscope*, 0

videotape *la vidéocassette*, 3

visit (a place) *visiter*, 9

volleyball: to play volleyball *jouer au volley(-ball)*, 4

W

wait for *attendre*, 9

Waiter! *Monsieur!* 5

Waitress! *Madame!* 5; *Mademoiselle!* 5

walk: to go for a walk *faire une*

promenade, 6; to walk the dog *promener le chien*, 7

wallet *le portefeuille*, 3

want *vouloir*, 6; Do you want . . . ? *Tu veux... ?* 6; Do you want . . . ? *Vous voulez... ?* 8; Yes, if you want too. *Oui, si tu veux.* 7

wash: to wash the car *laver la voiture*, 7

waste: a waste of time *zéro*, 2

watch *la montre*, 3

watch: to watch a game (on TV) *regarder un match*, 6; to watch TV *regarder la télé(vision)*, 1

water: to water ski *faire du ski nautique*, 4

wear *mettre, porter*, 10; I don't know what to wear for . . . *Je ne sais pas quoi mettre pour...* 10; Wear . . . *Mets...* 10; What shall I wear? *Qu'est-ce que je mets?* 10; Why don't you wear . . . ? *Pourquoi est-ce que tu ne mets pas... ?* 10

Wednesday: on Wednesdays *le mercredi*, 2

weekend: Did you have a good weekend? *Tu as passé un bon week-end?* 9; on weekends *le week-end*, 4; this weekend *ce week-end*, 6

welcome: At your service; You're welcome. *A votre service.* 3

well: Did it go well? *Ça s'est bien passé?* 11; Very well. *Très bien.* 1

went: Afterwards, I went out. *Après, je suis sorti(e).* 9; I went . . . *Je suis allé(e)...* 9

what *comment*, 0; What is your name? *Tu t'appelles comment?* 0; What are you going to do . . . ? *Qu'est-ce que tu vas faire... ?* 6; What are you going to do . . . ? *Tu vas faire quoi... ?* 6; What do you have to drink? *Qu'est-ce que vous avez comme boissons?* 5; What do you need for . . . ? (formal) *Qu'est-ce qu'il vous faut pour... ?* 3; What do you think of . . . ? *Comment tu trouves... ?* 2; What do you think of that/it? *Comment tu trouves ça?* 2; What kind of . . . do you have? *Qu'est-ce que vous avez comme... ?* 5; What's his/her name? *Il/Elle s'appelle comment?* 1

When? *Quand (ça)?* 6

where: Where? *Où (ça)?* 6; Where did you go? *Tu es allé(e) où?* 9

white *blanc(he)(s)*, 3

who: Who's calling? *Qui est à l'appareil?* 9

whom: With whom? *Avec qui?* 6

why: Why don't you . . . ? *Pourquoi tu ne... pas?* 9; Why not? *Pourquoi pas?* 6

win *gagner,* 9

window *la fenêtre,* 0; to window-shop *faire les vitrines,* 6

windsurfing: to go windsurfing *faire de la planche à voile,* 11

winter: in the winter *en hiver,* 4

with: with me *avec moi,* 6; With whom? *Avec qui?* 6

withdraw: withdraw money *retirer de l'argent* (m.), 12

without: You can't leave without . . . *Tu ne peux pas partir sans...* 11

work *travailler,* 9

worry: Don't worry! *Ne t'en fais pas!* 9

would like: I'd like to buy . . . *Je voudrais acheter...* 3

Y

yellow *jaune,* 3

yes *oui,* 1

yet: not yet *ne... pas encore,* 9

yogurt *le yaourt,* 8

you *tu, vous,* 0

young *jeune,* 7

your *ton/ta/tes,* 7; *vos,* 0; *votre* 7

Z

zoo *le zoo,* 6

GRAMMAR INDEX

A

à: contractions with **à** and **de**, p. 101; the prepositions **à** and **en**, p. 290

adjectives: adjective agreement and placement, p. 79; adjective agreement, p. 186; adjectives used as nouns, p. 265; demonstrative adjectives **ce, cet, cette,** and **ces,** p. 77; possessive adjectives, p. 181

adverbs: adverbs of frequency, p. 110; placement of adverbs with the **passé composé,** p. 240

agreement: adjective agreement and placement, p. 79; adjective agreement, p. 186

aimer, p. 33 (regular)

aller, p. 154 (irregular)

articles: the definite articles **le, la, l', les** and the gender of nouns, p. 28; the indefinite articles **un, une, des,** p. 73; the partitive articles **du, de la, de l',** and **des,** p. 208

avoir, p. 51 (irregular); **passé composé** with **avoir,** p. 239

avoir besoin de, p. 210

C

ce, cet, cette, ces: demonstrative adjectives, p. 77

c'est versus **il/elle est,** p. 274

choisir, p. 267 (regular)

contractions with **à** and **de,** p. 101

D

days of the week: using **le** with days of the week, p. 153

de: **de** after a negative verb, p. 104; **de** with expressions of quantity, p. 214; contractions with **à** and **de,** p. 101; possession with **de,** p. 180

de la, de l': partitive articles, p. 208

definite articles: the definite articles **le, la, l', les** and the gender of nouns, p. 28

demonstrative adjectives: **ce, cet, cette,** and **ces,** p. 77

des: indefinite articles, p. 73; partitive articles, p. 208

direct object pronouns le, la, and **les,** p. 247, p. 273

du: partitive articles, p. 208

E

en: the prepositions **à** and **en** p. 290; the pronoun **en,** p. 220

-er verbs, p. 33, 107

être, p. 187 (irregular)

F

faire, p. 104 (irregular)

frequency: adverbs of frequency, p. 110

G

gender: the definite articles **le, la, l', les** and the gender of nouns, p. 28

I

il est: **c'est** versus **il/elle est,** p. 274

imperatives, p. 136

indefinite articles: un, une, and **des,** p. 73

information questions, p. 165

-ir verbs: choisir, p. 267 (regular)

L

l': definite articles, p. 28

la: definite articles, p. 28; object pronouns, p. 247, p. 273

le: definite articles, p. 28; object pronouns, p. 247, p. 273; using **le** with days of the week, p. 153

les: definite articles, p. 28; object pronouns, p. 247, p. 273

leur, leurs: possessive adjectives, p. 181; object pronouns, p. 247

lui: object pronouns, p. 247

M

ma: possessive adjectives, p. 181

mes: possessive adjectives, p. 181

mettre, p. 263 (irregular)

mon: possessive adjectives, p. 181

N

ne... pas, p. 26
negative: de after a negative verb, p. 104
notre, nos: possessive adjectives, p. 181

O

object pronouns: le, la, les, lui, and leur, p. 247
oui: using si instead of oui to contradict a negative
    statement, p. 50

P

partir, p. 294 (regular)
partitive articles: du, de la, de l', and des, p. 208
passé composé: passé composé with avoir,
    p. 239; placement of adverbs with the passé
    composé, p. 240
possession with de, p. 180
possessive adjectives, p. 181
pouvoir, p. 213 (irregular)
prendre, p. 133 (irregular)
prepositions: the prepositions à and en, p. 290
pronouns: the object pronouns le, la, les, lui, and
    leur, p. 247, p. 273; the pronoun en, p. 220; the
    pronoun y, p. 323

Q

question formation, p. 103
questions: Information questions, p. 165

R

-re verbs, p. 245
répondre, p. 245 (regular)

S

son, sa, ses: possessive adjectives, p. 181
si: using si instead of oui to contradict a negative
    statement, p. 50
subject pronouns and -er verbs, p. 33

T

ton, ta, tes: possessive adjectives, p. 181

U

un, une: indefinite articles, p. 73

V

votre, vos: possessive adjectives, p. 181
vouloir, p. 160 (irregular)

Y

y: the pronoun y, p. 323

ACKNOWLEDGMENTS (continued from page ii)

EF Ecole Européenne de Vacances S.A.R.L.: From "Le rêve américain devient réalité, en séjour Immersion avec EF," photograph, and "Vacances de Printemps" "from" "Les U.S.A. en cours Principal: le séjour EF idéal" from *1993: EF Voyage: Hiver, Printemps, et Eté.*

Établissement public du Grand Louvre: Photograph, "Palais du Louvre," from *Les 34 Musées Nationaux,* 1992 edition.

Femme Actuelle: Text from "En direct des refuges: Poupette, 3 ans" by Nicole Lauroy from *Femme Actuelle,* #414, August 31-September 6, 1992. Copyright © 1992 by Femme Actuelle. Text from "En direct des refuges: Jupiter, 7 ans" by Nicole Lauroy from *Femme Actuelle,* #436, February 1993. Copyright © 1993 by Femme Actuelle. Text from "En direct des refuges: Flora, 3 ans" by Nicole Lauroy from *Femme Actuelle,* #457, July, 1993. Copyright © 1993 by *Femme Actuelle.* Text from "En direct des refuges: Dady, 2 ans; Mayo a trouvé une famille" by Nicole Lauroy from *Femme Actuelle,* #466, August 30-September 5, 1993. Copyright © 1993 by Femme Actuelle. Text from "En direct des refuges: Camel, 5 ans" by Nicole Lauroy from *Femme Actuelle,* #472, October 11-17, 1993. Copyright © 1993 by Femme Actuelle.

France Miniature: Illustration, phototgraph, and excerpt from *Le Pays France Miniature.*

France Télécom: Cover and excerpts from Minitel 2 : *Mode d'emploi modèle Alcatel.* Illustration from page 2048 from *Paris Annuaire Officiel des Abonnées au Téléphone,* Volume 2, f/m, April 1988.

Galeries Lafayette: Two photographs with captions of Naf-Naf products and four photographs with captions of Cacharel products from *RENTREE TRES CLASSE A PRIX PETITS: Nouvelles Galeries Lafayette.*

Grands Bateaux de Provence: Advertisement, "Bateau 'Mireio'," from *Évasion Plus.*

Grottes de Thouzon: Advertisement, "Grottes de Thouzon," from *Évasion Plus.* Photograph by M. Crotet, *Évasion Plus.* Provence, Imprimerie Vincent, 1994.

Groupe Filipacchi: Advertisement, "Casablanca," from *7 à Paris,* page 43, no. 534, February 2-18, 1992.

Hachette Livre: Title and descriptions from pages 67,68,77, and 78 from *Le guide du Routard-Provence Côte d'Azur 1994-1995.* Copyright © 1994 by Hachette Livre (Littérature générale: Guides de Voyages.)

L'Harmattan: Excerpts from French text and photographs from *Cheval de bois/Chouval bwa* by Isabelle et Henri Cadoré, illustrations by Bernadette Coléno. Copyright © 1993 by L'Harmattan.

Larousse: "Les monuments les plus visités" and "Les musées les plus visités" from *Francoscopie: 1993* by Gérard Mermet. Copyright © 1992 by Larousse.

Loca Center: Advertisement, "Loca Center," from *Guide des Services: La Martinique à domicile.*

Michelin Travel Publications: From Map #989: France/Francia. Copyright © 1994 by Michelin Travel Publications.

Ministère de la Culture et de la Francophonie: ticket, "Ministère de la Culture: C.N.M.H.S.: droit d'entrée."

Ministère de l'Education Nationale: Direction de l'Évaluation et de la Prospective (DEP): Table, "Bac 1991: 75% de reçus" from *Francoscopie 1993* by Gérard Mermet.

Musée du Louvre: Front of entry ticket for the Louvre.

NAF-NAF: Two photographs from *RENTREE TRES CLASSE A PRIX PETITS. Nouvelles Galeries Lafayette.*

Office Départemental du Tourisme de la Martinique: Map of Fort-de-France from *Martinique: Plan de Fort-de-France/Carte de la Martinique.*

OUI FM: Logo from OUI FM, 102.3 MHz (Paris).

Parc Astérix S.A.: Cover of *Parc Astérix,* 1992 edition. Advertisement for Parc Astérix from *Paris Vision,* 1993 edition, page 29.

Parc du Mont-Sainte-Anne: Cover of *Parc du Mont-Sainte-Anne: A Mountain of Summer Fun, 1993 Season.* Photograph by Jean Sylvain.

Parc Zoologique de Paris: Cover and map from *Parc Zoologique de Paris.*

Paris Midnight: French text and photograph from "Musée d'Orsay," text from "Notre-Dame de Paris," and text from "La Tour Eiffel" from *Paris Midnight,* no. 31, June 1993. Copyright © 1993 by Paris Midnight.

Paris Promotion: Map of Paris from *Paris: Mode d'emploi 93/94,* edited by Paris Promotion.

Paristoric: Advertisement, "Paristoric: Le Film."

Pomme de pain: Menu, "La carte pomme de pain."

Printemps: Illustration and Printemps logo from *Invitation.* From map of Paris from *Printemps: Plan de Paris/Map of Paris.*

PROSUMA: Société Ivoirienne de Promotion de Supermarchés: Illustration from *3 éléphants prennent votre défense!*

RATP: ticket, "Section Urbaine."

RCV: La Radio Rock: Logo from RCV: La Radio Rock, 99 MHz (Lille).

Réunion des Musées Nationaux: Text from "Palais du Louvre" from *Les 34 Musées Nationaux,* 1992 edition.

Réunion des Musées Nationaux, Agence photographique: Photograph, "Palais du Louvre" from *Les 34 Musées Nationaux,* 1992 edition.

Editions S.A.E.P.: Recipe and photograph for "Croissants au coco et au sésame," recipe and photograph for "Mousseline africaine de petits légumes," and "Signification des symboles accompagnant les recettes" from *La cuisine Africaine* by Pierrette Chalendar. Copyright © 1993 by S.A.E.P.

Société Anonyme Montparnasse 56: Cover of *La Vue Parisienne.*

Télé 7 Jours: From "Sport: La semaine en direct" from *Télé 7 Jours,* September 26-October 2, 1992. Copyright © 1992 by Télé 7 Jours.

Tourisme Québec: "Le Climat" from *Destination Québec: Guide Pratique de voyage,* Edition 92-93, page 11.

Trois Suisses: Text and photographs from "Le pull col montant," "Le pantalon de jogging," and "Les polos" from 3 Suisses le Chouchou, Autumn-Winter 92-93.

L'Union des écrivaines et écrivains québécois: Text and illustrations from "Les jeunes au micro" by F. Gagnon from *Vidéo-Presse,* vol. XX, no. 9, May 1991. Copyright © 1991 by UNEQ. From "Résultats de l'enquête VIP" from *Vidéo-Presse,* December 1993. Copyright © 1993 by UNEQ.

Village des Sports: Advertisement, "Village des Sports: c'est l'fun, fun, fun!" from *Région de Québec.*

PHOTOGRAPHY CREDITS

Abbreviations used: (t) top, (c) center, (b) bottom, (l) left, (r) right, (bckgd) background, (bdr) border.

FRONT COVER: (tr) HRW Photo by Marty Granger/Edge Productions, (c) Michael Howell/Photonica. **BACK COVER:** (tr) HRW Photo by Marty Granger/Edge Productions, (b) George Hunter/SuperStock **FRONT AND BACK COVER COLLAGE:** HRW Photo by Andrew Yates.

CHAPTER OPENER Background Photographs: Scott Van Osdol

TABLE OF CONTENTS: Page v HRW Photo by Sam Dudgeon, vi(tl), vi(bl), HRW Photo by Marty Granger/Edge Productions, vi(all remaining), HRW Photo by Scott Van Osdol; vii(tl), vii(tc), HRW Photo by Marty Granger/Edge Productions; vii(all remaining), HRW Photo by Scott Van Osdol; viii(inset), viii(tl), viii(br), HRW Photo by Marty Granger/Edge Productions; viii(bl), HRW Photo by Sam Dudgeon; viii(all remaining), HRW Photo by Scott Van Osdol; ix(tr), ix(bl), HRW Photo by Marty Granger/Edge Productions; ix(cr), ix(bc), ix(br), HRW Photo by Scott Van Osdol; ix(all remaining), HRW Photo by Sam Dudgeon; x(tl), x(br), HRW Photo by Marty Granger/Edge Productions; x(tr), HRW Photo; x(cr), x(bl), HRW Photo by Sam Dudgeon; x(all remaining), HRW Photo by Scott Van Osdol; xi(tc), xi(tr), HRW Photo by Marty Granger/Edge Productions; xi(cr), HRW Photo by Sam Dudgeon; xi(all remaining), HRW Photo by Scott Van Osdol; xii(tr), xii(bl), HRW Photo by Marty Granger/Edge Productions; xii(all remaining), HRW Photo by Scott Van Osdol; xiii(tr), xiii(br), HRW Photo by Louis Boireau/Edge Productions; xiii(all remaining), HRW Photo by Scott Van Osdol; xiv(tl), xiv(bl), HRW Photo by Marty Granger/Edge Productions; xiv(all remaining), HRW Photo by Scott Van Osdol; xv(tc), xv(br), HRW Photo by Marty Granger/Edge Productions; xv(all remaining), HRW Photo by Scott Van Osdol; xvi(tl), xvi(br), HRW Photo by Marty Granger/Edge Productions; xvi(all remaining), HRW Photo by Scott Van Osdol; xvii(tr), xvii(cl), HRW Photo by Marty Granger/Edge Productions; xvii(bc), HRW Photo by Sam Dudgeon; xvii(all remaining), HRW Photo by Scott Van Osdol.

Preliminary Chapter: Page v-1(tc), HRW Photo by Mark Antman; 1 (bc), HRW Photo by Marty Granger/Edge Productions; 1(tr), HRW Photo by Marty Granger/Edge Productions; (br), SuperStock; 2(tl), Sipa Press; 2(tr), Reuters/Bettmann; 2(c), Vedat Acickalin/Sipa Press; 3(cl), J. M. Jimenez/Keystone/-Shooting Star; 3(cr), Kathy Willens/Wide World photos, Inc.; 3(b), Archive photos; 4(tl), HRW Photo by Sam Dudgeon; 4(tc), Barthelemy/Sipa Press; 4(tr), Arianespace/Sipa Press; 4(cl), 4(c), 4(cr), HRW Photo by Marty Granger/Edge Productions; 4(bl), Robert Frerck/Odyssey Productions; 4(bc), David R. Frazier/David R. Frazier photolibrary; 4(br), Derek Berwin/The Image Bank; 5(both), HRW Photo by Marty Granger/Edge Productions; 7(tl), Clay Myers/The Wildlife Collection; 7(tc), Leonard Lee Rue/FPG International; 7(tr), 7(bc), Tim Laman/The Wildlife Collection; 7(bl), Jack Swenson/The Wildlife Collection; 7(br), Martin Harvey/The Wildlife Collection; 10(tl), HRW Photo by Daniel Aubry; 10(tr), HRW Photo by Ken Lax; 10(br), HRW Photo by Louis Boireau/Edge Productions; 10(all remaining), HRW Photo by Marty Granger/Edge Productions.

UNIT ONE: Page 12-13, HRW Photo by Marty Granger/Edge Productions; 14-15(bckgd), Terry Qing/FPG International; 14 (tr), Tom Craig/FPG International; 14(cl), 14(br) HRW Photo by Marty Granger/Edge Productions. 15(all)/HRW Photo by Marty Granger/Edge Productions. **Chapter One:** Page 16-17(all), HRW Photo by Marty Granger/Edge Productions; 18(tr-both) HRW Photo by Louis Boireau/Edge Productions; 18(all remaining) HRW Photo by Marty Granger/Edge Productions. 19(all) HRW Photo by Marty Granger/Edge Productions. 21(tc), HRW Photo by Sam Dudgeon; 21(br), HRW Photo by Alan Oddie; 21(all remaining), HRW Photo by Marty Granger/Edge Productions; 22(l), HRW Photo by John Langford; 22(r), HRW Photo by Marty Granger/Edge Productions; 22(cl), HBJ photo by Mark Antman; 22(c), HRW Photo; 22(cr), IPA/The Image Works; 23-24(all), HRW Photo by Marty Granger/Edge Productions; 25(tr), Toussaint/Sipa Press; 30(all), HRW Photo by Marty

Granger/Edge Productions; 34(tl), HRW Photo by Sam Dudgeon; 34(tc), HRW Photo by Marty Granger/Edge Productions; 34(tr), Robert Brenner/PhotoEdit; 34(cl), HRW Photo by David Frazier; 34(c), Capretz/Harbrace photo; 34(cr), M. Antman/The Image Works; 34(bl), Lawrence Migdale/Stock Boston; 34(bc), HRW Photo by Ken Karp; 34(br), HBJ photo by Mark Antman; 34(b), R. Lucas/The Image Works; 36(t), The Picture Cube; 36(tl), Richard Hutchings/PhotoEdit; 36(c), David C. Bitters/The Picture Cube; 37(t), 37(b), HRW Photo by Russell Dian; 37(tl), HRW Photo by May Polycarpe; 37(c), R. Lucas/The Image Works; 38(cl), David Young-Wolff/PhotoEdit; 38(all remaining), HRW Photo by Marty Granger/Edge Productions. **Chapter Two:** Page 42-45(all), HRW photo by Marty Granger/Edge Productions; 56(l), HRW Photo by Louis Boireau/Edge Productions; 56(both), HRW Photo by Marty Granger/Edge Productions; **Chapter Three:** Page 66-69(all), HRW Photo by Marty Granger/Edge Productions; 71(t), HRW Photo; 71(all remaining), HRW Photo by Sam Dudgeon; 72-73(all), HRW Photo by Sam Dudgeon.; 75(l), HRW Photo by Louis Boireau/Edge Productions; 75(c), 75(r), HRW Photo by Marty Granger/Edge Productions; 78(all), HRW photo by Sam Dudgeon; 80-81(all), HRW Photo by Sam Dudgeon; 88(both), HRW Photo by Sam Dudgeon.

UNIT TWO: Page (90-91), J. A. Kraulis/Masterfile; 92(all), HRW Photo by Marty Granger/Edge Productions; 93(t), 93(b), HRW Photo by Marty Granger/Edge Productions; 93(cl), Wolfgang Kaehler; 93(cr), Jean-Guy Kerouac/Hervey Smyth, Vue de la Prise de Quebec, le septembre 1759, 35.9 x 47.8cm, Musée du Quebec, 78,375. **Chapter Four:** Page 94-95(all), HRW Photo by Marty Granger/Edge Productions; 96(tr) HRW Photo by Edge Productions; 97(all) HRW Photo by Marty Granger/Edge Productions; 99(all), HRW Photo by Marty Granger/Edge Productions; 100(tc), David Young-Wolff/PhotoEdit; 100(tr), HRW Photo by Sam Dudgeon; 100(cl), PhotoEdit; 100(bl), David Lissy/Leo de Wys; 100(bc), 100(br), HRW photo; 100(all remaining), HRW Photo by Marty Granger/Edge Productions; 103(l), 103(r), M. Jacob/The Image Works; 103(cl), Robert Fried/Robert Fried photography; 103(c), R. Lucas/The Image Works; 103(cr), Mat Jacob/The Image Works; 105(l), Robert Fried photography; 105(r), 105(cl), HRW Photo by Sam Dudgeon; 105(c), HBJ photo by May Polycarpe; 105(cr), HRW Photo by Marty Granger/Edge Productions; 109(l), HRW Photo by Louis Boireau Edge Productions; 109(r), 109(c), HRW Photo by Marty Granger/Edge Productions.

UNIT THREE: Page 120-121(bckgd), Paul Steel/The Stock Market; 122(all), HRW Photo by Marty Granger/Edge Productions; 123(bl), Peter Menzel/Stock Boston; 123(all remaining), HRW Photo by Marty Granger/Edge Productions. **Chapter Five:** Page 124-127(all), HRW Photo by Marty Granger/Edge Productions; 134(l), 134(c), HRW Photo by Marty Granger/Edge Productions; 134(r), HRW Photo by Louis Boireau/Edge Productions; 138(l), 138(cl), HRW Photo by Russell Dian; 138(r), HRW Photo by Sam Dudgeon; 138(cr), HRW Photo by Robert Haynes; 142(t), HRW Photo by Stuart Cohen; 143(t), HRW Photo by Helena Kolda; 143(c), 143(b), Pomme de Pain; 143(br), Steven Mark Needham/Envision. **Chapter Six:** Page 148-149(all), HRW Photo by Marty Granger/Edge Productions; 150(tr), Sebastien Raymond/Sipa Press; 150-151(all remaining) HRW Photo by Marty Granger/Edge Productions; 154(bl), HRW Photo by Sam Dudgeon; 154(bc), Owen Franken/Stock Boston; 154(all remaining) HRW Photo by Marty Granger/Edge Productions; 156(top row), (1-3) HRW Photo by Marty Granger/Edge Productions; (4) Tabuteau/The Image Works; (center row) (1) Jean Paul Nacivet/Leo de Wys; (2) Greg Meadors/Stock Boston; (3-4) HRW Photo by Marty Granger/Edge Productions; (bottom row) (1) Robert Fried/Stock

Boston; (2) HRW Photo by Marty Granger/Edge Productions; (3) HBJ photo by Mark Antman; (4) R. Lucas/The Image Works; 158(l) HRW Photo by Louis Boireau/Edge Productions, 158(c), 158(r)/HRW Photo by Marty Granger/Edge Productions; 162(tl), Ulrike Welsch/PhotoEdit; 162(tr), HBJ photo by Mark Antman; 162(cr), HRW Photo by Marty Granger/Edge Productions; 170, HRW Photo by Capretz; 171, HRW Photo by Dianne Schrader. **Chapter Seven:** Page 174-175(all), HRW Photo by Marty Granger/Edge Productions; 176(cl), 176(cr), HRW photo by Edge Productions; 176(top), HRW Photo by Marty Granger/Edge Productions; 176(b), HRW Photo by Russell Dian; 177(b), HRW photo by Marty Granger/Edge Productions; 177(all remaining), HRW Photo by Edge productions; 178(tl), 178(bc) HRW Photo by Russell Dian; 178(all remaining), HRW Photo; 179(b), HRW Photo by Russell Dian; 180(Rows 1-2), HRW Photos; 180 (Row 3), (l) HRW Photo by Edge Productions, (2) HRW Photo by Marty Granger/Edge Productions, (3-5) HRW Photo by Russell Dian; 180 (Row 4), (l) HRW Photo by Cherie Mitschke; (2) HRW Photo by Marion Bermondy, (3) David Austen/Stock Boston; (4) John Lei/Stock Boston; 181(l), HRW Photo by Daniel Aubry; 181(r), HRW Photo by Sam Dudgeon; 181(cl), David Young-Wolff/PhotoEdit; 181(c), HRW Photo by May Polycarpe; 181(cr), Tony Freeman/PhotoEdit; 185(bc), Firooz Zahedi/The Kobal Collection; 185(br), TM © 20th Century Fox Film Corp/ 1992; 188(all), HRW Photo by Marty Granger/Edge Productions; 192(t), 192(b), Walter Chandoha; 192(c), HRW Photo; 193(t), 193(c), Walter Chandoha; 193(b), Gerard Lacz/Peter Arnold, Inc.

UNIT FOUR: Page 198-199, Nabil Zorkot/Pro Foto; 200(l), John Elk III/Bruce Coleman, Inc.; 200(tr), Nabil Zorkot/Pro Foto; 200(c), M. & E. Bernheim/Woodfin Camp & Associates; 201(all), Nabil Zorkot/Pro Foto. Chapter Eight: Page 202-205(all), HRW Photo by Louis Boireau/Edge Productions; 206(l), HRW Photo; 206(all remaining), HRW Photo by Louis Boireau/Edge Productions; 211(l), 211(r), HRW Photo by Marty Granger/Edge Productions 211(c) HRW Photo by Louis Boireau/Edge Productions; 215-216(all), HRW Photo by Louis Boireau/Edge Productions; 217(tl), HRW Photo by Lance Shriner; 217(tr), HRW Photo by Louis Boireau/Edge Productions; 217(bl), HRW Photo by Sam Dudgeon; 217(br), HRW Photo by Eric Beggs.

UNIT FIVE: Page 228-229, HRW Photo by Marty Granger/Edge Productions; 230(tr), HRW Photo by Cherie Mitschke; 230(cr), Erich Lessing/Art Resource; 230(bl), HRW Photo by Marty Granger/Edge Productions. **Chapter Nine:** Page 231(t), W. Gontscharoff/SuperStock; 231(cl), G. Carde/SuperStock; 231(b), HRW Photo by Marty Granger/Edge Productions; 232-235(all), HRW Photo by Marty Granger/Edge Productions; 236(r), Ermakoff/The Image Works; 236(all remaining), HRW Photo by Marty Granger/Edge Productions; 242(l), 242(r), HRW Photo by Marty Granger/Edge Productions; 242(c), Owen Franken/Stock Boston; 246(all), HRW Photo by Marty Granger/Edge Productions; 252(c), HRW Photo. **Chapter Ten:** Page 256-259(all), HRW Photo by Marty Granger/Edge Productions; 261(all), HRW Photo by Sam Dudgeon; 268(b), Paul Conselin/PhotoEdit; 269(c), 269(l), HRW Photo by Marty Granger/Edge Productions, 269(r), HRW Photo by Louis Boireau/Edge Productions; 273, HRW Photo by Sam Dudgeon; 276-277 (all), HRW Photo by Sam Dudgeon; 278(l), 278(r), Don Iron/Sipa Press; 278(c), Barthelemy/Sipa Press; 280(l), 280(r), HRW Photo by Sam Dudgeon. **Chapter Eleven:** Page 282-283(all), HRW Photo by Marty Granger/Edge Productions; 284(tl), HRW Photo by May Polycarpe; 284(cl), David Florenz/Option Photo; 284 (all remaining), HRW Photo by Marty Granger/Edge Productions; 285-286(all), HRW Photo by Marty Granger/Edge Productions; 292(c), 292(r) HRW Photo by Marty Granger/Edge Productions; 292(l) HRW Photo by Louis Boireau/Edge Productions; 295(l), 295(c), 295(r), HRW Photo by Marty Granger/Edge Productions; 295(b), Pierre Jaques/FOC photo; 297(both), HRW Photo by Marty Granger/Edge Productions; 298(cl) HRW Photo by Marty Granger/Edge Productions; 298(cr), Robert Fried/Stock Boston; 298(br), J. Messerschmidt/Leo de Wys; 298(bl), DeRichemond/The Image Works; 298(bc), Joachim Messer/Leo de Wys; 303(all), HRW Photo by Marty Granger/Edge Productions.

UNIT SIX: Page 306-309(all), HRW Photo by Marty Granger/Edge Productions. **Chapter Twelve:** Page 310-314(all), HRW Photo by Marty Granger/Edge Productions; 315(tl), Tony Freeman/PhotoEdit; 315(cl), HBJ photo by Patrick Courtault; 315(c), HBJ photo by Capretz; 315(cr), IPA/The Image Works; 315(bc), Robert Fried/Stock Boston; 315(all remaining), HRW Photo by Marty Granger/Edge Productions; 318(tl), 318(br), Chris Huxley/Leo deWys; 318(all remaining), HRW Photo by Marty Granger/Edge Productions; 321(cl), Helen Kolda/HRW Photo; 321(cr), HRW Photo by Sam Dudgeon/Duly authorized by CASTER MAN, Belgium; 321(bc), HRW Photo by Russell Dian; 321(all remaining), HRW Photo by Sam Dudgeon; 322(tl), Elizabeth Zuckerman/PhotoEdit; 322(tr), Amy Etra/PhotoEdit; 322(c), HRW Photo by Louis Boreau/Edge Productions; 322(bl), Robert Rathe/Stock Boston; 322(bc), Dean Abramson/Stock Boston; 322(br), Antman/The Image Works; 322(all remaining), HRW Photo by Marty Granger/Edge Productions; 324(all), HRW Photo by Marty Granger/Edge Productions; 328(c), Chris Huxley/Leo deW; 330(bckgd), HRW Photo by Mark Antman; 332(l), 332(cl) 332(cr) HRW Photo by Marty Granger/Edge Productions; 332(r), Chris Huxley/Leo de Wys.

ILLUSTRATION AND CARTOGRAPHY CREDITS

Beier, Ellen: 9
Bouchard, Jocelyne: 11, 23, 26, 102, 118, 155, 164, 180, 182, 220, 254
Bylo, Andrew: 47, 129, 131, 207, 212, 245
Cooper, Holly: i, vi, ix, xiii, xvii
de Masson, Anne: 317, 319, 320, 326, 327, 332, 334
Foissy, Jean-Pierre: 82, 140, 159, 161, 163, 186, 237, 238, 264, 265, 270, 274, 296, 321
Garnier, Pascal: 52, 184, 189, 190, 196
Kimani, George: 209, 220
Krone, Mike: 192-193
Larvor, Yves: 27, 31, 146, 157, 214, 226, 262, 280, 294,
Loppé, Michel: 73, 81, 83, 101, 108, 218, 219, 243, 262, 271, 293
Maestracci, Guy: 55, 139, 157, 182, 189, 241, 272, 288
Meyer, Camille: 28, 133, 208, 239, 289
Moore, Russell: 287
Petrus, Keith: 54
Rio, Vincent: 22, 33, 72, 79, 130, 132, 179, 183, 187, 190, 263
Roberts, Bruce: 6, 48, 50, 64, 105, 291
Stanley, Anne: 325, 328
Stevens, Brian: 48, 58, 74, 76, 106, 160, 185, 248, 268, 2, 323